Entrepreneurs
of Ideology

Entrepreneurs of Ideology

Neoconservative Publishers
In Germany, 1890–1933

Gary D. Stark

The University of North Carolina Press

Chapel Hill

© 1981 The University of North Carolina Press

Manufactured in the United States of America

Library of Congress Cataloging in Publication Data

Stark, Gary D   1948–
    Entrepreneurs of ideology.

    Bibliography: p.
    Includes index.
    1. Publishers and publishing—Germany—History.
2. Conservatism—Germany—History. 3. Germany—
Civilization. I. Title.
Z315.S8434   070.5'0943   80-14906
ISBN 0-8078-1452-0

To My Mother and Father

Contents

Preface

This study grew out of my dual interest in the German radical Right and in the social foundations of cultural life. On the one hand, I have been fascinated for some time with that ideological movement in late nineteenth- and early twentieth-century Germany which soundly rejected reason, democracy, technology, and so many of the other modern Western values and institutions which most of us rather facilely accept. On the other hand, I have been intrigued by the "external" determinants of cultural life—by which I mean those factors such as commercial and economic considerations, legal systems, institutional structures, and social or political forces, which influence the activities of intellectuals and help shape cultural development. Thus it was that I chose to explore the history of the German neoconservative movement from the perspective of the publishing industry and book trade.

From its inception, my work has benefitted from the guidance, encouragement, and admonishments of Vernon Lidtke. His sage advice on the peculiarities of publishers, both German and American, has been of immense help. Initial research for this study was conducted in 1972–73 with the aid of a generous grant from the Deutscher Akademischer Austauschdienst. Supplementary investigations were made possible in 1976 and 1977 by the University of Texas at Arlington Organized Research Fund. During my studies, Ulf Diederichs and Otto Spatz generously shared their time and their trust with me and readily granted me access to the records of the Eugen Diederichs and J. F. Lehmann publishing houses, respectively. Although these two individuals will probably disagree with my interpretation of their ancestors' activities, their hospitality and cooperative assistance toward me is deeply appreciated, as is their permission to cite in this book materials from their house archives. I am grateful, too, to Hennig Stapel, Renate Ullmann, and Dr. Walther Blunck for their permission to use the papers of Wilhelm Stapel, Hermann Ullmann, and H. F. Blunck. (My efforts to gain access to the archives of the Gerhard Stalling and the Hanseatische Verlagsanstalt firms, and to the Eugen Diederichs material in the Universitätsbibliothek Jena were, unfortunately, unsuccessful.) Rodler Morris was kind enough to share with me several drafts of his work in progress, while Dr. Adalbert Brauer of the Börsenverein des deutschen Buchhandels allowed me to exploit not only the holdings of the Börsenverein's Historisches Archiv, but also his own vast knowledge of and irrepressible enthusiasm for German publishing history.

My colleagues and former colleagues at Johns Hopkins and at the University of Texas at Arlington—Richard M. Golden, Frank J. Thomason, Douglas Richmond, Elliott West, Jerome Rodnitzky, and Glenn A. May —all read portions of my manuscript at one time or another and saved me from several embarrassing stylistic lapses and muddled passages. Roger Chickering carefully examined the work in its entirety and offered invaluable suggestions for its improvement.

Portions of this work appeared previously, although in different form, in *Archiv für Geschichte des Buchwesens* XVI, 2 (1976): 291–318, and in *German Studies Review* I, 1 (February 1978): 56–71. I am grateful to the editors of both journals for permission to reprint this material here. Publication costs of this book have been underwritten, in part, by a generous grant from the University of Texas at Arlington.

My greatest debt, however, I owe to my wife Mary Galen, who has endured with equanimity the incessant clatter of my typewriter and has borne with exemplary good humor my eccentric preoccupation with other obscure makers of books. Her support and understanding in this undertaking have been indispensible.

Arlington, Texas
January 1980

Abbreviations

ALV   Albert Langen Verlag

DAP   Deutsche Arbeiterpartei (German Workers Party)

DHB   Deutsch(nationale) Hausbücherei (German Home Library)

DHV   Deutschnationaler Handlungsgehilfen-Verband (German National Union of Commercial Employees)

DNVA   Deutschnationale Verlagsanstalt (German National Publishing Institute)

DNVP   Deutschnationale Volkspartei (German National Peoples Party)

DVP   Deutsche Volkspartei (German Peoples Party)

EDV   Eugen Diederichs Verlag

GMV   Georg Müller Verlag

GSV   Gerhard Stalling Verlag

HBV   Heinrich Beenken Verlag

HDVA   Hanseatische Druck- und Verlagsanstalt (Hanseatic Printing and Publishing Institute)

HVA   Hanseatische Verlagsanstalt (Hanseatic Publishing Institute)

JFLV   J. F. Lehmanns Verlag

LMV   Albert Langen—Georg Müller Verlag; Langen-Müller Verlag

NSDAP Nationalsozialistische Deutsche Arbeiterpartei (National Socialist Party)

SPD   Sozialdemokratische Partei Deutschlands (Social Democratic Party)

Entrepreneurs of Ideology

One

Introduction

Publishing and the Sociology of Knowledge

"The distribution of a book," Friedrich Schiller once wrote to his publisher Johann F. Cotta, "is almost as difficult and important a task as its creation."[1] As that branch of economic activity perhaps in closest contact to the world of ideas, the publishing industry does indeed cast publishers and bookdealers in a demanding role. Their social function is to mediate between intellectuals and society by producing an economically viable mechanism for the exchange and popular diffusion of ideas. Until the recent advent of electronic mass media, publishers served as one of the few concrete links between a writer and his audience. Consequently, the extent to which ideas have been communicated and the degree of rapport existing between intellectuals and the broader populace has depended in no small way on the structure of the book industry, its operation, and the behavior of publishers.

Indeed, the very existence of the modern professional writer has been contingent upon the organization of the book industry. Writers could exist as an independent social group, freed from financial dependency on traditional patrons or on a conventional occupation, only when they were able to derive a secure income from the proceeds of their writing. This, in turn, was possible only after publishers and bookdealers had managed to establish equitable copyright laws, provide a workable royalty system for authors, and suppress cheap, pirated editions of published works. Such developments did not occur in Germany, for example, until the early nineteenth century, which helps account for the relatively late emergence of an independent German intelligentsia. The mutual dependence between intellectuals and the book industry means that the structure and activities of the industry inevitably affect intellectuals, and thus, intellectual life.

Moreover, a medium of communication such as the publishing industry affects the very ideas which it communicates. Since the expression of ideas must in some way be adapted to the means by which those ideas are transmitted, authors and journalists structure their message to conform at least partly to the book and journal trade which must convey their pronouncements. In addition, the publisher who controls and operates the publishing medium continually selects which works will appear in print. He helps determine in this way which ideas gain public expression, how they are expressed, whether or not they reach a broad audience, and even—depending on the skill and energy with which he distributes and advertises his products—what effect they have on the reading public. For these reasons, publishers serve as "gatekeepers to the temple of literary success"[2] and influence the ideas and values which prevail in a society.

The organizational structure, material basis, personnel, ideological bias, degree of skill or success, and social standing of the publishing medium all help shape intellectual life. Since publishers often initiate, plan, commission, or sometimes even help write the books their firms issue, the ideas contained in published works are not necessarily identical with the ideas originally conceived by the authors. When examining the history of particular ideas or intellectual movements, therefore, it is often useful to explore their publishers and publishing history as well. The study of publishing in relation to a particular group of ideas can also enable one to determine how well certain books sold on the market, thereby allowing a better evaluation of just how extensively the ideas were disseminated. Study of publishing history and the book trade is thus an important aspect of the sociology of knowledge; it can—and has—yielded valuable new insights into cultural history.[3]

The present work is intended as a case study in this region of the sociology of knowledge. The complex interaction among publishers, writers, ideas, and the book industry will be illustrated by an examination of the relation of the publishing medium to one particularly important German intellectual movement, neoconservatism.

Neoconservatism in Germany

"Neoconservatism" is a general (and perhaps somewhat artificial) term which will be used in this study to designate what was admittedly an amorphous composite of several disparate cultural and political currents. The notion of neoconservatism has often been used by historians to identify the radical non-Nazi German Right between 1918 and 1933—those "Trotskyites of Nazism" who leveled a scathing critique from the right on Germany's postwar liberal, democratic order and called for a "conservative revolution" to overthrow the Weimar republic, but who at the same time were distinct from, often critical of, and after 1933 not infrequently persecuted by Hitler's National Socialist movement. Germany's postwar new conservative movement, although never effectively organized into a political force, nevertheless helped in a significant way to undermine the Weimar republic; it might be termed a kind of "cultural fascism"[4] which prepared the way for political fascism and the Third Reich. For this reason, radical right-wing ideology in the Weimar years has received considerable scholarly attention.[5]

While it was World War I and the revolution of 1918–19 which, by radicalizing many middle-class intellectuals and youths, sparked this new brand of radical conservatism after 1918, the origins of the movement reach well back into the prewar era. Many elements of post-1918 neoconservative ideology were but transformed versions of diverse phenomena such as cultural pessimism and radical *völkisch* nationalism which had sprung up in the Wilhelmian period, and the activities of many postwar neoconservative personalities and organizations were merely continuations, *mutatis mutandis*, of prewar endeavors. It was in the last decades of the nineteenth century that a series of cultural and political forces began to emerge which, although clearly antiliberal and conservative in nature, were at the same time distinct from and increasingly critical of the stance of traditional conservatives. The final break between this new Right and the old did not occur, however, until after 1914. Under the impact of the World War and the collapse of the conservative imperial order, the disparate prewar neoconservative stirrings converged and crystallized during the Weimar era into a new brand of radical, right-wing thought—the "conservative revolution." For the heuristic purposes of this study and for the sake of convenience, the term "neoconservatism" applies not only to the "conservative revolution" movement of the 1918–33 period, but also to those prewar forces which later culminated in the "conservative revolution."

Neoconservatism was a distinctly late nineteenth- and early twentieth-century phenomenon which differed markedly from traditional conservatism. In Germany, as elsewhere, conservatism was a manifestation of the secure and established classes which comprised the socioeconomic elite. During the latter half of the nineteenth century, this elite in Germany consisted of the agrarian aristocracy and the wealthy industrial bourgeoisie. This agrarian-industrial elite, which one might term the "old Right," was socially exclusive, believing that social and political power were properly reserved for a small elite based on birth and wealth. The one general, overriding goal of this established group was to protect the status quo, to conserve and defend the system under which it enjoyed disproportionate political influence, social prestige, and material benefits. Their traditional conservative ideology with its stress on discipline, authority, tradition, social hierarchy, and the rest, was designed to minimize change and shore up the values and institutions on which the preeminence of these propertied classes was based.

In defending the status quo, traditional German conservatives tended to be relatively pragmatic and flexible, often sacrificing abstract principles for concrete gains. The arch-conservative Junker aristocracy, after all, in order to preserve the greater part of its social and political privileges, had reached an accommodation with the industrial bourgeoisie in the mid-nineteenth century; this arrangement allowed features of feudalism and modern capitalism to coexist in Germany well into the twentieth century. In the process of adapting to and accommodating some modern, liberal developments such as capitalism, parliamentarism, and electioneering, traditional conservatives absorbed—perhaps far more than they realized —many of the liberal nineteenth-century trends which they originally opposed. Finally, the traditional German Right was fundamentally political in that it believed the social, economic, and cultural status quo could be most effectively preserved by gaining control of the political institutions of the state; thus, traditional conservatives organized themselves into political parties and economic interest groups through which they hoped to exert their influence on political life.[6]

By contrast, German neoconservatism in the late nineteenth and early twentieth centuries was largely a movement of insecure segments of the middle class, especially the cultivated intelligentsia and various marginal petty-bourgeois strata which felt threatened by the entire process of modernization; neoconservatism was, in essence, a manifestation of their anti-modern anxieties. Perhaps Henry A. Turner expressed it most succinctly:

> . . . The late nineteenth and early twentieth centuries marked, for most of western and central Europe, the great watershed of modernization, when the changes wrought by that process began to affect the life of the populace at large in a direct fashion. It was then that the old and settled patterns of life were first disrupted and displaced on a large scale. Only then, for example, did society's center of gravity shift from the countryside to the city; with unprecedented rapidity, millions were torn loose from the customary patterns of agrarian life and thrust into an alien, anonymous urban world. In that same process, venerable cultural values were subjected to widespread challenge and discreditation. Traditional religion, in particular, lost ground rapidly; secularism, previously reserved almost exclusively for the privileged and educated, became a mass phenomenon for the first time. Many of those torn loose from their

cultural and societal roots found a new secular point of reference in the socialist movement. But others remained uprooted and adrift in a threatening, brutal industrial world for which they were ill prepared. It seems scarcely surprising that some of the latter proved to be susceptible to movements vehemently hostile to that world.[7]

Neoconservatives represented a complete rejection not only of the political, social, and economic effects of modernity, but also the liberal values and assumptions which formed its very basis. Whether consciously or unconsciously, neoconservatives desired ultimately to reverse the social and intellectual processes which had produced modern industrial bourgeois civilization. This involved not merely a reform of modern political institutions, but a fundamental transformation of basic social and cultural values—of life itself. In the words of Turner, "what they proposed was an escape from the modern world by means of a desperate backward leap toward a romanticized vision of the harmony, community, simplicity, and order of a world long lost. Their thinking thus seems best characterized as a utopian form of antimodernism—utopian in the double sense of being a visionary panacea and being unrealizable."[8]

Unlike traditional conservatives, neoconservatives did not wish simply to cling fast to the status quo and conserve outmoded values and relationships against future change; rather, they were in a sense radicals who wanted to abolish the status quo, who called for a fundamental restructuring of culture and society so as to restore what they saw as its essential original or ideal features. German neoconservatives would have instinctively concurred with their Russian counterpart who said: "To be a conservative at this time means to be at least a radical, or rather, a revolutionary."[9] It was because they wished not to conserve, but to overturn existing modern realities that the later, postwar phase of the movement, in which the latent essence of neoconservative ideology emerged in full force, has been variously labeled the "Conservative Revolution," "Revolutionary Conservatism," "Radical Conservatism," or the "Revolution from the Right." It did not seem at all paradoxical for a leading neoconservative theorist of the time to characterize his ideas as standing "further left than the Left and further right than the Right."[10]

Unlike traditional conservatism, which tended to be directly and often unabashedly tied to the material interests of the conservative propertied elite, neoconservatism—at least on the surface—scorned individual or class interest and stressed instead certain ethical values and utopian communal ideals such as spiritual freedom, the creative personality, or social solidarity. To be sure, neoconservative ideology, like all ideologies, was conditioned by the specific interests of its proponents and served at once to disguise and to legitimize those interests. Nevertheless, because neo-conservatism tirelessly preached high-minded spiritual and national ideals and condemned selfish material interest, the link between neoconservative ideology and the class interests of those who professed it was more subtle, more indirect, and less apparent than was the case with traditional conservatism. This fact gave neoconservatism a popular appeal which the old Right lacked. Indeed, neoconservatism tended to draw its strongest support from the bourgeois and petty-bourgeois strata which resented the social, political, and economic supremacy of the narrow aristocratic and upper-middle-class elite, but who were at the same time terrified of radical left-wing movements such as Marxist socialism. Although they staunchly affirmed the need for authority, social hierarchy, and a controlling elite, neoconservatives resented the social exclusivity of the traditional conservative propertied elite; they hoped to replace the old elite of birth and wealth, from which they were excluded, with a new elite based on other selective principles such as the degree of one's ethical idealism, national consciousness, or racial purity. This new "spiritual" elite envisioned by neoconservatives would thus be open to members of the middle and lower classes who could not meet the geneological or material qualifications set by the traditional conservative elite. Moreover, the antimodern nature of neoconservative ideology also appealed to those marginal social groups which felt threatened by modernization and yearned for some form of economic and social protection against the vicissitudes of modern industrial mass society. Traditional conservatives, because of their reverence for the status quo and their opposition to social change, had little to offer these anxious, threatened masses. Neoconservatives, on the other hand, because they were more excluded from the benefits of the status quo, preached the need for extensive social and economic reform, and thus could offer the disaffected masses a positive alternative to the despised Left. Thus, while the reactionary, standpat ideology of the old Right appealed only to a small socioeconomic elite which profited from the status quo, neoconservatism struck deep roots within the broader populace by capitalizing on the desire of the demoralized middle and lower social strata for a program of non-Marxist social reform and economic protection against the ravages of the modern capitalist economy.

Finally, neoconservatism differed from the traditional Right in that it was less politically oriented—one might almost say "unpolitical." Neoconservatism rejected the established conservative political parties and interest groups as too socially exclusive and too subservient to the material interests of the upper-class elite. More importantly, however, neoconservative theorists—especially those from the cultivated German middle class which had traditionally remained aloof from political affairs—regarded political institutions and control of the state as but a secondary concern, and as a result, tended to avoid the political process altogether. For neoconservatives, like most radicals, looked to the very root of things and desired not merely a change in the political or social structure, but a fundamental reform of social values, cultural ideals, the human personality, and even human biology. Their ultimate goal was nothing less than a radical transformation of life itself, from the ground up. It was this all-encompassing, utopian nature of neoconservative aims which distinguished them from the more realistic, limited aims of traditional conservatives; neoconservatism was a form of cultural fascism which fed ultimately into totalitarianism.[11] Such utopian goals, and the absolute commitment to rooting out not only the effects but also the basic causes of man's modern ills made neoconservatives incapable of compromise and thus made them ill suited for the give-and-take of modern political life. As purists who clung tenaciously to a set of abstract antimodern ideals, they scorned the traditional conservative political organizations, which they believed violated "true" conservative principles by compromising with modern forces. Indeed, they generally regarded the entire political process as co-opted by modern liberalism, and so rejected traditional political activity out of hand.

Instead, neoconservatives preferred to organize networks of small clubs, associations, societies, and schools, and to work through the published media to preach their absolute ideals and utopian programs. Since zealotry was rampant and compromise or cooperation at a premium among neoconservative ideologues, the varieties of neoconservative thought, the number of neoconservative splinter groups, and the array of neoconservative publications reached bewildering proportions, especially after 1918. Neoconservatism was hardly a well-defined, coherent front, much less an organized political force; it was, rather, a loose collection of diverse groups and individuals moving toward roughly similar goals. The amorphous nature of neoconservatism, with its endless and at times even contradictory internal variations, precluded the movement from ever implementing its goals. It goes far in explaining why the German neoconservative movement was eventually overshadowed and skillfully shunted aside in the Weimar republic by the collateral, but more coherent, organized, and politically active National Socialist movement.

Neoconservatism and the German Publishing Industry

The significant role which neoconservative ideas played in Germany between 1890 and 1933 by unintentionally breaking the intellectual ground for Nazism would alone justify a study of their publishing history. Scholars have often noted that a history of neoconservatism from a publishing perspective would add much to our understanding of this important movement and is long overdue.[12]

The German neoconservative movement lends itself especially well to such a study and can serve as a valuable heuristic device to help point out the cultural role of publishing. For neoconservatism was bound up with the internal history of the German publishing industry in a way which other movements were not. It was supported primarily by publicists and writers, rather than by organized political parties or institutions, and was thus more dependent than other movements on the printed word. The neoconservative movement was a broad, somewhat amorphous phenomenon embracing a large number of authors from fields as varied as philosophy, literature, religion, politics, and economics. Precisely because of this fact, it offers a unique opportunity to examine the dealings between the publishing industry and diverse authors. Indeed, as shall become clear in the course of this study, publishers were instrumental in forging an identifiable neoconservative movement out of the many disparate neoconservative streams of thought.

There was no single publishing institution which dominated the production of neoconservative literature in the same way the Hugenberg-Scherl press empire promoted the cause of the traditional Right in the early twentieth century. (The "Hugenberg Concern," founded during World War I with financial backing from heavy industry, eventually controlled a series of metropolitan and provincial newspapers, mass circulation magazines, film production companies, and a telegraphic news service. During the Weimar years it was the leading producer of literature and information for the established parties and interest groups of the Right.)[13] Rather, neoconservative literature was disseminated by a great number of individual small and medium-sized publishing enterprises.

The interaction between the publishing industry and the German neoconservative movement can best be understood by examining the publishing houses which were well established in the professional book trade, which had a relatively broad and independent publishing program, and which were active in neoconservative publishing over a long period of time. Of the total number of publishing houses which were in some way involved in the production and distribution of neoconservative literature, only a few meet these criteria. A number of firms, for example, were ad hoc enterprises founded by a neoconservative journalist solely for the purpose of publishing his journal. Thus Ferdinand Avenarius founded the Kunstwart Verlag in 1887 to publish his *Der Kunstwart*, while Dietrich Eckart established the Hoheneichen Verlag in Munich in 1916 to issue his anti-Semitic journal *Auf Gut Deutsch*. The so-called June Club of Berlin created the Ring Verlag in 1918 to issue *Das Gewissen* and *Der Ring*, Rudolf Pechel founded the Deutsche Rundschau Verlag in Berlin to publish his *Deutsche Rundschau*, Ludwig Voggenreiter's Voggenreiter Verlag of Potsdam (also known as Der Weisse Ritter Verlag) was created in 1918 for the youth journal *Der Weisse Ritter*, and in 1927 Anna and Ernst Niekisch organized the Widerstand Verlag of Dresden solely to issue their journal *Der Widerstand*. These publishing houses might also produce an occasional book or two, usually written by one of the contributors to the house journal; not infrequently these volumes became important programmatic statements of neoconservative ideology.[14] Yet on the whole, such *Zeitschriftenverlage* were completely subordinate to the journal they were created to issue; once the journal ceased publication, the house itself also disappeared. Because almost none of these journals enjoyed a circulation of more than a few thousand copies and most expired after a few years, this type of neoconservative publishing house, while perhaps important for the internal development of neoconservatism, had only a peripheral and insignificant role within the German publishing industry. To study their publishing endeavors would be simply to study the respective journal and its small circle of contributors. As several scholarly studies of this type already exist,[15] it would be redundant to include these small, journal-dependent neoconservative enterprises in the present study.

Similar to the journal-dependent houses were those houses founded by individuals or groups who were active politically and who desired a publishing house in order to publish their programs and accounts of their activities. Such firms functioned as mere adjuncts or organs for groups whose primary interest lay beyond the field of publishing, and their publishing activities were fully determined by and subordinated to the founder's or sponsoring group's political interests. This was true, for example, of Ernst Jünger's Verlag der Aufmarsch (Leipzig), Alfred Roth's Deutschvölkischer Verlag (Stuttgart, founded 1924), of the Erich Ludendorff Volkswarte Verlag GmbH (Munich, founded 1929), and of the Deutschvölkischer Schutz- und Trutzbund's house, the Deutschvölkischer Verlagsanstalt (Hamburg). Likewise, the Verlag Friedrich Bruckmann of Munich fell under the influence of the Wagnerian Bayreuth Circle and of Wagner's son-in-law Houston S. Chamberlain, while the Deutscher Volksverlag Dr. Ernst Boepple and the Franz Eher Nachf. Verlag GmbH, both founded in Munich in 1919, were mere extensions of the Nazi party, producing the party newspaper, party platform, and works by leading Nazi theorists such as Alfred Rosenberg. One cannot speak of these firms as having genuine publishing programs; their publishing policy, instead, was identical to the parent organization's political program. Publishing enterprises of this type cannot be considered integral components of the commercial German publishing and book industry.

A number of small, short-lived, obscure publishing houses attached neither to a journal nor to a political group published neoconservative material, but they do not warrant inclusion in this study. Firms such as the Adolf Klein Verlag (Leipzig, founded 1926), the Deutschnationaler Volksverlag (Berlin, founded 1919), the Erneuerungs Verlag (Berlin), the Ernst Pieper Ring Verlag (Düsseldorf, founded 1909), the Frundsberg Verlag (Berlin, founded 1924), the Theodor Fritsch Verlag (Leipzig), the Jungdeutscher Verlag (Berlin), the L. Staackmann Verlag (Leipzig), or the Verlag für Zeitkritik existed solely to print and distribute neoconservative writings. Yet precisely because of this fact these firms were not completely a part of the regular German publishing industry and did not partake of its traditions. Rather, they were formed by and as a direct result of the neoconservative movement and consequently had too narrow a readership and too circumscribed an orientation to have an identity or function beyond the boundaries of the neoconservative movement. Almost without exception such houses were founded rather spontaneously by a neoconservative ideologue, published a handful of writings particularly dear to the founder, then sank, unnoticed, into oblivion (or more often, bankruptcy). The extremely limited professional nature and goals of these houses meant their participation in German publishing and intellectual life and their impact on the industry or on the reading public was marginal. Founders or directors of such houses were not professional publishers, but propagandists who dabbled in publishing; an examination of their publishing activities would tell us little about the various ways the established German publishing industry nurtured the neoconservative movement and helped acquaint the reading public with it.

Finally, there were a number of long-standing, reputable German firms which, as part of a broadly based publishing program, might include a work or two by some of the major neoconservative authors. The C. H. Beck'sche Verlagsbuchhandlung, an esteemed Munich firm established in 1763 and specializing in theology, law, history, philosophy, literature, and pedagogy, thus became the publisher of the young war novelist Walter Flex and of that cultural pessimist par excellence, Oswald Spengler. Ernst Jünger's radical war novels appeared under the imprint of E. S. Mittler (Berlin), a firm founded in 1789 with specialties in history, theology, philosophy, and military literature. The G. Fischer house in Jena, established 1878, issued works by the neoconservative political theorist Othmar Spann as part of its publishing program in the areas of economics, law, social science, natural science, and theology. Other titles by this same author also appeared from Quelle & Meyer (Leipzig), a newer house concentrating in psychology, literature, philosophy, history, religion, law, and natural science. Likewise, the writings of Carl Schmitt, theorist of "political romanticism," were published both by Duncker & Humblot (Berlin and Munich, established 1789) and by Junker & Dünnhaupt (Berlin, founded 1929). These two major houses specialized respectively in law, politics, economics, socialism, philosophy, and history; and in philosophy, pedagogy, German literature, and economics. None of these commercial houses can be said to have had a neoconservative orientation; the few conservative titles they produced were generally exceptions and were included not out of any ideological commitment to the neoconservative cause, but rather for commercial considerations or to balance out an extremely diversified list of authors. Perhaps nothing illustrates this type of fleeting association with neoconservative literature better than the case of the C. L. Hirschfeld Verlag of Leipzig, founded in 1834. This firm, publishers of legal and political literature, brought out Langbehn's *Rembrandt als Erzieher* (1890), a work which soon assumed scriptural significance for the early neoconservative movement and became a runaway bestseller, reaching its forty-ninth printing by 1909. After capitalizing on this work, however, the Hirschfeld firm sold the book rights to the A. Duncker Verlag and concentrated on the publication of left-wing socialist literature. By the 1920s it had become one of the leading outlets for the works of the Frankfurt School.

Neither the large array of basically "neutral" commercial houses which occasionally strayed into neoconservative publishing, nor the many small, short-lived firms whose only raison d'être was the neoconservative cause would thus provide much insight into the mutual relationship between the German book trade and the neoconservative movement. This study will therefore concentrate on only five German publishing houses, but ones which were particularly important in the creation, promotion, and dissemination of neoconservatism: the Eugen Diederichs Verlag (Jena); the J. F. Lehmanns Verlag (Munich); the Hanseatische Verlagsanstalt (Hamburg) and its many related enterprises; the Gerhard Stalling Verlag (Oldenburg); and the Heinrich Beenken Verlag (Berlin).

The publishers who founded or directed these houses were publishers by profession and regarded publishing, rather than politics or journalism, as their foremost activity. They were neoconservative publishers rather than simply publishing neoconservatives. As established members of the traditional book industry, these firms based their activity on more than merely the neoconservative movement. They were general publishing houses engaged in many fields of publishing, and were thus broad enough to have a distinct identity of their own extending beyond their neoconservative products. Because their existence was never completely dependent upon neoconservative undertakings, these houses remained closer to the mainstream of the industry. Ironically, it was perhaps precisely because these five firms devoted only a part of their energies to neoconservatism that they were more significant for neoconservatism than the houses which channeled all their resources in that direction. For with a basis and identity which existed previous to and beyond the boundaries of the neoconservative movement, these houses established a broader pool of respect from which neoconservatism could draw. By associating their houses with the movement, these publishers not only attracted to the movement readers from other fields of the firms' endeavors, but also lent greater respectability to the neoconservative movement. Even more importantly, these houses were not financially dependent on their neoconservative activities. They were able to use financial resources acquired from their other undertakings to support their neoconservative enterprises (which were often less remunerative than more neutral, conventional publishing). Hence they had greater freedom and more resources than did those small houses which were completely dependent on neoconservatism. The independent identity, prestige, and financial status of these five publishers meant that they were in a stronger position than were most other neoconservative houses to influence their authors and help shape those aspects of the neoconservative movement with which they dealt. Consequently, a study of these firms will better illuminate the involvement of publishers in the history of the German neoconservative intellectual movement.

Chapter 2 will examine the organizational structure of the five publishing establishments. The individual histories of the firms, the way in which these publishers' conceptions of their profession abetted their ideological commitment to causes such as neoconservatism, the manner in which they integrated neoconservative journals with their publication of books, and the interaction of the neoconservative houses with the broader German book trade will each be explored in turn.

Chapters 3 through 8 will discuss the way in which the publishers actually helped develop, disseminate, and promote neoconservatism in Germany during the Wilhelmian era, World War I, and the Weimar republic; the fate of these five firms after the Nazi seizure of power in 1933 is also related.

Finally, a concluding chapter will offer a general appraisal of the role these five publishers played within the neoconservative movement in Germany and will reflect on what the case of these five publishers can tell us about the broader role of publishers in modern culture.

Two

The Neoconservative
Publishing Houses

Origins and Institutional Development

Beyond the neoconservative cause which they so energetically championed, the five publishing houses examined in this study shared entrepreneurial characteristics. All were originally founded or reorganized during the book trade boom of the Wilhelmian era; all were independent houses producing for a general reading public (although this was true of the Hanseatic house only after 1920); and all were recognized as general rather than specialized publishing enterprises whose activities—and thus, financial basis—extended beyond the neoconservative movement.

Eugen Diederichs and the Eugen Diederichs Verlag (EDV)

Eugen Diederichs (1867–1930) was born into a family of Thuringian tenant farmers. Young Eugen was intensely interested in his ancestry and once undertook a pilgrimage to the family's original ancestral home near Braunschweig, where he rapturously reexperienced the milieu in which his forefathers had lived centuries before.[1] He remained forever proud of his rural heritage and felt that it had rooted him deeply in nature. Reflecting the emerging "blood and soil" ideology which came to dominate much of neoconservative thought, he was convinced that a closeness to the soil was more German and more profoundly spiritual than urban life. For Diederichs, the transition from peasant to publisher was internally consistent: "I thank fate that I stem directly from peasant blood and from it have stepped into the profession of spiritual plowing and sowing."[2] For this reason, he chose as the Diederichs Verlag's first insignia the image of a sower with his back to a rising sun.

Eugen's father was moderately prosperous and managed to accumulate a fair sum with which he hoped to purchase a small estate of his own.

More than half of this capital was lost, however, during the boom-and-bust "founding years" (*Gründerjahre*) of 1871–73, a misfortune which disturbed the family deeply.[3] This early encounter with economic distress in the frenetic 1870s may well have fathered Eugen's later rejection of laissez-faire industrial capitalism and his opposition to the growing materialism of German life.

Eugen was a bright, but poorly motivated student; after failing twice in secondary school, he withdrew two years early. His subsequent education, like that of so many other leading neoconservative publicists, was self-acquired through travel, lectures, and voracious (if dilettantish) reading. After his compulsory one year of military service and brief employment as agricultural inspector, the restless young man decided in 1888 to become a bookdealer's apprentice. He progressed rapidly, served with several different book firms throughout Germany, and established many important contacts in the literary world which were of great use to him later.[4] At the death of his father in 1895, a substantial inheritance (fifty thousand marks) passed to Eugen and he decided to establish a publishing house of his own. In September 1896, while making a grand tour of Italy, he announced the founding of the Eugen Diederichs Verlag: Publishing House for Modern Endeavors in Literature, Natural Science, and Theosophy. (The firm's designation was changed in 1898 to Publishing House for Modern Endeavors in Literature, Natural Science, Social Germanism, and German Cultural History.) The new firm headquartered in Leipzig, capital of the German book industry, until 1904; he then transferred it to Jena, a more congenial town and the center of the German classical tradition.

The eight years in Leipzig were difficult ones for the young house, for it faced stiff competition in its chosen fields from several similar firms such as the Albert Langen, Georg Müller, Insel, G. Fischer, and S. Fischer houses. A disastrous experience with an expensive, profusely illustrated, twelve-volume series on German cultural history nearly bankrupted the new enterprise; it took some fifteen years to recover the costs of this undertaking. This early failure was offset, however, by another substantial inheritance in 1902 and by the unexpected popularity of works by three of the house's young authors. By 1900 the EDV had attained a yearly turnover of one hundred thousand marks.[5]

The period from 1904, when the firm moved to Jena, until World War I was undoubtedly the house's finest. Not only did the firm enjoy great financial success, but it was coming to exercise an important influence on German cultural developments. By now Diederichs had settled on Donatello's Florentine lion as his permanent house insignia, and the portly, balding publisher with the immaculately trimmed goatee and drooping eyelids was himself respectfully referred to as the "Lion of Jena." The firm's influence was due in part to the acquisition of the journal *Die Tat* (see below, pp. 41–50), which provided Diederichs and his authors with a regular outlet for their opinions on current cultural and social problems, and in part to the firm's publication of several important multivolume series which attracted wide public interest. In addition, Diederichs developed into a gifted promoter who knew how to coin and use phrases which stuck in the public mind. He managed to create a distinct image for his house not only through the types of material he published, but also through his imaginative, programmatic catalogs, his provocative open letters to the public, and his own prolific essays on contemporary affairs.[6] Full of ambitious plans and driven by an urge to experiment, he published several unorthodox or controversial works by audacious young authors and more than once clashed with the censor or was charged with blasphemy or *lèse majesté*. Diederichs was quite skillful in keeping his firm before the public eye and in attracting favorable publicity. The firm's yearly catalogs and almanacs, for instance, were only partly intended to introduce the public to new house publications; they also contained essays by Diederichs and other prominent authors on the current and future state of German culture. Diederichs was well aware of the dual nature of his catalogs: "When these [abstract cultural essays] happen to touch on some of my house's own publications," he coyly told one author whom he commissioned to write such an essay, "so much the better."[7] Many of his catalog titles, for example "*Verlagsprogramm: Neuromantik*," became popular bywords for new cultural movements. The programmatic Diederichs house reports were soon recognized as important cultural manifestos.[8]

During the prewar years the house assembled an impressive collection of contemporary German and European authors, which included Ferdinand Avenarius, Henri Bergson, Anton Chekhov, Hermann Hesse, Thomas Masaryk, Carl Spitteler, and Sidney Webb. The EDV's publishing program, complemented by the house's pioneering, even revolutionary work in the area of book graphics (see p. 79), helped make it a renowned and highly respected publishing house both within Germany and abroad. At the 1906 Applied Arts Show in Dresden, the firm was cited as one of the foremost promoters of German culture, while the 1910 World Exhibition at Brussels awarded the house a gold Grand Prix medal as Germany's best publisher. During the 1914 International Exhibition of Books and Graphics in Leipzig, the Diederichs firm again captured highest honors. Prominent German cultural figures lavished praise on the house, and on the eve of World War I the noted writer Stefan Zweig said of Diederichs: "He represents in the best sense of the word the type of humanistic German whose intellect can scout out all directions with equal strength, who strives for that universality of cultivation of which Goethe remains the supreme, unattainable summit. . . . His catalogs are a small cosmos of cultivation and at the same time a monument of German culture, the portraits of a beautiful and creative personality."[9]

After 1914, the EDV—like so much of the German book trade—was plagued by economic problems. The sharp decline in demand during the war, an acute shortage of paper, skyrocketing production costs, disruptions in the transport system, and the public's "patriotic" reaction against foreign authors (who comprised a large share of the EDV offerings) all combined to cut the house's weekly income to less than 10 percent of the normal prewar level. While he was quick to include special war-oriented titles in his publishing program, unfavorable conditions during and immediately after the war prevented Diederichs from completing many of the undertakings he had begun during the previous decade. The postwar inflation was, as Diederichs complained, "catastrophic" for German publishers; in 1923 he estimated that publishers like him were losing 90 percent of their capital through the rapid deterioration of the currency.[10] Even though he viewed the economic situation as increasingly bleak, he was determined not to restrict his publishing activity. While conditions improved after 1924, the world economic collapse of 1929 brought on a new crisis for the firm. That year, Diederichs feared that the survival of his publishing house might necessitate abandoning his cultural program. Although Diederichs's debilitating illness in 1929 and his death a year later undoubtedly played a role, the firm's new publications during the years 1929–32 fell off by 30 to 50 percent from the level of the 1920s.

From 1914 until Diederichs's death in 1930, the house continued its publication of belles lettres and avant-garde cultural books, but also added to its lists more works on current political and social problems. Several monumental multivolume series were initiated or continued. Among the authors joining the firm during the 1920s were Lou Andreas-Salomé, Lujo Brentano, Ludwig Klages, Hendrik de Man, Paul Natorp, Hermann Nohl, and Hugo Preuss. The reputation of the house remained high, and respected men such as Ernst Troeltsch and Theodor Heuss praised its work.[11] In 1924 the University of Cologne awarded Diederichs an honorary doctorate, the Weimar republic's equivalent of a patent of nobility. By Diederichs's death, the EDV had published more than seventeen hundred titles. To be sure, not all were neoconservative in nature. Diederichs was a man of wide-ranging interests who was involved in many avant-garde cultural movements; before World War I, when his interests were more eclectic, he relished issuing works by cultural nonconformists of all sorts and he counted liberals, democrats, and not a few maverick socialists among his friends and authors. During the last decade and a half, however, his publishing program became less and less varied and more narrowly focused on works with a neoconservative bent.

But whatever the subject matter, the books issued by the EDV were of almost uniformly high intellectual quality and were intended for the well-educated, cultured circles; the firm could, in fact, boast that no less than six of its authors held the Nobel Prize. As a house in contact with leading intellectuals of the day and striving to uphold some of the noblest traditions of European culture, the Eugen Diederichs Verlag by 1930 had become a cultural institution in Germany. It was this leading position which made the firm's extensive neoconservative activities so significant.

Julius F. Lehmann and the J. F. Lehmanns Verlag (JFLV)

Julius Friedrich Lehmann (1864–1935) was born in Zurich as the son of an exiled 1848 revolutionary. The nationalism of mid-century German liberalism permeated the Lehmann family, which stressed its ties to the German, rather than to the Swiss nation. The Lehmann children attended a special school for German exiles in Zurich. In 1871 the entire family scuffled with French-Swiss citizens of Zurich over a celebration of the Sedan victory, an experience which made a deep impression on young Julius.[12] It has often been noted that some of Germany's most fervent nationalists—E. M. Arndt, H. S. Chamberlain, Arthur Moeller van den Bruck, Alfred Rosenberg, Hans Grimm, Adolf Hitler—were "foreign-Germans" (*Auslandsdeutsche*) born either outside the German Reich or in "endangered" border areas containing mixed nationalities. As men who were in a sense outsiders to Germany, having grown up where their German heritage was threatened or had to compete with other ethnic groups, these figures suffered identification problems. They consequently developed an exaggerated consciousness of their German nationalism and had to prove themselves and to others that they were, indeed, ardent members of the German *Volk*. In the same way, Lehmann's later radical nationalism was no doubt due in part to his childhood identification with, and his physical separation from, the German Reich.

Like Diederichs, Lehmann became dissatisfied early with formal education, ultimately rejecting it for the path of self-education. His school attendance was irregular and he withdrew from school after completing only two-thirds of the normal secondary program. His early separation from the formal world of learning (a separation in which he took some pride in adult life) probably prompted Lehmann's later distrust of intellectuals and his preference for direct, forceful action over reasoned argument. As he expressed it: "I have never considered myself a thinker; rather, I console myself with the saying that a small mind and a bold heart can also accomplish great things."[13] Indeed, Lehmann seemed rather prone to asocial, even violent tendencies. After his marriage, his family lived more or less in isolation from Munich society.[14] At the turn of the century, as his house was engaged in an intense anti-Catholic publishing campaign, he suspected that both Catholics and Jews were plotting to destroy him; he kept himself continually armed so that he might fend off assassins at any time.[15] Likewise, after the World War Lehmann believed his life was in danger from those who opposed his nationalistic publishing activities. At various times he carried a loaded revolver, heavy stick, rubber truncheon, or brass knuckles, all of which he intended to use "ruthlessly." The publisher advised some of his authors to do likewise, and offered one writer detailed instructions on the proper use of brass knuckles.[16]

After leaving school Julius, like Diederichs, became a bookdealer's apprentice and worked for various German firms. During that time he coauthored a practical handbook for apprentices, from which he earned substantial royalties. But he had the urge to become independent and establish a firm of his own. The opportunity to do so arose when his cousin, who was editor of the respected *Münchener Medizinische Wochenschrift* (*Munich Medical Weekly*), became dissatisfied with the journal's publisher and approached Lehmann with an arrangement whereby Lehmann would found a new publishing house in Munich to take over publication of the *Wochenschrift*. With a capital of five thousand marks, on 1 October 1890 Lehmann established the J. F. Lehmanns Verlag; he set up shop on Munich's Landwehrstrasse and began business with one assistant and one packer.

During its initial years, the JFLV engaged solely in medical publications and in promoting the *Wochenschrift*. Within a decade Lehmann had succeeded in tripling the medical journal's circulation, establishing it as the most widely circulated professional organ in the German language. The *Wochenschrift* formed one of the strongest pillars of the Lehmann house. Other important fields of JFLV medical publishing included the translation of medical books and publication of lavishly illustrated medical atlases. These latter volumes were an instant success and were translated into fourteen languages for extensive distribution abroad. (An American publisher once placed an order for one hundred thousand copies, a remarkable amount for the nineteenth century.) Revenues from these early sales firmly established the financial security of the J. F. Lehmanns Verlag at a relatively early date, and the popularity of the works gave the young house a worldwide reputation in the field of medicine before World War I. Both gains proved important for the house's racial activities.

Although the firm prospered and expanded (by 1906 Lehmann had been forced three times to move to larger quarters, finally settling in the Paul Heysestrasse), Lehmann was interested in more than publishing medical materials. From the very founding of his house he desired to publish political material but was forced to postpone these plans because of limited financial means. As a young man, he had adopted his father's liberalism and was associated with the Progressive (*Freisinnige*) party; but he soon abandoned that outlook and turned instead to more right-wing, nationalistic causes. To enable his firm to carry out its "national duties without consideration of financial profit," Lehmann wanted first to insure that the house was supported by profitable undertakings.[17] He consciously and deliberately used his revenue from medical publications to engage in nationalistic activities: "As soon as my medical house drew in enough so that the concern over daily bread was no longer pressing, I concentrated my energies in the service of the national cause. I sought to further nationalist strivings through a great number of works; and though these often meant a successive chain of losses for the house, I have also had the joy of seeing many of these attempts fall on fruitful ground."[18]

The ideological activities of the JFLV, then, were based financially on its medical work; without the latter, the former would not have been undertaken. The house began its publication of political material in 1896 and over the next four decades divided its energies about equally between medical-scientific and political-racial works.

Before World War I, the house issued a total of some seventy books as well as several journals. After 1918, the JFLV expanded rapidly, producing between fifty and one hundred titles each year (out of approximately one thousand manuscripts submitted annually), plus twelve journals. By the early 1930s the firm employed some fifty to sixty people, and Lehmann had admitted three partners to help supervise the house's widespread activities: Fritz Schwarz, a trusted employee, became a partner in 1911; Lehmann's nephew Friedrich Lehmann attained partnership in 1920 (Lehmann's only son was killed at the front in 1916); and Lehmann's son-in-law Otto Spatz was made a full partner in 1930. Lehmann himself, however, always retained control over publishing policy.

The two to three hundred neoconservative books published by Lehmann between 1890 and 1933 were of a far different type than the books of the EDV and touched different areas of the neoconservative movement. Diederichs had high intellectual aspirations and hoped to make his house a respected cultural force in Germany. He thus produced refined works in philosophy, literature, or religion which explored the intellectual foundations of neoconservative theory and which generally appealed only to the more educated, cultivated readers. Lehmann, by contrast, disdained theory and had in mind a much different audience; for he hoped to motivate Germans to concrete action. His firm's products, consequently, were usually straight-forward agitational tracts which aimed at a broader, less educated readership and dealt with the neoconservative social, political, and military tasks at hand.

The German National Union of Commercial Employees (DHV) and the Hanseatic Publishing Institute (HVA)

The Hanseatic Publishing Institute (Hanseatische Verlagsanstalt, HVA) was founded in Hamburg in 1920 through the consolidation of several smaller book enterprises; within a decade, it had developed into an extensive and diversified publishing empire. The HVA's close relationship with another important neoconservative institution, the German National Union of Commercial Employees (Deutschnationaler Handlungsgehilfen-Verband, DHV) distinguishes it from the other publishing enterprises of this study. Although the Hanseatic house directors remained relatively autonomous and the HVA never functioned as a mere mouthpiece for the DHV, the activities of the house were linked to those of the union. A brief look at the DHV is therefore necessary.

The DHV championed the social, economic, and ideological interests of many salaried white-collar employees and sales clerks (*Angestellten* and *Gehilfen*). White-collar employees numbered some two million in imperial Germany. Their status and working conditions distinguished them from the approximately fourteen million industrial workers; for they generally earned more than laborers, received a salary rather than a wage, did not engage in manual labor, and were covered by a separate social insurance law. Most importantly, they enjoyed closer contact with their employers, and indeed, tended to identify with management. Many a sales clerk or office employee in a small commercial firm hoped one day to gain economic independence by founding and operating his own business, while those employed in larger companies expected eventually to enter the upper ranks of management. Intensely proud of their independent status and thoroughly imbued with middle-class values and aspirations, white-collar employees hardly considered themselves employees, much less members of the industrial proletariat, which they disdained.

By the last decade of the nineteenth century, however, technical change, rationalization, and concentration in industry were undermining the status, and more importantly, endangering the future of white-collar employees and clerks. As small enterprises were squeezed out by larger ones, and as increasing specialization restricted upward mobility within the larger companies, many white-collar employees saw their opportunity to rise on the social ladder being cut off. Increasingly, they faced the prospect of remaining forever an employee, condemned to perpetual economic dependence. The more their future came to resemble that of the common wage laborer, the more the distinction between their status and that of the industrial working class was erased and the greater became their fear of proletarianization. Predictably, they sought all the more desperately to maintain their traditional status and distinct social identity as a "middle stratum" (*Mittelstand*) between the wealthy bourgeoisie and the working class.

As both big business and organized labor learned to flex their growing muscles in Wilhelmian Germany, many white-collar employees felt crushed between the Scylla of their wealthy bourgeois employers and the Charybdis of the socialist working class. On the one hand clerks and white-collar employees rejected the Marxist contention that petty-bourgeois intermediary strata like their own were destined to disappear, and they feared sinking into the egalitarian mass proletariat. Instead, they clung to the notion of a hierarchically structured, antiegalitarian social order in which their social superiority over the working class would be assured. On the other hand, they opposed exploitation and social reactionism by capitalistic employers, and desired a system of social protection which would insure their social and economic security. They advocated a kind of "socialism for the little man" which would strengthen the intermediate petty-bourgeois classes (*Mittelstände*) against the wealthy, powerful business elite and at the same time would preserve the distinction between their class and the organized socialist proletariat.[19]

Thus the German Union of Commercial Employees (Deutscher Handlungsgehilfen-Verband) was founded in Hamburg in 1893 "to protect our class, which comprises the greatest segment of the *Mittelstände*, from proletarianization, from ruin," and to "oppose the Social Democratic trade union movement with the idea of a nationalistic union movement."[20] The DHV charter pledged the organization to repulse all attempts by socialism to win followers from among the clerks and office employees of Germany.

According to the charter, Jews were also excluded from membership in the DHV. For, to many clerks and white-collar employees, the bewildering industrial changes which endangered their present social status and future economic prospects seemed to be the result of a general decline of hallowed German values and traditions, the product of an alien, un-German capitalist system introduced into Germany by liberals, Marxists, and Jews. Strengthening German national and racial consciousness and rooting out all Marxist and Jewish influence, they believed, was the key to the preservation and future prosperity of their class. Thus the young DHV stood on a strange, contradictory program which, on the one hand, preached anti-Marxism, antiegalitarianism, militant nationalism, and middle-class unity in the face of the Red threat, and on the other hand advocated a populist anticapitalism, militant *Mittelstand* consciousness, social protection against reactionary employers, and a hierarchic social order in which clerks and white-collar employees and other members of the *Mittelstand* would hold an honored place. The antisocialist and anticapitalist elements of the DHV platform were held together by a virulent, racial anti-Semitism. In 1896, the organization changed its name to German National Union of Commercial Employees (Deutschnationaler Handlungsgehilfen-Verband), *deutschnationale* being one of the era's euphemisms for anti-Semitic.

Under the direction of Wilhelm Schack, and after 1909 of Hans Bechly, the DHV grew to more than one hundred thousand members by World War I, making it a formidable pressure group and the foremost representative of white-collar interests. Politically, the organization formed a series of fleeting alliances with various anti-Semitic and imperialist groups such as the German Social Reform Party and Pan-German League (Alldeutscher Verband) which advocated social protection for the *Mittelstand* and a more vigorous pursuit of German national and economic interests at home and abroad.

World War I brought sudden economic misery to clerks and commercial employees and put them face-to-face with the dreaded prospect of proletarianization. For between 1914 and 1918, salaries lagged significantly behind the rapidly rising cost of living, and men faced competition from women who were induced into the labor force as part of the war effort. The hours and working conditions of white-collar employees came more and more to resemble those of manual workers, whose wages rose steadily during the war. In short, clerks suffered both an absolute and a relative decline in relation to the working class; the line which separated them from the proletariat became increasingly blurred. Peace brought little respite however, for the ravages of inflation in the early 1920s, the impetus toward increased rationalization and routinization of industry in the later 1920s, and the devastating unemployment brought by economic depression in the 1930s, hit this group particularly hard and placed the cherished goal of economic independence hopelessly beyond the reach of all but a few. Anxious, demoralized, and slipping ever closer to the dreaded mass proletariat, white-collar employees and clerks after 1914 clung all the more desperately to their distinctive *Mittelstand* consciousness and life-style. Although they continued to fear the Social Democratic labor movement and to denounce Jewish-Marxism as un-German, they also became more militantly hostile toward what they considered their reactionary capitalist employers. Their hatred of big business, the rich, and the powerful within the bourgeoisie was coupled with increasingly radical demands for control over private property, greater social and economic equality with the upper bourgeoisie, and a comprehensive system of social protection for the *Mittelstand* to forestall their proletarianization.[21]

As the socioeconomic problems of commercial employees intensified and their militancy rose, so too did membership in the DHV. From one hundred forty-seven thousand members in 1918, the union claimed some four hundred nine thousand in 1931. After 1914 the organization functioned more and more as a union, lobbying for the interests of its constituents. In politics, it followed a course of flexible noncommitment and neutrality, cooperating with any non-Marxist party which would support a program of social protection for the *Mittelstand*. Throughout the 1920s, the DHV was most often allied with the conservative parties which were critical of the "Weimar system": primarily the German National Peoples Party (Deutschnationale Volkspartei, DNVP), and to a lesser extent the German Peoples Party (Deutsche Volkspartei, DVP), the Catholic Center Party (Zentrum), and other middle-class splinter groups.

With the advent of the depression in 1929, however, the DNVP fell under the control of the reactionary Hugenberg wing and came to reflect the interests of big business; it turned a deaf, if not hostile ear to the social demands of white-collar employees, for whom the effects of the economic collapse were especially painful. Thus in the early 1930s the DHV rank and file turned in ever-increasing numbers to the radical Nazi party, which offered them both an intensely nationalistic anti-Semitism and a non-Marxist policy of social protection. At the same time, the membership began pressuring DHV leaders to abandon their independent political stance. Faced with growing competition from the Nazis for the allegiance of white-collar employees, the DHV leadership drifted further and further to the right after 1929 in a desperate attempt to maintain the union's independence and prevent a desertion of its membership to Hitler.[22]

Throughout its history, the DHV was more than a union pressing for limited socioeconomic interests; it claimed also to be the vanguard of a broad ideological and social movement. According to the DHV, the *Mittelstand* could truly prosper only in a Germany which had been totally restructured and rejuvenated—culturally, politically, socially, and economically. The ultimate goal of the DHV was a comprehensive neoconservative transformation of national life, a kind of peaceful *Mittelstand* revolution which would create a society attuned to white-collar interests and ideas. Educational and propaganda work, directed first at the *Mittelstand* and then to the entire nation, was thus a crucial part of the DHV's activities. To assist in its ideological campaign, the DHV acquired several publishing and book distribution enterprises.

When Friedrich Raab and Johannes Irwahn founded the DHV in 1893, they also established a small printing house in Hamburg, the Hanseatic Printing and Publishing Institute (Hanseatische Druck- und Verlagsanstalt GmbH, HDVA). The firm, at first independent from the DHV, published several anti-Semitic journals but was soon contracted also to print the DHV stationery and the union newspaper. By the turn of the century this printing firm had come to be almost completely dependent on the DHV for its business. Between 1903 and 1909 the DHV purchased more than thirty thousand marks worth of HDVA stock and a DHV officer, Christian Winter, was installed as the firm's director. Sometime between 1913 and 1917 the DHV acquired total ownership of the small publishing house, whose capital now stood at three hundred fifty thousand marks.[23]

In 1904, as the DHV had begun to consolidate its control over the HDVA, the union also established its own Union Bookstore (Buchhandlung des DHV) to handle technical literature and practical vocational handbooks for union members. In addition, the store distributed the agitational literature of various anti-Semitic organizations with which the DHV was associated. The purpose of operating a union bookstore, the DHV claimed, was "to provide the intellectual tools for the unionized clerk."[24] By 1913 the Bookstore enjoyed yearly sales of more than ten thousand marks. After the outbreak of the war, the store changed its name to the German National Bookstore (Deutschnationale Buchhandlung GmbH) and concentrated on distributing nationalistic literature to soldiers on the battlefield (many DHV members, the store's primary market, now being in the army), and began publishing a few nationalistic books and pamphlets under its own imprint.

In April 1917, with a capital of three hundred fifty thousand marks, the DHV founded a third, separate publishing house, the German National Publishing Institute (Deutschnationale Verlagsanstalt, DNVA). This new enterprise took over the publishing activities of the union's bookstore, assumed publication of the union's new journal *Deutsches Volkstum* (*Germanic Volk Character*) from the HDVA, and began publication of another union periodical. As by-products of these journals, the DNVA also published belletristic books so as "to furnish our circle of journal readers with a broad but thorough fare of literature."[25] When the war ended, the publishing undertakings of the DHV proliferated even further. A special art publishing house, the Hanseatic Art House (Hanseatischer Kunstverlag), was founded in December 1918 with twenty-one thousand marks capital; and when Wilhelm Stapel assumed editorship of the *Deutsches Volkstum* in January 1919, he demanded the journal be given its own independent publishing house, the Verlag des Deutschen Volkstums.

By 1920, then, the DHV owned the HDVA and the German National Bookstore outright, and was closely associated with the operation of three other firms, the DNVA, the Hanseatischer Kunstverlag, and the Verlag des

Deutschen Volkstums. But that year the directors of the DNVA discovered that the recent formation of the German National Peoples party was creating a mistaken public impression that their own German National Publishing Institute was but an organ of the political party, a belief which the directors found "detrimental to the development of the DNVA as an independent publishing enterprise."[26] The DHV decided to remedy this situation and at the same time completely reorganize the union's far-flung publishing enterprises by consolidating them all into one firm. Thus, a new house, the Hanseatic Publishing Institute (Hanseatische Verlags-anstalt, HVA) was founded in 1920; it superseded the old DNVA, HDVA, Hanseatischer Kunstverlag, Verlag des Deutschen Volkstums, and the German National Bookstore. Beginning with a capital of nearly two million marks, the new HVA grew rapidly into a major publishing enterprise in its own right. By the end of the decade the house was publishing some thirty-five new titles each year, employed nearly four hundred people (although most of these were in the printing rather than the publishing division), enjoyed annual sales of almost eight million marks, and realized an annual profit of over three hundred thousand marks.[27] The firm was directed first by a Mr. Ulrich, then by Emil Schneider, Karl Bott, and after 1931 by Benno Ziegler; prominent DHV officers such as Bechly, Winter, Christian Krauss, and Max Habermann inevitably sat on the HVA's board of directors. Because his journal *Deutsches Volkstum* appeared in the HVA, Wilhelm Stapel also played an important role in the house. A special department for cultural and political literature (*kulturpolitische Volkstumabteilung*) was created within the HVA in 1926 and placed under Stapel's direction; in this capacity and in his role as official policy advisor for the HVA, Stapel drew up guidelines for and exercised an enormous influence over the house's publishing program.

During the late 1920s, the HVA took advantage of economic difficulties in the German book trade to acquire other publishing houses of its own, and in this way succeeded in assembling a far-reaching publishing empire. Numerous small publishing firms, hit first by the postwar printers' strikes and rising production costs, then by the 1922–23 inflation, and finally by the disastrous depression with its declining book prices and the drying up of capital and credit, faced bankruptcy and liquidation. The large, prosperous HVA seized the opportunity to acquire several insolvent houses such as the Verlag Alfred Roth of Augsburg (March 1928), the Benno Filser Verlag (November 1928), the Eduard Avenarius Verlag (December 1928), the Volksverein Verlag, Duisberger Verlagsanstalt, and Flammenzeichen Verlag (1929), and the Albatros Verlag of Berlin.[28] Another important acquisition was the Ring Verlag, a small publishing house and book club which served the network of neoconservative institutions and journals of

Arthur Moeller van den Bruck's Ring Movement. By gaining control of this key neoconservative firm, the HVA acquired rights to the writings of several leading neoconservative theoreticians, including Moeller's works.[29] In order to propagate its ideological program effectively through these cover houses, the HVA sought to keep its control over them secret.

Of greatest importance to its publishing empire and to German cultural life, however, was the HVA's procurement of two respected German literary houses, the Georg Müller Verlag (GMV) and the Albert Langen Verlag (ALV). After Müller's death in 1918, his Munich house had fallen under the control of the ultraconservative August Scherl newspaper empire and was given a new, right-wing direction. By the late 1920s, however, the firm had amassed debts of some two million marks and another change of ownership, perhaps to the liberal Ullstein publishing empire, appeared imminent. E. G. Kolbenheyer, a longstanding member of the Nazi Fighting League for German Culture (Kampfbund für deutsche Kultur), feared the firm would fall into ideologically unsympathetic hands and he appealed to his friend Wilhelm Stapel for help. Stapel, in turn, convinced the leaders of the DHV and HVA to acquire the GMV for seven hundred thousand marks in February 1928. Karl Bott, director of the HVA, assumed the post of manager of the GMV, while Stapel and Max Habermann (director of the DHV's cultural and political departments) were installed on the house's board of directors.[30] Under their inexperienced management, however, GMV losses mounted and it became clear that a professional bookman was needed to run the enterprise. Kolbenheyer suggested the DHV approach Gustav Pezold, owner of the prestigious Osiander'sche bookstore in Tübingen. Pezold had no previous DHV ties, but did possess impeccable radical right-wing and anti-Semitic credentials.[31] The DHV told Pezold it wanted him "to build up a respected German literary house" and "erect a strong front of German-national literature so that when the approaching political and cultural collapse comes, at least something of German value will survive."[32] After receiving assurances from the DHV that the house would enjoy immunity from the union's meddling, Pezold assumed direction of the Georg Müller Verlag in September 1930. He hoped to use his new post to erect a nationalistic publishing concern large and powerful enough to counteract the influential liberal Jewish houses such as S. Fischer and P. Zsolnay.[33]

Pezold quickly concluded that, despite large financial subsidies from the DHV, the GMV could avoid liquidation only by acquiring the Albert Langen Verlag of Munich, another bankrupt house but one which enjoyed a greater reputation and a more prestigious list of authors. This bold move, Pezold believed, would lift up the failing GMV and enable it to carry out its ambitious ideological publishing program.[34] With the support of

Stapel and Kolbenheyer (who was also an ALV author), Pezold convinced
the DHV to purchase the ALV in May 1931 for five hundred thousand
marks; in March 1932, the GMV and ALV were merged into the Albert
Langen—Georg Müller Verlag (LMV) and given a capital of 1.4 million
marks.[35] Again, although ultimate responsibility over the LMV rested with
the DHV and the HVA men in Hamburg, Pezold was given an extraordinary
degree of autonomy in running the Munich firm. To prevent the HVA and
the LMV from working at cross purposes, a division of labor was established
under which the latter concentrated on belles lettres, while the former
handled political, historical, cultural, military, and commercial publications. The Langen-Müller Verlag, drawing on the extensive catalogs
of the old GMV and ALV and publishing some two hundred new titles
annually, was one of Germany's foremost literary houses in the 1930s.
It quickly became a kind of south German rallying point and literary
counterweight to the large, liberal Berlin houses like Fischer, Ullstein, or
Rowohlt.

Despite its close relation to the DHV, the Hanseatic house and its related
publishing firms cannot be considered merely an extension of the union's
political activities. To be sure, the DHV and the houses of the Hanseatic
empire held similar ideological and programmatic goals. But the HVA and
its affiliates were publishing houses in their own right and produced for
a general market, not merely for DHV members. As the DHV asserted,
"the goals of our publishing houses must reach out far beyond the immediate needs of the Union."[36] Moreover, the key men in the Hanseatic
publishing empire were either professional bookmen or had extensive
book trade experience before coming to the DHV; this was true not only
of Gustav Pezold, but of Max Habermann, Albert Zimmerman (who
founded the DHV Bookstore), Stapel, and Emil Schneider. Pezold, especially, was very much a "professional" who resented and, on the whole,
successfully resisted any meddling by the DHV in the affairs of his LMV.[37]

Besides supporting a network of publishing houses, a large organization
like the DHV was also excellently suited for the distribution of books
among its members—and not only its members. This was done passively
through the DHV Bookstore, but also in a more active manner through a
book club. Because the large DHV membership formed a stable, secure
market, the union could, at minimal financial risk, produce expensive
books and distribute them for mass consumption. For that reason the DHV
in 1916 founded the German National Home Library (Deutschnationale
Hausbücherei, DHB, renamed simply German Home Library in 1923).
The DHB was Germany's first genuine book club, and its creation was
significant both for book trade and for German social history.

Book clubs originated not among readers of the educated middle class, but in the semieducated lower classes. In Germany (and elsewhere), the consumption of books—and to an even greater extent, the actual ownership of books in the prepaperback era—has been largely a reflection of social status, a trait closely identified with the respectable, educated bourgeoisie. The purchase and consumption of books is regarded as a prime means of acquiring the bourgeois cultivation necessary for middle class respectability; books are, if not a means of social mobility, at least an outward sign of middle-class status for those who aspire to a higher social standing. The rapid growth of the book market in nineteenth-century Germany was thus closely linked to the aspirations of the lower middle classes.[38] Book clubs developed in Germany as a way of making inexpensive books—and hence, middle-class cultivation—available to social groups which normally did not buy or could not afford them. Working-class educational societies in imperial Germany, for example, created the Society for Book Lovers (Verein für Bücherfreunde) in 1891; a forerunner of later book clubs, the Society sought to introduce aspiring socialist laborers to the world of books.

The DHV's book club was similarly linked to the needs of white-collar employees who, especially after 1914, feared they were sinking into the proletariat and who desperately sought to identify with the respectable middle class. Ownership of books could provide them with the symbol of social prestige they needed. Indeed, the consumption patterns of white-collar families in the Weimar era, especially those at the lowest income levels, reveal they spent a significantly larger proportion of their income on reading matter than did either the workers below them on the social scale or the government officials above them.[39] Hard-pressed clerks could not afford the high-priced books of the traditional book trade; yet cheap, shoddy books or the pulp novels of the mass reading public would not bring the required social respectability. What anxious clerks and white-collar employees needed was inexpensive editions of reputable, high-quality books, preferably of the respected (but lighter) classics. This is precisely what the German Home Library was created to provide. By joining it, the aspiring commercial employee could acquire decent books inexpensively, without having to set foot in the unfamiliar (and expensive) bookstores.[40] Using the facilities of the HVA, the Library at first reprinted low-priced editions of previously published works or, in the later 1920s, commissioned and published new titles of its own.[41] Subscribers to the club paid a yearly sixty mark membership fee and were entitled to receive six (later eight) titles. Of these, four (later six) were determined by the Library, while the remaining two could be selected by the subscriber from a recommended list. An advisory committee, comprised of DHV officials, scholars, and noted writers, decided which books would be offered.[42] Subscribers also received a small magazine which contained reviews and recommendations of the DHB books as well as books from the HVA and other publishing houses.[43] In practice, the DHB was sometimes used to "push" the various books produced in the HVA publishing houses, and if need be, to dispose of remainders by placing them on the mandatory list.[44]

The DHB clearly appealed to the cultural aspirations of lower-middle-class readers. When the club was formally announced to DHV members, for example, they were told that white-collar employees are superior to manual laborers in that they use their heads and are in closer contact with the realm of the spirit and intellect; "being a good German-national [commercial employee]," the DHB proclaimed, "and having the need to read books is one and the same."[45] Subsequent advertisements assured potential subscribers that while its books were inexpensive, they were also objects one would be proud to own and display:

> The German Home Library is neither a book distribution agency nor a book factory; it is, rather, a dedicated community (*Gesinnungs-gemeinschaft*) with cultural goals. It produces no sensationalist books, nothing shallow or racy, but rather books with inner value, books which enrich and strengthen the reader. Our bindings are not sham or shoddy; we encourage solid German workmanship. Our volumes are beautiful, because they are genuine. . . . The German Home Library provides a library for the German family which has a lively interest in German culture, which is seeking to guard itself against the mass leveling which threatens personal life, and which still values noble frugality.[46]

Home Library membership increased steadily and included not only DHV members, but interested readers from other nationalist circles. The accompanying table indicates the growth of subscriptions; since each subscription represented distribution of eight books by the DHB, the club must be considered a significant factor on the German cultural scene.[47]

GERMAN HOME LIBRARY SUBSCRIPTIONS

Year	Members	Year	Members
1919	600	1926	6,458
1920	880	1927	13,998
1921	1,200	1929 (Jan.)	23,174
1924	2,960	1929 (June)	34,130
1925	3,755	1930 (Feb.)	40,251

SOURCE: "Entwicklung der DHB, Nach dem Privatakte von Emil Schneider," Box 561: DHV, Forschungsstelle für die Geschichte des Nationalsozialismus in Hamburg, Hamburg.

The DHV operated one additional book distribution enterprise. Throughout the 1920s, the union purchased some twenty local bookstores across Germany and formed them into a retail network, the Bücherborn Buchvertriebstelle. This retail chain carried books published by the HVA, LMV, and the other DHV-related houses and promoted them with aggressive advertising. The stores served not only local DHV members, but appealed to the broader public as well. In this regard, they were in direct competition with the retail stores of the regular book trade, a situation which eventually caused serious problems for the DHV and HVA (see pp. 53–56).

The intellectual quality of books produced by the DHV and the HVA network lay somewhere between the level of the Diederichs house and that of the Lehmann firm. Hanseatic books were predominantly political; less agitational and demagogic than the political publications of the JFLV, they were at the same time more practical and journalistic than the theoretical, intellectualized works of EDV authors. The fiction produced by the HVA empire and the DHB ranged from works of lasting quality to shallow, sentimental, nationalistic novels of dubious content. The Langen and Müller firms had both brought with them a reputation for high quality literary production, and the prestige of the old Langen-Müller circle of authors helped increase the respectability of the HVA.

The Heinrich Beenken Verlag (HBV) and the Gerhard Stalling Verlag (GSV)

The two remaining neoconservative publishing establishments treated in this study will receive less attention than the Diederichs, Lehmann, and Hanseatic houses. The Heinrich Beenken Verlag and the Gerhard Stalling Verlag conducted more limited neoconservative activities, had less impact on the movement and the public, and because of the ravages of World War II left behind far fewer historical documents.

The HBV of Berlin arose from the small Friedrich Zillessen Verlag. Zillessen (1837–i915), an evangelical pastor deeply disturbed by liberal attacks on parochial education during the 1870s, founded a small publishing house in 1888 in order to produce an antiliberal educational periodical. The firm soon acquired other nationalistic and conservative journals and began publishing occasional folklorish books on historical or social themes. A growing hatred of socialism during the Wilhelmian years drove the publisher toward a more extreme conservatism.

Heinrich Beenken (1882–?) entered the firm in 1904 and was made a partner in 1912; when Zillessen died, Beenken assumed control and in 1920 changed the house name to the Heinrich Beenken Verlag. Beenken was more politically motivated than his predecessor, and after the national trauma of 1918–19, he dedicated his firm to nationalistic publications. He continued the HBV's traditional struggle against Marxism and socialist unions, printing all the pamphlets for the militantly antisocialist German Employers' League (Deutscher Arbeitgeberverband) and the League Against Social Democracy (Reichsverband gegen die Sozialdemokratie). However, the HBV remained small and was at least as dependent on income from its printing business as on its actual publishing activities.

The Gerhard Stalling Verlag of Oldenburg was, by contrast, a large house with a much longer history. Founded in 1789 by Gerhard Stalling, the GSV published in a variety of areas from local history, folklore, law, administration, and church hymnals, to agricultural handbooks, fiction, and yearbooks for various organizations. In 1889 the brothers Paul and Heinrich Stalling, Jr. inherited the house, which by then employed some sixty people. The two brothers decided to devote the GSV's major energies to the new and financially promising field of technical military literature. While retaining the house's older activities, they concentrated now on the publication of officer's handbooks, military journals and newspapers, training manuals, military histories, and similar material. Within two decades the GSV was the recognized leader in the field of military literature. Through these publications, however, the firm also became active in various contemporary political and economic questions. Paul Stalling's involvement in county politics brought him into contact with several political figures, and eventually with Hjalmar Schacht and the Reich Finance Ministry. These connections served the GSV well, for during the hectic inflationary years of 1922–23, the government commissioned the GSV to help print emergency currency, a task which kept the firm's presses working overtime.

The publications of the HBV were, in both quality and quantity, similar to those of the JFLV and included agitational books on specific political or economic issues which were aimed at a broad, only modestly educated readership. Products of the GSV, on the other hand, resembled those of the HVA and its affiliates, and were competent, semijournalistic treatments by reputable authors. If one ranked the intellectual quality of the five firms or the approximate educational level of its readers, the Diederichs house would be highest, followed by the Hanseatic and Stalling firms; the Lehmann and Beenken houses would be on the lowest, most popular level. A ranking of the quantity of neoconservative literature published by the firms over the 1890–1933 period would again place the EDV first, followed by the JFLV and the HVA empire, with the GSV and HBV far behind.

The Professional Ethos of Neoconservative Publishers

To Eugen Diederichs, J. F. Lehmann, the men of the HVA publishing empire, and those of the Beenken and Stalling houses, publishing was far more than a mere business or vocation. Neoconservative publishers, like so many of their fellow German bookmen, regarded publishing quite literally as a calling. The notion of calling is rooted deeply in the German Protestant tradition which stresses individual will, social responsibility, and service. To the neoconservative bookmen, all of whom were Protestant (Lehmann almost fanatically so), publishing was their imperative calling and neoconservative publishing activity was the means by which they could fulfill the personal moral obligations and duties which that calling entailed.

For the man who feels he has a calling, a close relationship exists between his sense of individual fulfillment and his vocational activity. Eugen Diederichs is a case in point. After a restless, directionless youth, he realized "almost overnight" that publishing was his calling.[48] To him, publishing was a psychological outlet, a means of self-realization by which he might overcome the "dark powers" within himself.[49] His publishing house became Diederichs's alter ego; the firm's activities exactly paralleled and reflected his own personal development. "My publishing house rests entirely on my personality and my personal opinions," he said; "I commissioned many works [for the firm] simply because I personally wanted to know something more about that particular topic."[50] One young author, meeting Diederichs for the first time, was astonished at how the publisher "spoke of his business dealings and his plans as though they were affairs of the heart."[51] Moreover, Diederichs's personality became so immersed in his career that his publishing activities displaced and eventually came to serve as a substitute for any active involvement in public political life: "As soon as I discovered my goal in life," he later confided, "Reichstags and elections no longer held any claim over me; I felt that I could not be very effective in those areas."[52] Diederichs tried instead to establish the closest possible relationship with his authors, a "spiritual marriage," as he called it; at other times he spoke of his authors as his "publishing-house sons" (Verlagssöhne).[53] "Personal relations with my authors," he reflected, "and the feeling of being able to help them gave me the heightened sense of life which I needed. Out of this feeling of solidarity with my authors I was led . . . to spiritual self-realization."[54] J. F. Lehmann fused his individual personality with his publishing house in much the same way: "My house," he once wrote to a prospective author, "is a piece of my person, of my name, of my honor."[55]

Neoconservative publishers believed the calling of publisher entailed a unique opportunity and obligation to serve German culture. According to the DHB and to Diederichs, a publisher makes artistic treasures accessible to the public, thereby rescuing and preserving the "cultural goods" and "spiritual heritage" of the nation.[56] The DHB, especially, claimed to be retrieving great cultural creations from obscurity. Because the book club felt less bound by economic considerations than were the more traditional book firms, the DHB professed an ability to distribute unknown but deserving works which might, under normal circumstances, be unprofitable to produce and which, therefore, might otherwise never be published or read.[57] Since they, as publishers, were responsible for handing down cultural creations to future generations, the neoconservative bookmen portrayed themselves as "culture bearers" (*Kulturträger*), "transmitters (*Weitergeber*) of ideas," and "mediators (*Vermittler*) of cultural forces."[58] As Heinrich Beenken expressed it, "the publisher, through his work, is more deeply involved in the cultural texture of his nation than is any other profession. For he decides what will be published, and thus, what will pass into the feelings and thought not only of the present, but of coming generations. Therefore, the publisher bears an unusually great human, moral, and political responsibility toward his people; he determines which, of all the nation's cultural achievements, will see the light of day."[59] The ultimate role of the publisher, according to Diederichs, the DHB, and the DHV Bookstore, was that of a "trustee" (*Treuhänder*) who administered cultural goods for the entire national community. "I don't conceive of my calling simply as a businessman," Diederichs declared, "but rather as one who conducts cultural policy (*Kulturpolitik*)."[60] Pezold concurred that the book trade was "*the* most crucial factor in cultural life," and he believed bookmen must therefore invest their complete conviction, diligence, talent, and judgment in their calling.[61]

Given the great cultural importance they attributed to their profession, neoconservative publishers were not content to serve as passive agents who merely decided among the manuscripts which reached their office. To these publishers, the book trade was more than a simple medium through which ideas flowed haphazardly; rather, the resources of a publishing house were a malleable instrument which could be placed at the disposal of specific authors or groups and which could be specially attuned to their particular ideas. The publisher's function, according to the neoconservative bookmen, was to offer the publishing medium to specific writers and to adjust it to the writers' needs so as to give their ideas wider impact. Diederichs, for example, was convinced that the isolation of creative individuals from one another was a major problem of modern mass culture; because they lacked the supportive company of peers and public reinforcement, their individual efforts were too often ineffectual.[62]

The Jena publisher hoped to provide the various creative personalities with an arena within which they could exercise and display their talents and receive supportive reinforcement. He intended the EDV to be a "meeting point," a "point of crystallization" which would collect these isolated individual forces and bring like-minded writers into contact with one another's works. By helping to concentrate the efforts of diverse creative men, Diederichs sought to give them greater visibility and to heighten their effect upon the public.[63] "No other calling," he claimed, "offers such rich opportunities to establish links between one soul and another . . . and to help break a path for creative forces."[64] Similarly, Lehmann and the leaders of the HVA felt the role of publisher entailed aiding certain writers or forces to gain a wider hearing. Lehmann saw his function as that of "a squire who is always ready to carry the standard for those who are greater."[65] The leaders of the HVA saw their firm "as a means of . . . preparing and consolidating a new [national-conservative] front and helping it exert greater influence;" the house sought to help the "right" authors by bringing them a "ready-made literary audience," the DHV membership.[66]

Because of their close identification with authors and their sense of responsibility for the transmission of culture, neoconservative publishers sought to mobilize the resources of their houses so as to achieve both the maximal dissemination and most effective impact of their authors' ideas. Annual EDV catalogs, for example, were intended not merely to promote the firm's books, but "to agitate for the ideas represented in the books."[67] Gustav Pezold knew that simply producing good books and hoping for favorable reception was not enough; the book trade must energetically promote the works as well. By this, he meant more than mere advertising. According to Pezold, an author and publisher must form a "spiritual front" which would "push through" (*durchsetzen*) the work in covert ways unnoticed by the general public. He tried, for example, to preempt unfavorable reviews by currying the favor of influential journalists and key book critics and by arranging meetings between them and his house's authors.[68] Lehmann, too, believed in organizing the resources of his house "to confer power and strength to a new idea, to conduct heroic guerrilla warfare (*Kleinkrieg*) on its behalf."[69]

To Eugen Diederichs, a publisher must even go beyond assisting in the spread of cultural movements—he must actively organize them. "I attempt," he confided to one author, "to make the activity of the publisher into *organizational* activity. I try to pave the way for intellectual currents by, on the one hand, leading together into my house individual forces which are striving in the same direction, and on the other hand, by 'breaking the ground' among the reading public through an effectual organization of the book trade."[70] By this, Diederichs meant combining together within his publishing house different schools of thinkers or writers from different intellectual fields in order to establish and emphasize the relations between their ideas and to inspire readers to draw analogical conclusions from them. A publisher thus could magnify a weak movement—or in some cases even create a movement where none previously existed—by drawing together diverse ideas under a common label or by connecting the writings of theoreticians on a topic with those of practical men of action. Diederichs hoped to create a "phalanx of thinkers" and concentrate that force on the reading public in order to make an opening for the ideas and causes his firm supported.[71] Pezold's notion of a "spiritual front," or Stapel's talk of creating a "totally unified spiritual effect" (*vereinigten geistigen Gesamtwirkung*)[72] had the same aim. The leader of the LMV once tried literally to create such a front by organizing a congress of like-minded authors and journalists in 1930 at Gera, as well as a series of "author evenings" (*Dichterabende*) in Berlin for nationalist writers.[73] Forming a harmonized phalanx of authors at other times required a publisher to entice an author away from another house. Thus the HVA, to cite but one example of many, tried to convince H. F. Blunck to leave his current publisher (Diederichs) and become a member of the Hanseatic house because he would "fit our house's publishing program perfectly."[74]

Besides organizing authors to help push through new ideas, Diederichs desired to organize the book trade. By this he meant using all possible formats available to a publisher—pamphlets, monographs, anthologies, a series of related books issued over a longer period of time, and journals—in such a way that each would complement and supplement the others, thereby achieving maximum effectiveness for all. Diederichs believed that a single book seldom had significant impact; a lasting effect could be achieved only by forming "cells" of similar books, by a series of related books. For him, a well-organized publishing firm was like an army whose various parts must be arranged into mutually supportive functions and formations.[75] The EDV, as well as other neoconservative houses, made extensive use of various publishing formats, especially multivolume series. This not only gave the houses greater flexibility and magnified their effectiveness, but it also led to their involvement in organizational activity for the neoconservative movement.

A theory current in some German publishing circles underlay this multifaceted publishing program. According to this view,[76] if one regards the substances with which publishers work as being not books, but rather "unit messages" (*Mitteilungen*), then an individual book or pamphlet becomes a single message by one author on a single occasion. A way of increasing the number of messages communicated to the public is to publish anthologies or single volumes of collected essays. Such works embody messages by several individuals at a single time. Multivolume series of books then become the next higher level of increased message units, for they represent pronouncements by several people appearing at widely spaced intervals. Finally, a journal or periodical provides a publisher with his greatest organizational activity in that it enables publishers to collect a distinct, tangible, and cohesive circle of contributors and readers. From this circle, actual societies, congresses, and work groups can be organized. The close connection between publishing activity and group formation was clear to neoconservative publishers. Diederichs, for example, proclaimed that his house, after having created the proper public climate through its publications, planned to move into the creation of practical organizations.[77]

Neoconservative bookmen, then, believed they could best fulfill their imperative cultural obligations by aiding and organizing those who addressed and sought to influence the general public. But what, if any, responsibilities did the publisher's calling imply with regard to the receptive audience? These publishers, like many of their fellow German bookmen, assumed that the book industry must serve as the nation's tutor. Diederichs, for example, believed publishing and educational work were inseparable. A publisher must, he said, "run ahead of his times," clearing a path for the future by paternalistically directing the public away from momentary fads or inferior reading matter and guiding readers instead toward enduring works of high cultural merit. For him, the bookman's task was essentially one of "ministerial work" (*Seelensorge*); to carry out that task more effectively, he advocated formation of a Cultural Office by the Commercial Union of the German Booktrade.[78] Likewise, the DHV claimed that since books had become powerful weapons in the struggle against German decay, the union could not be indifferent to what Germans read.[79] "Our duty toward those people for whom we are responsible," it maintained, "is to keep a loyal vigil so as to resist mercilessly all trashy literature and to see to it that good reading matter is spread to our members."[80] In all the DHV's many book enterprises, the union therefore sought to have educational activity and publishing activity "mutually penetrate and promote one another."[81] The establishment of the DHV Bookstore in 1904, for example, and the creation shortly thereafter of a Literary Advisory Center within the Bookstore, were intended as "a further step on the road to a spiritual uplifting [of the *Mittelstand*]."[82] Perhaps the most pedagogically useful of all DHV book activities was the German Home Library book club. The club was able to exercise "ideological guidance" over readers and to "lead [our] subscribers to the right literature"[83] because the books on the DHV mandatory list as well as those which subscribers could choose from the optional list were all selected by the advisory committee. Thus, a 1919 directive sent by the DHV directors to educational and propaganda chiefs in local DHV branches called their attention to the German Home Library. The DHV memo wanted "especially to point out . . . that with the distribution [of DHB books] a strong tool is placed at your disposal for directing the education of youth in the proper direction and thereby opening the souls of youth to the 'German essence' in literature and life."[84]

When neoconservative publishers spoke of "guiding" or "educating" the reading public, they usually meant imposing their own views. Wilhelm Stapel of the HVA regarded publishing as "pushing through a belief," while Pezold of the LMV believed a bookman not only can, but should make his own values prevail upon his customers.[85] Lehmann, with his more characteristic bluntness, believed it a publisher's duty to impress political "truths" upon the public,[86] while the DHV admitted that its entire publishing empire was a determined attempt to inject political persuasion into the realm of literature.[87]

Neoconservative publishers considered the actual initiation of literary production as another imperative of their calling, one which followed logically from their role as popular educators. For if the literature necessary for guiding and teaching the reading public was insufficient or nonexistent, a publisher could not fulfill his preceptorial responsibilities. It then became incumbent upon the publisher to help generate the proper material. Thus, Diederichs considered it part of the publisher's function to encourage writers to work on certain themes and to popularize specific ideas; Lehmann held similar views.[88]

To call forth the kinds of works they desired, the publishers sometimes used indirect means, such as offering prizes for manuscripts on a particular topic, or approaching prominent conservative authors and inviting them to submit their next manuscript to the publishing house.[89] At other times, neoconservative bookmen formulated their own ideas and sought out authors to carry out those plans.[90] Lehmann, for example, claimed always to be full of plans for books he wanted written which would rejuvenate the German *Volk*, but he complained of the difficulty in finding the "right" people to write them.[91] In fact, many of the books produced by these neoconservative houses were directly instigated or commissioned by the respective publisher. Lehmann boasted that most of the works published by the JFLV were the result of his own personal inducement and that for many others, he had determined at least part of the content: "Only when I am unable to find an author to do the work for me do I occasionally take up the pen myself; but I have always laid it down again when I found [a writer] who could do it better."[92]

Leading, rather than following public opinion not only required a publisher to become active in the creation of cultural works. It could also involve him in financial sacrifices if public tastes and purchasing patterns did not correspond to the kinds of literature he considered worthwhile for the public. Because of this, neoconservative publishers stressed that idealistic commitment was another inherent part of the publisher's calling: a publisher must be willing to accept financial losses in the interest of attaining his higher cultural goals. German bookmen traditionally maintained that publishing was far more than merely a business, and that a publisher had duties and cultural obligations which reached far beyond the profit ledger. Diederichs, for example, insisted that he had not entered publishing for material gain, but because it was a profession where he could do what he believed in.[93] "All the plans which welled up in me concerning my profession," he said, "came from my instinct. I decided on all manuscripts which were offered to me according to whether or not they still appealed to me after I had finished reading them. I never cared about public tastes nor did I calculate in advance the chances of a book's success. It was enough for me that I realized a book had been written from an inner necessity of the author's and that the experience of reading it had kindled something within me."[94] The Jena publisher proudly maintained that he never resorted to publishing rubbish or compromising with economic fads in order to gain enough revenues to print the kind of quality literature he was most interested in. Hermann Hesse confirmed that Diederichs "spoke of his books not as a businessman speaks about his wares, but as a preacher about his ideals."[95] Lehmann, on the other hand, claimed to be a cool and calculating businessman when it came to general publishing. But when it concerned a political goal of his or a book which touched the *Volk* and fatherland, then his mood changed to one of "fiery enthusiasm" and he behaved not as a merchant who hopes for a profit, but as a political fighter striving to achieve a higher goal. He was willing to absorb a financial loss if in so doing he could help educate the people to national and racial truths. "Just as I would never print a book which represents views I consider to be bad," he told an author, "even if it might be quite profitable commercially, so I am as happy as a child when I succeed in helping to create a beautiful work, a work which is of value to my *Volk* and which brings honor to my publishing house."[96] And to a friend, Lehmann confided: "For years, I have been sacrificing one-fourth of my income in order to publish nationalistic materials."[97] Similarly, director Pezold of the LMV felt that conservative literature must, "under all circumstances," be brought to the public. Any book his firm sold, "even if it subsequently means a loss for us," was ultimately working toward that conservative goal, for it drove a book from a liberal house out of the market. "A nationalistic publishing house," Pezold told the auditors, "must reckon on significant financial sacrifices and must be prepared to expend large sums in order to win over and to support powerful authors and bring out their promising works. A literary house like ours has almost no prospect of making large profits with its products. To the business directors of the LMV house I *most strongly emphasize* that this house strives *not for egotistical profit, but only for effectiveness in a nationalistic sense.*"[98]

To be sure, such expressions of selfless idealism were often self-serving rhetoric; many—but not all—were made for public consumption and were intended to embellish the public image of the respective firms. Unless they were also astute businessmen able to run a profitable enterprise, few publishers could have stayed in business as long as men like Diederichs, Lehmann, or the Stalling brothers did. Indeed, we have seen that men like Diederichs displayed an expert and subtle sense of marketing. Yet, the neoconservative publishers' claims of financial sacrifice must not be completely discounted. While their own self-characterizations were usually more generous than their actual behavior warranted, they were anything but cynical hypocrites; there can be little doubt they sincerely believed in the idealistic, self-sacrificing commitment they preached. The very notion of fulfilling one's calling involves a belief that the task is no easy one and that the calling places demands on the individual. Although the financial records of all but the Langen-Müller house have been lost, and we thus have no way of determining definitely just what the publishers gauged the financial prospects of potential publications to be, nevertheless we do have some evidence that they published works which they believed would entail financial losses but which they considered ideologically necessary.[99]

Of the neoconservative publishers then, at least the three most important (the EDV, the JFLV, and the HVA/LMV) shared a professional ethos which interpreted the calling of publisher as entailing a didactic relationship toward the reading public, a sense of idealistic self-sacrifice in propagating certain ideas regardless of financial return, and the necessity of playing a central, directive role in the formation and dissemination of cultural movements. Because of the conception they held of their cultural function, these publishers served as committed agents of the neoconservative cause in Germany.

Publishers and Periodicals

Neoconservative publishing houses found journals to be an effective supplement to their publication of neoconservative books. Among them, the five publishers examined in this study produced over twenty journals as part of their neoconservative publishing program. Three of these journals—the Diederichs house's *Die Tat* (*The Deed*), the Lehmann house's *Deutschlands Erneuerung* (*Germany's Renewal*), and the Hanseatic firm's *Deutsches Volkstum* (*Germanic Volk Character*)—became central organs of the German neoconservative movement.

Journal publication is a natural complement to book publication. Of the various ways a publisher can organize the "unit messages" of his authors, the periodical represents the highest synthesis. As a collection of messages appearing regularly and interminably, a journal represents the largest quantity of authors' pronouncements and communicates them to the public over the longest possible time. Since journals require minimal capital and the audience of a journal provides publishers with a fairly stable and predictable market, this medium is among the least expensive and most secure for an entrepreneur. A publishing house's authors already form a fairly distinct group which can serve as a journal's basic circle of contributors. If a house has a distinct publishing program, it becomes all the more natural to transfer that orientation to a programmatic journal. A journal can also provide an effective means of introducing a house's authors to the public. Obviously, a publisher can use a periodical for outright advertisement of his books, a most effective form of publicity, as Diederichs discovered.[100] Reviews of, excerpts from, or subtle references to a house's books can also be included in the journal.

Periodicals, moreover, enable a publisher to widen his house's publishing program. Contributors to a journal are easily persuaded by a publisher to expand their articles into books which will then appear in the publishing house. New authors can be attracted to a house from the circle of a journal's contributors, just as a journal can gain new contributors from a publishing house's list of authors. In the same way, readers can be attracted from one medium to the other. The more a house's ideological program coincides with that of its journal, the more likely such mutual reinforcement will be. Thus, organizing a distinct group of writers and readers around a programmatic journal is one more way an activist publisher can direct, control, and stimulate the reading market and at the same time heighten the impact of his house's ideological program. Because of their natural affinity, more periodicals in Germany were affiliated with publishing houses than with independent organizations or with private individuals.[101]

Neoconservatism was a cause particularly well suited to the journalistic medium. Neoconservatives generally scorned the traditional political party system as hopelessly corrupt, inefficient, and captive to economic interest groups. Thus, to implement their ideas, they chose other, extra-political means such as loosely knit groupings of publicists and a network of small brotherhoods, clubs, and paramilitary societies. The journal, which has been called the "little man's true means of expression,"[102] seemed just the right organ for the anxious, disenchanted, petty-bourgeois neoconservative spokesmen who railed against the increasing rationalization and centralization of modern life. To them, newspapers were a manifestation of mass culture; economic and technological developments and the desire for mass readership were forcing the daily press to become ever more concentrated and intellectually superficial. Journals, by contrast, were still small-scale enterprises with more limited, elitist goals. Cultural and political journals, each with a distinctive character and program, offered an attractive alternative by means of which the "little man," be he publisher, journalist, or reader, could resist the monopolistic, manipulative features which seemed to characterize modern newspapers.

Because of the advantages and opportunities which journals offered as a supplement to their neoconservative publishing programs, Diederichs, Lehmann, and the HVA were eager to acquire periodicals for their publishing houses. Eugen Diederichs purchased the small journal *Die Tat* in 1912. Founded as an organ of the Monist League in 1909 by the two young free-thinking Nietzsche disciples August and Ernst Horneffer, this religious and ethical monthly was already bankrupt by 1911; it was saved from extinction only by being transferred to the EDV. The HVA's journal, too, was acquired from a publisher facing financial difficulties; in October 1913, the DHV and HDVA purchased the fifteen-year-old theatrical and literary monthly *Bühne und Welt* (*Stage and World*) from a firm in liquidation. Under the new editorship of Wilhelm Kiefer, the DHV used the journal to campaign for theater reform and to spread the union's radical nationalistic, anti-Semitic ideology. Circulation of *Bühne und Welt* rose from two hundred to nearly three thousand, partly because of the ready-made market of DHV members and partly because the journal, despite low honoraria, was able to attract prominent *völkisch* contributors.[103] In January 1917, amidst the nationalist fervor of the World War, the periodical was renamed *Deutsches Volkstum: Monatsschrift für das Kunst- und Geistesleben* (*Germanic Volk Character: Monthly for Artistic and Intellectual Life*). Only J. F. Lehmann created his own journal. After he was approached in 1916 by the right-wing journalists Erich Kühn and Houston S. Chamberlain with the idea for a new nationalistic journal, the Munich publisher contacted the Pan-German League (of which he was an officer) and the East Prussia Aid Society (Ostpreussenhilfe) to see whether a political journal could count on these organizations' support. Assured that the undertaking could, Lehmann then promised to finance the journal. Thus, the *Deutschlands Erneuerung: Monatsschrift für das deutsche Volk* (*Germany's Renewal: Monthly for the German Volk*) was born in April 1917.[104]

Once he had acquired his journal, each publisher faced the task of integrating it into his publishing house and harmonizing his intentions with those of the journal's editors. Diederichs made it clear to his readers from the outset that "the goals of my journal and those of my publishing house are one;" "*Die Tat*," he proclaimed, "will uphold the same ideas as my house . . . and will carry the house's endeavors to wider circles."[105] He hoped the journal would serve as a central collection point and platform, not only for his house's authors, but for all neoconservative forces.[106] Diederichs interpreted the function of a journal editor in the same aggressive way he conceived of the publisher's calling: it demanded the total commitment of one's personality and required active involvement in intellectual production. "The chief of a journal," he said, "must never wait until something is accidentally sent in to him; rather, he must recognize latent forces and then actively direct them."[107] To insure that *Die Tat* would be run aggressively, he personally took on the post of coeditor (with Karl Hoffmann) in October 1913. Hoffmann was soon dropped, and after September 1915 Diederichs exercised total editorial responsibility. To attract the high-quality contributors he wanted for the undertaking, he raised the honorarium to three marks per page.[108] In 1928 Diederichs's failing health, plus his realization that the public was beginning to find his esoteric cultural and literary journal too abstruse, prompted the publisher to turn the daily editorial duties of *Die Tat* over to the younger, more politically minded Adam Kuckhoff. Within a year, however, Kuckhoff was replaced by the young newspaper journalist Hans Zehrer. Zehrer collected around himself a small cell of radical authors, the famous "*Tat* Circle" (*Tatkreis*), which called for a "revolution of the Right." The *Tat* Circle's elaborate ideological program, its forceful analysis of all major political, economic, and international issues of the day, and its ties to powerful political figures soon made *Die Tat* an intellectual haven and the leading platform for Germany's radical right-wing intelligentsia.[109]

Unlike Diederichs, Lehmann did not personally assume the editor's chair for *Deutschlands Erneuerung*. He briefly considered appointing Wilhelm Kiefer of the DHV's *Bühne und Welt* as editor, but finally decided on the *völkisch* activist Erich Kühn as editor-in-chief; Kühn was assisted by an editorial board drawn primarily from the Pan-German League.[110] This did not mean, however, that Lehmann was not active in his journal's affairs. He believed a journal was "a wagon hitched to two horses, editor *and* publisher," and that both must pull with equal force.[111] Consequently, he maintained close supervision over the journal, passing judgment over individual articles. Like Diederichs, Lehmann was convinced that an editor must be active and aggressive; he made it clear to Kühn that "success can come only when one sets the guidelines [for articles] one's self and more or less compels people to write what one personally considers good and desirable."[112] Thus, Lehmann often requested authors to write articles on specific topics, or informed them of specific points he wanted made in their essays. Nor was he hesitant about altering an article or changing the journal's final layout without notifying either the article's author or the journal's editor. While such actions insured the closest possible coordination between the JFLV and *Deutschlands Erneuerung*, they inevitably created tensions between Lehmann and his journal's contributors. On the other hand, Lehmann offered contributors very generous honoraria and royalties for reprints.[113]

In contrast to the journals of the EDV and JFLV, the *Deutsches Volkstum* remained institutionally independent from the HVA. After the old *Bühne und Welt* was transformed into the *Deutsches Volkstum*, the former editor (Kiefer) was replaced in 1918 by the young publicist Wilhelm Stapel. Stapel, a central figure of the radical Right in the Weimar republic,[114] had worked before World War I as a bookstore clerk's apprentice, as a writer for one of the Progressive Peoples party (Fortschrittliche Volkspartei) newspapers, and as editorial assistant for Ferdinand Avenarius's conservative cultural journal *Der Kunstwart*. His service there and his membership in several neoconservative organizations such as the Dürer League (Dürerbund), the Hamburg Peoples Home (Hamburger Volksheim), and the Fichte Society (Fichtegesellschaft)[115] brought him to the attention of the DHV, which tapped him to edit *Deutsches Volkstum*. Stapel accepted the post on the condition that he be allowed complete freedom.[116] Despite its formal independence from the publishing house, the *Deutsches Volkstum* was, like the other neoconservative journals, thoroughly integrated into the book publishing activities and ideological program of its parent HVA. Stapel's personal involvement in both the HVA and the DHV served to bind the journal to the publishing house in any case. When he was appointed leader of the HVA's section for *Volkstum* in 1926, an even closer association was established between the HVA and the *Deutsches Volkstum*. Calling this new relationship a "personal union," Stapel proudly noted that "from now on, the *Deutsches Volkstum* no longer stands as an isolated, accidental enterprise within the publishing house, but rather advances to the center of a publishing department. The authors [of the HVA] now have a coherent unity (*Zusammenhalt*) in the journal, and the house's books form a continuity (*Zusammenhang*) with the goals of our journal."[117]

Interplay between the two media was keen. Contributors to the journal published books with the HVA, and HVA authors wrote for the journal. The HVA often asked its more well-known authors to write laudatory endorsements for the journal, which were then used in advertisements for *Deutsches Volkstum*.[118] Lengthy reviews and recommendations of HVA books appeared in every issue of the journal. Reviews of neoconservative books published in the journal were periodically collected and reprinted in one comprehensive reference volume by the HVA, which was then distributed through the Fichte Society. And the *Deutsches Volkstum*, "in order to extend [its] work beyond the limitations which a journal necessarily sets," created the two multivolume book series, *From Old Bookcases* (*Aus alten Bücherschranken*) and *Our Volk Character* (*Unser Volkstum*). These were selected by editors of *Deutsches Volkstum* but published and distributed by the HVA.[119]

All three neoconservative journals were flexibly structured, allowing for an emphasis on personal relationships and the maximum utilization of various publishing techniques. *Die Tat*, for example, claimed an ability to meet national cultural needs because, its editors claimed, the journal "opens itself up to 'outsiders' of any orientation if they have fruitful ideas to contribute."[120] Indeed, Diederichs often turned over entire issues of the journal (so-called *Tat-Sonderhefte*) to prominent individuals or groups and allowed them to explore a particular theme in depth. Diederichs would then attempt to extract from such undertakings those ideas which would encourage a neoconservative renewal of Germany. He also fostered a sense of "internal solidarity" in the journal. For Diederichs tried to convey to the circle of readers a special sense of identity and at the same time to involve them actively in the journal.[121] This was accomplished by specifically requesting readers to comment on particular articles or by soliciting readers' opinions through questionnaires. Diederichs continually organized cultural meetings, discussion sessions, and workshops where he wanted the journal's readers and authors to meet each other. Apparently some group identification did develop among *Die Tat* readers. During the World War, a "*Tat* war fund" was instituted to provide free subscriptions to those readers serving at the front; the fund was generously maintained through reader contributions. Likewise, Zehrer utilized novel means to establish firmer links between his *Tat* Circle, the journal's readers, and leading political and economic figures. He encouraged the formation of some fifty local *Tat* circles across Germany where readers met to discuss the latest issue; he also sent out "*Tat*-Circle-Letters" to keep in closer contact with these local groups, and after 1932, issued regular communiqués about the local circles' activities.[122] The *Deutsches Volkstum*, too, sought to foster a "united feeling of common activity" among its readers and journalists.[123]

Lehmann also organized his journal flexibly to integrate it with his broader publishing activity. He intended the journal to have a thematic organization of its contributors' unit messages, like that of the occasional *Tat-Sonderhefte*; each monthly issue of *Deutschlands Erneuerung* would form a "chapter" and treat one specific topic.[124] His organizational thinking for the journal was influenced by his publication of books and anthologies, where messages on a single topic gave the work an underlying unity. Lehmann also extracted certain contributors' messages from the journal for separate publication as pamphlets. Some one hundred of these pamphlets (*Flugschriften*) were printed, and most enjoyed a far wider circulation—as high as two hundred fifty thousand copies—than did the journal itself. During the World War, Diederichs did much the same. The EDV issued a *Tat-Flugschriften* series of individual pamphlets written by *Tat* contributors, and published a series of special anthologies (*Feldpostbücher der Tat*), each volume containing reprinted articles from *Die Tat* grouped around a single theme. When *Die Tat* came under the control of the *Tat* Circle after 1929, the EDV again issued a series of books which were explicitly related to the journal. These *Tatschriften* were works written by members of the *Tat* Circle or works dealing with a topic in which the *Tat* Circle was particularly interested.

All three neoconservative periodicals were formally associated with an organization of conservative and nationalist journalists known as the Workgroup of German Journalists for the Interests of Border Germans and Germandom Abroad (Arbeitsgemeinschaft deutscher Zeitschriften für die Interessen Grenz- und Auslandsdeutschtum). The group was founded in 1921 by Rudolf Pechel, editor of the *Deutsche Rundschau* (*German Review*), for the purpose of "using common, simultaneous action and a division of labor (*verteilten Rollen*) to handle the burning issue of borderland Germans and Germandom abroad." This was to be done in such a way "that the impression arises [among readers of the member journals] that each journal is treating the topic simultaneously, due to the strong outrage in German public opinion over the issue."[125] The Workgroup served as a clearing house to coordinate publication of nationalistic propaganda and material on specific political issues such as the French occupation of the Rhineland. It operated in cooperation between the individual editors and publishers of the member journals, and had links to other neoconservative organizations such as the Ring Movement and the German-*Völkisch* Defense and Offense League (Deutschvölkischer Schutz- und Trutzbund). By 1925, the Workgroup contained some fifty-seven member journals.[126]

Diederichs, who enrolled *Die Tat* as one of the Workgroup's charter members, utilized some of its suggested propaganda material in the early 1920s. An article on the Rhineland occupation which appeared in the March 1922 issue of *Die Tat*, for example, came directly from the Workgroup.[127] But because of *Die Tat*'s basically independent policy, the journal soon drifted away from the organization. After November 1921, *Deutschlands Erneuerung* was also a member of Pechel's Workgroup, but was more actively committed to the organization than was *Die Tat*. The editor of the Lehmann house journal frequently requested essays from the Workgroup on specific nationalist issues; if none were readily available, the Workgroup composed the needed article. At other times, as part of a carefully planned national propaganda campaign, the Workgroup would contact Lehmann, asking him to help distribute special brochures prepared by the Workgroup by including them in issues of *Deutschlands Erneuerung*.[128]

Circulation of these three journals varied over time, but was consistently too low to make them profitable undertakings for their publishers. To be sure, the average circulation for all German journals in the 1890 to 1933 period was quite low; seldom did a journal sell more than a few thousand copies.[129] When Diederichs acquired *Die Tat* in 1912, it had a circulation of barely 1,000 copies; it remained at this level until 1915–16 when it rose to about 2,500. During the early postwar years, the journal sold 3,000 to 4,000 copies, with some individual *Sonderhefte* reaching as high as 6,000. Circulation again sank to near 1,000 in the late 1920s, which was one reason Diederichs decided to alter the orientation of the periodical and turn it over to Kuckhoff and Zehrer. Under Zehrer's *Tat* Circle, circulation skyrocketed after 1929 to around 30,000. Although circulation was low throughout most of the 1920s, Diederichs believed the number of actual readers was much higher—he calculated that for every subscriber, the journal reached six readers[130]—and thus, he was confident that its neoconservative message was receiving a fairly wide hearing. Yet, the financial basis of the undertaking was a persistent problem. By 1918 Diederichs complained of the journal's unprofitability, but he continued it "out of love." *Die Tat* cost the EDV money every year of its publication; by 1929, it required yearly subsidies of 29,000 marks from the publishing house.[131]

With its lower intellectual pretensions and militant appeal to wider sectors, the early *Deutschlands Erneuerung* enjoyed a larger circulation than *Die Tat*. Lehmann (in a calculation which was also probably applicable to the other journals discussed here) estimated he needed 4,000 subscribers to recover the costs for his journal.[132] He succeeded in capturing 3,500 firm subscribers within three months of the first issue, and by 1919 was circulating 9,000 copies, a level he was able to maintain throughout the early 1920s. Only when economic and political life in Weimar Germany stabilized after 1923 did circulation fall dramatically, hovering during the mid- and later 1920s at 2,000 to 3,000 copies. Thus, Lehmann too was plagued by financial losses from his journal; in the late 1920s he claimed the serial cost his house 12,000 marks per year.[133] Still, he told his readers that "our journal was not created for profit, but rather solely to prepare for and assist in Germany's spiritual renewal. The weapon which our journal represents must and will be maintained, even if it can be preserved only by absorbing great losses over a long period."[134]

During the late 1920s and early 1930s, the *Deutsches Volkstum* attained a circulation of between 3,000 and 5,000, making it among the most widely read of all neoconservative journals.[135] But this fact did not spare the periodical from financial difficulties; like the other publishers, the HVA had to subsidize *Deutsches Volkstum* heavily for several years, especially during the inflation years.[136]

Long-range subsidization of these neoconservative journals by the large neoconservative publishing houses helped preserve not only the existence, but also the ideological integrity of these important neoconservative organs. Many of the small independent cultural or political journals in Germany which tried to serve as their own publishers were often forced to cease publication because of sagging circulation and mounting financial losses. Some two-thirds of the 150 new political journals founded in Berlin during 1918–19, for example, disappeared within two or three years.[137] Others had to be taken over by a larger, more solvent publisher to insure their survival. Quite frequently, this entailed subordination of the journal to the hard-headed commercial policies of the new publisher, a change in the journal's original orientation, and a loss of ideological independence. Both the liberal *Neue Merkur* (*New Mercury*) and Pechel's conservative *Deutsche Rundschau*, for example, were forced to abandon part of their ideological program in order to survive financially.[138] Because of their special relations with neoconservative publishing houses, however, *Die Tat*, *Deutschlands Erneuerung*, and *Deutsches Volkstum* managed to avoid such problems and maintain their ideological stances.

Contributors to the pages of these journals form a Who's Who of the German radical Right, especially after 1920. A significant number of authors wrote for two or for all three journals, some on a regular basis.[139] *Die Tat*, *Deutschlands Erneuerung*, and *Deutsches Volkstum* were part of a large network of neoconservative groups and organs within which individuals moved freely. Not only did the journals and neoconservative publishing houses often actively support each other's work,[140] but major contributors to the journals were often officers or activists in the Ring Movement, the Dürer League, the Pan-German League, various paramilitary Free Corps, and other neoconservative organizations.

Because of their association with major neoconservative publishing houses, *Die Tat*, *Deutschlands Erneuerung*, and *Deutsches Volkstum* could serve the neoconservative cause in ways which other journals usually could not. The publishers used their journals to explore in timely, concrete, and action-directed ways the themes and issues which the houses' books treated in a more abstract, suggestive, exploratory or theoretical manner.

In this sense the journals helped crystallize the neoconservative movement and channel its energies toward more active involvement in national affairs. Moreover, the journals similarly prompted engagement on the part of individual authors. Perhaps because of their association with the culturally minded publishers, these journals tended to combine both literary-cultural and political-social themes in each issue. Artists and abstract theoreticians who published books with one of these publishers were usually encouraged to become involved with the house's journal as well, thus drawing them closer to the concrete issues being treated in the journals. At the same time, "outside" contributors to the journal—that is, those not previously associated with the publishing house—became acquainted through the journal with the publisher's broad neoconservative program and the house's panorama of neoconservative books. Similarly, readers who were attracted to the journal because it contained an article by one of the house's well-known cultural authors would at the same time be exposed to the journal's political or social articles, and vice versa. The journals thus served to bring the disparate branches of the neoconservative movement into closer contact.[141]

Journals such as these also provided a firm link between abstract neoconservative theory and concrete organizational activity. A distinct, tangible, cohesive circle of contributors and readers collected around the journals, and from this circle, it was possible to organize actual neoconservative associations and societies. Diederichs, for example, formed a series of Lauenstein Cultural Congresses comprised largely of contributors to *Die Tat*. Likewise, the Fichte Society was founded by the DHV journal *Bühne und Welt*, and a number of parapolitical groups became linked with the JFLV journal *Deutschlands Erneuerung*. By joining together the different levels (publicistic and organizational) of the neoconservative movement, the journals served as connecting links on a continuum which led from neoconservative thought to neoconservative action and thereby helped the movement gain coherence and expression.

Neoconservative Publishers
and the German Book Trade

A mutually reinforcing relationship existed between these publishers' neoconservativism and the German book trade. On the one hand, the bookmen used the book trade as a medium for disseminating their personal neoconservative ideology; on the other hand, that very ideology arose, at least in part, from their professional experiences within the book industry.

Two of the men associated with the neoconservative publishing houses attributed their conversion to neoconservatism to specific encounters they had as professional bookmen. Friedrich Zillessen, founder of what later became the Heinrich Beenken Verlag, suffered revenue losses of one hundred thousand marks during a socialist printers' union strike in 1891–92. As a result, he became a vehement antisocialist, founded or joined several prominent antisocialist organizations, and devoted a large share of his house's production to anti-Marxist literature.[142] Max Habermann, later a director of the HVA, said he first realized how much Jewish literature was flooding Germany when he was employed in a bookstore. That sudden perception prompted him to join the anti-Semitic DHV and to become active in its educational and publishing work.[143]

More frequently, experiences in the book trade merely reinforced the neoconservatism of these publishers. From developments in the book industry, they became all the more firmly convinced that Germany stood in need of a total neoconservative rejuvenation. The rapid rise of bulk paper prices in the 1920s, for example, as well as the growing demands of militant labor unions were proof to J. F. Lehmann that Germany was falling prey to Jewish greed. He believed that such crass materialism, fostered by the liberal Weimar republic, was destroying German culture because publishers were finding it increasingly difficult to print and distribute books. Unless immediate steps were taken against Jewish "exploiters," Lehmann predicted imminent cultural catastrophe. When the government raised postal rates for books and journals in 1922, Lehmann became convinced that the men of the Weimar republic were "sucking the last marks [a pun on 'money' and 'marrow'] from the bones of the German nation."[144] The former bookdealer Wilhelm Stapel charged that the traditional idealistic bookdealer who helped transmit German culture was being ruined by modern, rationalized, profit-hungry publishing concerns which mass-produced cheap reading matter and pandered to crude, popular tastes with crass advertising. Forgetting momentarily that the HVA and DHB itself might fit these epithets, Stapel went on to proclaim that a struggle was taking place within the book trade between new, mass democratic, capitalistic forces and the older, aristocratic, idealistic bookmen; this struggle simply mirrored a similar struggle going on within German society. For Stapel, to resist materialistic, mass-oriented "democratic" publishing was to champion German idealism and conservatism in general.[145]

Diederichs shared these sentiments. As the economic interests of the various branches of the German book trade (publishers, retail bookdealers, printers, etc.) diverged ever more sharply in the late nineteenth and early twentieth century, each faction organized its own interest groups to press its material concerns. To Diederichs, this indicated that the dreaded social struggle was entering the book trade. Materialism among some bookmen, he felt, was destroying the profession's noble ethos, just as idealism in general was perishing in the modern age.[146] When the German Writer's Academy (Deutsche Dichterakademie) demanded a revision of the copyright laws in the 1920s so as to restrict the number of works becoming public domain, Diederichs charged that self-serving, materialistic literati were trying to sacrifice the cultural needs of the community for their own selfish gain. Such an attitude, he said, represented a "mechanistic-American" trend which must be resisted if the traditional ideals of German culture were to survive.[147]

His experiences with the German book market convinced Diederichs that German culture could be rescued only by drastic neoconservative reform. Twice Diederichs was deeply disturbed by the poor public reception his firm's books received: once when he published a four-volume novel he considered to be a literary masterpiece but which the public ignored, and upon another occasion when his house's massive multivolume historical series *Germanic Volk Identity* (*Deutsche Volkheit*) met a similarly disappointing reception. The poor sales of these great undertakings, Diederichs charged, was caused ultimately by the serious ills of the modern age. According to him, cheap, short dimestore novels (*"billige Ullsteinbände"*)[148] which flooded the market, artificial best-seller lists, and the advertising of the mass press had all exhausted the reading public and led to superficial and capricious literary tastes. This "literary Americanization" was a result of the frantic pace of modern civilization. Diederichs charged that the mass media, especially the modern press which inundated the public with transient trivia, had created a mediocre mass culture geared to the fleeting needs of the moment. Germans no longer had time for multivolume works, no longer had an interest in their historical heritage, and had neither the time nor the desire for self-cultivation. Since books require slow, thoughtful digestion and provide distance and perspective, Diederichs believed, they no longer seemed to have a place in the mass media "film culture" (*Kinokultur*) sweeping Germany. To him, the declining interest in good books was thus both symptom and cause of the cultural malaise of frantic urban civilization. Germany was losing its inner spirit, he believed, and mechanization and "Americanization" were leading the nation to the brink of spiritual chaos.[149] Experiences in the book trade, then, reinforced Diederichs's cultural despair and drove him, as it did other neoconservatives, to seek radical solutions for Germany's salvation.

The concern which Diederichs and Stapel voiced over newspapers and mass publishing made reference to neoconservative bookmen's constant bogey, the left-wing press empires of Ullstein and Mosse. Most of Weimar Germany's liberal newspaper publishers (e.g. the Mosse, Ullstein, and Sonnemann firms), as well as major liberal avant-garde publishing houses such as S. Fischer's, were controlled by Jews.[150] Some of the largest concerns, like the Ullstein house, combined cheap paperback book publishing with a network of mass circulation newspapers and illustrated periodicals; through reviews and advertisements in their papers, these liberal, Jewish-run empires could successfully market their books to an immense urban audience. Conservative bookmen were convinced that the liberal Jewish press and leftist Jewish publishing houses worked hand in hand to monopolize the German book trade, dictate literary life, and suppress conservative literature. Pezold in particular believed that these "antinational" press empires were responsible for the success of the liberal Jewish authors like Zweig, Döblin, Werfel, and Remarque who were, to his mind, undermining authority, morals, and patriotism in Germany.[151] Throughout the Weimar era conservative-nationalist publishers and the large left-wing houses waged a running battle. In 1931, this conflict broke out into heated warfare, with Pezold's Langen-Müller Verlag as a leading combatant.

It will be recalled that during the 1920s, the DHV acquired a chain of retail bookstores to provide an outlet for "German" literature and to break the Jewish-leftist book monopoly. Traditional bookdealers resented the union's growing involvement in the book trade; they complained that the DHV's large membership and extensive resources gave it an unfair competitive advantage and that it was in any case inappropriate for a union to be engaged in bookselling. Opposition to the DHV retail chain became so strong in book trade circles that the union was reluctantly forced to abandon its plan for an extensive bookstore network. Nevertheless, the DHV proceeded with its purchase of failing publishing houses like the Avenarius and Georg Müller firms. Although the union tried to keep these acquisitions secret, rumors of them continued to arouse criticism from the commercial book trade and the liberal press.

When the formerly liberal Albert Langen Verlag fell into the HVA publishing empire and was about to be merged with the GMV, pent-up resentment toward the DHV erupted into a bitter press feud. On 14 June 1931, Mosse's liberal *Berliner Tageblatt* (*Berlin Daily*) reported that Karl Krause, a genial fourteen-year employee of the GMV and beloved figure in Munich literary circles, had committed suicide after receiving a summary dismissal from the publishing firm. The *Tageblatt* believed "the dismissal of Krause can be traced back to the ideological struggle between Right and Left which has been going on in the Georg Müller Verlag for some time. The new directors of the house [the DHV had just placed Pezold in charge of the firm] found Krause to be far too liberal. The financial backing of the house has recently been moving further and further to the right, and the firm is now being financed by the DHV and perhaps also by Hugenberg." A few days later the journalist Werner Richter published a longer article in the *Tageblatt* attacking the DHV's publishing empire, criticizing especially the secrecy of the union's dealings and its dilettantish use of its members' hard-earned money to support economically questionable enterprises like the GMV and ALV. He warned that the entire GMV-ALV undertaking was an attempt by reactionary industrial and military interests to amass a secret, influential right-wing publishing empire just as the right-wing press magnate, Hugenberg, had done earlier with German newspapers. Richter complained further that DHV acquisition of the Müller and Langen houses would ruin and degrade these two respected liberal firms. He warned that the DHV, in building a publishing empire, was politicizing literature and seeking a "literary dictatorship;" for since most bookstore clerks and employees were members of the DHV, the union would soon be able to pressure and browbeat them into suppressing democratic books and peddling only right-wing literature.[152] Leftist newspapers throughout Germany immediately picked up the Krause story. They spared no rhetoric in criticizing the DHV's secret publishing empire or in attacking the GMV for brutally hounding the martyr Krause to his death. One paper even characterized Krause as "the first visible victim of the coming fascism";[153] others advised their readers to boycott all GMV books.

Pezold, closely advised by Stapel, reacted quickly to these charges. He issued a public statement on 16 June denying that politics had played any role in Krause's dismissal from the GMV; in fact, Pezold said, Krause was not a liberal at all as the *Berliner Tageblatt* implied, but was rather a pro-Nazi who had been dismissed solely for his moral turpitude.[154] Pezold vehemently denied the accusation that the GMV was in any way responsible for Krause's suicide, and that Hugenberg money was behind the publishing house. The director of the Müller house then filed a libel suit against the *Berliner Tageblatt* and the *Münchener Post*, another liberal newspaper which had repeated the *Tageblatt*'s charges.

A number of right-wing papers, including the Nazi *Völkischer Beobachter*, saw propaganda opportunity in this affair and rallied to the defense of the GMV. These papers sought to "expose" the liberal newspapers as mere propaganda outlets for the Jewish circles which were out to ruin upstanding, patriotic German publishing houses. The conservative papers ridiculed the way the liberal press had distorted the facts of the Krause case, and gloated when the liberal papers were forced to withdraw some of their accusations. "It is typical," wrote one right-wing paper, "for the 'highbrow press' like the *Berliner Tageblatt* and similar newspapers to ridicule, persecute and blindly hate anything that is German. It is typical for them to try to use an unfortunate, but purely private affair like this to make propaganda against nationalistic circles."[155]

The Krause affair, the GMV, and the DHV's publishing empire aroused such controversy during the summer of 1931 that the German Publishers Union (Deutscher Verlegerverein) and the Commercial Union of the German Booktrade (Börsenverein des deutschen Buchhandels) began an investigation into DHV and other union involvement in the book trade. But the announced investigation merely fanned the raging fire. Through a polemical tract written by their hack, Rudolf Borchardt, the GMV attacked Richter, the *Berliner Tageblatt*, and other liberal newspapers as stooges of big-business publishing circles like the German Publishers Union. These circles, Borchardt charged, were jealous of the DHV's publishing success and were out to ruin the GMV, ALV, and HVA simply to protect their own selfish commercial interests; the liberal-Jewish press campaign over the Krause affair had been instigated for purely materialistic motives.[156] Richter promptly responded by suing Borchardt for libel. This vitriolic publishing feud finally climaxed in January 1932 when decisions were handed down in the two libel suits. Borchardt was ordered to pay Richter 600 marks damages, but the editors of the *Berliner Tageblatt* and *Münchener Post* were also forced to pay the GMV 500 marks. The settlements, of course, simply unleashed another round of mutual denunciations and gloating self-justifications between the leftist and rightist newspapers.

Besides further polarizing the publishing world along ideological lines, the entire conflict had important ramifications for the new Langen-Müller Verlag and its DHV overseers. Because of bad publicity and boycotts, sales of the GMV and ALV dropped by 60 percent during 1931–32, exacerbating the already serious financial problem of the houses. When Langen-Müller house sales continued to languish during the next few years, Pezold was convinced it was because of the unseemly Krause affair and he believed the bitter press feud had made German booksellers hostile to all LMV books. Moreover, several of the oldest and most popular GMV and ALV authors, disturbed over the great controversy and over the DHV's secretive acquisition of the firms, nearly bolted the houses for other publishers. Only with the greatest effort did Pezold persuade the authors to remain with the new LMV. Pezold and the other HVA bookmen, of course, blamed all their difficulties on the Jewish liberals in the press and publishing world who had engineered and manipulated the Krause controversy. The men of the DHV publishing empire thus emerged from the struggle all the more firmly convinced of the necessity of a militant neoconservative reform of German life. They also noted that the *Völkischer Beobachter* had been one of their few supporters throughout the affair.[157] Thus, just as the DHV membership was falling prey to Nazi blandishments during the final months of the Weimar republic, leaders of the union's publishing empire were also becoming more favorably disposed toward the Nazi movement.

If developments within the German book industry served to intensify the neoconservative convictions of these publishers, it is also true that the bookmen attempted to model the book trade itself along neoconservative lines. Lehmann, for example, tried to convince all German publishers to eliminate foreign words and place names.[158] Diederichs, on the other hand, sought a more thorough reform of the institution through the creation of a new self-consciousness among bookmen. As mentioned above, the Jena publisher was disturbed by the growing commercial materialism and conflicting economic interests within the book trade; profit-hungry bookmen unwilling to cooperate with their colleagues in the trade and ignorant of their duties toward the larger community were creating economic chaos within the industry. But even more seriously, he believed this spritual decay in the book trade was also aggravating the general crisis of German culture, for the book trade's internal problems and its growing commercialization made it incapable of providing its traditional cultural leadership and of furnishing its uplifting cultural products. Only a rebirth of idealism and solidarity among bookmen, said Diederichs, could overcome the industry's own internal problems and help remedy Germany's larger cultural crisis. Publishers and bookdealers must come together, he believed, first to formulate common economic policies, and second to reestablish the profession's traditional idealistic ethos so that it can carry out its cultural responsibilities for the nation.[159]

To revivify idealistic cultural commitment within the booktrade, Diederichs founded a series of Summer Academies where young bookmen met to discuss common professional problems. Held in idyllic rural settings to escape the material influences of modern urban culture, these academies were intended to embody many of the principles of the romantic German youth movement. A close comradeship among participants, the singing of folk songs for inspiration and German consciousness, and long forest hikes were supposed to create an intense communal living experience for young bookmen and inspire them to a new idealism. From such an atmosphere, Diederichs hoped a new spirit of professional solidarity would arise in the book trade and that young bookmen would feel a new dedication to the cultural needs of the national community.[160] The first academy was held at Burg Lauenstein in 1922, with two or three held each succeeding year until 1926. At each session, Diederichs not only examined the internal, financial, and organizational problems of the book trade, but also instructed the participants in recent cultural and political developments. For he felt that if young German bookmen were to fulfill their calling as national spiritual leaders, they must become more culturally conscious and idealistically committed. To assist him in these cultural-political sessions, Diederichs often called in prominent neoconservative speakers, including Stapel. The participants in Diederichs's academies soon came to view themselves as a phalanx of idealistic young reformers struggling against the entrenched interests and outmoded outlooks of the book trade establishment, and the meetings came to be known as the "Lauenstein Movement." Diederichs placed his publishing house at the disposal of the movement and founded two journals specifically to champion the movement's goals.[161]

While Diederichs's Lauenstein movement may not have reformed the German book industry, it did create a sense of solidarity among many young German bookmen in the 1920s and heightened their sense of cultural commitment. Participants in the movement became more "intuitively conscious of [their] calling" and were prompted to convert their new idealism into practice through the publication of high-quality cultural works.[162] The same professional ethos which inspired the neoconservative publishers and made them such energetic and committed agents of neoconservative ideology was thus successfully spread to other members of the German book trade as well.

Three

Cultural Pessimism and National Regeneration: Eugen Diederichs and German Culture, 1896–1914

Voices of Decline and Renewal

The five or six decades before World War I were years of dramatic intellectual and material advance in Europe. Specialized scholarly research in the humanistic and especially in the natural sciences produced an exhilarating explosion of knowledge and technology, while the growth of the capitalist economy and the emergence of the centralized industrial state brought an unprecedented material prosperity. The intellectual progress, economic prosperity, and international peace of the age made most Europeans optimistic over the direction of modern civilization.

Yet there was a significant minority of observers who did not share this optimism. Cultural pessimists, particularly in Russia and Germany, regarded the advance of modernism with an uneasy sense of impending doom. Cassandras such as Fyodor Dostoevsky, Leo Tolstoy, Jakob Burckhardt, and Friedrich Nietzsche rejected the notion that man was inherently rational and good; the evil, irrational forces which lurked deep within the psyche, they said, made human perfectibility and progress impossible. These thinkers were convinced that the modern industrial world had unleashed blind, satanic forces which destroyed values, perverted true culture, and spelled the end of meaningful human existence. For in their eyes, modern science and reason ultimately negated free will, traditional moral values, and the very existence of God, leaving only a spiritual vacuum. Modern civilization, founded on crumbling spiritual foundations and the superficial philistinism of the masses, was but a decadent pseudo-culture where individual cultivation and fulfillment was all but impossible.

To these apocalyptic prophets, the moral corruption and spiritual emptiness of modern bourgeois civilization was merely a prelude to an even
darker cataclysmic future. "What I relate," wrote Nietzsche in his last
work, "is the history of the next two centuries. I describe what is coming,
what can no longer come differently: the advent of nihilism. . . . For some
time now, our whole European culture has been moving as toward a catastrophe, with a tortured tension that is growing from decade to decade:
restlessly, violently, headlong, like a river that wants to reach the end, that
no longer reflects, that is afraid to reflect."[1] Only a fundamental spiritual
rebirth, these pessimists believed, could prevent the impending cultural
catastrophe. For Tolstoy, this meant a return to a simple, almost primitive
belief in God and a correspondingly primitive lifestyle; for Dostoevsky,
only a new religious mysticism could save man; Nietzsche demanded
nothing less than a radical revaluation of all values in order to create a
heroic, intensely individualistic new morality; and Burckhardt, perhaps
the most pessimistic of all, could only look with sadness on the modern
age of mass mediocrity and with nostalgia on the creative elites who
inspired past eras.

In the years between 1890 and World War I, Eugen Diederichs shared
this pessimistic assessment of modern civilization. Much of his cultural
pessimism he contracted from reading Burckhardt, whose ideas made a
deep and lasting impression on the young publisher.[2] Echoing Burckhardt's
complaints about the age of the common man, the publisher warned on
the eve of the war that "it is a deception to believe that we are perpetu-
ally ascending. . . . Despite more universities and greater educational
opportunities, the German people are on the road to spiritual impoverish-
ment. . . . The masses are becoming more and more uncultured and are
sinking into tastelessness and superficiality."[3] He believed that Germany,
despite the external success of the Second Reich, actually faced a "spiritual
crisis" and "cultural bankruptcy," a condition all the more serious because
it went unrecognized. To him, the apparent well-being of Germany and
Europe at the end of the nineteenth century was mere appearance, a facade
behind which all values were being leveled, where seriousness, sincerity,
and spirituality were being rapidly pushed aside by philistinism and the
frantic pursuit of material goods.[4] Hoping to make his contemporaries
aware of the cultural crisis they faced, Diederichs's early publishing program included works like Adolf Bartels's *The Stupid Devil* (*Der dumme
Teufel*, 1898) which, according to the EDV, "scornfully exposes all the
festering tumors of our public and spiritual life."[5]

But it was in the writings of Nietzsche that Diederichs saw the most
penetrating critique of modern Europe's spiritual predicament as well as
the best suggestions for its resolution. Diederichs venerated Nietzsche as a

brilliant prophet and sought to heighten this writer's impact on Germany in any way he could. "In my effort to prepare a new German culture," the publisher confessed, "I have been strongly influenced by Nietzsche. I see in him one who . . . struggles against his times to champion a new age; . . . I have used Nietzsche's ideas . . . as the foundation of my early publishing activity."[6] During the 1890s while he was writing a series of travel reports on Italy for a German paper, Diederichs consciously mentioned Nietzsche in every article because he believed Germans should become more familiar with the philosopher.[7] Later, the publisher established a friendship with Nietzsche's sister Elisabeth and was among the few participants invited by her to Nietzsche's funeral in 1900. Diederichs used the opportunity to discuss with Nietzsche's publisher the possibility of the EDV issuing a new edition of the philosopher's works. These negotiations proved unfruitful, however. Instead, Diederichs hit upon the idea of reissuing the works of Nietzsche's favorite authors: Stendhal, Taine, Lichtenberg, and the pre-Socratic philosophers. Diederichs advertised these works, which he began publishing in 1900, as "Nietzsche books" and stressed their influence on the philosopher's thought.[8] In addition, the EDV published several studies of Nietzsche by admiring disciples such as August and Ernst Horneffer, Karl Joel, and C. A. Bernoulli.

Diederichs, however, was more acutely disturbed over decadence in Germany than over the general European conditions about which Burckhardt and Nietzsche had written. Consequently, he was captivated by the doctrines of an early prophet of German cultural pessimism, Paul de Lagarde. Lagarde was among the first to draw attention in the 1870s and 1880s to the cultural hollowness behind the external pomp of imperial Germany; his particular brand of radical cultural criticism set the tone for nearly all later cultural pessimists.[9] Lagarde saw the nineteenth century as a time of alarming moral decline in Germany. He acrimoniously identified the many elements of this decline: loss of religious faith and moral stamina; violation of traditional German values; laziness caused by excessive material comfort; widespread mediocrity, philistinism, pedantry, and lack of creativity in the educational system; the disappearance of heroic German individualism; democracy and urbanism; political corruption; and worst of all, a fundamental lack of unity among Germans. Most of these phenomena he attributed to the growing influence of Jews in German life. Lagarde was a prophet as well as critic, prescribing radical reforms to reverse the German cultural decline and to regenerate national life. He called for the reforging of a new unified community based on common Germanic values, a new religion, a radical reorganization of political life, a new aristocratic elite to direct the nation, and the recovery of vital, pristine Germanism.

Eugen Diederichs regarded Lagarde as both a brilliant diagnostician of Germany's ills and an idealistic advocate of a national rebirth. He worshipped Lagarde like a patron saint and established a close filial relationship with Lagarde's elderly widow, even calling himself "her son." The publisher once asked Mrs. Lagarde for some sort of personal keepsake of her late husband's, an object which Diederichs promised to "hold holy" and reverently pass down in his family.[10] He took it upon himself personally to champion Lagarde's ideas by exhorting the German public to take heed of the cultural critic's warnings and prescriptions. Diederichs in 1907 laid plans to form a Lagarde Society in Germany (nothing came of it however), and when he was given the responsibility of outfitting a small chapel at the 1914 International Book and Graphics Exhibition in Leipzig, the Jena publisher turned it into what he called a "Lagarde temple."[11] Numerous articles on Lagarde appeared in the early issues of the EDV journal *Die Tat*, and the journal's first special issue (the *Sonderheft* for April 1913) was devoted exclusively to his ideas. Above all, Diederichs undertook a republication of Lagarde's works. Worried that Lagarde's writings were "sleeping" under their original publisher, who was doing little to promote them, in 1913 Diederichs issued a new, inexpensive anthology of Lagarde's most important essays in order to make them more accessible to readers. The book was highly successful, selling an impressive 27,300 copies over the next two decades.

By 1914, Diederichs found his publishing activity "increasingly permeated . . . by the task of actualizing the work to which [Lagarde] devoted his life"; reflecting later, he regarded the EDV's reissuing of Lagarde's works as one of the firm's most important endeavors to reverse the German cultural decline.[12] Diederichs's attempts to popularize Lagarde's ideas paid high dividends, for they helped spark a Lagarde revival after World War I. The ideologues of the Ring Movement, for example (Germany's leading neoconservative organization in the 1920s), credited the EDV Lagarde anthology with reawakening their appreciation for this writer.[13]

Behind Diederichs's cultural pessimism lurked a messianic urge to rescue Germans from their impending doom, to reverse modern trends before they become fatal. This could be done, he believed, only through a dramatic spiritual revolution, an inner renewal which would overcome modern decadence and revitalize cultural life. Contemporary conditions, he wanted to believe, were merely part of a transitory culture (*Übergangskultur*); Germany stood on the verge of a spiritual breakthrough to a new era, a cultural revolution which would break out of the reigning superficiality and materialism of life. In this new "culture of the soul" man would regain the inner freedom and creative individuality he had lost in the modern world. A complete reform of social values, morals, and the Germans' fundamental relationship with life would take place.[14]

Given Diederichs's professional ethos and sense of calling, the publisher considered the book trade as one of those institutions which could and should do most to launch a new culture and thus save the German nation from spiritual collapse. Most of the books appearing in his house, he claimed in a 1904 catalog, "consciously seek the path to a new German culture."[15] To stimulate interest in a national rebirth (and perhaps also to support Burckhardt's thesis that Western culture had declined since the fifteenth century), Diederichs published several studies of the Italian Renaissance, an era which he saw as the model for a similar cultural rebirth in Germany. He hoped to spark this renewal by synthesizing the values of the Renaissance with native German traditions.[16] The Diederichs house's first programmatic catalog, moreover, was entitled "Toward a New Renaissance" (*Zu neuer Renaissance*, 1900).

Spiritual Unity and a New Idealism

What was it in German culture that so disturbed Diederichs? What ills of modern life did he want cured, and how was the new cultural age he envisioned to differ from his own? Of the many afflictions of German national life which this critic found intolerable, one of the most distressing was the lack of spiritual and cultural unity.

Nietzsche once wrote that true culture required a unity of artistic style in a people's various cultural activities; "abundant knowledge and learning . . . might sometimes be characteristic of the very opposite of culture, of barbarity—that is to say, of a complete lack of style or a chaotic confusion of styles."[17] Nietzsche's concern for cultural unity and synthesis has been shared by many Germans, especially those who have been unable to tolerate the diversity, pluralism, and continual clash of opposing interests which often characterizes the modern liberal era. To escape the conflicts of posttraditional society and the discord which results when traditional authorities or outmoded sociopolitical relationships confront modern realities, German thinkers have repeatedly exhibited a "propensity for synthesis," a tendency to resort to some final, comprehensive, and often authoritarian resolution which would eliminate conflict per se.[18] Sophisticated theorists frequently hoped to accomplish this through an idealized, utopian state of harmony in which values and institutions would command universal allegiance and where all elements would be harmoniously integrated into a single, unified whole; divisions and conflicts had to be reconciled, disunity transcended, and an ultimate, unified synthesis achieved.

While this "propensity for synthesis" (or, as another scholar has called it, this "hunger for wholeness")[19] has been evident in many German thinkers from both the Left and the Right,[20] it has proved especially alluring to those conservatives who fundamentally opposed the diversity and inherent conflicts of the modern age. Many who were unable to tolerate the transition from a stable, hierarchic world to the pluralistic dynanism of modern liberal society have longed for some sweeping synthesis or unity which would somehow surmount the supposed social, political, and moral dissolution of the traditional order. In this way, laments about the disintegration of "the whole" and calls for a "new synthesis" to overcome the atomization of modern culture have often served in German cultural history as "almost purely an escapist device, a herald of spiritual renewal and an ally of the conservative revolution."[21]

Eugen Diederichs, like Nietzsche, came to believe that no true culture was possible where ideas, systems, values, individuals, and social groups were in perpetual conflict. According to the publisher, culture could not flourish where selfish individualism reigned, but only where there was a union of the individual with the whole. The 1904 EDV catalog asserted that "culture means . . . organic wholeness . . . a unity"; since modern Germany lacked this spiritual unity, the author concluded, "one can not speak of a real German culture."[22] Diederichs harked back to an earlier age where, he believed, the realm of the spirit and intellect had formed a coherent and unified whole, where all knowledge had been synthesized. By contrast, he was convinced that modern rational science had analyzed, dissected, and sundered the world of knowledge; the increasing specialization of learning had fragmented the whole into isolated, independent units. To his eyes, developments in the various branches of knowledge had been so rapid and uncoordinated that they had come to conflict with and negate each other. Individual intellectual achievements had thus lost their relation to and proper subordination within the whole. To overcome the dissolution of the spirit, Germany had to regain its lost sense of the unity of culture and of life; "better than too much knowledge," Diederichs was fond of saying, "is a recognition of the unity of all knowledge."[23]

After the lack of spiritual unity, Diederichs identified materialism as the next most serious aspect of the modern cultural crisis. On the one hand, he used the term "materialism" to mean that scientific viewpoint which saw the world in positivistic, empirical terms and which considered material reality as the only true reality. He categorically rejected any such view because he was convinced that social life and human behavior were not determined by the material bases of life.[24] On another level, he meant by materialism a mode of vulgarized behavior based on material interests rather than on spiritual values. To Diederichs, as to many other cultural critics, materialistic behavior was but the inevitable result of materialist epistemology. A materialist view of the world—especially natural science —concentrated only on empirical natural phenomena at the expense of the spiritual dimension of reality. Materialism cut off the transcendent or "inner" realm of the spirit, the realm which gave human existence its meaning and which served as the supernatural unifying force of the cosmos. Because it was antagonistic to the spirit, materialism was seen as antagonistic to life itself. By disdaining metaphysical speculations and spiritual considerations, materialism and positivism closed man off from the deeper essence of life, destroyed true culture, and made human existence shallow, one dimensional, and spiritually empty. Diederichs viewed this "flattening of life" as one of the most alarming characteristics of the modern cultural crisis, and he dedicated his house to resisting it "by offering [books which would be] lofty pinnacles."[25] Indeed, from the very outset he proclaimed that his house and his journal *Die Tat* would champion antimaterialism and would work to establish a "new intellectual superstructure, a new idealism."[26] He hoped also to create among Germans a more "metaphysical attitude." For if materialism concentrated on the concrete and the empirical and disdained all abstract speculation, then by contrast idealism represented abstraction and speculation, a concern for the infinite, the transcendent, and the metaphysical. The materialist view of reality, he maintained, culminated in the pursuit of (natural) science, while idealism meant the pursuit of philosophy. When Diederichs boasted that he had "a closer relationship" to philosophy than other publishers and that the task of his house was "to carry philosophy to a wider circle of readers," he was but expressing his house's commitment to a neoidealism.[27] Through his firm's many publications in the area of philosophy, he hoped to provide that new idealistic spirit.

To acquaint educated laymen with neoidealist philosophy, Diederichs in 1906 planned an anthology of idealist essays.[28] The plan, however, was never implemented. Instead, inspired perhaps by Paul Natorp's pathbreaking 1903 book on Plato, Diederichs began reissuing new editions of a number of Platonic and neoplatonic texts, and he published several scholarly studies of Platonic and neoplatonic idealism as well as many related works on Greek philosophy. More importantly, the publisher sought to revive classical German idealist philosophy. In its 1908 catalog, the EDV announced that its publications were "consciously seeking a resumption of our ties to the romantic age of German Idealism in order to reintroduce the ideals of that period."[29] By issuing new abridged editions of works by classical idealist philosophers such as Fichte, Schelling, and Hegel, Diederichs tried to make these texts easier for the public to understand "and therefore easier for readers to become involved with and to apply"—

even when he felt, as was the case with his editions of Hegel, that the EDV's new abridgments amounted to a "violation" of the original text.[30]

Diederichs's pursuit of a new sense of life's unity and his campaign for a neoidealist revival drew him toward the philosophical school of monism. Monism, developed by the Jena zoologist Ernst Haeckel, sought to overcome the traditional dualistic view of the world and to reconcile science and religion by stressing the ultimate unity of all reality. All phenomena, all present plurality, this school maintained, could be traced back to a single original force. As Haeckel expressed it, "we unambiguously proclaim our conviction that there lives 'one spirit in all things,' and that the whole cognisable world is constituted, and has been developed, in accordance with one common fundamental law. We emphasize . . . in particular the essential unity of inorganic and organic nature. . . . Simultaneously, we regard the whole of human knowledge as a structural unity."[31] In its early stages, the monist school interpreted the ultimate essence of all existence as primarily material, and Haeckel's movement preached a crude form of Darwinistic materialism. But after 1900, monism evolved in a direction almost diametrically opposed to its original materialist stance. For Haeckel and the Monist League (founded in 1906) began to drop their material interpretation of reality and to stress instead the mysterious, pantheistic nature of the cosmos's basic substance. As Haeckel moved increasingly closer to idealism and vitalism, monism took on a semireligious character and became a virtual mystery cult preaching a kind of nature-mysticism which (so its adherents believed) was able to reconcile materialism and vitalism.[32]

Diederichs, who always believed the cosmos was "fundamentally unified" (*einheitliches*),[33] was first attracted to monism through the work of Wilhelm Bölsche, one of the movement's foremost popularizers and one of its most antimaterialist members.[34] After reading Bölsche's influential *Developmental History of Nature* (*Entwicklungsgeschichte der Natur*), Diederichs commissioned him to write another monistic natural history, *Love Life in Nature* (*Das Liebesleben in der Natur*, 1898–1902). This three-volume work proved extremely successful and provided one of the earliest financial windfalls for the young EDV. Besides publishing other works by Bölsche and volumes by leading monists such as Bruno Wille, Albert Kalthoff, Hans Driesch, Ludwig Woltmann, and the Horneffer brothers, Diederichs also issued a basic anthology of monist essays in 1908 and a major scholarly study of monism in 1912.

Reason vs. Life: The Revolt Against Rationalism

Max Weber, one of the twentieth century's most perceptive social analysts and a friend of Eugen Diederichs, identified rational systematization as the distinguishing characteristic of modern Western culture. Writing at the end of the nineteenth century, Weber pointed to the inexorable process of intellectualization and rationalization in all aspects of social life as "the fate of our times." This inescapable phenomenon, closely linked to the emergence of capitalism, was accompanied by a progressive "disenchantment" of the world, a steady erosion of the magical, religious, and irrational aspects of life. Among the most striking manifestations of this "specific and peculiar rationalization of Western culture," Weber said, was the relentless bureaucratization and impersonal organization of modern secular life.[35]

Whether they greeted or loathed that process of rationalization, European liberals, radicals, conservatives, and neoconservatives all concurred with Weber that the growing domination of reason was both the fundamental basis and determining feature of modernity. Those who saw modernity as a curse rather than a blessing were thus quick to attack rationalization and rationalism as the pernicious source of the modern malaise. In the tenacious neoconservative campaign against liberal modernity, the denunciation of reason and the glorification of irrationalism necessarily played a central role.

Eugen Diederichs was among those who pointed to rationalism as a primary source of Germany's cultural crisis. Life was essentially nonrational, he maintained, and human behavior was determined predominantly by instinct, not rational deliberation. In his eyes, reason not only ignored but actually stifled man's "inner daemon," those imaginative, nonrational, mystical elements which gave life its beauty and richness.[36] Rationalists were mistaken when they assumed there existed universally valid principles or rational laws by which life could be comprehended. Rational scientific objectivity, when it attempted to apply the logical rules of the intellect to the diversity of actual life, inevitably violated the individuality of the phenomena it studied and, in contrast to the instinct, was unable to distinguish what was truly essential from what was not. To Diederichs, then, rationalism cast a dull, cold pall over anything it touched. For this reason, he believed, rationalism was a dead-end street for Western civilization; it had no future and must be abandoned. Less reliance on intellectual knowledge and more confidence in intuition and the unconscious, he maintained, would bring modern man greater freedom and creativity.[37]

The publisher, who proudly claimed that his own decisions in business and in life were based on his instinct and intuition, regarded his firm as part of the "upsurge of irrationalism against intellectualism" which was occurring throughout Europe at the end of the nineteenth century. He sought to make the EDV a "point of crystallization for all those who oppose the domination of reason and who champion life's primal feelings."[38] The Diederichs house championed irrationalism on a number of fronts. Individual EDV publications such as Leopold Ziegler's *Western Rationalism and Eros* (*Der abendländische Rationalismus und der Eros*, 1905) attacked rationalism as inimical not only to love, but to life itself. On a more abstract level, the EDV promoted new modes of irrational thinking such as academic "life-philosophy" (*Lebensphilosophie*), vitalism, religious mysticism, aestheticism, and a new romanticism; and on yet another plane the firm sought to foster certain prerational impulses and primordial bonds which Diederichs believed shaped (or rather, should shape) man's social existence. Such forces included ancient communal myths and legends, a sense of rootedness in primal nature, the historical traditions which link together successive generations, and the primeval ties of heredity which weld a collection of individuals into one national community or *Volk*.

As two of the pillars of a new irrationalism, Diederichs sought to promote the philosophical movements of vitalism and life-philosophy. Both intellectual currents represented an attempt to subordinate the human faculties—especially the conscious intellect—to the larger, irrational "experience of life."

According to vitalists, living organisms possessed a vital internal force which was neither explicable in rational terms nor reducible to scientific, natural laws. This mysterious life-force governed the organism's behavior according to its own unfathomable precepts, thus making life self-determining. The instinctual drives which directed the evolution of this vital force also shaped and determined all other manifestations of life, including consciousness and rational thought.

The Diederichs house was active in spreading vitalist philosophy. Around the turn of the century the publisher conceived the idea for an anthology on vitalism which would explain that outlook and its relation to late nineteenth-century academic "life-philosophy."[39] While he never carried out this plan, in 1901 Diederichs did begin issuing a multivolume series, *God-Nature*, which was intended to "overcome mechanistic natural science and intellectualized philosophy" by repopularizing the pantheistic natural philosophers whom Diederichs considered to be the precursors of modern vitalism.[40] The series, which was not completed until 1928, contained new editions of works by Giordano Bruno, Paracelsus, Lamarck, and Goethe, the major writings of the early nineteenth-century physiologist and psychologist Carl-Gustav Carus, the works of German romantic philosophers of nature, and original scholarly studies of these various figures. Through the series, Diederichs hoped to "resurrect" the forgotten forerunners of vitalism and "help them achieve a greater contemporary effect."[41]

In the years before World War I, the EDV also produced a number of works like Hans Schlieper's *The Rhythm of the Living* (*Der Rhythmus des Lebendigen*, 1909) and Gertrud Prellwitz's *On the Wonder of Life* (*Vom Wunder des Lebens*, 1909) which explored the mysterious rhythm and supernatural enigmas of life. The Jena bookman accepted the vitalist principle that the laws and truths of the rational intellect were determined by life's biological necessities; EDV books such as R. Burckhardt's *Biology and Humanism* (*Biologie und Humanismus*, 1907), or Wilhelm Fliess's *Of Life and Death* (*Vom Leben und vom Tod: Biologische Vorträge*, 1909) thus stressed the biological framework within which human actions occur.

An early twentieth-century movement in academic philosophy known as "life-philosophy" demanded even more ardently than did vitalism that irrational life must have primacy over the conscious intellect. The foremost of the life-philosophers was Henri Bergson, a French academician who is generally considered the epitome of the antiintellectual movement in European philosophy. In Germany, Bergson's ideas were further developed by Ludwig Klages, Max Scheler, Hermann Graf Keyserling, Georg Misch, and Friedrich Gundolf. Life-philosophers maintained that the rational intellect and the objective scientific approach, because they relied on abstractions and fixed symbols and concentrated on the external, mechanistic manifestations of reality, were capable of comprehending only the static and spatial aspects of the universe. The flow or "duration" which strung together the many separate instances of time and matter could not be perceived by reason, however. The intellect, they said, could not grasp the inner consciousness and dynamism which permeated reality but which lay hidden behind external existence. This flow of reality and the continuous process of becoming was life itself, and could be experienced only by means of intuition and instinct. To apprehend the richness of life, these thinkers claimed, men must discard rational thought in favor of irrational, intuitive experience.

Diederichs was strongly attracted to life-philosophy. When he first became aware of Bergson's works around 1905, the publisher believed he had at last found the man "who will implant in Germany the new philosophical ideas which we need."[42] In Bergson's philosophy, Diederichs saw a significant new force which would help overcome hyperrationalized thought and "give back to intuition its rightful precedence."[43] Eager to introduce Bergson's works to the German reading public, Diederichs contacted the French philosopher in 1908, and soon paid him a personal visit to arrange for translation and publication rights. The Jena publisher confessed that his own training in formal philosophy was poor, but that he nevertheless had a deeply personal, eclectically acquired *Lebensphilosophie* of his own. Diederichs assured Bergson that he was seeking to make the EDV a center for all who preach life over rationalism, and that the works of the great philosopher would therefore find a sympathetic home in the Diederichs house.[44]

Bergson agreed to Diederichs's offer and in 1908, the Eugen Diederichs Verlag became Bergson's sole publisher in Germany. Over the next two and a half decades, the EDV published translations of all seven of Bergson's major works, as well as two of the earliest scholarly studies of his ideas. In the numerous EDV catalogs and in his own prolific articles, Diederichs tirelessly promoted Bergsonian life-philosophy to the German reading public. It was a "pressing necessity," he proclaimed, "for us Germans to overcome rationalism with the help of Bergson," whom he portrayed as "the chief representative of the entire neoidealist movement."[45] His attempts to have Bergson widely read were repaid with some success. By 1933, the Bergson translations had sold a total of 31,468 copies, an impressive achievement considering the difficulty of the philosopher's esoteric writing. This widespread dissemination of Bergson's ideas in Germany was a direct stimulus to the development of a German *Lebensphilosophie*, and may have been a factor in Bergson's winning the Nobel Prize in 1927.[46] At any rate, the French thinker expressed his deep gratitude to the EDV not only for its work on his behalf, but also for promoting philosophy in general through its many publications in this area.[47] While Diederichs also helped promote the school by eventually publishing works by other life-philosophy authors such as Keyserling, Hans Driesch, and Bergson's mentor Emile Bourtroux, and by working closely with Georg Misch on a new journal, it was his introduction of Bergson's books into Germany which Diederichs considered among the most important of all his publishing accomplishments.[48]

A New Religious Mystique

As another means of promoting irrationalism in German life, Diederichs strove to apply the principles of vitalistic life-philosophy to the realm of religion. Throughout the nineteenth century, leading German thinkers had interpreted God less and less as the highest form of rationalism and increasingly as a pantheistic, irrational force of nature.[49] By positing the supremacy of a mysterious cosmic life-force, life-philosophy contributed immensely to the reconceptualization of God. Some men like

Diederichs hoped to complete the process and create a new religion in Germany in which God would be completely replaced by the irrational, vital life-force of the cosmos. The publisher's search for a new religious mystique led him ultimately to occult spiritualism and mysticism.

For Diederichs, heightened religiosity was a valuable weapon in the struggle against rational modernity. He defined religion not as a relationship between man and some personal savior, but as communion between the individual soul and the infinite, supernatural life-spirit which permeated the cosmos and was present in all living beings. God, in other words, meant to him simply the cosmic life-force.[50] Since that force was fundamentally irrational, Diederichs was convinced that "being truly religious means being antirational," and that genuine religion must be grounded on a subjective, intuitive metaphysics.[51]

Religion was to provide modern man with a new mystique, and would thereby free him from the deadening hand of rationalism. To Diederichs, the disenchantment of modernity had mercilessly stripped away all the dark mysteries which enveloped the universe. This loss had uprooted and estranged man by tearing him from the unconscious, irrational web of cosmic life. To overcome rationality and modern alienation, man had to regain his feeling for the mysteries and irrational myths in which true existence was enshrouded. Only through a new mystique (*Mythos*) could man restore his contact with the primal life-force and again become firmly anchored in the cosmos.[52] The publisher was convinced a new religious mystique could overcome other modern evils as well. Worship of the cosmic spirit which permeated the material world would, for example, help elevate the spirit over matter and thus defeat modern materialism. Because religion meant reestablishing contact with the fundamental life-force which unified all forms of existence, Diederichs believed a new religious culture would also help Germans regain their sense of spiritual unity and wholeness.[53] For these reasons he considered it absolutely essential to "push the irrationalist character of religion into the foreground" and to help create "a new mystique."[54] By publishing works such as Arthur Bonus's *Of a New Mystique* (*Vom neuen Mythos*, 1911), which he considered the most important religious book of the decade, the publisher hoped to call forth this new religious mystique which modern man so desperately needed.[55]

Orthodox, organized Christianity in Wilhelmian Germany—especially the Protestant church, which encompassed some two-thirds of the population—bore little relation to the inspiring religious mystique which Eugen Diederichs envisioned. Attacks upon Christian tenets by nineteenth-century science, liberal skepticism, and by the "higher criticism" of academic circles who subjected traditional Christian dogma to a relentless rational and historical critique had all seriously undermined orthodox theology. "Modernist" or liberal theologians within the church had tried to adapt to these intellectual currents, but their efforts had merely caused, as one scholar terms it, "a watering-down of dogma and theology to a point where the Protestant religion threatened to become nothing but a bundle of ethical rules, inspired not by divine authority but by social utility."[56] The Roman Catholic church was more successful at resisting the fashionable modernist movement, but only by clinging obstinately to old dogmas and traditions which a growing number of educated believers were coming to view as outmoded and irrelevant. Both denominations were experiencing declining membership. This was due in large part to the fact that the church hierarchy, especially the Protestant state churches, were becoming more socially reactionary. They identified closely with the monarchy, the conservative ruling classes, and the status quo, and not only discouraged but also (as in the case of the Evangelical Supreme Church Council decree of 1895) expressly forbade social work by the clergy. As a result, the Marxist working class in Germany's rapidly growing cities was increasingly rejecting Christianity altogether.[57]

When concerned cultural critics like Diederichs surveyed religious life in Germany at the turn of the century, they concluded (with much justification) that the established church was failing to satisfy the deeper spiritual and emotional needs of the nation. Orthodox Christianity's sterile theological formalism on the one hand, and its institutional rigidity and secularism on the other, were killing the very spirit of true religion. Eugen Diederichs went so far as to identify the "torpidity and petrification of religious life within the church" as the chief obstacle to any spiritual revival in Germany. Despite overwhelming evidence of declining popular interest in religion, he charged, orthodox churchmen refused to recognize the need for a fundamentally new conception of God; by clinging to outmoded historical forms and intellectualized dogmas, scholastic theologians had completely lost touch with man's real religious needs.[58] The church, whether Protestant or Roman Catholic, had become a conservative, iron bureaucracy which stifled sincere religious feeling. The organized, orthodox Christian church, the publisher concluded, was "spiritually bankrupt" and had to be "cast off" to make way for a genuine religious revival.[59] To rescue man's religious spirit from the established church and to pave the way for a new mystique, the EDV initiated a publishing campaign in 1902 which was intended to promote a more subjective, personalized religiosity against institutional Christianity.

At first the house concentrated its attentions on the Protestant church. By energetically soliciting and publishing works by dissident clergymen and unorthodox theologians such as Arthur Bonus, Gottfried Traub, Karl

König, Carl Jatho, Fritz Bredow, Paul Göhre, Hermann Kutter, Rudolf Penzig, and Julius Rupp (many of whom had clashed with the church hierarchy or had been expelled from the church for their social activism or nonconformist beliefs), the EDV became closely associated with the "free" wing within the church which felt the established Protestant structure too confining.[60] Diederichs and many of his authors hoped instead that itinerant preachers would form "free religious congregations" (freireligiöse Gemeinde) which would be free of all formal church control and would serve as focal points for a new religiosity.[61] The Jena publisher supported, both personally and financially, the loosely grouped independent Protestant congregations which arose, and participated in the free religious congress held in Munich in 1910. His firm, moreover, published works by "free religious" leaders such as Arthur Drews, Ernst Horneffer, and Gottfried Traub.

Beginning in 1908 Diederichs also turned his attentions to the Roman Catholic church; for he sensed there a deeper, more emotional and mystical religious sentiment and believed that the antipapal "reformed" wing within the Catholic church held greater possibilities for the future than did its "free religious" counterpart within the Protestant church.[62] Thus the EDV issued the two-volume Reformed Catholic Essays (Reformkatholische Schriften) in 1908 and a work by the nonconformist Catholic theologian George Tyrell the following year. In all these activities, Diederichs sought to give the antichurch movement "more outward visibility." By 1909 he claimed the EDV had become the focal point, and to a certain extent the organizer of the various Protestant and Catholic religious movements which were taking place outside the churches and which were preparing for a religious revival in Germany. Were it not for his house's initiative and active involvement, he boasted, most of these dissenting religious views would never have been published or have had the great impact they did.[63]

Diederichs's criticism of the orthodox churches eventually extended to basic Christian tenets as well. He published works by radical theologians such as Arthur Drews, Albert Kalthoff, Samuel Lublinsky, and others who denied the historical authenticity of basic Christian myths and dogmas, who demonstrated that Christian doctrine was actually a patchwork of corrupted teachings purloined from various Eastern mystery cults, or who charged that the contemporary church had hopelessly adulterated original Christian teachings. As part of its challenge to Christian dogma, the EDV issued a number of outright heretical attacks on the figure of Christ. Personally, Diederichs admitted he was "always nervous" when Christ was mentioned and did not want to "burden" his house with Christ's name, for the concept of Jesus was associated with many principles "that humanity must overcome."[64] To facilitate this process, he published two famous studies, Kalthoff's *The Problem of Christ* (*Das Christusproblem*, 1903) and Drews's *The Myth of Christ* (*Die Christusmythe*, 1909) which debunked the figure of Christ. Both of these prominent, if unorthodox theologians denied the historical existence of Jesus, asserting that He was merely a mythical invention derived from astral Eastern mystery sects. The two tracts gained a wide readership and generated heated controversy in the years before World War I. Diederichs followed up these heretical volumes by issuing some nine additional works which, he hoped, would eventually reduce the figure of Christ to a mere symbol for the cosmic life-force.

By "casting off" the institutional church and the greater part of Christian dogma, Diederichs was simply clearing the way for his ultimate goal: a new irrational religious mystique which would bring Germans salvation from the oppressive evils of rationalized modernity. As examples of the deepened personal religiosity he hoped to anchor in Germany, Eugen Diederichs held out to his readers several specific religious models. One was the American transcendentalist Ralph Waldo Emerson, whose works the EDV published in seven volumes between 1902 and 1907. A second was the saintly religious prophet Leo Tolstoy, who had been expelled from the Russian Orthodox church for his denunciation of all Christian dogmas and sacraments and for his intense, almost radical form of primitive Christianity. Tolstoy combined a simple religious outlook with a vehement rejection of materialism, capitalism, and other evils of modern bourgeois society, a fact which made his ideas all the more attractive for cultural pessimists such as Diederichs. To him the undogmatic Tolstoy seemed to be just the strong, spiritualistic personality who could lead Germans back to profound, "free," inner religious experiences and thus spark that national spiritual rebirth for which Diederichs longed.[65] Between 1900 and 1912 therefore, the EDV undertook the massive task of publishing all of Tolstoy's writings. This enterprise, the first German edition of Tolstoy's collected works, eventually comprised some thirty-two titles in fifty volumes. Because publication of some of Tolstoy's more radical religious works was still forbidden in Russia, the Diederichs house also published these in Russian for distribution in Tolstoy's homeland. One of Tolstoy's essays, "My Answer to the Synod," provoked German authorities in 1902 to prosecute Diederichs and the translator for blasphemy, of which they were eventually acquitted, however.[66]

Another religious figure Diederichs introduced to Germans was Sören Kierkegaard. There was much in this Danish thinker's work which appealed to cultural pessimists. For Kierkegaard, too, had attacked the established Christian church and the entire notion of institutionalized religion in the name of personal, individualized religious experience. He considered religious truth to be totally unlike rational, intellectual truth; it could be gained only by rejecting all intellectual theories, immersing oneself totally in the experience of life, and extracting from that encounter a unique, subjective insight. And Kierkegaard, too, had rebelled against modern collectivity and against the disappearance of heroic individualism. For these reasons, Diederichs considered Kierkegaard a powerful prophet who had to be liberated from his obscurity in stuffy scholastic circles. In 1905, after consulting with other nonconformist theologians in his house such as Bonus, the Eugen Diederichs Verlag thus began issuing a thirteen-volume German translation of Kierkegaard's collected works, which was soon supplemented by two scholarly studies of the Danish thinker. This EDV undertaking—the first time Kierkegaard's complete works had appeared in a major European language—had a tremendous impact on subsequent intellectual history, for it inaugurated the great Kierkegaard revival in Europe which lies at the heart of modern existential thought.

Eastern spiritualism was yet another means by which Diederichs hoped to revive an antirational religious feeling in Germany. To arouse interest in Eastern religions, in 1912 the EDV initiated two multivolume series, *Religious Voices of the Nations* (*Religiöse Stimmen der Völker*) and *The Religion and Philosophy of China* (*Religion und Philosophie Chinas*), under which he brought out German translations of the Upanishads, the Bhagavad Gita, and other oriental religious texts. In the years immediately preceding the war, the firm also published a number of sympathetic studies of Indian theosophy and the mysterious "Eastern soul."

By popularizing the mystery religions of the East, Diederichs hoped ultimately to inspire similar occult currents such as theosophy and anthroposophy in the West. The publisher, who in 1896 had originally designated his firm as a "Publishing House for Theosophy," established a close working relationship with Rudolf Steiner, General Secretary of the German Theosophical Society (founded 1902) and later head of the Anthroposophical Society. Diederichs solicited theosophical manuscripts from Steiner, who in return praised the EDV highly for its various theosophical activities. The prominent theosophist was particularly impressed with Diederichs's efforts to revive interest in gnosticism (an early Christian heresy which laid the foundations for all later theosophical movements) by publishing between 1903 and 1910 two important gnostic source books and a major study of the sect by Drews.[67] The Jena publishing house was no less energetic in championing anthroposophy, an obscure occult offshoot of theosophy founded by Steiner, for the EDV issued the works of Gertrud Prellwitz, leader of the anthroposophical cult "St. George's League."

Diederichs was a devoted pantheist who practiced sun worship and sought to spread religious pantheism in Germany. He regarded the rays of the sun as the source of all life; coming from the cosmos beyond, they represented to him the invisible life-force which permeated and sustained the world.[68] Believing that ancient Germanic tribes had practiced sun worship, Diederichs hoped to revive the rite by introducing it into his circle of youthful devotees. From 1906 to World War I, the portly publisher and his "Sera Circle" (see pp. 104–5) assembled annually in the Thuringian foothills for the midsummer solstice. Carrying banners depicting the ancient Germanic "sun wheel," the group sang Germanic ballads, recited pantheistic poems and "fire prayers," and ended their celebrations by leaping through a bonfire.[69] The publisher also tried to spread pantheism through the publishing medium; in 1911 he developed plans for a popular reader in pantheism which, he hoped, would "make pantheistic ideas known to far larger circles."[70] The volume, however, did not appear until 1929 under the title *From Origin to Consummation: A Reader in Cosmic-Religious Ties* (*Vom Ursprung zur Vollendung: Ein Lesebuch kosmisch-religiöser Bindung*).

The quest for a new spiritual mystique which could overthrow rationalism led ultimately to religious mysticism, however. Diederichs expressed a general interest in mysticism ever since he founded his house in 1896. But he first became a serious devotee of mysticism after he published Bonus's *Religion as Creation* (*Religion als Schöpfung*) in 1903, a book which had a profound impact on his religious conceptions. It was at this point that Diederichs decided "Germans must now pass into mysticism in order again to sense the world as a whole."[71] To his mind, the famous medieval German mystic Meister Eckehardt was Germany's greatest religious figure, Luther notwithstanding.[72] He decided that the times demanded a revival of Eckehardt's brand of mysticism, and that it was his "high moral duty" to publish new editions of medieval German mystic texts so that these ideas might gain a new hearing.[73] In 1903 he consequently launched a *Mystic Library* (*Mystische Bibliothek*) series which, over the next decade, republished nearly all the basic writings of the old German mystics: Eckehardt, Angelus Silesius, Sebastian Franck, Heinrich Seuse, and Johannes Tauler. Works by other European mystics (St. Francis of Assisi, Blaise Pascal, Immanuel Swedenbourg), A. Spamer's 1912 anthology of fourteenth- and fifteenth-century mystic writings, Martin Buber's anthology of Jewish mysticism *Ecstatic Confessions* (*Ekstatische Konfessionen*, 1909), and several scholarly studies of mystics or mysticism were also published as part of this program.[74] Diederichs had hoped to include a new edition of Jakob Böhme's works as well, but finally abandoned the plan because he could not find an editor who was willing to stress strongly enough the relevance of Böhme's mysticism for twentieth-century Germans.[75]

In trying to revive interest in the medieval German mystics, Diederichs subtly reminded the reading public that mysticism had formed a central element of that medieval German culture which many modern Germans idealized as a high point of their national heritage. Irrational mysticism, in contrast to "alien" Western Christianity, was represented as an appropriately German mode of thought. A cultural rejuvenation through German religious mysticism, he implied, would dethrone modern rationalism, lead the nation out of the spiritual wilderness of modernity, and rescue the German *Volk*'s cultural identity from the corrupting influence of Western liberalism.

The Cult of Art

"One could say," Richard Wagner once wrote, "that when religion becomes artificial, it remains for art to salvage its true essence by perceiving its mythical symbols . . . according to their figurative value, in order to make us see their profound, hidden truth through idealized representation."[76] Eugen Diederichs, too, saw art as the modern executor of a declining religious heritage. Art, he declared in 1900, was intimately linked to the yearning of the human soul to find a meaning and purpose in life; simply put, "art must transform man's soul."[77] In turning to art and aestheticism as another redemptive agent for modern man, as a kind of secular religion, Diederichs drew on a popular German tradition which associated art closely with both national political consciousness and antimodern protest.

In the mid-nineteenth century Richard Wagner, and Julius Langbehn a generation later, firmly established the image of art as a revolutionary force capable of redeeming both the individual soul and the national community from the throes of the modern bourgeois age. Wagner's two 1849 essays "Art and Revolution" and "The Art-Work of the Future," and Langbehn's enormously popular book *Rembrandt as an Educator* (*Rembrandt als Erzieher*, 1890) portrayed art as an irrational, antiintellectual force which was the very antithesis of modern science and reason. Both writers believed art represented individuality, spontaneity, freedom, passion, subjectivity, and a simplicity capable of profound intuitive insight. Wagner suggested, and Langbehn later insisted, that art was by nature rooted in the primeval national soul and was an expression of a nation's distinctive racial genius. Langbehn was even audacious enough to declare that true art was uniquely Germanic, since the mystical life-forces of the cosmos were more perfectly embodied in the simple rural traditions of the German peasant than they were in any other people. Both thinkers lamented that art and creativity were being destroyed by commerce, industry, and the shallow material progress of modern bourgeois society. They saw this artistic degeneration as being linked to the erosion of the German *Volk*'s distinctive cultural identity and social unity. Both believed this national cultural decline could be halted only by means of an artistic revolution. To their minds, the artist was both a religious prophet and national savior. The artist (by whom Wagner meant primarily himself, while Langbehn had in mind models like Rembrandt) was singularly capable of apprehending and expressing the simple, unspoiled essence of the national character; he alone could lead the nation back to its primal origins and inspire his fellow men to a new social unity through universal participation in aesthetic experience. The "art-work of the future," Wagner proclaimed, would be a "total art" which alone could grasp the totality of human existence and ultimately usher in both a new spiritual age and a new, harmonious social order. To allow artists to work their miraculous regenerative powers, Langbehn demanded the subordination of all politics to art. A new age of passionate "art-politics" (*Kunstpolitik*) must replace cold, rational realpolitik before artistic leadership could guide the German nation out of the morass of decadent modernity. Wagner and Langbehn both contended that the revolutionary rejuvenation of art—and thus of national life—by the artist-hero required a revival of man's contact with the mystical forces of primeval nature and a heightened consciousness of the cultural heritage and organic unity of the German national community.[78]

The ideas of Wagner and Langbehn on art captivated cultural pessimists like Diederichs. The publisher was a Wagner devotee who made it a point to attend the Wagnerian festivals in Bayreuth. In 1912 he even postponed a major trip to Russia and the Balkans so that he could squeeze in a Bayreuth performance of Wagner's "Parsifal."[79] Diederichs hailed Langbehn's book on Rembrandt as one of the "first blossoms" of the new irrational age that would overcome German dissipation and decay. He considered Langbehn "one of the fathers of our modern intellectual life"; "I openly confess my debt to him," said Diederichs, "and I have attempted, through my professional and organizational activities, to administer his spiritual heritage."[80]

Following Wagner and Langbehn, Diederichs embraced art as the antipode of modern rationalism. Since art was governed by principles of noble beauty rather than rational utility, it seemed to be an expression of values and morality over selfish materialism. Grounded in genius—which was by nature instinctive, spontaneous, and totally subjective—art represented the free, creative expression of instinctive truths. In practicing art, man gave voice to all the idealism, sincerity, and passionate intensity of the human soul. Precisely because it was an irrational experience, art seemed capable of embracing the total man, thereby restoring that fundamental unity of existence which modern rational analysis was destroying. By promoting art, cultural pessimists believed they were providing an outlet for the repressed inner spirit and a powerful antidote to the cold rational intellect. "No longer shall dead, scientific learning govern life," proclaimed Diederichs; "rather, art . . . must shape man's emotions and direct his practical activity."[81]

Diederichs's house used a variety of means to champion art and inspire an artistic revival in German life. Before 1914 the EDV published some twenty treatises exploring the metaphysical bases of art, the nature of artistic genius and creativity, the relation of art to culture and to national identity, and the need for a greater aesthetic sensibility. The firm published another twenty-five works by noted artists or critics such as da Vinci, Isadora Duncan, Hermann Muthesius, Dante G. Rosetti, John Ruskin, Fritz Schumacher, Paul Schultze-Naumburg, and Karl Söhle treating specific aspects of the visual and performing arts.

Because he regarded the artistic outlook as so crucial for cultural renewal, Diederichs wanted to see art manifested in all aspects of daily life and he desired to establish a new aesthetic consciousness among Germans. In this regard he was consciously following in the footsteps of one of his contemporaries, Ferdinand Avenarius. Avenarius, son of the publisher Eduard Avenarius (whose firm the HVA eventually acquired), nephew of Richard Wagner, and like Diederichs an autodidact, was a minor poet and novelist in imperial Germany. But he gained his greatest notoriety as editor of the journal *Der Kunstwart* (*The Artistic Guardian*), which he founded in 1887. Avenarius and *Der Kunstwart* were critical of the general cultural tone of Wilhelmian Germany. He condemned the materialism, artificiality, and superficiality of the times in which he lived, and launched an outspoken attack on the pomp, the concern with externals, and the general lack of taste exhibited by his countrymen. Through the *Kunstwart* and its parallel organization the Dürer League, Avenarius campaigned tirelessly for a new culture based on genuineness, ethical idealism, and above all on a higher level of aesthetic taste. Only a nation with a more highly developed sense of the aesthetic, he believed, would spawn the strong, creative personalities which were so desperately needed to resist the dulling, flattening effects of modern mass civilization. For this reason he and his circle of followers assumed the function of educating Germans in matters artistic and of carving out a larger role for aesthetics in daily life.[82]

Eugen Diederichs regarded Avenarius not only as a close friend, but as a spiritual mentor and trusted advisor; he later admitted that Avenarius and *Der Kunstwart* had been part of the two strongest influences on his early life.[83] Diederichs hailed Avenarius as "one of the driving forces in the recovery (*Gesundung*) of the German *Volk*," and he modeled the EDV journal *Die Tat* as well as his own activities on Avenarius and *Der Kunst-wart*.[84] The very first book published by the newly founded Diederichs house in 1896 was a collection of Avenarius's poems, *Live! Poems (Lebe! Gedichte)*; by 1900 the EDV had issued three more works by this writer. Indeed, the Diederichs house drew many of its early authors (Adolf Bartels, Carl Spitteler, Paul Schultze-Naumburg, Leopold Weber, and Karl Söhle) from Avenarius's *Kunstwart* circle, and when Avenarius founded the Dürer League in 1903, Diederichs sat on the Board of Directors.

Following Avenarius's lead, the Jena publisher used a variety of imaginative new policies in an attempt to heighten aesthetic experience in Germany. Through the use of book graphics, Diederichs sought to infuse art into all the objects his house produced. For to him, every book was an individual work of art with its own unique cultural mission. He believed that not only the written content of a book, but also its external form and design must carry a cultural message to the public. Each book had to be given a soul of its own, a unique form which distinguished it from all others. This outward aesthetic form, however, must be in complete "organic" harmony with the book's content. By making every EDV volume a unified artistic object, Diederichs hoped to bring deeper spiritual content and greater synthetic unity to the superficial material world around him. Aesthetic book graphics, he believed, because it represented an "external expression of inner forms," could play a crucial role in "the search for the spiritual vestments of our times."[85] Thus, shortly before the turn of the century, Diederichs's firm began experimenting with new book layouts, type styles, colored paper, novel dust jacket designs and house insignia, and avant-garde textual illustrations. The Jena publisher sought especially to apply to book graphics the new artistic movement of *Jugendstil*, that distinctly German branch of Art Nouveau which sprang up alongside the German Youth Movement. He provided several generous commissions to struggling young *Jugendstil* artists such as E. R. Weiss, Melchoir Lechter, F. H. Ehmcke, and Fidus, many of whom first gained public recognition through their design work for the EDV.[86] In this way, Diederichs not only patronized individual artists, but also provided *Jugendstil* art with a new outlet of expression, and helped popularize this new artistic movement both in Germany and abroad. Conversely, Diederichs believed that his house's *Jugendstil* designs had gained a whole new circle of readers for EDV books (and probably made them sell better).[87] If this were true, then his pioneering work in book graphics also helped disseminate his emerging neoconservative ideology to a wider reading public.

To heighten the role of art in German daily life, Diederichs also joined with Avenarius and other prominent cultural figures in 1907 to found the German Work League (Deutscher Werkbund). This organization, which stood under the influence of Langbehn and of Avenarius's Dürer League and which was part of the broader "arts and crafts" movement in Europe, believed that modern industrialization and mechanization were destroying artistic culture and were giving rise to a plethora of shoddy, tasteless goods. Werkbund members hoped somehow to bridge the widening gulf between art and industry by reestablishing high standards of quality workmanship and aesthetic taste. By providing a meeting place for artists, designers, and industrialists, the Werkbund intended to apply the principles of art to daily life, especially to consumer goods. It was the goal of the Werkbund to raise the aesthetic level of the national environment and at the same time create a harmonious national style, thereby restoring moral and ethical unity to German culture.[88] Hermann Muthesius, guiding spirit and first leader of the group, summed up the Werkbund as "a product of German Idealism" which sought, first, to achieve "a coherent, unified artistic style" out of Germany's "confused, disharmonious cultural chaos," and second, to "bring industrial and commercial activity into accordance with artistic goals."[89] Diederichs, a founding member who saw the Werkbund as the vanguard of a larger movement which would encompass all creative people and would overcome Germany's cultural decline,[90] lent it support by publishing the organization's manifesto, by issuing the Werkbund's widely distributed annual reports between 1911 and 1914, and by helping to organize the Werkbund's 1913 festival in Leipzig.[91]

It was not merely the antimodern irrationalism of art which impressed Eugen Diederichs, but its relation to national consciousness as well. Wagner and Langbehn had both emphasized the *völkisch* roots of artistic creativity, and had seen art as heightening Germanic identity. Diederichs, too, believed German art was an expression of the nation's unique soul. He was convinced that Germans had a deeper, closer appreciation for the world of art than did people of other nations and that the fortunes of the inner German spirit were directly linked to the fate of the German artistic style. This became particularly clear to him in 1910–11 as a controversy swept German publishing and aesthetic circles as to whether or not Germans should abandon their idiosyncratic Gothic script (*Fraktur*) and adopt the more modern, universal Roman script (*Antiqua*). In an impassioned article in the German book trade journal,[92] Diederichs argued that a nation's script, like its language, was but an outward expression of that *Volk*'s deeper inner essence. The drive for one uniform script in the world, he said, was similar to the drive to create one universal language—and would be just as disastrous, for it would destroy the rich diversity of the world and force all peoples into one uniform straitjacket. He maintained (largely incorrectly) that Roman script was primarily a product of the eighteenth-century French Enlightenment and represented the rational clarity, cosmopolitanism, intellectualism, and utilitarianism of that age. German *Fraktur*, on the other hand, was associated in his mind with the Renaissance—the height of German art—and was an expression of the uniqueness, creativity, fantasy, and profound inwardness of the German *Volk*. The debate over which script Germans should adopt was, in his eyes, actually a debate over whether the German *Volk* should abandon its own unique artistic weltanschauung for an alien, Western one: "The question of whether *Antiqua* or *Fraktur* [should dominate] ultimately involves the following: should the intellect, which is only one aspect of life, violate (*vergewaltigen*) the creative life-style, or do the laws of artistic life stand above the fanatic utilitarianism of shortsighted rationalists?"[93]

For those who might be inclined to doubt the prospect of a new religious revival in an age of pervasive liberal skepticism and disbelief, then, art provided an attractive surrogate. Diederichs's glorification of art, his emphasis on the relationship between art and the *Volk*, and his efforts to heighten appreciation for German art styles were all elements of his larger struggle against modern rationalism. These efforts merely reinforced his campaign for a new religious mystique. Indeed, they helped transform aestheticism into a new secular religion which promised the German nation salvation from the modern predicament.

Romanticism and Neoromanticism

Out of an aversion to modern rationalism, many disaffected members of the Wilhelmian intelligentsia like Eugen Diederichs looked to such remedies as instinct and emotion, pantheistic nature-mysticism, immersion in the organic stream of life, faith in a spiritualistic religious mystique, and the cult of the creative artist. In these respects and others, their outlook bears a striking resemblance to the rebellion a century earlier by romantics against the Enlightenment. Indeed, German cultural pessimists at the end of the nineteenth century borrowed heavily from the romantic heritage and men like Diederichs were consciously reenacting the original romantics' revolt against enlightened reason, although now with a heightened sense of last-chance urgency. He not only sought explicitly to identify his own goals and activities with those of the original German romantics, but he also attempted, quite literally, to launch a new romanticism in Germany.

Late eighteenth- and early nineteenth-century German romanticism was (like the neoconservative movement of the late nineteenth and early twentieth century) an extremely amorphous and frequently contradictory phenomenon. Despite nearly a century and a half of intensive scholarly research, there is yet no consensus of interpretation—much less a satisfactory definition—of the romantic movement. However, since World War II, many cultural historians, looking perhaps for the roots of fascism, have tended to view the early phase of German romanticism as a revolt against the principles of the eighteenth-century Enlightenment, and have seen the later phase which began around 1800 as a specific reaction against the upheaval of the French revolutionary era.[94] According to this interpretation, Germany at the end of the eighteenth century was confronted with a series of forces which threatened to replace the old social order, traditionally based on caste and absolutism, with a new order founded on class and constitutionalism. This crisis of change emanated primarily from the West, first in the form of French Enlightenment philosophy, and later in the guise of the French Revolution and Napoleon. To meet this all-inclusive threat of reason and revolution to the traditional order, many German intellectuals reacted (either consciously or unconsciously) by developing a comprehensive system of ideas designed to surmount or escape from the general crisis facing German society.

Many romantics were convinced that the glorification and application of abstract reason by the Enlightenment was the ultimate source of the revolutionary challenges which threatened the traditional order in which they lived. They responded by idealizing the antithesis of reason: the heart, feelings, emotion, the supernatural, the mystical. Threatened both socially and psychologically by the age's thrust toward egalitarianism—and by the resultant loss of individual identity—romantics turned toward passion, intense subjectivity, and the cult of the individual personality, for these seemed to offer a means of expressing and preserving one's unique identity in the midst of the dreaded leveling they saw around them.

German romantics also lamented Enlightenment rationalism and the French Revolution for disturbing the traditional relationship between the individual and the social whole. Too much emphasis on the individual, they complained, was causing a disintegration of the social order and the outbreak of anarchic turmoil. In hopes of reintegrating society under some higher authority, romantics focused a new attention on the notion of the whole. A particular, they concluded, was always part of some larger whole; indeed, to fulfill its own existence an individual unit must partake of the whole. Yet wholes, too, were individuals. Any whole, such as the state or society, was always greater than the sum of its parts and functioned as a single organic entity. It had, in the eyes of the romantics, a life and will of its own and obeyed only its own unique laws of development. Within such a homogeneous entity, the romantics maintained, individual elements must of necessity be hierarchically related to one another and be subject to some ultimate authority to insure that the whole functioned as a single organic entity. Any authoritarian hierarchy, however, implied an inequality of individual members. Romantics could (and did) justify such inequality, especially social inequality, by claiming it was founded on the unique individuality of each particular; the subjectivity and singularity of each individual unit made it incomparable—and thus unequal—with every other unit. By positing in this way the necessary subordination of conflicting individual elements to some larger whole, and especially by stressing the ties of cultural, racial, or historical heritage which bound men together into one harmonious national community, German romantics hoped to reintegrate the sociopolitical order and ultimately restore stability to their age.

It was the yearning for stability and for permanence which prompted the German romantics also to turn to the past for consolation. From the historical process, romantics attempted to sift out what was transitory and erratic from what was constant and enduring. They discovered in the distant past—especially the Christian Middle Ages—the security, the continuity of lasting values, and the permanency which to their minds was so lacking in the bewildering, even chaotic changes of their own age. In history, for example, some romantics found the eternal entity of the *Volk*, that cultural identity which persisted through all the ephemeral changes of political and social institutions. Others searched for some eternal, infinite, nontemporal reality beyond the transient material world. This search, symbolized in German romantic literature as the pursuit of the elusive "blue flower," led many to a new appreciation for pristine nature, where they believed they saw a level of existence untouched by change or by the baffling complexity and mournful decadence of human civilization. In nature, too, romantics found a pantheistic manifestation of an infinite, mystical Spirit rather than the mechanical Newtonian universe which Enlightenment philosophy saw there.

In short, the comprehensive new view of reality presented by German romanticism at the end of the eighteenth century was often a manifestation of the inherently conservative, even reactionary proclivities of its adherents. Romanticism served as a means of deliverance for those caught up in the midst of transition from traditional to modern society around 1800. As one scholar has recently written, "Emerging in the wake of a disaster originating from without, which left what little remained of shared traditions and institutions in shambles, romanticism provided Germans, and especially middle-class Germans . . . with an orientation that seemed more appropriate—and more manageable—than any other in an otherwise meaningless and menacing world."[95] The vague fluidity of its concepts and its origins as an ideology of reactive opposition made romanticism easy to apply to other crisis situations. For precisely because romanticism never developed a clear, consistent program of action of its own, "it could remain from that day to this the most readily available cultural outlet for discontent, since it possessed the ambiguous advantage of not having to risk defeat or disillusionment. And nowhere more so than in Germany, where fewer alternatives for expressing discontent existed than elsewhere."[96]

At the end of the nineteenth century, therefore, cultural pessimists like Eugen Diederichs who felt caught up in another cultural crisis fathered by rationalism quite naturally reached back to the original romantic tradition as a means of combating the more deeply entrenched evils of their own age. Diederichs, who admitted he was inwardly inclined toward the "romantic weltanschauung," declared when he founded his publishing house in 1896 that the firm would work "toward romanticism" as a means of opposing modern materialism, and he later proclaimed that he hoped someday to create a new German culture based largely on romanticism.[97] He saw in the romantics models who had "something to say" to modern Germans and who could serve as spiritual allies in his own struggle to create a new synthesis and wholeness for modern man. Diederichs pointed, for example, to the poet Hölderlin (who had gone insane at an early age) as a figure relevant to Germany's modern cultural crisis; for Hölderlin, Diederichs reminded his readers, "had already long before us been deeply distressed over the disunity and disintegration of our nation and of the Western world. Because of this, he ultimately suffered personal psychic ruin."[98] And in his house's first programmatic catalog, Diederichs declared that "in the strivings of the new [cultural] era, one can recognize the revivification of the ideals of our old romantics concerning the unity of art and knowledge . . . and the desire for a universal man."[99]

In 1898 Diederichs began republishing the works of major romantic authors in order, as he put it, to create a new interest in romanticism, make the writings of romantics more accessible to the German public, "resurrect the living impact" of these writers, "and thereby help shape and broaden the essential basis of our culture."[100] Many of these romantic works, especially those by the German romantics, were grouped into a series which Diederichs didactically entitled *Mentors for German Cultivation* (*Erzieher zu deutscher Bildung*, 1904–7). Even though the EDV's romantic publishing program meant some of his other publishing activities had to be curtailed, Diederichs proceeded with this plan because of a "personal fondness" for these authors. The reissuing of romantic works, he emphasized, was being undertaken "not for some aloof academic goal and still less out of some romantic-poetic wallowing in nostalgia. Rather, it is an attempt to dig down to the roots of our original, Germanic essence in order to retrieve—by means of these popular, national (*volkstümlich*) publications—a new, living source of power for our flat, materialistic, and spiritually impoverished times."[101] The Jena publisher decided to include a new anthology of Rousseau's essays in the program, for example, because he felt the romantic-sentimental Rousseau rather than the rational Voltaire should inspire modern man.[102] Ultimately the EDV published three major anthologies of romantic texts plus individual works by such German romantics as Schlegel, Wackenroder, Herder, Schleiermacher, and Bettina von Arnim. The complete works of the two major romantic poets Novalis and Hölderlin were also republished by the EDV and served as the cornerstone of the firm's series of romantic texts. Hölderlin had been virtually ignored throughout the nineteenth century. Largely through the efforts of the Diederichs house, this poet's works were rediscovered by scholars and general readers shortly before World War I, and he quickly became one of the most popular of all German romantic authors.[103]

Besides romantic texts, Diederichs also produced a number of scholarly studies of romanticism such as Marie Joachimi's *The World-View of German Romanticism* (*Die Weltanschauung der deutschen Romantik*, 1905), a work which the publisher confessed was intended as "a scholarly vindication" of romantic ideas.[104] Through studies such as these, Diederichs hoped to redirect the attention of modern scholars and scientists back to romantic principles. He approached a young scholar, for example, requesting him to write a book on the medical ideas of the German romantics. Such a treatise, Diederichs confided, might help steer modern medicine out of its "dead end" of empirical chemical experimentation and more toward romantic goals and procedures.[105]

Diederichs, however, was not content merely to revive earlier ideals. His entire cultural approach was distinguished by its attempt to give older conservative traditions new force by adapting them to modern conditions. Thus he realized that while romanticism may have been an appropriate means of expression for early German conservatism, the new conservatism of the late nineteenth and early twentieth century required a new form of romanticism. The EDV therefore worked to develop a distinctive Neoromantic movement.

The term "New" or "Neoromanticism" is often ambiguously applied. Because so many of the principles of the neoconservative movement resemble those of the earlier romantics, some scholars have used the term "Neoromanticism" to connote simply the entire ideology of cultural pessimists such as Diederichs.[106] In truth, Neoromanticism was a more circumscribed phenomenon in German culture; it was a distinct literary movement around 1900 by a group of authors who explicitly rejected both the realistic style and rather seamy subject matter of German literary naturalism.[107] This group included such writers as Ricarda Huch, Ina Seidel, Maurice Maeterlinck, Gertrud von le Fort, the early Hermann Hesse, Börries von Münchhausen, Agnes Miegel, Lulu von Strauss und Torney, Carl Spitteler, Paul Ernst, and Wilhelm Schäfer (although the last three are sometimes also classified as Neoclassicists).

Neoromantic authors drew direct inspiration from the earlier romantic movement. One group (von Münchhausen, Miegel, and von Strauss und Torney) deliberately sought to revive lyric poetry and epic balladry as a German art form after a decade of naturalist drama and prose, much as the original romantics had rebelled against Enlightenment prose in favor of poetry. In contrast to literary naturalism, Neoromanticism placed greater emphasis on feeling, emotion, the senses, and inner psychic experience. It sought to portray life as one unified totality infused with joy and beauty. Neglecting the material and temporal realm, it turned for its subject matter to the supernatural, the holy, the mystical, and the exotic, often utilizing pagan, Oriental, and legendary motifs. Although strictly a literary movement, Neoromanticism carried politically conservative overtones. Admirers of the movement portrayed it as an aristocratic, irrational reaction against the liberal, egalitarian modernism of the naturalists. As the neoconservative historian Georg Steinhausen explained in his 1930 survey of German cultural history, literary Neoromanticism represented a healthy attempt "to turn away from the problems of the time by returning to the eternal, untimely themes and currents of the past."[108]

The Eugen Diederichs Verlag did more than any other single agent to establish and promote the Neoromantic movement. One literary scholar has in fact concluded that "the sole figure who may be termed a genuine Neoromantic and who has left clear and lasting tracks in our literary life is the publisher Eugen Diederichs."[109] For reasons of marketing and public image, Diederichs was eager to associate his newly founded firm with an identifiable new literary current in the successful manner that his great rival, the S. Fischer Verlag, had identified itself with naturalism in the 1890s. Such an opportunity presented itself in 1899 while Diederichs was negotiating with a young author named Hermann Hesse over publication of the writer's first book. In one of his letters to Diederichs, Hesse offhandedly included a short literary manifesto he had composed which he thought the publisher "perhaps can make use of in some way." This manifesto, entitled "Neoromanticism" (*Neuromantik*), stated:

> Neoromantic literature reaches back to Novalis. It acknowledges him, who was for so long unknown. It has rediscovered him and sees him as a venerated figure standing far above all modern squabbling

and cheap artistic hucksterism. Neoromanticism also has his "blue flower" as its symbol; but it understands the meaning of this symbol far better than Novalis himself did. . . . The history of true Romanticism, interrupted by Novalis's death, is about to begin again. The term, which was once . . . used as a term of ridicule, has now purified a new youth and will now bring honor to all those who have dreamed enthusiastically about their unhappy and luckless predecessors [the Romantics].[110]

Diederichs had the keen sense immediately to seize the term "Neoromanticism" and adopt it as his house's slogan for the new century. In his catalog for 1900, "For the Turn of the Century. House Program: Neoromanticism" (*Zur Jahrhundertwende. Verlagsprogramm: Neuromantik*), Diederichs further elaborated on the concept. The time had come, he wrote, to overthrow the increasingly specialized, fragmented, one-sided rationalistic-materialistic culture of the nineteenth century and grasp the cosmos as a whole once again. Neoromanticism, Diederichs declared, was uniquely capable of accomplishing this and would help prepare the new era; for it proceeded intuitively and would thus help Germans recover their "universality of experiencing" (*Universalität der Welterfassung*).[111] In 1906 the EDV published Ludwig Coellen's *Neoromanticism* (*Neuromantik*), a treatise which served as the movement's first comprehensive statement of principles. Coellen defined Neoromanticism as the upsurge of a new pantheistic mysticism; because naturalism had been based on rationalism, he declared, Neoromanticism was inherently antirational.[112]

Besides helping to develop and popularize the general concept of Neoromanticism, the Diederichs house became a haven for nearly every prominent Neoromantic author. Works by Huch and Miegel, and some ten major works by Spitteler, appeared under the EDV imprint between 1900 and 1914. (The publisher believed that Spitteler's writings perfectly complemented the firm's other religious and philosophical publications.)[113] Diederichs also issued the complete works (some twenty titles) of Maeterlinck. These volumes became best-sellers and reaped handsome profits for the EDV; by 1932, the Diederichs house had sold a total of 525,830 copies of Maeterlinck's books. After divorcing the "hearth-and-homeland" poetess Helene Voigt (see p. 97), Diederichs married the Neoromantic lyricist Lulu von Strauss und Torney in 1917 and subsequently published ten volumes of her works. The publisher also sought to aid other Neoromantic authors. After issuing Hesse's first work, *An Hour Behind Midnight* (*Eine Stunde Hinter Mitternacht*, 1899), Diederichs tried to procure a better position for the struggling young writer, who was at the time

employed as a bookstore clerk. The publisher knew the director of the
Leipzig Booktrade Museum and offered to get Hesse a job there which
would allow him to devote more time to his writing.[114]

The publisher's many efforts on behalf of Neoromantic literature would,
he hoped, ignite a general resurgence of romanticism in German life. In
the early nineteenth century German romanticism had served, rather successfully, as an ideological bulwark against the advance of French rationalism, and a comprehensive intellectual foundation from which to combat
the Western forces of modernization which threatened the "unique" German character. By reviving the romantic outlook in the twentieth century,
Diederichs believed he was reconstructing that bulwark, refurbishing that
foundation for a new counteroffensive against rational modernity.

The *Volk* Mystique

During the first decade and a half of his publishing career (1896 to
approximately 1910), Eugen Diederichs concentrated his efforts on "*innere
Bildung*," the cultivation of Germans' inner, subjective natures. By promoting various esoteric philosophical, religious, and aesthetic outlooks, he
hoped to create a new "personal culture" (*Persönlichkeitskultur*) in which the
sensitive, integrated, creative personality would once again feel at home.

Beginning around 1910, however, Diederichs began shifting his attention from the inner spiritual education of modern man to the communal
bonds which link individuals. For true culture, he came to realize, required
there to be a "spiritual commonality" (*seelischer Gemeinsamkeit*) between
individuals; all members of the culture must be integrated into a larger
whole in which some higher form, order, or organizing principle pre-
vailed. Only when individual Germans felt a new sense of attachment to
the whole, he declared, could German cultural life be rejuvenated.[115]
Diederichs now believed it imperative to focus more attention on the
social dimension and public responsibilities of modern man. He declared
in a 1912 programmatic catalog, for example, that "the present cultural
superstructure (*Überkultur*) of aestheticism, with its stress on individualism, requires a sharper eye for the increasingly rapid transformations in
social life if there is to be a healthy functioning of all members within the
civic whole. . . . I want to spur the educated middle class . . . to concern
itself more with the problems of social life, and I want to help them realize
that observing the events of the social sphere can be . . . as satisfying and
enriching as contemplating a work of art."[116] In the years immediately
preceding World War I, therefore, he undertook a publishing campaign

designed to promote the civic cultivation of Germany's educated elite and to heighten its social consciousness.

When Diederichs had earlier contemplated the fate of the internal self, he had lamented the spiritual disunity and intellectual fragmentation of modern life and had turned to abstract schools of thought such as monism, life-philosophy, mysticism, and romanticism because these seemed to offer a comprehensive view of reality which could restore a synthetic totality to spiritual life. Similarly, when he now focused on the external relationships and communal existence of Germans, he detected a breakdown of social and political unity—caused, he believed, by excessive hedonistic individualism—and the need for social reintegration.[117] For Diederichs, the restoration of Germany's communal solidarity had to be achieved on an ideal, subjective level through heightened national consciousness, and on a material, objective plane by means of a new socioeconomic order.

In his search for a sense of community and solidarity, Diederichs was drawn initially to the interpersonal ties of tradition and race. As he matured he confessed to becoming more and more conscious of what he called "the bonds of blood and of the past" ("*Blutserbe und Gebundenheit an der Vergangenheit*"), bonds which exercised a strong, inescapable, and yet largely unconscious hold over every individual's life.[118] In Diederichs's view, every member of a culture inherited a complex of historical traditions which inevitably shaped his outlook and actions. The sharing of a common heritage and common experiences gave individuals a sense of tradition and served as a spiritual cement which held men together and produced a feeling of solidarity. "As soon as one cuts one's self off from tradition," Diederichs realized, "one loses the commonality of heritage."[119] Conversely, it was clear to him that heightening man's awareness of a shared historical heritage might help foster a new consciousness of solidarity and common destiny. By reawakening interest in the German past, the Jena bookman hoped to inspire a renewed sense of national community which might rescue Germans from the individual egotism and civic fragmentation of modernity. To him, the study of history was not some detached scholarly undertaking, but rather served as a means of arousing in Germans a high degree of enthusiasm for their common identity and as a tool with which to fashion a new national outlook.[120] "The future of our nation," Diederichs was convinced, "depends on our listening to the voices of the past"; his house's publications in the area of history, he admitted, were all designed to lay a strong new foundation of German consciousness and to create a common sense of identity.[121]

Because he recognized from the outset the potential value of history in strengthening national solidarity, Diederichs's firm had begun issuing a number of works before 1910 on Germany's past. Inspired by Lagarde's earlier call for a collective history of German folk customs, for example, Diederichs in 1899 conceived the plan for a multivolume series of *Monographs on German Cultural History* (*Monographien zur deutschen Kulturgeschichte*) and persuaded Georg Steinhausen, University librarian at Jena, to serve as general editor. But Diederichs continued to play an active role in the project, undertaking two extensive research trips to collect material for the volumes.[122] Although the enterprise, which eventually ran to twelve volumes and extended over six years, proved at first a commercial burden for the EDV, by 1933 nearly ninety-five thousand volumes from the series had been sold. Prominent writers such as Börries von Münchhausen claimed the series provided them with "a substantial part of [their] historical education."[123] The EDV also produced, both before and after 1910, a number of individual popularized historical studies such as *The German Past in Pictures* (*Deutsches Leben der Vergangenheit in Bildern*, 2 vols., 1908) and Ernst Lissauer's *1813* (1913).

Besides shared tradition Diederichs looked to race as another natural bond which inextricably linked individuals together into a larger unified community. By 1900, his study of the German past had convinced him that "German blood" was the key to understanding why German historical development differed so from that of other European peoples.[124] The publisher became increasingly interested in racial anthropology and briefly considered purchasing the journal *Anthropologische Revue* (*Anthropological Review*), a Social-Darwinistic organ whose racial orientation he believed to be closest to his own.[125] Because of his special concern over such problems as the effect of social structures on the health of the race and the ways in which racial factors determined social development, in 1901 Diederichs published a study by Haeckel's disciple Heinrich Driesmans on German racial mixing, *The Elective Affinities of German Racial Compositions* (*Die Wahlverwandtschaften der deutschen Blutmischung*). Eight years later he issued Ludwig Woltmann's influential *Political Anthropology* (*Politische Anthropologie*), which argued that Germany's modern social ills were the result of racial pollution and could be overcome only when racial purity was regained. Woltmann's volume laid the groundwork for later theories of Nordic racism and inspired many of the leading racial theorists in the postwar era, especially those associated with the J. F. Lehmann house.[126] After 1910, Diederichs expressed the desire to devote more of his attention and publishing resources to the "racial question," and on the eve of World War I emphasized to his readers that a conscious sense of race was the logical and inevitable outcome of heightened national consciousness.[127]

In Diederichs's mind (as in many Germans'), shared historical experiences or traditions on the one hand, and a common biological or racial

heritage on the other, formed the two distinguishing characteristics of a
Volk, a national cultural and ethnic community in which successive generations and contemporary individuals were welded together into a coherent
people. Since the beginning of the nineteenth century, the notion of *Volk*
and *Volkstum* symbolized to many Germans a perfectly integrated social
whole, the epitome of harmonious communal existence. Friedrich Jahn,
whose 1810 book *Germanic Volk Character* (*Deutsches Volkstum*) first anchored
the term *Volk* in the German consciousness, maintained that:

> *Volkstum* is nothing less than the unifying force of the highest,
> greatest, and most comprehensive of all human associations, the *Volk*.
> *Volkstum* is that which the *Volk* has in common, its inner existence, its
> movement and life. Because of it, there courses through all the veins
> of the *Volk* a folkish way of thinking and feeling, loving and hating . . .
> intuition and faith. It is *Volkstum* which brings all the individual
> members of the *Volk*, through a many- and all-encompassing unity
> with every other member, into a beautifully unified community. And
> it does so without abolishing [individual] freedom and autonomy.
> On the contrary, these are even more strengthened in the process.[128]

Membership in the *Volk* presumed an all-inclusive integration of individuals into one natural, organic, and harmonious social entity. In the face
of the deepening social divisions of nineteenth-century society, the idea of
the *Volk* provided a growing number of Germans with that satisfying
sense of unity and community which they lacked in real life, and the
popularity of *völkisch* ideology grew accordingly. To Diederichs, the *Volk*
was an especially attractive symbol of the ideal, harmonious social community. For the *Volk* was commonly regarded as an entity based on non-
utilitarian, nonrational foundations. As the concept evolved in Germany,
each *Volk* was assumed to possess some intangible essence or unique inner
soul (*Volksgeist*). This mysterious *Volk* spirit was easily formulated as an
unconscious, biological, or vitalistic force which arose "organically" or
intuitively from nature. Thus to many Germans, " '*Volk*' signified the
union of a group of people with a transcendental 'essence.' This 'essence'
might be called 'nature' or 'cosmos' or 'mythos,' but in each instance it
was fused to man's innermost nature, and represented the source of his
creativity, his depth of feeling, his individuality, and his unity with other
members of the *Volk*. The essential element here is the linking of the
human soul with its natural surroundings, with the 'essence' of nature."[129]
This relation of a *Volk* to the irrational forces of nature gave *völkisch*
ideology a semimystical, nearly religious aura and hence made it easily
adaptable to Diederichs's principles. The *Volk* mystique also proved irresis-
tible to him because it was idealistic: since a community such as the *Volk*

presupposed subordination of individual egotism to the greater ends of the whole, the notion of *Volk* served as a source of moral self-sacrifice and seemed to offer the perfect antidote to modern materialism. Moreover, the concept of *Volk* was largely an imaginary ideal yet to be realized, a utopian, perhaps unattainable goal. The romantic, Novalis, whom Diederichs "rediscovered," recognized this at the outset of the nineteenth century when he proclaimed: "The *Volk* is an idea. We should become a *Volk*."[130] Even Lagarde, Diederichs's idol, admitted that "the German *Volk*, which we love and which we long to see, has never existed and will perhaps never exist."[131]

In the two or three years immediately preceding World War I, Eugen Diederichs placed his house squarely behind the "*Volkstum* movement," which sought to restore German social solidarity through heightened *völkisch* consciousness. He claimed in 1912–13 that his firm and his journal would be committed to the cultivation of *völkisch* ideas because these "sought the path to community" and helped, "through biological-hereditary means (*Blutsanlagen*), to heighten the communality of feeling, thought, and action." A strengthening of the *Volk* and of national consciousness, he added, could be achieved only through a "heightened racial feeling" (*rassenhafte Gefühl*).[132] There may also have been a commercial reason behind Diederichs's inauguration of a conscious *völkisch* program around 1913. The public, he complained, was losing interest in the EDV's religious publications, and he hinted that a new slogan such as the "*Volkstum* movement" might attract more attention from the press.[133] At any rate, in the months before the outbreak of war the EDV produced books such as H. Staudinger's *Individual and Community in the Cultural Context* (*Individuum und Gemeinschaft in der Kulturorganisation*, 1913) or D. Bischoff's *The German Disposition* (*Deutsche Gesinnung*, 1914) which explored the concept of a German *Volk*. The publisher also devoted two special issues of *Die Tat* to German national consciousness and to Fichte, one of the intellectual forerunners of German *Volk* ideology.

Diederichs had reminded contemporary Germans of their common historical heritage in order to raise their *völkisch* consciousness and thus perhaps restore to them a sense of social solidarity. He hoped that creating a new awareness of German historical mythology, its folklore and legends, might also serve that purpose. For folktales, it was commonly believed in Germany, were expressions of a people's innermost values and beliefs; since mythical folklore was a preliterate manifestation of ancient communal experiences, it could also reveal a *Volk*'s fundamental disposition. The famous brothers Grimm, for example, had religiously collected German fairy tales because they were convinced that "in these folktales can be found the original, undefiled German mythos which we thought had been lost."[134] Similarly, *völkisch* enthusiasts like Diederichs regarded folktales and popular legends as clear, direct reflections of the eternal German *Volksgeist*. Beginning with publication of a new edition of the famous Till Eulenspiegel saga in 1899 (two additional versions were later published by the EDV, one of which sold more than fifty thousand copies), Diederichs by 1910 had committed his house to collecting and reissuing as many German folktales as possible. He personally planned several anthologies and multivolume series in this area and sounded out appropriate authors to carry out the projects.[135] Two major collections of German folktales, *The German Folk Books* (*Die deutschen Volksbücher*, 6 vols., 1910–13) and *Old German Legends* (*Alte deutsche Legenden*, 1910) were issued by the Diederichs firm, as well as the collected tales of Hans Christian Andersen and two individual volumes on German folklore.

The Jena publisher became particularly fascinated with the folklore produced by the ancient Germanic tribes. These heroic, pagan, Teutonic peoples who were just entering the stage of European history provided cultural pessimists like Diederichs with a *völkisch* model which seemed the perfect antithesis of modern social life. As described by Tacitus in his *Germania*, the ancient Germanic peoples were pure, simple, genuine, young, and vital. Their primitive simplicity and vigor made these Germanic pagans strong, heroic, idealistic, and virtuous and placed them in the sharpest possible contrast to the weak, decadent, "modern" Christian-Western civilization they soon encountered. Because ancient Teutons had not yet experienced contact and mixing with other peoples, they were still a distinct, unique, and completely homogeneous *Volk*. These old Germanic people, in the eyes of many latter-day Germans, provided the clearest picture of the original German *Volk* essence and of perfect, harmonious social communities. Prehistoric Germanic tribes had been closely related to the other ancient Gothic peoples of Northern Europe. They were part of a general Nordic culture which shared many of the same pagan gods, values, and customs. The virtues, strengths, and communal ideals which later cultural pessimists admired in the ancient Germanic peoples were also found in other Nordic tribes. In fact, many Germans came to believe that the ancient Germanic qualities which the German *Volk* eventually lost had survived in other Nordic peoples; isolated Nordics like those in Iceland, for example, had been spared much of the corrupting contact with civilization which had so weakened the Germans over the ages. Nordic peoples, it was believed, had thus remained closer to ancient Germanic roots.

It was not surprising, then, that Diederichs's search for German historical identity would eventually lead him to the primitive Nordic cultures such as Iceland. Shortly after the turn of the century, he published books by Driesmans, Woltmann, and W. Pastor which treated early Germanic-Nordic cultures. Pastor's book, *The Drive from the North* (*Der Zug vom Norden*, 1906), the publisher told his readers, convincingly demonstrated that the Nordic peoples of the northern regions of the planet have historically served as the "sole incubators of culture."[136] In 1909, while on a tour of Iceland, Diederichs developed a deep interest in old Icelandic sagas, which he believed embodied the "pure essence of the Germanic soul." He concluded that Icelandic sagas, because they pointed out especially clearly the original loyalty and tribal sanctity of the early German *Volk*, "can perhaps fulfill a cultural task in our own modern life: they can make us more conscious of what our own genuine nature is and can give us the courage we need to again profess and embrace it."[137] He began therefore to collect and republish the ancient Nordic "Thule" sagas of Iceland, for he saw these texts as a "literary monument" of pre-Christian Teutonic peasant culture which would serve as "a source of new power" for the German *Volk*.[138] The massive twenty-four-volume *Thule* series, issued by the EDV between 1911 and 1930, became the cornerstone of the firm's efforts in the field of Nordic literature and culture. By 1933, more than ninety-eight thousand volumes had been sold from the series. To bring the modern German *Volk* closer to its Nordic neighbors and ancestors, from 1913 to 1922 Diederichs also published the journal of the "Friends of Iceland Society" (of which Diederichs was treasurer), and a yearbook devoted to German-Nordic cultural exchange.

In surveying the original qualities of the German *Volk* as manifested in ancient Nordic culture, Diederichs and others who shared his *völkisch* assumptions concluded that modern Germans had all but lost the exemplary characteristics of the primal German tribes and that these must somehow be regained if the German *Volk* were to surmount the social and spiritual crises of the modern world. It was, above all, alien influences such as Christianity, the publisher came to believe, which had sapped the strength and destroyed the character of the ancient Germanic *Volk*. The introduction of this intellectualized, rigidly theological Roman-Hebraic religion had snuffed out the healthy, natural, pantheistic paganism of the Nordic peoples and thus weakened the original *Volk* spirit. This negative assessment of orthodox Christianity led the publisher, as we have seen, to reject much of Christian doctrine (especially in its Pauline formulations), and to attempt to "free" Christianity from its historical theology.[139] It also made him sympathetic to efforts by *völkisch* theologians such as Houston S. Chamberlain and Arthus Bonus who hoped to articulate a unique new "Germanic Christianity" which would allow for the Germans' "innate" pagan mysticism and pantheism. Although Diederichs considered Chamberlain somewhat of a dilettante, the publisher claimed to have been "deeply enriched" after reading Chamberlain's influential *The Foundations of the 19th Century* (*Die Grundlagen des XIX. Jahrhunderts*, 1899), a massive, rambling tract which interpreted Western history in racial terms, proclaimed the supremacy of the German-Aryan race, and is generally credited with founding Nordic ideology.[140] Diederichs asked Chamberlain to participate in some of the "free religious" conferences organized by the EDV; he also invited the renowned author to write introductions for books published by the EDV, and hoped (albeit in vain) that Chamberlain would play an active role in a new journal he was planning.[141] More important, however, were Diederichs's relations with Bonus. In 1911 he published Bonus's *Toward the Germanization of Christianity* (*Zur Germanisierung des Christentums*), a book which argued that Christianity must be made to conform more closely to the innate Germanic essence. This volume, Diederichs told his readers, called for a "ruthless and decisive break with all those aspects of our inherited religion which are alien to and have no deep, inner relationship to our *Volk*."[142] And Arthur Drews, another early proponent of a Germanic Christianity, proclaimed that all his works, especially his *The Further Development of Christianity* (*Weiterbildung des Christentums*) fit perfectly into the program of the EDV "because they corresponded to [Diederichs's] own religious orientation, which was directed toward a Germanization and internalization of religion."[143]

German ethnic traditions, then, whether historical or mythological, were cultivated by Diederichs in hopes of strengthening the *Volk*'s sense of communal solidarity. He tended to romanticize the *Volk* past as an idyllic era with all the communal harmony and pristine heroic idealism so lacking in the modern age. This idealization of the past and of Germans' racial heritage reflected not only the publisher's modern cultural pessimism, but also his desire to escape from liberal modernity and his longing for some new order which would recapture the *Volk*'s lost utopia.

Back to Nature

Of the traditions of the German *Volk*, many *völkisch* ideologues valued the rural above all. For in the German concept of *Volk*, a crucial link was assumed to exist between an individual, the social community, and some natural cosmic force. According to *völkisch* ideology, the way this cosmic force was manifested in the natural landscape of a particular region shaped the character of those living there. As George Mosse has noted, "the landscape thus became a vital part of the definition of the *Volk* through which it retained continuous contact with the life spirit of the transcendent cosmos. . . . Not within the city, but in the landscape, the countryside native to him, was man fated to merge with and become rooted in nature and the *Volk*. And only in this process, taking place in the native environment, would every man be able to find his self-expression and his individuality."[144] The *Volk*'s essential rural nature was especially popularized by the nineteenth-century writer Wilhelm H. Riehl, who founded the study of German folklore (*Volkskunde*) and turned it into an arch-conservative, antimodern discipline.[145] Riehl's widely read works maintained that the German *Volk*'s character and culture arose directly from its natural environment. Since that landscape was eternal and unchanging, Riehl concluded, any deviation from the *Volk*'s original agrarian socioeconomic system was an artificial violation of the nation's spiritual essence.

In the Wilhelmian era, cultural pessimists such as Diederichs were slowly coming to the conclusion that the modern social and spiritual crisis was a consequence of man's having been uprooted from his native soil by the forces of liberal modernity. Deprived of the communal ties and natural roots which lent security and stability to life, modern man had become disoriented and society atomized. This process of cultural decay, they believed, was especially evident in Germany's large cities.

Indeed, the process of urbanization in imperial Germany had been both rapid and extensive. Between 1880 and 1910, the urban population grew by nearly twenty million, while the proportion of Germans living in rural areas declined from 64 to 40 percent. Many Germans were unable to adjust to the ugly industrial metropolises which suddenly seemed to scar their once idyllic countryside, or to the new urban lifestyles, which many found decadent and immoral.[146]

To Diederichs, modern urban life represented a tragic break with the *Volk*'s most hallowed spiritual traditions; life in the impersonal city was making Germans more superficial and materialistic, and less and less like their simple, heroic Germanic forefathers. "Where in our large cities," the publisher lamented, "does one still see serious, profound people, people who are at peace with themselves and who, in their old age, have the searching eyes of a Rembrandt or a Goethe, or the faces which we see in the art of the old Flemish and German masters? [In the big city] one works, one amuses one's self—but one does not 'live.'"[147] The spirit and ideals of the small community, Diederichs proclaimed, must be upheld against those of the modern big city. These antiurban principles were in his mind closely associated with the Germanic heritage and with the age of classical German idealism and romanticism. Returning to the *Volk*'s premodern rural roots, moreover, meant resurrecting a tradition in which the ancestors of nearly all Germans had shared; this new consciousness of shared tradition might therefore also serve to heighten German social solidarity.[148]

Diederichs, who in 1904 relocated his firm to the small university town of Jena in order to escape the stifling urban environment of metropolitan Leipzig and to establish closer contact with the older humanistic cultural traditions which Jena represented,[149] undertook a publishing program designed to awaken a new interest in nature and to reverse the tide of Germany's urbanization. The EDV, for example, reissued works such as J. H. Fischbeck's *Natural History, or a Short Sketch of the Principal Wild Animals in the Duchy of Bremen* (*Naturgeschichte, oder kurtzgefasste Lebensabrisse der hauptsächlichsten wilden Thiere im Hertzogthum Bremen*, 1899) which idealized the German landscape, native fauna, and idyllic small "hometowns." The publisher also placed his house behind Ebenezer Howard's "Garden City Movement," which sought to overcome urban alienation through communal settlements in utopian natural settings. In 1907 he published Howard's manifesto on garden cities, and later issued four other major volumes dealing with the need for a new "garden culture." When a model garden city was founded in Germany at Hellerau in 1908 by Wolf Dohrn, Diederichs greeted it as a momentous cultural event and made the EDV the primary outlet for literature about the Hellerau experiment.[150]

To bring Germans back to nature, Eugen Diederichs also promoted the "hearth and homeland" literary movement (*Heimatskunstbewegung*). This turn-of-the-century movement represented a revolt against urbanism, cosmopolitanism, and the values and art styles which emanated from industrial Berlin. "Hearth and homeland" writers sentimentally glorified Germany's rural landscape and idyllic hometown communities, which they portrayed as wellsprings of the German *Volk* spirit. The movement was institutionalized in 1904 when Paul Schultze-Naumburg founded the League for the Preservation of the Native Homeland (Bund für Heimatschutz) to protect Germany's ancient environment and *Volk* shrines from further spoilation.[151]

The EDV became one of the leading publishers of "hearth and homeland" literature. Diederichs joined the Jena chapter of Schultze-Naumburg's League and issued works of such homeland authors as Ferdinand Avenarius, Adolf Bartels, Hans Thoma, and Wilhelm Holzammer. The publisher established particularly close ties to two authors of the homeland movement before the war. In 1893 he married Helene Voigt (they were divorced in 1911) and subsequently published nine volumes of her poetry and prose. He became a close personal friend also of Hermann Löns and issued several of his books. After Löns's own marriage broke up in 1911, Diederichs befriended the penniless author, provided him with outright monetary gifts so that he might purchase Christmas gifts for his children, and assumed the role of paternal benefactor toward the author's widow and children after Löns's death in 1914.[152]

Because *völkisch* cultural pessimists placed such importance on rural traditions and on the native *Volk* soil, they nostalgically idealized the peasant as the archetypical representative of the German *Volk*. For the peasant had remained closest to the cosmic forces which permeated the natural landscape; in him, the *Volk*'s primitive rural heritage had survived unspoiled. Thus Riehl had proclaimed that "peasant work and peasant customs are the backbone of the *Volk* personality. . . . The peasants *are* what we *were*."[153] To Diederichs, likewise, the peasantry was the very antithesis of the modern, urban, industrial world and was a source of hope and regeneration for the German nation. The peasantry, he declared, was "an eternal fountain of youth and health for our *Volk*."[154]

Diederichs's publishing house consequently produced a number of works, especially "peasant novels" (*Bauernromane*), glorifying the peasant heritage and idealizing the peasant as the German *Volk* hero. The most successful of these works was Löns's *The Werewolf, A Peasant Chronicle* (*Der Wehrwolf, Ein Bauernchronik*). After the manuscript, which dealt with German peasant life during the Thirty Years War, had been rejected by several publishers because of its many indecent passages, Löns offered it to Diederichs, claiming it was "a weltanschauungs novel" which combined "agrarianism, the peasantry, aestheticism, mysticism, and realism."[155] The EDV published the work in 1910 and sold nearly three hundred seventy-five thousand copies by 1933. Six other works on the peasantry, including Bartels's *The Peasant* (*Der Bauer*, 1900) and W. S. Reymont's *The Polish Peasants* (*Die polnische Bauern*, 1912) were issued by the EDV before the war.

Toward a New Social Order

However much Eugen Diederichs hoped a mere revival of the *Volk* mystique and its agrarian heritage might restore a sense of solidarity among Germans, he nevertheless realized there could be no true and lasting national community until the nation's social injustices were remedied. In contrast to the more obtuse conservatism of the old Right, neoconservatives like Diederichs displayed a social consciousness which recognized that modern social conflict could be ultimately overcome and social unity reestablished only when legitimate lower-class grievances were met. A study of German history and society as presented through his firm's publications, he told his readers, demonstrated that "no social estate (*Stand*) is conceivable without the others. If one estate falls ill, the others will fall ill as well; for the malady easily overtakes the entire organism, the nation."[156] It was no accident, then, that since 1898 he had designated the EDV as a "Publishing House for Social Germanism."

It became clear to Diederichs in the decade before World War I—as it was becoming clear to a growing number of "progressive" members of Germany's educated middle class—that the political apathy and naïveté of the German bourgeoisie presented one of the foremost obstacles on the path to social reform. Since the late 1870s, the reactionary coalition which Bismarck had forged between agrarian Junkers and the wealthy industrial bourgeoisie had impeded even moderate social reform in the Reich. This ruling coalition, founded on the mutual protection of each partner's economic interests, was able to justify and preserve its uncompromising social policies largely by two means. On the one hand, it encouraged the German middle classes in their traditional indifference toward political life; on the other hand, the Junker-industrial coalition played upon the fears of the more moderate bourgeoisie by continually harping on the danger of social revolution which the growing and radical Social Democratic movement seemed to present. By the late 1890s, however, internal tensions and economic conflicts were disintegrating the Bismarckian coalition and rapidly eroding its hegemony. In the years around 1900, therefore, progressive and left-liberal forces which had chafed under the social obstructionism and political authoritarianism exhibited by the ruling elite during the 1880s and 1890s emerged in new strength, both within and without the established political parties. Of the leading progressive spokesmen, many—such as Friedrich Naumann, Max Weber, Theodor Barth, or Hugo Preuss—were loyal monarchists, fervent nationalists, and opponents of full-scale democracy (and have thus been labeled "liberal elitists").[157] All, however, denounced the exclusivity and stifling reactionary policies of the old Junker-industrial coalition, advocated a greater degree of popular participation in national affairs, and espoused sweeping social reforms and some form of accommodation with Social Democracy to forestall the threat of revolution.

Diederichs was first attracted to the progressive movement for social reform in 1903 when one of his house's religious authors introduced the publisher to the circle of activists in Friedrich Naumann's Evangelical-Social Congress (Evangelisch-Sozialer Kongress). This group of liberal Protestants preached a social gospel which sought to reconcile the German bourgeoisie and the working class. After attending the Congress's 1903 meeting in Darmstadt, Diederichs established a friendship with Naumann. Inspired by the goals of Naumann's organization, he commissioned Paul Göhre, the Congress's General Secretary, to edit a series of "worker monographs" for the EDV. (Göhre had achieved notoriety in 1891 when he left his pastorate, worked for several months in a factory, and published a popular account of his experiences.) Diederichs, who had come to accept the working class movement as a "political necessity" but who was nevertheless strenuously opposed to Social Democracy because of its radical, egalitarian ideology, intended with this new series of workers' autobiographies to help bridge the yawning gulf between the middle class and the workers. On the one hand, the EDV advertised the series as books "which communicate the thoughts and feelings of the working class to the educated class," while on the other hand, the publisher instructed Göhre to cast his introductions to each volume in such a way as to deemphasize anything relating to Social Democracy and to stress instead to readers "the need to fulfill [our] social duties."[158] The first of these worker autobiographies, Carl Fischer's *Memoirs and Memories of a Worker* (*Denkwürdigkeiten und Erinnerungen eines Arbeiters*) appeared in 1903; over the next eight years, the EDV issued another four volumes of workers' memoirs.

The Jena publisher was drawn still deeper into the progressive camp in 1909–10, when the dissolution of the conservative "Bülow Block" in the Reichstag and the unification of several progressive forces into a formidable Progressive People's party (Fortschrittliche Volkspartei) under T. Barth opened up dramatic new opportunities for social reformers. These political events precisely coincided, moreover, with Diederichs's personal rejection of what he called "overgrown aestheticism" (*überwuchernde Ästhetizismus*)[159] and his new concern for man's social existence. (Indeed, these events may have provided the impetus for his reorientation.) In a sudden outburst of activity, between 1910 and 1912 Diederichs poured forth a series of ringing manifestos, circular letters, questionnaires, and programmatic catalogs in which he declared that Germany stood at a crucial turning point with regard to social policy. Policymakers must overcome their long-standing dependence on economic interests, and the public must overcome its fixation with rigid party slogans in order to carry out long overdue (but unspecified) social reforms. Otherwise, Diederichs warned, the nation's natural evolution would be thwarted and Germany would lag further and further behind the other progressive nations. The publisher believed no social reform was possible, however, until the German middle class was cured of its traditional political apathy and backwardness. For too long, he declared, the educated bourgeoisie had been frightened and intimidated by the Red bogey; as a result the German middle class had been deterred from active involvement in social and political affairs and had remained— in comparison with the bourgeoisie of other nations—politically naive and immature. What was most desperately needed, therefore, was the "political cultivation" (*politische Bildung*) of the educated middle classes. Civic education, Diederichs hoped, would lead to a new middle-class involvement in public affairs and ultimately to social reform.[160]

Diederichs, of course, never doubted that it was his duty as a publisher to enlighten the German reading public about political life. (His important manifesto of 1912, in which he committed the EDV to the civic education of the German middle class, was entitled "The Publisher as Educator.") To accomplish this task, he sent out a questionnaire in 1911 to leading intellectuals, soliciting their opinions on the social and political issues of the day; he then forwarded the replies to newspapers and bookdealers in hopes they would gain wider publicity.[161] But more importantly, his house launched two major multivolume series dealing with the problem of civic reform: the *Political Library* (*Politische Bibliothek*, 18 vols., 1910–18) and the *Civic Pamphlets* (*Staatsbürgerliche Flugschriften*, 7 vols., 1911–12). Even though Diederichs knew political books did not sell well, and that these two projects might well "get [him] in over [his] head" financially, the Jena publisher was convinced that such series were necessary as forums for people who wanted to address contemporary social and political issues but who, for one reason or another, chose to stand outside of political life.[162] Indeed, he intended these two series to transcend completely the old slogans and hackneyed phrases of party politics which so many educated middle-class Germans found repulsive.

The foremost goal of the EDV series (as, indeed, of all Diederichs's efforts in the realm of social reform) was to achieve a reconciliation between the German middle class and the German working class; he hoped, like Barth and Naumann, to bring about a strong new progressive block by unifying the bourgeois Left with the more moderate elements of the labor movement.[163] To effect this convergence of socialism and middle-class progressivism, Diederichs employed two tactics: on the one hand, he sought to educate the bourgeoisie about the problems of the working class and to allay their fears about socialism; and on the other hand, he attempted to support within the workers' movement those tendencies which aimed at deradicalizing socialism and transforming it from a revolutionary to a reformist force. Thus, in announcing his new *Political Library* in 1911, the publisher declared:

> Socialist party literature lives only for itself. It has no effect on the middle class, and will never have any, because it no longer bears any relation to the ideas of the leading socialist thinkers today. It represents an anachronism, or what will soon become an anachronism: namely, materialism. With the *Political Library* I want to collect the forces which conceive of socialism in biological terms, and which want, through a socialized literature, to promote the further development of Social Democracy into a party which will affirm the national state. At the same time, I want to spur middle-class

citizens—to the extent that they are not philistines, and thus hopelessly sterile—to interest themselves more in the problems of social life.[164]

Because he wished to help "deproletarianize" German socialism, wean the workers away from radical Marxism, and instill in the workers' movement a sense of nationalism,[165] Diederichs collaborated with Eduard Bernstein's revisionist movement within the Social Democratic party (SPD). Like Diederichs, the revisionists were rebels against the domination of scientific positivism and historical materialism and advocates of philosophical idealism; and like the publisher, they rejected the notion of class struggle, proclaiming in its stead the need for a larger, all-encompassing national community in which workers would enjoy full integration. Social Democracy, as Bernstein professed it, "does not want to dissolve society and proletarianize all its members. Rather, it works ceaselessly to raise up the worker from his social position as a proletarian to that of a citizen (*Bürger*), and thus seeks to generalize . . . the enjoyment of citizenship in the nation."[166]

Perhaps through the mediation of Paul Göhre (who was active in the revisionist movement), Diederichs met the two most prominent revisionist leaders, Bernstein and Georg von Vollmar, at the Social Democratic meeting in Jena in 1905, two years after the SPD had formally rejected the revisionist platform.[167] When the publisher launched his two political series in 1910, therefore, he not only convinced Bernstein to serve as coeditor for the *Political Library* but also to write the first volume of the *Civic Pamphlets* (a revisionist study of the SPD entitled *From Sect to Party*). The EDV eventually published several other volumes by revisionist socialists such as Richard Calwer, Gerhart Hildebrandt, Jean Jaurès, and the Swede Gustav Steffen. Diederichs presented these volumes to his readers with the recommendation that these were works by socialists who had "overcome Marxism," combined socialism with biology and Bergsonian philosophy, and who proclaimed a healthy nationalist patriotism.[168]

While Diederichs promoted a revised, nonrevolutionary version of Social Democracy for the working class, he was also seeking to win over the progressive middle class to a comprehensive yet respectable program of social reform. He eventually came to see English Fabianism as the perfect model for educated Germans. The English Fabian Society, whose social policy sprang like Diederichs's from a desire for a moral and ethical regeneration of society and was aimed at a utopian new life-style, had been weaning middle-class British intellectuals away from laissez-faire capitalism for two decades, demonstrating to them the necessity and value of a non-Marxist state socialism. Time and again between 1910 and 1913

Diederichs expressed his deep admiration for the Fabians, and declared that what Germany needed was a German Fabian movement.[169] He sought to propagate Fabianism in Germany by publishing works by the Fabian leaders Sidney and Beatrice Webb, and by the former Fabian and cofounder of the independent British Labor party, Ramsey Macdonald. Diederichs also commissioned the young left-wing academic Karl Korsch, who was residing in London at the time, to write frequent reports on the activities of the Fabian Society for the EDV journal *Die Tat*.[170]

The effect of the EDV's prewar campaign for civic awareness and social reform was ambiguous. On the one hand, the *Political Library* and *Civic Pamphlets* series made a deep impression on many intellectuals. One observer, for example, recalled over a decade and a half later: "I still remember how surprisingly effective it was when, in 1911, Diederichs called upon the aesthetically inclined educated middle classes (*Gebildete*) to recognize their civic duties and at the same time offered them such compelling and intellectually valuable reading matter."[171] But on the other hand, the two series proved a commercial disappointment to Diederichs. By 1913 he was already bemoaning the apathy of the German public and the lack of support and demand exhibited by the press and by intellectual circles for EDV publications. He decided, therefore, to terminate the *Political Library* series and "put the political side of my house to rest."[172]

Youth Leads the Way

After his brief, but largely disappointing foray into the area of progressive civic reform, in 1913 Diederichs turned back again to the cultural arena to concentrate his efforts on what he considered a more promising force for national regeneration: the German Youth Movement. Springing up suddenly in the 1890s, the Youth Movement, whether in its early *Wandervögel* ("Roamers") or its later Free German Youth phase, represented a passionate protest by alienated urban adolescents against the stilted, authoritarian atmosphere of the German family and the pedantic intellectualism of the secondary school system. Rejecting the complacent materialism and hypocritical values of established bourgeois society, those in the Youth Movement sought to reassert adolescent independence, honesty, and naturalness. To escape the stifling environment of urban industrial life, the youth groups advocated a return to simple nature and launched a populistic rediscovery of the common *Volk*.[173]

In the Youth Movement, Diederichs saw the concrete embodiment and practical application of all the new cultural and social ideals which the older generation of cultural reformers only talked about. He believed

Nietzsche's ideas had taken root among these youth and that they were among the few in Germany who had a real sense of life's deepest meaning. The publisher admired the freshness, honesty, and genuineness of the German Youth Movement; these young people, he believed, had recovered an appreciation for the spiritual and irrational side of human existence and for the pantheistic nature of the universe. He praised the movement for rebelling against the bankrupt values of the elder generation, for rejecting urbanism, selfish individualism, intellectualism, and the effete material trappings of modern civilization. Their attempts to infuse poetry, music, and art into their weekend nature roamings, he declared, was helping to surmount the "boredom of daily life." And the revival of old folk dances by the movement was an excellent way of preserving German folklore and respect for the *Volk* heritage. But Diederichs was perhaps most profoundly impressed by the close comradeship which existed within the Youth Movement; he saw the youth groups as small, closed, unified communities where adolescents from different social backgrounds used "Du" with each other and where communal solidarity took precedence over individual egotism.[174] In short, as Diederichs proclaimed a few years later, the Youth Movement was "visible proof that Germany was beginning to soar again. It was therefore the duty of the older generation to help the development of this movement by all possible means."[175]

Diederichs had been personally involved in Youth Movement affairs for many years, and eventually became one of the few adults whom the movement's adolescent leaders accepted and respected. In 1904, at the age of thirty-seven, the publisher had founded his own youth group, the Sera Circle, which attracted young Jena students and artists, as well as a few white-collar and working-class youths. The group, soon known as the "aristocrats of the *Wandervögel* movement," hiked through the Thuringian countryside before the war performing folk songs and dances, Hans Sachs plays, solar solstice celebrations, and other forms of nature worship.[176]

When leaders of various youth groups decided in 1913 to hold a national youth festival on the Hohe Meissner, Diederichs's Sera Circle hosted the preliminary planning session and the publisher—the only adult present—played an influential role in planning and organizing the festival. He suggested which speakers should and should not be invited and which symbols and colors the festival should adopt. He assumed the task of composing the important "*Aufruf*," the proclamation which formally announced the festival and stated its goals. In an accompanying circular which he sent out to his authors and to leading national figures, he requested, as "solicitor" (*Anwalt*) for the Youth Movement, that the recipients endorse the *Aufruf* and compose brief statements of support for the upcoming festival "so that the [event] will find the press coverage it deserves."[177] During the four-day Meissner festival in October—the climax of the prewar German Youth Movement and the single most important event in the movement's history—Diederichs acted as press agent, explaining its goals to the public.

Throughout 1913, as he was disengaging the EDV from political publications, Diederichs placed his house's resources behind the Youth Movement in other ways as well, thereby lending the movement important publicistic support. For Youth Movement material circulated mainly within the youth culture, making it generally an unprofitable publishing venture which standard publishing houses were reluctant to touch. Consequently, most Youth Movement journals and reading matter were issued by small houses which concentrated exclusively on youth literature and which had an audience drawn primarily from the Youth Movement.[178] Firms like Diederichs's, however, were general publishing houses with a much broader circle of readers. When Diederichs or other neoconservative publishers lent their imprint to Youth Movement material—at some financial risk to themselves—they helped carry the ideas of the movement to a much broader adult audience. Diederichs's house in 1913 issued some of the most important works to come out of the prewar Youth Movement, such as the programmatic festschrift of the Hohe Meissner festival, an immensely popular collection of folksongs and folk music for youth groups (which by 1922 was in its fortieth printing), and Eduard Heimann's controversial *The Sexual Problem of Youth* (*Das Sexualproblem der Jugend*). During the year before the war, Diederichs was also transforming his journal *Die Tat* into what he termed "a central organ for the Youth Movement," making it a forum for both *Wandervögel* and Free German Youth authors. And he personally approached Hans Blüher, foremost historian and analyst of the movement, and convinced him to abandon his former publisher and enter the ranks of the EDV. Blüher accepted because of Diederichs's "inflamed interest" in the Youth Movement and because Blüher knew that Diederichs would do everything possible to promote it.[179]

Diederichs regarded his various efforts on behalf of the German Youth Movement to be among his most important contributions to the renewal of German culture. His modest claim later that he had served as a "sponsoring godfather" (*Pate*) at the movement's birth and that he had offered paternal guidance during the movement's formative years[180] did not do his role full justice. For Youth Movement activists later recalled how Diederichs had "dominated and consummated the Youth Movement in its earliest years . . . and had pulled us youth in his wake."[181] At his death in 1930, one Youth Movement leader paid tribute to the publisher by acknowledging that "the Youth Movement is immeasurably indebted to him. He helped unloose all the powers of the movement . . . everything was instigated and summoned forth with his help." Another leader maintained that "without the influence of Eugen Diederichs, the history of the prewar Youth Movement is totally unthinkable."[182]

Summary: Cultural Reform in Wilhelmian Germany

Eugen Diederichs's desperate struggle for cultural renewal in imperial Germany at once mirrored and articulated the plight of many educated middle-class Germans. Bismarck's founding of the Second Reich in 1871 was greeted enthusiastically by most national-minded Germans. Middle-class liberals and entrepreneurs welcomed the Reich because unification fulfilled their nationalistic aspirations, provided a representative (although hardly democratic) form of parliamentary government which was more responsive to the needs of the industrial bourgeoisie, and encouraged the nation's economic modernization. Conservative agrarian aristocrats hailed the new state because behind its liberal facade stood an authoritarian structure which not only preserved but also in many ways increased their own political and social powers. A large segment of the cultivated, traditionally nonpolitical educated middle class was hopeful that Germany's new political and economic ascendancy under the imperial order would also evoke a brilliant cultural upsurge. While the expectations of the first two groups were largely fulfilled in the years after 1871, and they consequently became the Reich's most loyal supporters, many sensitive *Bildungsbürger* were soon disenchanted with the Reich and with its ruling agrarian-industrial elite. For it gradually became apparent to these idealistic observers that the external success of the new Germany— and the pomp of its quintessential Kaiser, Wilhelm II, in particular— were founded on no inspiring new cultural ideals. Indeed, the calculating realpolitik, material success, and the ensuing complacency of the empire seemed to them to stifle rather than stimulate the nation's creative urges.

As apprehension over the cultural barrenness of imperial Germany mounted within certain segments of the intellegentsia, so too did alarm over the nature of the modern, industrial, mass society which emerged after 1871. Industrialization, economic rationalization, and urbanization combined with mass education, popular journalism, and new egalitarian political forces such as democracy and social revolutionary movements to destroy traditional life-styles and to create a new, mass-based technological society which many Germans, especially members of the traditional cultural elite, found alien, dehumanizing, uncontrollable, and threatening to both their individual and social identity. Groping for new ideals to fill what they perceived as a spiritual vacuum, yet at the same time repelled by the values of the modern bourgeois industrial society emerging around them and horrified at the concomitant rise of the Marxist Left, many educated German mandarins felt alienated, estranged, and increasingly forlorn in Wilhelmian Germany.[183]

Although these disaffected individuals sought an alternative to liberal, technological modernity, they could find none in traditional conservatism. For under the Reich, the traditional Right consisted essentially of an opportunistic alliance of the Junker aristocracy and the wealthy industrial bourgeoisie, two groups whose material interests were well served by the imperial order and who therefore strove not to change it, but to uphold it. This conservative agrarian-industrial coalition, founded on crass economic interest and a mutual desire to preserve the status quo, held little appeal for those alienated middle-class intellectuals who were thirsting for new values with which to fill the spiritual void of liberal mass society. The forces of the old Right could offer at best self-serving slogans, but no inspiring ideals. Moreover, since the traditional conservative parties and interest groups held a fairly tight grip over political life in the Reich, some members of the disillusioned *Bildungsbürgertum* channeled their discontent into avenues which lay not merely beyond the ideas and institutions of traditional conservatism, but outside of the conventional political sphere altogether.

Thus it was that the spiritual distress, antimodern anxieties, and general dissatisfaction with the existing order harbored by many educated, bourgeois Germans found cultural rather than political outlets in the last decades of the nineteenth century. There arose within the Second Reich a "cultural opposition" which rejected most of the established values on which the new Germany was based. This cultural opposition, unlike other oppositional currents in the Reich, did not aim to restructure the German state or to carry out mere social and economic reforms. Rather, as a means of overcoming what they perceived as the crisis of modern civilization, the Reich's cultural critics desired to transform spiritual values and regenerate the entire cultural foundation of human existence, from the bottom up. "Their critique was of a specific and of a very fundamental nature: it was directed not only at the pressing contemporary problems of technical civilization, but at its underlying conditions in general: technologization, industrialization, urbanization."[184]

This broad urge in Wilhelmian Germany for a reform of culture and of the basic conditions of life sought release from the artificiality, spiritual emptiness, and socially threatening implications of modern industrial civilization by returning to simpler, more harmonious and "natural" values and life-styles. Cultural opposition in Wilhelmian Germany took many forms, of which the Youth Movement, rural "garden city" communes, the Werkbund, "free religious" and "Germanic Christian" movements, theosophy, spiritualism, and the various other movements in which Diederichs participated are only a part. It was manifested even more bizarrely in the dizzying array of eccentric cults and reformist fads such as nudism, vegetarianism, antialcohol and antitobacco clubs, coldwater cures, Schultze-Naumburg's clothing reform movement, and various occult and parapsychological practices which swept the educated German middle class around the turn of the century. All these were part of a variegated antimodern subculture which posited, in one form or another, a "backward-oriented utopia"—some ideal, "natural" existence which was to be recovered or somehow reestablished. The utopian vision underlying these various attempts at cultural reform was regressive and escapist, in that it yearned for the return to a premodern era. But it was also revolutionary, for (in the words of one scholar) "over against the existing social reality it set up a forward-looking alternative model which could be considered as a phenomenon of resistance against both the structure and the order of the present society. The cultural reform movement's ambivalent combination of regressive and utopian-revolutionary tendencies is shared with other endeavors of the educated middle class and places it in the vicinity of the 'conservative revolution.'"[185] But however radical its goal, the movement for cultural reform in prewar Germany remained apolitical. It not only scorned the traditional political parties and interest groups, but also circumvented the entire political process, for it assumed that a basic transformation of the internal self and of the cultural milieu would, ipso facto, also bring about a general reform of social and political life. For Germany's traditionally nonpolitical *Bildungsbürgertum*, then, cultural opposition and cultural reform seemed a most fitting outlet for their vague fin de siècle anxieties.

In many ways, Eugen Diederichs was typical of the cultivated Germans who felt like outsiders in the new Reich and who expressed their estrangement and antimodern fears through opposition to "official" imperial culture. Deeply disturbed over what he considered the spiritual void behind Wilhelmian Germany's vibrant, progressive exterior, he struggled unremittingly to move German culture off dead center, to infuse it with some new spirit. If his vision of the new culture he desired seems vague, eclectic, and at times even contradictory, it is because he was not yet sure just what he wanted to replace the present culture with. He was convinced, however, that virtually any new direction would be preferable to imperial Germany's lack of spiritual purpose, any fresh cultural stirrings would be better than the intellectual turpor and inner decay of liberal, bourgeois, industrial civilization. It was for this reason that Diederichs's interests were so broad, his activities so diverse, his general ideological orientation so ambiguous and difficult to classify. In his frenetic quest for new forces which might spark a rejuvenation of German culture, Diederichs traversed an extremely wide spectrum of ideas and movements: from highbrow, scholarly schools such as life-philosophy and Neoromantic literature, to less seemly movements such as the occult, Germanic Christianity, and racism; from ideas which were clearly nostalgic, regressive, and anti-democratic, to those such as liberal theology, *Jugendstil* art, and revisionist socialism which were decidedly progressive and avant-garde. Although they had little influence on his publishing and were thus not discussed in this study, Diederichs also took a deep personal interest in such eccentric fads as "bodily culture" (*Körperkultur*), abstinence and health foods, cloth-ing reform, school reform, and avant-garde literary movements such as naturalism.

A fundamentally conservative outlook lay behind all Diederichs's en-deavors. He rejected most of the conditions and trends—such as rational-ism, materialism, or egalitarianism—of modern industrial civilization, and he exhibited a pervading antidemocratic elitism and a nostalgic desire to return to a more natural, idealistic, and simple premodern system of values and mode of life. But his brand of conservatism had little in common with imperial Germany's traditional established Right, for Diederichs rejected the values of the Reich's conservative ruling elite. On the one hand, as a member of the educated middle class, he considered the Junker agrarians as too anachronistic, boorish, socially snobbish, and crassly material to serve as a conservative model, while on the other hand he realized that the triumph of the modern industrial bourgeoisie was creating a mass society which seriously threatened the mandarin class to which he belonged and the elite cultural ideals in which he so ardently believed. Diederichs's conservatism was of a new, more radical and more modern type than that of the established German Right. He hoped to preserve and revive earlier, premodern values and traditions, but unlike old-style conservatives he recognized that these must be given new, more modern forms if they were to meet the needs of the times. Thus he sought to revive religion in Germany not by shoring up the established church, but by creating a dramatically new mystical religion which broke almost completely with traditional Christianity. He longed not merely to rescue the conservative romantic outlook, but to create a distinct "New" or "Neoromantic" move-ment. And unlike traditional conservatives, Diederichs so completely re-jected the modern culture in which he lived that he was willing to resort to extreme means—including certain modern, liberal, or left-wing tendencies such as rational biblical criticism or revisionist socialism—if these could be of use in overturning the modern status quo and opening the way for the kind of utopian, antimodern order which he envisioned. In short,

Four

Radical Nationalism: Julius F. Lehmann and German *Volk* Militancy, 1890–1914

If estrangement, cultural pessimism, hazy antipolitical idealism, and passionate albeit vague yearnings for some fundamental cultural and social regeneration were characteristic of the cultivated but alienated circles of the *Bildungsbürgertum* with whom Diederichs identified, then self-confident optimism and assertive, even militant aggrandizement often characterized imperial Germany's propertied and office-holding middle class which, with the old aristocracy, shared power in the new Reich. As insiders to the imperial order, the industrial, commercial, and bureaucratic bourgeoisie enjoyed material prosperity from Germany's rapid economic modernization, and great social prestige from the nation's political ascendancy. They therefore tended enthusiastically to affirm the conservative Bismarckian Reich and were generally its most dependable supporters.

Beginning around 1890, however, a small but steadily growing number of patriotic middle-class Germans came to the conclusion that the material, social, and political benefits which they enjoyed under the Reich could be protected and ensured for the future only if German national interests, especially economic interests, were more aggressively promoted abroad and if the preeminence of the German *Volk* vis à vis other national minorities were more vigorously affirmed at home. But their nationalist demands, particularly their calls for imperial expansion abroad, were sometimes more radical, uncompromising, and diplomatically dangerous than the major conservative parties and the imperial government (both of which still stood under the influence of aristocratic agrarians) could accept. Consequently, many of the radical nationalists in imperial Germany became increasingly impatient with the traditional conservative political system and struck out on their own by founding a series of independent leagues, societies, and interest groups to promote their demands and to pressure the government into adopting a more aggressive national policy. These radical nationalists, most of whom came from the industrial, commercial, professional, and bureaucratic middle classes, emerged as a distinct new force on the right around the turn of the century and, like the cultural pessimists from the educated middle class, came to represent a source of conservative opposition within the established imperial order.[1] Although they arose for different reasons, expressed different grievances, and often had widely differing goals, these two oppositional currents on the right (cultural pessimism and radical nationalism) preached new, more radical brands of conservatism than the traditional conservative parties. These currents frequently intersected one another and contained such common ideological elements as the *völkisch* mystique, the need for a distinct Germanic religion, and the desire for a general rejuvenation of German life and values.

Pan-German Expansionism

Julius Lehmann, the rather crude autodidact and prosperous publisher of medical-scientific literature, clearly identified not with the alienated, idealistic aesthetes with whom Diederichs associated, but with imperial Germany's materialistic, self-assured, up-and-coming entrepreneurs and officials. He shared little of Diederichs's cultural pessimism, but rather exhibited great nationalist pride over the material and political accomplishments of the new German Reich. His house's first political publication, for example, was J. Sepp's *Germany Then and Now* (*Deutschland Einst und Jetzt*, 1896), a paean to the Bismarckian state. It was soon followed by other patriotic works such as R. Deye's collection of poems *To Germany's Honor* (*Zu Deutschlands Ehr*, 1898), Paul Dehn's reverential *Bismarck as Educator* (*Bismarck als Erzieher*, 1903), and Max Liebermann von Sonnenberg's *From the Happiest Days of My Life: Memoirs of the Great German War 1870–71* (*Aus der Glückzeit meines Lebens: Erinnerungen aus dem grossen deutschen Kriege 1870/71*, 1911).

Like Diederichs, Lehmann recognized the potential value of the study of history for strengthening nationalist consciousness and pride. Thus, in 1899 the J. F. Lehmann house, in cooperation with the Pan-German League, launched a fourteen-volume series of popularized historical pamphlets for younger readers entitled *Julius Lohnmeyer's Patriotic Youth Library* (*Julius Lohnmeyers Vaterländische Jugendbücherei*). An advertisement for the new series proudly announced that:

A number of nationally minded men and trusted friends of youth have cooperated [on this series] in order to deepen nationalistic education among our growing youth. Through masterful tales by popular national writers, scenes from the lives of our heroes and thinkers and meaningful segments from our national history will be presented to the youth of the nation. [Readers of this series] will comprehend what is noble, good, and true, what "German" means in the best sense of the word. They will be inspired by the greatness of our past and our future. [The series] will awaken a sense of duty in readers [which calls upon them] to place their entire being in the cause of the nation.[2]

The publisher was even willing to risk financial loss to publish hagiographic patriotic studies. When Felix Dahn submitted his *Armin the Cherusker* (*Armin der Cherusker*), a study of the old Germanic warrior-hero Arminius, to the JFLV in 1908, the author expressed grave doubts that the work would be popular and warned Lehmann that the JFLV would probably suffer a heavy loss if it published the manuscript. Nevertheless, Lehmann proceeded with publication (and soon proved Dahn wrong: the book sold ten thousand copies the first year alone).[3]

If there were any aspect of Bismarck's national state with which Lehmann was dissatisfied, it was the fact that the Second Reich was a "small-German" solution to the problem of German unity and failed to encompass the entire German *Volk*. By excluding millions of ethnic Germans in Austria and other border areas, Lehmann worried, the imperial state as constituted actually thwarted true national unity.

Lehmann's concern over the fate of German minorities abroad, and in Austria in particular, led him into the Pan-German League (Alldeutscher Verband). This organization was founded in 1891 by members of the nationalistic professional classes, civil servants, and industrial interests who believed the Reich government was not doing enough to protect the German minorities outside the Reich which, cut off from the protection of the German state, were being threatened by foreign (especially Slavic) domination and were thus in danger of being lost to the German *Volk* forever. The Pan-German League, intended as a "nonpolitical" organization above the traditional parties, sought to lend moral, diplomatic, and financial support to these "endangered" ethnic brethren, and envisioned the creation of a "greater-German" empire in central Europe which would finally unite all Germans into one political entity. The League, although modest in membership (which had reached twenty-two thousand at the turn of the century, but by 1914 had fallen to seventeen thousand), had important connections to leaders both in industry and government and became a powerful pressure group.[4]

J. F. Lehmann put his publishing house completely behind the Pan-German cause and played a central role in the development of the movement. "Wherever the German *Volk* was endangered," he reminisced later, "I have tried to focus the attention of wider circles on the situation and, through my publishing work, have tried where possible to create the means for alleviating this plight."[5] After he cofounded the Munich chapter of the Pan-German League, Lehmann was elected to the League's national Executive Committee in 1898, where he served until the mid-1920s. Upon his suggestion, the League established a special "war fund" in 1903 "to directly assist Germans wherever their nationality is threatened." The fund, financed through voluntary member contributions, became one of the most important bases of all the League's subsequent activities. It was used, as Lehmann suggested, "to strengthen Germandom on our language borders and abroad, to support German settlers, students, libraries, and economic enterprises, and for the settlement of German colonies throughout the world."[6] The publisher also persuaded the League to join with a sister organization, the Society for Germandom Abroad (Verein für das Deutschtum im Ausland) in acquiring the castle of Persen in South Tyrol, which the two organizations then converted into "an outpost of German culture and language" and a "rallying point for the threatened German communities" in this Austro-Italian province. By 1918, Lehmann claimed to have personally contributed more than seventy thousand marks to renovate and outfit Persen.[7] When the League's first president Ernst Hasse died in 1908, it was Lehmann who nominated Heinrich Class as his successor; under Class's long leadership, the Pan-German League became increasingly militant and openly embraced racism.

Lehmann's strong Pan-German convictions were reflected in his publishing activities. Besides publishing the Leauge's official yearbooks and handbooks, between 1896 and 1913 the JFLV issued a thirty-one-volume *Flyers of the Pan-German League* (*Flugschriften des Alldeutschen Verbandes*) series for the organization. The pamphlets for this series, some of which Lehmann helped ghostwrite,[8] were inexpensively priced so that they might reach a wider audience. This resulted in a substantial financial loss for the house. However, as many as sixty thousand copies of certain titles in the series were distributed, and the undertaking became more important than even the League's official newspaper for propagating Pan-German ideology before the war.[9] League president Ernst Hasse's monumental *German Policies* (*Deutsche Politik*, 2 vols., 1907–8), a comprehensive and influential statement of Pan-German goals, was also published by the JFLV.

The Munich publisher issued a number of books on the plight of German minorities abroad, especially in eastern Europe. He joined again with the Pan-German League to produce a nineteen-volume series on this topic entitled *In the Struggle for Germandom* (*Im Kampf um das Deutschtum*, 1897–1902). According to one JFLV advertisement, this series depicted "in an exhaustive manner the condition of Germandom on the entire globe. . . . Here, for the first time, are individual reports about all the German settlements in the world as well as suggestions as to how these members of our *Volk* can preserve themselves and enjoy a strong, healthy development in the future."[10] "My main goal in producing these writings [on German minorities]," Lehmann claimed, "is to increase national feeling and to awaken a sleeping German nation in order to inspire people to fight against the enemies of our *Volk*."[11] Indeed, financial considerations seemed secondary. The twenty-two thousand marks he earned from Franz von Defregger's *The Germans of Austria* (*Die Deutschen Österreichs*, 1896), for example, he donated to the endangered German minorities in Cilli, while sales of A. Geiser's *The German Balts* (*Die deutsche Balten: Zu Hilf und Ehren eines bedrohten Bruderstammes*, 1906) enabled him to contribute eighteen thousand marks to support Baltic German communities.[12]

Lehmann was particularly concerned over the Germans in Austria-Hungary. Ethnic minority problems were acute in this multinational empire; in mixed border areas such as Bohemia and Moravia, Germans and Czechs battled continuously for political, cultural, and economic ascendancy. Germans in these areas grew increasingly alarmed in the 1890s as the Roman Catholic church began assigning Czech priests to Bohemian parishes with mixed populations. Indeed, many Germans in the Austro-Hungarian empire feared that a coalition of Slavs and Catholic clerics was gaining control of the entire imperial bureaucracy, and that this seriously threatened the traditional German position within the empire. When the imperial government decreed in 1897 that Czech would replace German as the official language in Bohemia and Moravia, and that henceforth Czech priests would be allowed to fill vacancies in traditionally German parishes, the German population in these border areas were outraged.

Lehmann, who had followed these developments closely from neighboring Bavaria, condemned the decrees as a plot to destroy the German *Volk* in Austria-Hungary. Czech priests in German communities, he charged, would be "agents of Czechification" who, by inviting more Czechs to settle there and by exercising control over the schools, would eventually be able to gain complete dominance over the German population.[13] In the summer of 1897, after a trip to Bohemia to investigate the situation, he therefore initiated what soon became known as the "Break With Rome" (*Los-von-Rom*) movement, an attempt to convert Germans in Austria to Protestantism, thereby freeing them from the domination of "Slavic" Ca-

tholicism and drawing them, at least culturally, closer to the predominantly Protestant Prusso-German Reich.[14] Lehmann approached the German Evangelical League (Deutscher Evangelischer Bund) and convinced it
to establish a special "war chest" to be used for sending Protestant mission-
aries to Austrian-German communities. Since he believed this religious
campaign would rescue Austrian-Germans from alien, un-German Catholicism and establish a new Pan-German solidarity on a Protestant basis,
he sought also to involve the Reich's Pan-German League in the Break
With Rome movement. After heated debate, however, the League decided
in 1898 not to associate itself formally with the movement for fear of
antagonizing Catholic Pan-Germans.[15] Lehmann's campaign, however,
did gain the enthusiastic support of Georg Ritter von Schönerer, leader of
the Pan-German movement in Austria. Schönerer, who considered Austrian Catholicism an obstacle to closer ties with the Reich, hoped the
conversion of Austrian Germans to Protestantism might remove the religious barrier to such contact.

Working closely with the Austrian pastor Paul Bräunlich, the German
Evangelical League, and Austrian Pan-Germans, Lehmann used all the
resources of his publishing house to induce Austrian-Germans to break
their ties with the Roman church. In 1902 he helped found the journal
Wartburg (*Wartburg: Amtliche Zeitschrift des Deutschen Evangelischen Bundes
für die Ostmark*). This organ, which became the focal point for much of
the German-Czech conflict within the Austrian empire, was issued by the
JFLV until 1909. The house also produced the twenty-volume series of
Reports on the Break With Rome Movement (*Berichte über die Los-von-Rom
Bewegung*) between 1899 and 1908, as well as some fourteen individual
works, all of which attacked Catholicism, ultra-Montanism, and cleri-
calism as un-German and sought to convince readers that Protestantism
served the best interests of a united German *Volk*. Two of these tracts,
L. Wahrmund's *Catholic World View and Academic Freedom* (*Katholische Weltanschauung und freie Wissenschaft*, 1908) and *Ultra-Montanism* (*Ultramontan*,
1908) enjoyed a combined circulation of more than seventy thousand
copies and unleashed a bitter controversy which shook the Austrian universities and government. Before the dispute ended, student riots had
broken out, a papal nuncio was dismissed, and two government ministers
had fallen. Lehmann, as publisher of Wahrmund's tracts, proudly claimed
a large share of the credit for the affair.[16] Indeed, the JFLV was so closely
identified with the Break With Rome movement that the publisher received
numerous personal threats from Catholics in Munich and was requested
by "high officials" there to move his house to another city. Lehmann
responded characteristically by carrying firearms for protection during
those years.[17]

While his campaign to rescue the *völkisch* heritage of Austrian Germans by leading them away from Catholicism was hardly the "new Reformation" he had envisioned, Lehmann's Break With Rome movement nevertheless did awaken the *völkisch* consciousness of many young Austrians—including Adolf Hitler—and gained nearly one hundred thousand converts to Protestantism. After World War I, these converts became among the most vocal proponents for Pan-German contact with the Reich. Without the aid of Reich Germans such as Lehmann, the Break With Rome movement in Austria would have been far less successful.[18]

Pan-Germans were concerned not only with the fate of German minorities in Europe but also with that of the millions of Germans who had emigrated overseas in the nineteenth century, Germans who might lose their *völkisch* identity. Pan-Germans therefore urged the Reich government to take a greater interest in the problems of Germans living overseas, and demanded a more aggressive foreign policy to advance German interests throughout the world. They called upon the nation to adopt a "world policy" which would raise Germany to the status of a world power. To accomplish this, the League agitated for the acquisition of a larger colonial empire for Germany, for in its view, only by securing a world empire could the German *Volk* compete for survival with other imperialist nations. Moreover, by providing an outlet for Germany's growing population, Pan-Germans believed a formal colonial empire would also preserve *völkisch* solidarity: emigrating Germans, rather than being permanently lost to the *Volk*, would be able to settle in German colonies where they could retain their ethnic identity. Germany could exert its influence in world affairs and gain and protect overseas colonies, however, only if the nation were a strong naval power. For this reason, the Pan-German League and organizations such as the German Naval Society (Deutscher Flottenverein) crusaded for a massive naval buildup to make the Reich a mighty sea power.

Pan-German calls for German naval expansion, colonialism, and an imperial "world policy" found relatively broad support among Germany's industrial, commercial, and bureaucratic bourgeoisie. For at the turn of the century, many within these groups were coming to the conclusion that their elite position within the Reich was threatened by ominous economic and sociopolitical developments. On the one hand, after 1896, members of the entrepreneurial middle class feared that the rapid growth of the population, changing patterns of international trade, and declining opportunities for investment might bring on a recurrence of the economic depression which had plagued Germany and other industrialized nations from 1873 to the mid-1890s, unless new markets, new supplies of raw materials, and new investment opportunities were found which could insure Germany's economic expansion in the future. On the other hand, conservative members of the middle classes and the aristocracy viewed with alarm the growing movement for liberal, democratic reform within the Reich, and feared especially the threat of social revolution which the steadily growing Social Democratic party represented. To meet these threats and secure their dominant position in domestic affairs, many members of Germany's ruling classes were drawn to imperialism and naval expansion. For, they believed, acquisition of a large world empire and the crash construction of a huge navy with which to attain this empire, would assure Germany's continual economic expansion and bring prosperity to the entire nation. And, it was hoped, as the material benefits of a world empire filtered down, the working classes would abandon their social and political radicalism and rally patriotically around the monarchy and the German imperial order. This "social imperialism," then, would serve the dual function of relieving the grievances of the lower classes by sharing with them the material benefits which a German world empire would bring, and of deflecting or diverting domestic tensions outward by focusing national attention on international colonial problems and policies. In this way, the endangered conservative social and political structure of the German Reich was to be stabilized and protected from social and political reform.[19]

Julius Lehmann committed his firm to the promotion of a German "world policy" of imperial expansion. JFLV publications such as Hasse's *World Policy, Imperialism, and Colonial Policy* (*Weltpolitik, Imperialismus und Kolonialpolitik*, 1908) or Theodore Reismann-Grone's *Overseas Policy or Continental Policy?* (*Überseepolitik oder Festlandpolitik?*, 1905) called for German expansion overseas. To awaken public interest in specific German African colonies or potential colonies, Lehmann issued the following: *In the Golden Land of Antiquity* (*Im Goldland des Altertums*, 1902) by Carl Peters, president of the Society for German Colonization (Gesellschaft für Deutsche Kolonisation); a work by E. von Liebert, governor of German Southwest Africa; several pamphlets treating Morocco; and a tract on *Germany's Claims to the Turkish Inheritance* (*Deutschlands Ansprüche an das türkische Erbe*). The publisher maintained regular contact with Bernhard Dernburg, head of the Foreign Office's Colonial Department, and cooperated closely with him on the publication of colonial literature. Some of these publications Lehmann distributed free of charge to the political parties, nationalist organizations, and German newspapers; for others he charged only a nominal price in hopes of motivating German bookdealers to distribute them free of charge.[20]

The Munich publisher was no less energetic in agitating for the means necessary to acquire and maintain a world colonial empire: a large German fleet. As he wrote to Adolf Lehr, head of the Pan-German League's special committee for naval expansion, Lehmann considered the "naval question" to be "the main life-question of the nation," and he pledged to do "all within [his] power to assist the naval movement."[21] Shortly after the Reichstag passed the first Naval Bill in 1898, thereby adopting Admiral Tirpitz's program of crash naval construction and expansion, Lehmann planned and produced a definitive annual handbook, Weyer's *Pocket Guide to the German War Fleet* (*Taschenbuch der deutschen Kriegsflotte*, 1900) to provide lay naval enthusiasts with the specific data they needed to discuss naval affairs intelligently. During the book's initial stages, Lehmann worked closely with Lehr, who had direct contacts within the government's Naval Office (Reichsmarineamt); Lehr supplied Lehmann with important official data, who in turn passed it along to the handbook's editor.[22] Although the JFLV lost money on the project, updated editions of the handbook continued to appear annually for over three decades.[23] The firm also produced a number of agitational naval tracts such as Lehr's *Why the German Fleet Must be Enlarged* (*Warum die deutsche Flotte vergrössert werden muss*, 1899); D. Schäfer's *What Does History Teach Us about the Importance of Sea Power for Germany Today?* (*Was lehrt uns die Geschichte über die Bedeutung der Seemacht für Deutschlands Gegenwart?*, 1900); and H. Petersen's *Germany's Most Glorious Days at Sea* (*Deutschlands Ruhmestage zur See*, 1898).

Most German imperialists, including Lehmann, realized that expansion of the German navy would inevitably bring Germany into conflict with England, which considered its own naval supremacy as the only guarantee of survival. Lehmann, who after the turn of the century viewed England as Germany's foremost enemy in world affairs,[24] published belligerent works such as Eisenhart's *The Showdown with England* (*Die Abrechnung mit England*, 1900) or Moulin-Eckart's *England's Policies and the Great Powers* (*Englands Politik und die Mächte*, 1901) which attacked English diplomatic and naval policy. The outbreak of the Boer War in 1899 provided Lehmann with an irresistable opportunity to arouse further and exploit anti-English feeling in Germany. In 1902 his firm undertook a four-volume series entitled *The Struggle Over South Africa* (*Im Kampf um Südafrika*) which was blatantly pro-Boer and anti-British. Lehmann, with great difficulty, finally convinced Transvaal President Paul Krüger to include his memoirs in the series, although the volume incurred a fairly large financial loss for the JFLV. However, another JFLV publication on the war, F. Bley's *The Boer War in Picture and Word* (*Der Burenkrieg in Bild und Wort*, 1901), was highly successful, and eventually enjoyed thirty-four printings; proceeds from this work enabled Lehmann to donate twenty thousand marks to the war's Boer victims.[25]

The Quest for Germanic Purity

The radical nationalism professed by Lehmann and other Pan-German expansionists reflected the Darwinistic spirit which permeated so much of the age. They assumed the existence of a universal struggle for survival among peoples and concluded that the German *Volk* could avoid extinction in this struggle only by aggressively asserting its interests. Externally, the German people had to insure its position in the world and secure the resources necessary for its well-being. And internally, many of these extreme nationalists deduced, the *Volk* must gain ascendancy over the alien forces which supposedly threatened its identity and homogeneity. If the first imperative led Lehmann and many of his fellow Germans to imperial expansion, the second drew him toward racism.

Lehmann was first attracted to racial theory through his house's publications in the area of medicine and genetic biology. After publishing medical texts by the noted Munich hygienist Max von Gruber, who was investigating the areas of demography and public health, Lehmann at the turn of the century became interested in general problems of eugenics, especially the relationship of hygiene to the national birth rate and the prevention of hereditary mental or physical illness through premarital examinations.[26] These interests were soon reflected by such JFLV publications as Senator & Kaminer's *Sickness and Marriage* (*Krankheit und Ehe*, 1904) and A. Reibmayr's *Racial-Biological Essays* (*Rassenbiologische Aufsätze*, 1908). The Eugen Diederichs house's publication of racial anthropologists such as H. Driesmans at this time also caught Lehmann's attention—and envy. EDV publications on the "Indo-Aryan world view," Lehmann told one author, would have fit very nicely in the JFLV, and he regretted that his own name was not on these books; "moreover," the Munich publisher continued, "I would rather have seen [these books] in the hands of an Aryan than of those Semites [at the EDV]." Nevertheless, Lehmann expressed grudging respect for Diederichs as a well-meaning and earnest man whose pioneering activity in the racial area was having a positive effect.[27]

It was not until 1911, however, that Lehmann firmly committed his house to a racial program. In that year von Gruber set up a special display on racial hygiene at the International Hygiene Exhibition in Dresden, and convinced Lehmann to publish the catalog for the exhibit. That volume, *Propagation, Heredity, Racial Hygiene* (*Fortpflanzung, Vererbung, Rassenhygiene*, 1911) launched the JFLV on an intensive three-decade campaign to propagate racial thought and practice in Germany. By 1913–14, Lehmann was personally attending meetings of the German Society for Racial Hygiene (Deutsche Gesellschaft für Rassenhygiene, founded 1905) and was issuing such works as L. Kuhlenbeck's *The Historical Development of Roman Law*

(*Die Entwicklungsgeschichte des römischen Rechts*, 1913), which the publisher claimed proved that "the racial factor determines the direction [of a nation's] legal development, a notion which is thoroughly new in the literature of legal history."[28] Other JFLV works such as G. von Hoffmann's *Racial Hygiene in the United States of America* (*Die Rassenhygiene in den Vereinigten Staaten von Nordamerika*, 1913) or F. L. Gerngross's *Sterilization and Castration as a Remedy in the Fight Against Crime* (*Sterilisation und Kastration als Hilfsmittel im Kampfe gegen des Verbrechen*, 1913) agitated for the application of eugenic techniques as a means of solving social problems and of strengthening the biological foundations of the German race.

Once Lehmann came to view the international struggle in racial terms and to value racial health as an essential element of the German *Volk*'s wellbeing, he grew alarmed over foreign influence in German life, which he believed obscured genuine Germandom and undermined *Volk* strength and unity. So obsessed did he become with the dissolution of the ancient German essence and adulteration of the *Volk* spirit by alien, un-German forces that he routinely chided any of his authors who used foreign words or phrases, not to mention non-German concepts or viewpoints.[29] And it was for this reason, too, that Lehmann and the Pan-German League adopted a staunchly anti-Semitic stance; "we are not conducting a pogrom (*Judenhetze*)," the publisher explained, "but we seek, as much as possible, to exclude [Jewish] influence from the League as well as from political and cultural life."[30]

Lehmann's desire to rid German cultural life of alien, especially Jewish influence, led him eventually to the same conclusion which the cultural pessimists and *völkisch* ideologues around Eugen Diederichs had reached by a somewhat different route: namely, that religion in Germany had to be purged of its Judaic foundations and a new "Germanic Christianity" established. Like Diederichs, Lehmann was disillusioned with the orthodox Protestant church in imperial Germany. Personally, he rejected such church teachings as the literal truth of the Bible or the divinity of Christ and His equality with the Father. Indeed, Lehmann not only rejected the Old Testament almost in its entirety, but wished to see the greater part of orthodox Christian dogma "cast off like dross (*wie Zunder abfallen*)."[31] The established Protestant church, he believed, had lost Luther's original dynamism and become stultified, bureaucratized, and intellectually petrified; it needed new forms and new ideas to attract modern believers. Thus, like Diederichs, he published works by unorthodox liberal theologians such as Otto Pfleiderer, who specifically addressed one of his JFLV volumes, *The Origins of Christianity* (*Entstehung des Christentums*, 1905) to those "who have outgrown the traditional Christian faith."

The Munich publisher called for nothing less than a "New Reformation" which would "rejuvenate and deepen" modern religion. This could be accomplished, Lehmann concluded, only by liberating Christianity from its Jewish and Roman foundations and linking it more intimately with the spiritual essence of the German *Volk*.[32]

Like Diederichs, Lehmann turned to Houston S. Chamberlain as the founder and prophet of a new Germanic Christianity. In 1904, after reading Chamberlain's *Foundations of the Nineteenth Century* (which maintained that Christ was Aryan rather than Jewish), Lehmann became convinced that Chamberlain was the new religious leader the German *Volk* needed.[33] The publisher, who had been planning a major treatise which would lay the groundwork for a new Germanic religion, approached Chamberlain with the plan and begged him to write this work which, Lehmann maintained, would serve as "the cornerstone of a New Reformation" and the "starting point for a new spiritual movement."[34] "The times yearn for a general renewal," Lehmann told the author; "all that is lacking is a man with the power and spirit . . . to point the Germanic race in the right direction. You are that man, and God willing, I will be your shield bearer."[35] The publisher devised an elaborate scheme for the distribution of the planned religious book. Lehmann promised Chamberlain a more lucrative contract (25 percent more royalties) than the author enjoyed with his present publisher, Bruckmann. The JFLV would print three quality editions of Chamberlain's book, from which an income of at least twenty thousand marks was expected; part of those proceeds would then be used to subsidize publication of an inexpensive (1 to 3 marks) popular edition— which, Lehmann declared, would be "largely a mere give-away." Lehmann hoped to distribute more than five thousand copies of the mass edition to specially chosen professionals "who are particularly disposed and well-suited to spread the ideas to the *Volk*: teachers, pastors, and librarians." He planned, finally, to win the Kaiser's endorsement for the new work ("just as Luther had the support of his prince"), to launch a prepublication campaign in the press, and to have Chamberlain undertake an extensive lecture tour to promote the work. "I have never in my life been so enthused over an undertaking as I am over this one," Lehmann confided; "I promise to devote my best energies to the ideas you represent and to help them to a breakthrough. . . . I am certain I will . . . succeed in effecting for them a tremendous dissemination."[36]

Unfortunately, Chamberlain pleaded that because of his chronic ill health and other commitments, he could not undertake Lehmann's ambitious project. Undaunted by his first rebuff, Lehmann over the next several years sought tirelessly—at times almost desperately—to woo this noted *völkisch* author over to the JFLV. He kept up a regular correspondence with Chamberlain and exchanged ideas with him on religious, cultural, and political issues.[37] Aware that Chamberlain was dissatisfied with the Bruck-mann house, Lehmann applied a combination of sycophantic flattery, professional, and personal favors to convince Chamberlain to transfer to the Lehmann house. While on business trips to France, Italy, and America in 1905, Lehmann voluntarily sought out publishers to produce editions of Chamberlain's works in these respective nations. He not only advised the author on negotiating the subsequent translation and publication con-tracts with these foreign publishers, but even sought Chamberlain's power of attorney to act on his behalf in the future. While Lehmann claimed his efforts were merely "service by a devoted admirer who wants to help make your ideas more widely known," at the same time he subtly men-tioned that his negotiations on Chamberlain's behalf would be much sim-plified if Chamberlain were one of the JFLV authors.[38] The Munich pub-lisher kindly offered to use his influence with the Mülhausen theatrical company to have one of Chamberlain's lesser known dramas, *Antonie*, performed there, and he later sponsored Chamberlain for membership in the Pan-German League.[39] Lehmann also served as intermediary between Chamberlain, who resided in Vienna, and his estranged, destitute, and seriously ill wife Anna, who lived in Munich. In Chamberlain's absence (and probably without his prior knowledge), the publisher arranged for medical treatment for Mrs. Chamberlain and regularly reported on her condition to (a largely indifferent) Chamberlain.[40] Throughout the decade preceding World War I, Lehmann constantly sent Chamberlain free copies of new JFLV publications in which he thought the author might be inter-ested; occasionally he would ask Chamberlain to write endorsements for the works, compose favorable reviews of them for journals, or even to simply mention them in passing in one of Chamberlain's many articles so as to gain publicity for them.[41] The publisher regularly (but to no avail) expressed his interest in publishing Chamberlain's collected works, a single Chamberlain book, or even a hastily composed pamphlet from the famous author's pen. He once, in desperation, suggested that Chamberlain merely dictate some short tract for the JFLV; if the author had no stenographer of his own, Lehmann pleaded, he had only to drop a postcard to the publisher and the next day one would be placed at his disposal.[42] Finally, Lehmann made a veiled offer to serve as Chamberlain's patron: if he were granted the privilege of publishing a religious book—or any book—by a thinker of Chamberlain's stature, he said, "then I will be inclined to provide the author, for his eminent spiritual achievement, with the appropriate material rewards which will enable him henceforth to be completely free from pecuniary cares so that he can place his mind in the service of the community."[43]

Lehmann believed a militant assertion of German interests, both at home and abroad, was imperative for the German race. His view of a Germanic Christianity which would symbolize a new racial consciousness and a liberation from alien influences was but one component of this broader vision. As he negotiated unsuccessfully with Chamberlain after 1905, Lehmann and the entire Pan-German movement were also becoming increasingly impatient with the imperial government for not pursuing vigorously enough German expansion abroad. Radical nationalists like the Munich publisher harbored a growing, but still relatively latent frustration with the traditional conservative ruling classes of Germany, for they saw those in control of the Reich's affairs as dangerously oblivious to the domestic needs and world interests of the German race. In the years before World War I, Lehmann's disappointment with the moderate policies of the government and with the lack of racial consciousness among his countrymen became increasingly acute, and at times could erupt in quasiapocalyptic yearnings for a dramatic radical nationalist awakening among Germans. In 1907, for example, he proclaimed that:

> We need a man who can give to the twentieth century what Luther offered to the fifteenth and sixteenth centuries. He will bring on a struggle which will shake our very foundations, a struggle which will compel the entire nation—indeed, the whole world—to take a stand on the great questions of our time. It is certain that whoever undertakes such a task will be cursed by thousands, and that they will seek to make his life miserable. But it is also certain that this man will understand how to articulate the innermost feelings of millions in such a way that all those who strive for higher ideals will say: "Yes, this is what I, too, have wrestled with inwardly; this is what will finally overcome the narrow letter of the law and make the inner spirit live once again."[44]

While Lehmann for a time envisaged Chamberlain as this national messiah and was willing to serve as his John the Baptist and lay the resources of the JFLV at his disposal, the author's recalcitrance eventually convinced Lehmann to look elsewhere. After World War I finally shattered his last vestiges of respect for the established conservative order, the publisher concluded that only a radical outsider, an impassioned *völkisch* demagogue, could save the German race from domestic and international extinction and lead the nation to its glorious world calling.

Five

A Glimpse of the Millennium:
The Experience of World War I

The outbreak of World War I in August 1914 was a critical turning point in the history of German neoconservatism. By suddenly throwing into question the values of nineteenth-century bourgeois civilization and fracturing the stability of the conservative Wilhelmian Reich, the war opened up tantalizing new opportunities for antimodern cultural reformers and radical *völkisch* nationalists to realize their dreams, whether at home or abroad. Yet the more fervently they yearned, and the more energetically they worked for the utopia which drew nigh, the more impatient they became with the established imperial order which seemed to block the path to their envisioned millennium.

The war not only revolutionized neoconservative expectations; it also radicalized and politicized the neoconservative movement and dramatically accentuated the differences between neoconservatives and traditional conservatives. For the war threw up grave domestic and international problems for Germany which, on the one hand, forced the cultural opponents of the prewar Reich to focus their attention on more concrete social, economic, and political concerns, and on the other, caused the radical nationalists and Pan-German expansionists to more frequently and openly challenge the specific policies of the Reich leadership. Thus before the revolution of 1918 swept away the Reich, the neoconservatives' vague and implicit opposition to the conservative imperial order had crystallized into explicit hostility. While the old Right lamented the loss of the Wilhelmian order in 1918 and hoped for its restoration, the new Right was glad to see the Second Reich go and worked instead for a "conservative revolution" which would create a radically new political order.

Finally, if the war itself was a formative experience for neoconservatism, so too was Germany's loss of the war in 1918. Because of that defeat, neoconservatives remained transfixed by the 1914–18 war experience throughout the postwar period.

The War and German National Power

Like all their countrymen, the neoconservative publishers greeted the outbreak of the war enthusiastically and were swept up in the general flood of patriotic delirium which engulfed the nation. Before the war was a fortnight old, Eugen Diederichs was already soliciting patriotic war material from his most prominent authors, and the other houses soon followed suit.[1] Diederichs, who sought "to carry [his] firm right into the trenches,"[2] issued a special series of inexpensive volumes, the *Tat Field-Mail Library* (*Tat-Feldpostbücherei*, 1914–15), especially for front-line troops. His firm also "discovered" and published the songs and novels of a group of "proletarian war poets" which included Karl Bröger, Heinrich Lersch, Max Barthel, Alfons Petzold, and H. F. Blunck. The Union Book-store of the DHV established a special Section for War Bibliophiles; for a fee of 3 to 5 marks per month, subscribers could receive all the latest war literature.[3] The DHV also issued a *War Pamphlets* (*Kriegsblätter*, 1914–16) series which was "meant not only for commercial employees. . . . They are, rather, flaming calls for nationalistic thinking and for nationalist action, and belong in the hands of everyone who does not want this war to be fought in vain."[4] Julius Lehmann, to supplement his extensive patriotic publications, also helped organize and finance a lecture and slide show presentation which toured southern Germany to arouse public support for the war.[5] During the four years of the world conflict, the Eugen Diederichs Verlag, the Gerhard Stalling Verlag, the Hanseatic Publishing Institute and its various corporate predecessors, and the J. F. Lehmanns Verlag produced some eight new multivolume series devoted exclusively to the war, plus nearly fifty individual volumes of patriotic war songs, war sermons, war poems, war letters, and various political justifications for the German cause. Some of these undertakings, such as the EDV's *War Songs* (*Kriegslieder*, 1914–15) series, attained sales as high as one hundred twenty-seven thousand copies; others such as the HVA's *War Poems* (*Kriegs-dichtungen*, 1915) or the Stalling house's *Germany's War Songs* (*Deutschlands Kriegsgesänge*, 1915) received national recognition and were placed in librar-ies and public reading halls throughout the nation.[6]

The war was welcomed by several of the neoconservative publishers because it offered the possibility of expanding German national power, especially German economic power. The DHV, representing the interests of hard-pressed commercial employees whose future was directly tied to the strength of German world trade, saw the war primarily as a show-down between Germany and her foremost commercial rival, England. Accordingly, the Union's DNVA publishing subsidiary issued a multi-volume *England and the Nations* (*England und die Völker*, 1915–16) series which sought, first, to "expose" England's historic economic exploitation of other nations, and second, to encourage still neutral nations such as the United States not to cast their lot with England and her allies.[7] Others, however, had more ambitious war aims than merely the defeat of English commercial supremacy. Despite government efforts to suppress public discussion of German war aims lest it hamper official moves to reach a negotiated settlement, many sectors of German society immediately began raising increasingly militant calls for German annexations, particularly in the east, where early German military victories opened up exciting new opportunities.[8] In varying degrees, neoconservative publishers contributed to this growing debate over war aims and German expansion. Diederichs, for example, issued four works by Gustav Steffen on Germany's international objectives in the war. These works, the publisher told his readers, "plead the realpolitik view that no living, dynamic state can let itself be bound by theoretical principles of law or justice." After reading the volumes, he said, Germans would reach the conclusion that world peace could only return after Germany had established its superiority over the other continental powers of France and Italy and had anchored itself militarily and economically as a "great power" in central Europe.[9] Through his journal *Die Tat*, Diederichs elaborated on what he saw as the appropriate German war aims. The Reich, he believed, should deepen its economic interests in western Europe, but its basic expansionist urge should be directed eastward. After some outright annexations along the Baltic Sea, Germany, according to Diederichs, should establish its indirect domination over central and eastern Europe by means of a loose federation consisting of Austria-Hungary, the Balkan states, and the non-Russian minorities (Poles and Ukranians) of western Russia. As the economic blockade of Germany intensified in 1915, Diederichs—like his friend Friedrich Naumann—became increasingly convinced that Germany's future depended on establishing economic hegemony and indirect political dominance over Middle Europe, and that Russian influence must be pushed back eastward.[10] More specific demands for territorial annexations in the east and for German hegemony over Europe were raised by Houston S. Chamberlain's *German War Aims* (*Deutsche Kriegsziele*), published by the Gerhard Stalling house in 1916. This work, by one of Germany's most prominent spokesmen for pan-German expansion, sold more than forty thousand copies.

J. F. Lehmann, however, was the publisher most active in the war aims debate. Although before the war Pan-Germans like Lehmann had advocated acquisition of an overseas colonial empire as the solution to the nation's problems, initial German successes on the eastern front soon convinced them that Germany's imperial future lay in eastern Europe.

Thus Lehmann was soon proclaiming that Germany's "life necessities" were to be found in the east, and that it was "a matter of life and death for Germany to win the new land she needs to become strong and agriculturally and industrially independent from foreign influence."[11] Yet he and his fellow Pan-Germans feared that incorporation of the native non-German peoples living in those eastern lands would introduce alien, hostile elements into the German Reich; therefore the Pan-German League proclaimed that Germany's goal must be "de-populated land" (*Land ohne Leute*). This slogan, which Lehmann boasted he first introduced through his house's publications, meant the native Slavic populations in the areas Germany would acquire in eastern Europe were to be "resettled" or "emigrated."[12]

Lehmann's advocacy of expansionist war aims quickly involved him in a running battle with the Wilhelmian state. The first clash came in late 1914 when Lehmann published Heinrich Class's *On German War Aims* (*Zum deutschen Kriegsziele*), an official statement of the Pan-German League's war aims which called for German economic hegemony in Europe and German annexation of Belgium, the Baltic, and large parts of Poland. Some two thousand copies of this provocative tract were distributed before Chancellor Theobald von Bethmann Hollweg ordered it confiscated in 1915.[13] The action enraged Lehmann, who now became convinced that Bethmann Hollweg's reluctance to formulate clear territorial demands to insure Germany's postwar security and his attempts to censor public discussion of war aims were harming German interests and leading the nation "toward an abyss." The Munich publisher agreed with officials of the Pan-German League that the chancellor had become "the foremost danger to Germany's survival."[14] Privately, Lehmann was even more hostile toward Bethmann Hollweg: "For our chancellor, too, the hour of reckoning will come," he said; "we should leave final judgment to God, although I would not criticize anyone who shot down a man who was destroying his *Volk*."[15] For the time being, however, the publisher declared his house's foremost task would be to "topple" the chancellor by any means necessary. In the remaining war years, a great deal of the revenues and energies of the JFLV were devoted to that goal.[16]

In order to "make clear to the German *Volk* and to the Kaiser that the fate of Germany lies in incompetent hands," Lehmann decided to publish a volume which would "clearly expose all [Bethmann Hollweg's] disastrous policies."[17] The publisher commissioned Hans von Liebig of the Pan-German League to compose the work, and supplied him with material. Expenses for the undertaking (which ran to several thousand marks) were borne completely by the JFLV, since the booklet was to be distributed free of charge.[18] Lehmann printed the first part of Liebig's vitriolic *The Policies of Bethmann Hollweg* (*Die Politik Bethmann Hollweg*) in late 1915; using an elaborate system of deception to get the work past government censors, he managed to distribute some three thousand copies to leading politicians, including the Kaiser's personal entourage.[19] Several copies of this scurrilous attack even found their way into the trenches, where they undermined military confidence in the chancellor. Bethmann Hollweg was enraged over the episode; he ordered the work confiscated and tight police surveillance placed on both Lehmann and Liebig. During subsequent months, Bavarian police searched the JFLV premises with increasing regularity. In hopes of evading the censorship of the regular book trade, Lehmann began printing the firm's antigovernmental literature under the label of "Private Manuscript" or "Confidential Material." In this way he succeeded in slipping another vehement attack on Bethmann Hollweg, J. Alter's *The Reich on the Path to Historical Episodes* (*Das deutsche Reich auf dem Weg zur geschichtlichen Episoden*) past the government in 1916.

By 1917, Lehmann's disgust over the government's war policies led him to attack the entire spirit of the prewar Reich as well. In the first issue of his new *Deutschlands Erneuerung* journal in April, Lehmann proclaimed that Germany's timid, compromising prosecution of the world war and her reluctance to aggressively pursue territorial spoils revealed that over the past decades, the Wilhelmian Reich had lost its will to fight. Behind its façade of economic and technological vitality, he now realized, the empire had suffered from cultural decadence, ethical decline, and spiritual nihilism; the soul-destroying atomism, rampant egotism, and complacent materialism of the prewar years had made the German race soft and lazy. He blamed this situation ultimately on the Reich's conservative founder. For Bismarck's calculating realpolitik and his willingness to compromise and negotiate, Lehmann said, had destroyed Germans' capacity for bold, passionate action. The conservative leadership of the Reich, he charged, had allowed alien and inferior elements to sap the strength of the German *Volk*. "The noble ones (*Edle*) are guilty, when the inferior rise to the top. Men of excellence must defend themselves—with all possible authority and power, and, if need be, by vile means—against the vile (*das Niedrige*)." It was necessary, Lehmann proclaimed, to undertake a fundamental national renewal and to spark a German awakening which would reestablish the supremacy of national interests and of the German race before it was too late. This historic task, of which the new JFLV journal was to be an instrument, was one which could not be left to the upper-class elite; rather, it must be grasped and implemented by the entire nation.[20] Lehmann was even more blunt in private: he confided to a friend that *Deutschlands Erneuerung* would "unite all those currents which will wash out the German Augean stables."[21]

Privately, the Munich publisher was convinced that the Reich's fundamental problem was racial in nature: there existed an international Jewish community of interests, he believed, which worked to prevent the German nation from attaining the legitimate territorial and economic gains needed for its survival. German Jews, regardless of their patriotic intentions, inevitably fell under the influence of this international Jewish community. Thus the German press, because it was largely controlled by Jews, conspired to stifle open discussion of Germany's war aims and imperial needs. Finally, Lehmann believed that the ruling elite of the Reich had itself been "Jewicized" or had fallen under the influence of the international Jewish community, and therefore no longer represented or promoted the interests of the Germanic race.[22] For these reasons, Lehmann declared in midwar that "in the future the [Lehmann] house will devote special attention to the area of racial science. Through the war, the lessons of racial hygiene have been fundamentally deepened and transformed."[23] The racial publisher donated three thousand marks to the Anthropological Society and to the Society for Racial Hygiene to promote the collection of portraits of "pure" German racial types, and he convinced the Pan-German League in 1918 to establish a special "Jewish Committee" (on which he served) to discuss the general "Jewish problem."[24] He also fulfilled his long dream of winning over Houston S. Chamberlain to the JFLV when he commissioned the author to compile a pamphlet, *Race and Nation* (*Rasse und Nation*, 1917) which exposed the international Jewish influences and personalities at work in various spheres of German life and contrasted these with representatives of the racially pure German spirit. This work sold some fifteen thousand copies by the end of the war; by 1930, it had gone into its ninth printing and had sold more than forty thousand copies.[25] In addition, the JFLV issued several other racial or anti-Semitic works such as G. von Hoffmann's *War and Racial Hygiene* (*Krieg und Rassenhygiene*, 1916); F. Siebert's *The Völkisch Idea and the Realization of Zionism* (*Der völkische Gedanke und die Verwirklichung des Zionismus*, 1916); and F. Lenz's *Race as a Principle of Value* (*Die Rasse als Wertprinzip*, 1917).

Meanwhile, Lehmann continued publishing sharp attacks on Bethmann Hollweg's conduct of the war. Although some works, such as the secretly printed second installment of Liebig's tract, were seized before they could be distributed, the JFLV did manage to distribute several other books, both licit and illicit, which denounced the chancellor. These works did their share in turning much of public and military opinion against Bethmann Hollweg and hastened his downfall. (They also on one occasion exposed Lehmann to blackmail by one of his firm's collaborators.)[26] By July 1917 Bethmann Hollweg's popularity had sunk so low that the Supreme Command, strengthened by numerous Pan-German petitions, could pressure the Kaiser into dismissing the chancellor.[27] In later years, Lehmann boasted of his role in toppling Bethmann Hollweg and in opening the way for the military dictatorship of Hindenburg and Ludendorff.[28]

After the restraining influence of Bethmann Hollweg was removed, the public debate over war aims flourished virtually unchecked. When the bellicose Fatherland party (Vaterlandspartei) was founded in September 1917 to help orchestrate the increasingly ambitious demands for German annexations and continental hegemony, Lehmann became one of its most zealous participants. With censorship now relaxed on the war aims controversy, his firm inaugurated a special series of annexationist tracts entitled *German Works of Enlightenment for the Army and Volk* (*Deutsche Aufklärungsschriften für Heer und Volk*, 1917–18). As part of this series he issued new editions of previously banned works like Class's manifesto, of which thirty-five thousand copies were soon distributed. By using clever printing techniques to point out which patriotic passages the censors had earlier ordered deleted from these works, Lehmann hoped further to arouse public opinion against the "stupid" and timid policies of the government's more moderate leaders.[29] The house also brought out works such as F. Lezius's *Germany and the East* (*Deutschland und der Osten*, 1915) and sponsored the journal *Osteuropäische Zukunft* (*East European Future*), which were designed to direct public attention to the potential rewards of eastward expansion.[30] In addition, the publisher issued two works glorifying the military leadership of Hindenburg and contrasting him with the weak and cowardly policies of the Reich's civilian leaders.

To demonstrate the absolute necessity for a peace settlement which would permit extensive German territorial expansion, Lehmann in late 1917 composed *Germany's Future Under a Good and a Bad Peace* (*Deutschlands Zukunft bei einem guten und einem schlechten Frieden*). Reviving graphics techniques his firm had used so successfully in its illustrated medical atlases, Lehmann employed a series of colored maps in this booklet to stake out the territorial claims which must be met by a "German peace"; any settlement allowing for less, he declared, would be a "rotten peace" and "treason to German blood."[31] The Munich publisher donated some eighteen thousand copies to the army, which Ludendorff then had distributed to every unit. Within two years, a total of two hundred twenty-five thousand copies of this agitational work had been circulated among the German public. This brochure, like all war aims literature published by the JFLV and other neoconservative houses, probably helped prolong the war by raising unrealistic expectations in Germany and encouraging military leaders to hold out for a total German victory rather than accept a less advantageous negotiated peace.[32] More importantly, the wide circulation of such material before 1918 made it psychologically impossible for many Germans to accept either the terms of the Versailles settlement in 1919, or the new republic which signed it.

The War and German Culture

While frustration over the Reich's external policies radicalized Lehmann during the war, Eugen Diederichs, after an initial euphoria, also became disillusioned and embittered with the imperial order, but for very different reasons. For Diederichs was far less concerned with the diplomatic and military gains which the war might bring Germany than he was with the domestic cultural effects of the conflict, especially the spiritual impact. Indeed, the Jena publisher maintained that rabid Pan-German annexationists like Lehmann, because they could think only of expanding Germany's economic and political power, were misguided materialists who missed the point completely: not material power, but cultural and spiritual considerations were the key to the nation's well-being, and the only means by which Germany could overcome the crisis she faced. Diederichs condemned Pan-German expansionist demands as serving only the interests of mammonistic industrialists, and he charged that much of the war aims debate was created by those who wished to divert public attention away from Germany's more serious internal problems. Moreover, the ambitious war aims of the annexationist circles and their insistence on a total victory merely prolonged the war and made a negotiated peace of reconciliation impossible. Finally, he decried the narrow, xenophobic chauvinism of the Pan-German League, the Fatherland party, and similar circles as harmful to German culture because it would cut Germans off from the spiritual influences of other peoples and eventually render German culture sterile.[33] Diederichs's frequent attacks in *Die Tat* on the radical nationalist and Pan-German patriots naturally aroused the ire of Lehmann, and throughout the autumn of 1917 these two neoconservative publishers carried on a running battle through the pages of their respective house journals.

Rather than the material gains it could bring Germany, Eugen Diederichs looked to the larger spiritual meaning of the world conflict. To him—as to many other anxious members of the educated German middle class—the war represented an historic cultural turning point, an apocalyptic reckoning with man's modern social and spiritual ills.[34] On the one hand, the war marked for Diederichs the dramatic beginning of the long-awaited radical rejuvenation of German life; on the other, it raised the struggle against Western liberalism and modern bourgeois civilization to a larger stage.

For cultural pessimists like the Jena publisher, the heady ecstasy and patriotic solidarity unleashed by the war seemed to signal the end of a complacent, materialistic, and spiritually barren age and to inaugurate an exhilarating new era of heroic idealism, self-sacrifice, and civic unity. The inspiring experience of the war cleansed and purified the tired, decadent Wilhelmian age and gave life a new meaning. With one lightning stroke, the selfish, mundane concerns, the personal isolation, and the social atomism of bourgeois existence gave way to a new shared national purpose. Political disputes between Germans were forgotten as the *Burgfrieden*, the "party truce within the fortress," was declared; long-standing social and economic divisions seemed overcome under the centrally directed communal war economy which arose to cope with the hardships imposed by England's blockade. Indeed, one of the greatest attractions of the war was that it brought political and spiritual unity to the German people, to a far greater extent than even the creation of the Reich in 1871 had. Thus, Diederichs believed that "those great days in August 1914 were a true revelation. For they made us recognize that, despite all the petty disagreements of everyday life, the whole of our *Volk* was capable of a common experience of exhaltation, of deep inwardness, and of reconciliatory power. In opposition to the many forces which try to stress our differences, we must always seek to nurture and exalt this power of a common experience, common feeling, and common thinking."[35] He also believed the tight-knit sense of comradeship, mutual dependence, and loyalty which the front-line soldiers were experiencing in combat would form the basis of a new postwar sense of national solidarity.[36]

In short, during the first months of the war Diederichs and many others sensed an exciting new spirit arising in the nation, a mood which would at last push through the fundamental cultural reforms which he and others had been advocating for so long. The war, the publisher believed, had called forth "the buds (*Keime*) of the future"; the nation stood on the eve of a "New Reformation." Whatever the final outcome of the war, Diederichs was convinced, Germans must seize this unique opportunity which had been thrust upon them and use it to break with the decadent past and the morass of contemporary civilization in order to construct a radically new culture.[37]

If neoconservatives like Diederichs were convinced the war would reintegrate and rejuvenate the nation, they also considered the war as a summons to a larger crusade against liberal modernity. In seeking a deeper philosophical meaning to and justification for the war, neoconservative theorists and prominent German intellectuals came to see it less as a political and diplomatic struggle than as a conflict between two fundamentally opposed spiritual systems, between profound German culture and the superficial, liberal "civilization" of the Western Allies.[38] According to these writers, the war represented a cosmic struggle between the German "Ideas of 1914"—youthful idealism, heroic sacrifice, communal solidarity, and intense national consciousness—and the West's liberal "Ideas of 1789"—individual egotism, selfish materialism, utilitarianism, democratic egalitarianism, and cosmopolitanism. England, France, and America were seen as Germany's spiritual and cultural, as well as her political enemies; the war, as one writer summarized it, was a war of the shallow English merchant mentality against the idealistic spirit of the German hero. Germany was thus fighting to protect its own superior culture against the degenerate liberalism of the Western Allies. Some ideologists even dared claim that in this war, Germany had a universal mission to free all humanity from the grips of Western modernity.[39]

The EDV, and to a lesser extent the DHV's German National Publishing Institute, eagerly promoted this interpretation of the war. Diederichs, for example, was convinced that Germany's world mission was to make moral rather than territorial conquests, and to establish a cultural superiority sufficient to protect Europe from both "Anglo-Saxon utilitarianism" and "Slavic indolence."[40] His house and the DNVA issued such works as G. Misch's *On the Spirit of the War* (*Vom Geist des Krieges*, 1914), *The Holy War* (*Der Heilige Krieg*, 1914), H. Wette's *Heroes and Merchants* (*Helden und Händler*, 1915), and Paul Natorp's *Germany's World Mission* (*Deutscher Weltberuf*, 1918). This latter work, one of the most influential statements of the "Ideas of 1914," preached that Germany's mission was to rescue true culture "by crushing the leveling, world-pervading civilization [of the West]," while another EDV book declared that "if we are defeated, then along with the death of German creativity will die any hope for a higher, peaceful, and blessed future for humanity."[41] Thus in World War I, neoconservative publishers helped propagate an elaborate ideological justification not only for resisting the advance of liberal modernity, but also for mounting a militant counterattack against it.

Given the importance of the war for German culture (and of German culture in the war), Diederichs redoubled his efforts for comprehensive cultural reform. He confessed in November 1914 that "all sorts of plans about defining our postwar cultural tasks are racing through my head," and that he hoped to begin organizing the people who would help fashion the new Germany he envisioned.[42] To herald the new cultural order which was to arise out of the war, the EDV issued titles such as E. Everth's *Inner Germany After the War* (*Das innere Deutschland nach dem Kriege*, 1916) or

Wolfgang Heine's *Toward Germany's Renewal* (*Zur Deutschlands Erneuerung*, 1916), and created a new multivolume series entitled *Pages for the New Times* (*Blätter zur neuen Zeit*). Indeed, the EDV catalog for the early war years was optimistically entitled *Toward the New Orientation of German Culture After the War* (*Zur Neuorientierung der deutschen Kultur nach dem Kriege*).

Before the war, the publisher merely speculated, in a vague sort of way, on the general outlines of the new culture he desired. Now, however, as the importance of cultural reform became more pressing and the concrete possibility of it came within grasp, he became more mindful of the mechanisms and institutions through which the reforms might be implemented. For instance, he developed an elaborate plan calling for the reorganization of Germany into several independent cultural provinces. These regions, which were either to replace or coexist with the various federal states (he never made clear which), would each encompass one of the traditional distinct Germanic tribes and would be centered around two poles: a small university town and a large metropolitan city. Each province would have its own representative body, budget, taxes, and control over the administration of its schools. In each of these cultural provinces Diederichs desired a small organized elite of culturally aware men who would found a cultural newspaper to educate the populace and direct the province's cultural policies. Lastly, Diederichs desired that the separate provinces culminate in one central organ to be located in Berlin; this organ, the "Cultural Council" (*Kulturrat*), would have close contact with and exert influence over the traditional state political structure.[43]

Diederichs next issued a public call for the formation of small cultural societies comprised of civic leaders and practically oriented academics who would transform German idealism into a "cultural world power" and "help realize God's kingdom on earth" by "debating what forms the holy German spirit will take in the future and by seeking to apply that spirit to the problems of the day."[44] In 1915 he personally founded a "Beneficial Society 1914 in Jena" (Gemeinnützige Gesellschaft 1914 zu Jena), a discussion and lecture forum for young academics from the University of Jena which was intended as a southern counterweight to the more conservative, patriotic "German Society 1914 in Berlin." In 1916, he expanded this society into the "Patriotic Beneficial Society 1914 in Thuringia" (Gemeinnützige Vaterländische Gesellschaft 1914 zu Thüringen), which he hoped would become an umbrella organization for all the smaller cultural reform groups in Thuringia and which, by attracting representatives from all classes and occupations, was to serve as a microcosm of the larger *Volk* community. With a three thousand mark donation from the publisher and the aid of a young EDV author, Max Mauernbrecher, the Society sponsored a series of lectures across Thuringia during 1916–18 which were designed to counteract the rising tide of vulgar chauvinism and annexationism among the middle classes and to spark an idealistic revival by enlightening the citizenry on the cultural tasks and the spiritual meaning of the war. (Many of these lectures later appeared in the EDV journal *Die Tat* or were issued separately by the Diederichs firm as pamphlets.) When Mauernbrecher began steering the Society closer to the political, annexationist line of chauvinist groups such as the Fatherland party in mid-1918, Diederichs withdrew from the organization in disgust.[45]

Finally, in 1917 Diederichs created the "Lauenstein Cultural Congresses" (Lauenstein Kulturtagungen), a series of intensive seminars held at Burg Lauenstein in 1917 and 1918 to discuss cultural and political issues such as "The Meaning and Tasks of our Times," or "The Leadership Problem in Cultural and State Affairs." Diederichs hoped these meetings would serve as "fixed abodes (*Stätte*) for the new German spirit, whose mission it is to make moral conquests . . . and to hammer out a new lifestyle [for the nation]."[46] Through his far-ranging contacts in the cultural world, the publisher convinced politicians, academics (including such notables as Max Weber, Theodor Heuss, and Friedrich Meinecke), artists, and various maverick intellectuals to participate; leading neoconservative theorists such as Wilhelm Stapel also attended and spoke.[47] Some participants, such as Ernst Toller and Paul Ernst, later regarded these congresses as important personal turning points. For others, such as Max Weber, the Lauenstein meetings served as a crucial catalyst in their final break with the entire Wilhelmian cultural and political order.[48]

While Diederichs's institutional vehicles for cultural reform may have been novel, his general cultural objectives were essentially the same ones he had articulated before the war. He continued, for example, to stress the importance of overcoming materialism with a new idealism. The upsurge of idealism at the outbreak of the war, he believed, meant that in the future the power of the spirit would decide not only political issues, but even economic affairs; for his part, he hoped "to mobilize German idealism, so that it can step in at the proper time to shape the future of Germany."[49] The publisher now considered it all the more important for his house and journal to communicate the ideas of German idealists such as Fichte and Lagarde to the masses, and to this end he published such works as G. Dost's *Paul Lagarde's National Religion* (*Paul Lagardes nationale Religion*, 1915).[50] The publisher's scorn for rationalism became even more manifest after 1914: he now rejected intellectual truth as "merely relative," and reaffirmed his conviction that for the individual, "the only truth is that of the instinct."[51] By 1917 Diederichs claimed that the EDV's circle of collaborators were all more or less "tuned in" to mysticism and transcendental idealism. By the end of the war he was predicting the dawn of a new pantheist age which would be founded on the mystical ideas of Meister Eckehardt and which would achieve a final, higher synthesis between all opposites.[52]

As they had before the war, Langbehn's ideas on art continued to play a central role in the Jena publisher's ideology after 1914: "the deceased Rembrandt German [Langbehn]," Diederichs declared, "means more for the Germany of the future than all the German bank directors alive today."[53] The Diederichs house continued its artistic publications (over ten titles dealing with aesthetics or drama appeared during the war), and even created a new multivolume artistic series, *Pages for German Style and Art* (*Blätter für deutsche Art und Kunst*, 1915–20). Diederichs also took a personal, although rather brief interest in the new literary movement of expressionism, in which he saw many of the same principles which animated his own work: a messianic urge for purification and renewal, rebellion against established cultural conventions, and a passionate desire to break out of the confines of intellectual civilization and to return to "natural" instincts. "I am presently moving nearer and nearer to expressionism," he wrote in 1917, "for I see it as the borderline between the old and the new, as a kind of geological fault which will heave up a new layer of life."[54] After Georg Kaiser's expressionist drama *The Coral* (*Die Koralle*) was poorly received in Jena, Diederichs rose to its defense with a lengthy newspaper article in which he hailed the piece as a major artistic breakthrough and a work with deep religious implications.[55] This prompted not only Kaiser, but other young expressionist authors such as Johannes Baader to approach Diederichs with requests that he publish their avantgarde works.[56] He did, in fact, toy with the idea of devoting at least part of his publishing program to expressionist literary movements, for (as he confirmed to a friend), "in general I am opposed to letting Kurt Wolff [the leading publisher of expressionist literature] take over leadership of the German literature of the future. Rather, I favor setting up a more cosmically and personally anchored brand of literature in direct opposition to the world of letters of the Wolff people, who are mostly Jews."[57] Thus, after bringing out a volume of poems in 1917 by the young expressionist Curt Corrinth, the EDV between 1918 and 1920 created and published the literary journal *Nyland*, which served as an organ for a short-lived circle of young "proletarian" or "social expressionist" writers who called themselves "Working People from the House Nyland" (*Werkleute auf Haus Nyland*).[58]

Finally, Diederichs continued to support the Youth Movement, but with a new intensity. More than ever he became convinced that the spirit of the "new Germany" being born in the war was perhaps best embodied in the followers of the Youth Movement who, shortly after the 1913 Hohe Meissner festival, volunteered almost en masse when the war broke out. For German youth groups, he believed, had a deeper appreciation than older Germans for the social whole; they represented "a new way of thinking, a new feeling for life—and correspondingly more honor and a deeper experimental power than the older generation."[59] Throughout the war, therefore, the EDV promoted the Youth Movement by publishing four major works by Hans Blüher, the foremost authority on the movement, including his classic *The Role of the Erotic in Male Societies* (*Die Rolle der Erotik in der männlichen Gesellschaft*, 1917), which eventually sold more than fourteen thousand copies. Besides issuing some six other book-length volumes on the Youth Movement, the Diederichs house also created a short-lived youth journal, *The Awakening* (*Der Aufbruch: Monatsblätter aus der Jugendbewegung*, 1915), as well as a thirty-title series *Pamphlets for German Youth* (*Flugblätter an die deutsche Jugend*, 1915–19), of which more than one hundred sixty-five thousand individual copies were sold. And whenever asked, the Jena publisher willingly served as a fatherly adviser for young editors such as Arno Steglich who issued Youth Movement journals of their own.[60]

While mysticism, art, the fresh outlook of the Youth Movement, and other means of cultivating the personal inner spirit continued to have a central place in Diederichs's cultural program, we have seen that, in the years before the war, he was coming to regard the social dimensions of man's existence as increasingly important. The sense of national solidarity and social reintegration generated by the experience of war in 1914 merely reinforced his growing awareness that not only the individual private self, but man's communal relations had to be fundamentally transformed: "the world historical meaning of the present war," he declared, "is that we, as Germans, are to forge a stronger, deeper spirit of living *Volk* unity."[61]

Diederichs's new concern for the social elements of culture and the bonds of social coherence is perhaps best illustrated by the way in which the war fundamentally altered his conception of religion. At the turn of the century, although he often held novel views about the form which religious expression should take, the publisher nevertheless conceived of religion in a fairly traditional way—namely, as the relation of the individual soul to the larger forces of the cosmos (i.e., God). But the experience of the war convinced Diederichs that Nietzsche was correct about the "death" of God. Old concepts of "religion" and "God," not to mention the entire Christian church and its theology, now became meaningless and superfluous in his eyes, and he proclaimed that postwar German culture would need a fundamentally different conception of religion.[62] The Jena publisher found a new object for his religious yearnings in the notion of the national community. For him, as for many Germans, the inspiring sense of national solidarity and common purpose which swept Germany in 1914 was a mystical experience, almost religious in nature. As national unity and patriotic inspiration assumed sacred importance, and as the established church rushed to lend its sanction to the national cause, religion and nationalism tended to fuse into one. For Diederichs, religion thus took on an entirely new meaning after 1914: he now defined the essence of religion as "contact between souls," or simply as "a feeling for community" (*Gemeinschaftsgefühl*).[63] By 1915, individual religiosity for Diederichs had become inseparable from consciousness of and service to the national community; "to me," he confided, " 'religion' is a cognate of 'nation,' as both are forms of a communal, coherent (*verbindende*) feeling for life."[64] The publisher declared that after the war, Germany must embrace this new religious spirit which "seeks to transcend the individual soul and strives instead for a sense of community," and he warned that anyone who violated or undermined the new sense of national community would be demonstrating their alienation from God.[65]

To promote his new concept of religion, Diederichs's firm issued some twelve religious titles during the war, including such works as *German Faith* (*Deutscher Glaube*, 1914), F. Gogarten's *Religion and Volk Character* (*Religion und Volkstum*, 1915), and Dost's *Paul Lagarde's National Religion*. In 1915 the publisher also issued a public call for the establishment of a new national religious holiday for the "new Germany." He suggested that midsummer's day (St. Johannistag), an observance which reached back to the pantheistic practices of the ancient Nordic tribes, be declared a "Festival of the German Soul" on which "the unity of the *Volk* and its willingness to sacrifice" could be celebrated annually. Diederichs hoped this religious holiday would become "a symbol of the great feeling of community among all Germans and Nordics, a symbol of our love of nature, of our loyalty, and of our yearnings for the infinite."[66]

As a result of the war, then, religion assumed a new function in Diederichs's thinking: it was no longer merely a means by which to counter rationalism and inspire idealism, but a new force for social cohesion. For religion united individuals into a common community of believers, and a shared religious faith in which all Germans participated helped preserve and intensify Germany's newfound sense of unity and solidarity. Indeed, Germans' feeling of belonging to a unified national community tended itself to become the object of religious adoration.

As conscious membership in the German *Volk* community assumed a larger and larger role in Diederichs's ideology, he became increasingly interested in the nature of German national identity. Nietzsche once observed that "characteristic of the German is that his question 'What is

German?' never dies out."[67] After 1914, the EDV contributed a number of works to this perennial question by issuing studies which explored the nature of the German *Volk* spirit, and the essence and uniqueness of the German national character. These titles included: *Germanic Volk Character* (*Deutsches Volkstum*, 1914), *The German Man* (*Der deutsche Mensch*, 1915), R. Buchwald's *The Science of German National Character* (*Die Wissenschaft vom deutschen Nationalcharakter*, 1917), and G. Schmidt's *Our Mother Tongue as a Weapon and Instrument of German Thought* (*Unsere Muttersprache als Waffe und Werkzeug des deutschen Gedankes*, 1917). One EDV publication in particular, Wilhelm Stapel's *Education to Volk Citizenship* (*Volksbürgerliche Erziehung*, 1917), quickly became a catechism of the twentieth-century *Volkstum* movement and exerted a profound influence on neoconservative organizations such as the DHV.[68] Stapel, who picked up many of the ideas for his book from other EDV publications,[69] argued that the *Volk* was the ultimate human reality and the fundamental unit of life; notions such as "the individual," "the state," or "humanity" were merely artificial abstractions. He rejected traditional patriotic attachment to the state (and, by implication, to the Wilhelmian Reich), and declared instead that the ultimate loyalty of Germans must be to the *Volk*, which existed above and beyond the political state. When Stapel was chosen editor of the DHV journal *Deutsches Volkstum* in 1918 (largely, no doubt, because of the popularity of his recent book, the rights for which were later transferred from the EDV to the HVA), he used this new journal to carry on the program laid out in his *Volksbürgerliche Erziehung*. The first issue of the *Deutsches Volkstum* proclaimed, for example, that "Germanic *Volkstum* describes both our work and our wish: *Volkstum* is our true goal; the political state is merely a form, but the *Volk* is the real content. *Volkstum* is the source of our energy, and in it is found everything which inspires and heightens our national existence. It is both a creed and a summons to arms."[70]

Like Lehmann, Diederichs and other neoconservative publishing firms such as the new German National Home Library were concerned about the purity of the German *Volk* and the effect of foreign influence on the German essence. Thus when the Home Library was founded in 1916, it proclaimed itself to be a "bulwark against the infiltration of un-German elements," while the EDV advertised one of its own books as a volume "which proves the 400-year self-alienation (*Selbstentfremdung*) of the German spirit under the domination of Romanic elements," and which promised to point the way toward a recovery of "a German *Volk* perception."[71] Through publications such as *Germanic Heroism* (*Germanisches Heldentum*, 1915) and his (unrealized) plans for a new Nordic cultural journal, Diederichs also sought to steer Germans back to their original Nordic roots.[72] Unlike Lehmann, however, the Jena publisher no longer conceived of the

German *Volk* in racial terms. In Diederichs's mind, a German outlook, not racial criteria, determined whether one partook of the German essence; this meant that full membership in the German *Volk* community was open to those of non-Germanic racial stock, such as Jews, if they but adopted the *Volk*'s spiritual orientation. He asserted that he was not an anti-Semite, and warned others that "it is entirely wrong to lump together Jewish descent, cultural sterility, and the spirit of negation all in the same pot."[73]

The Eugen Diederichs Verlag's wartime publications on *Volk* character, as well as those on German history and folklore, were intended to emphasize the distinctive "Germanness" which every German shared, and thereby to heighten Germans' consciousness of their common *Volk* experience and of their communal solidarity. Yet Diederichs had recognized before the war that lasting national unity and solidarity could be insured only through social and political justice for all segments of the *Volk*. The conservative ruling elite's continued exclusion of the lower classes from full political participation in the Reich and from a larger degree of material security within Germany's economy would, he knew, almost certainly guarantee the reappearance of the resentments and divisions which plagued the nation before the war. The publisher therefore demanded that the nation's new wartime solidarity be used to push through a long overdue "reorganization of [Germany's] social and economic relations." Through his house journal and through other EDV publications such as H. Potthoff's *War and Social Policy* (*Krieg und Sozialpolitik*, 1915) or H. Mehner's *Europe's Capital and Labor After the War* (*Europas Kapital und Arbeit nach dem Kriege*, 1918), he called for the formation of a new socioeconomic order which would be founded on social solidarity and social justice.[74] Diederichs soon reached the conclusion that the only alternative to the prewar laissez-faire capitalist system, where individual social classes and interest groups promoted their selfish interests at the expense of the common good, was a form of socialism—which he defined as "the voluntary subordination of subjective interests to the needs of the social whole."[75] Attempting to steer a "middle path" between liberalism, conservatism, and Marxist socialism, he spoke during the war of a new "community of labor" or a "national socialism" in which the material interests of all groups would be harmonized with each other and with the larger needs of the *Volk*. As envisioned by this utopian publisher, such a socioeconomic order would overcome the chaotic disunity, atomistic individualism, class antagonisms, and social insecurities of capitalism, yet at the same time avoid the oppressive mass collectivism and egalitarianism of proletarian Marxist socialism.[76]

Diederichs turned to corporatism as one model for the new harmonious economic order he believed Germany needed. Corporate theory, popular in imperial Germany, revolved around the notion of the occupational corporation or social estate (*Stand*).[77] Corporatists regarded the occupational estate as a natural social grouping founded on the shared interests of those engaged in the same economic pursuit. A corporate estate represented a kind of integrated microcommunity within which members' interests were harmonized and which could present a single, united front in encounters or direct negotiations with other corporations. Those who feared that mass leveling and the atomization of modern industrial society were robbing them of their traditional socioeconomic status found corporatist theories particularly attractive. For corporatism assumed that each occupational estate performed a unique economic function which was indispensable to the general welfare of the *Volk*; the well-being of the social whole depended on the well-being of each of its essential units, the occupational *Stände*. Corporatists, because they stressed the need to preserve the distinct identity of each estate and to protect its social and economic standing, thus sought to prevent the undifferentiated egalitarianism of mass society and to maintain instead some sort of social hierarchy. As Eugen Diederichs explained, corporatism provided a "measured gradation" (*abgewogener Schattierung*) for social and political life.[78]

While corporatism would protect the *Volk*'s traditional occupational subgroupings from the leveling aspects of modernization, many believed it would also achieve comprehensive *Volk* solidarity. For corporate theory assumed the conflicting socioeconomic interests of individuals would be harmonized within the estate, which represented a natural community of interest; each estate would stand as one united entity. But since each individual corporate estate performed a unique function within the *Volk* whole, there could be no real conflict of interest between the various estates either; the *Stände* were independent, "organically" interrelated units of the larger social body. Thus corporatism seemed inherently *völkisch*, for in a society organized along corporate lines, a hierarchical structuring of the estates would subordinate each to the larger *Volk* whole. Harmonious social integration would then exist both within and among the corporations, thus creating a unified *Volk* community.[79] Moreover, a state based on corporate representation would overcome the divisive party squabbling and selfish interest politics which so many educated middle-class Germans considered characteristic of liberal parliamentarism. For to many conservative Germans, parliaments and political parties were products of modern industrial society and served only the private interests of the industrial bourgeoisie. A supreme governing assembly comprised of representatives of the various estates, by contrast, was seen as a more appropriate structure for a *Volk* community. Such a corporatively organized state would not only provide for a form of popular representation, but would unite political and economic direction in one centralized body, thus better harmonizing interests within the social whole.

Diederichs concluded during the war that a restructuring of Germany according to corporatist principles would restore the social and political health of the nation and lay the foundation for the new, postwar "community of labor" which he envisioned.[80] He advertised the EDV's first publication on corporatism, E. Krieck's *The German Idea of the State* (*Der deutsche Staatsidee*, 1917), as a work which proved that an organic corporate political structure would not only serve the German *Volk* by overcoming modern individualism, but would lead it back to its historic *völkisch* roots as well.[81] Through M. Planck's *The Occupational State* (*Der Berufsstaat, nach der Rechtslehre K. Chr. Planck*, 1918), he sought to popularize the thought of Karl C. Planck, an early German corporate theorist; the war, Diederichs told his readers, had at last made Germany "ripe" for Planck's ideas.[82] Finally, during the closing months of the war the publisher developed a plan for a corporate state. He envisioned a series of provincial assemblies and a central national organ in which all the major corporate estates—agriculture, industry and commerce, bureaucrats and administrators, and of course "cultural occupations" such as academics, artists, and journalists—would be represented according to a strict formula.[83] (After November 1918, he continued to publicize this plan through special issues of *Die Tat* in hopes that the new Weimar National Assembly would adopt it.)[84]

The indefatigable Lion of Jena found yet another model for a radically new communal-socialist economic order in the centrally directed war economy which arose in Germany after 1914. Neoconservatives like Diederichs greeted the mobilization of the economy for war because it required all Germans to sacrifice their individual material interests to the national cause. During the first year of the war, when the impulse toward patriotic self-sacrifice was the strongest, both the DHV's DNVA and the Diederichs house produced works such as W. Lambach's *The Mobilization of Labor* (*Mobilmachung der Arbeit*, 1914) or G. Brost's *Economic Mobilization* (*Wirtschaftliche Mobilmachung*, 1914) which extolled the benefits of centralized mobilization of the nation's social and economic forces. As the war progressed, Walther Rathenau and Wichard von Moellendorf, the two architects of the German war economy, developed a comprehensive closed economic system which soon came to be known as the "social" or "communal economy" (*Gemeinwirtschaft*). Defined by its founders as a system which incorporated the principles of material sacrifice, duty, loyalty, solidarity of economic interests, and social justice, this communal economy represented to many neoconservatives the perfect solution to Germany's socioeconomic problems. Diederichs, for example, eagerly adopted the concept of "communal economy" and in the spring of 1917 began to preach that Germans must develop a permanent communal economy as a means of realizing a true *Volk* community.[85] To popularize the principles of this new German economic order, he persuaded Rathenau's secretary and editor, Erich Schairer, to edit an eighteen-volume series for the EDV entitled *German Communal Economy (Deutsche Gemeinwirtschaft)*. Appearing between 1917 and 1920, this series sold more than forty-four thousand individual pamphlets and played an important role in the early history of the Weimar republic. For when the war ended, Moellendorf entered the new Weimar Ministry of Economics, where he and his colleague R. Wissel worked desperately to have a system of social economy adopted by the nascent republic. Moellendorf and Wissel utilized the EDV's *German Communal Economy* series as their chief forum to mobilize public support for their policies. Although this 1918–19 crusade for a communal economy was unsuccessful, it represented an important non-Marxist contribution to postwar German social policy.[86]

Eugen Diederichs's wartime vision of a rejuvenated Germany presumed not only economic security, but also a greater degree of political integration for the lower social classes. In August 1914, the working classes had proved their loyalty and patriotism by supporting the German war effort, but they made it clear that, in return for this support, they expected extensive political reforms to be carried out in the Reich. Diederichs, like many middle-class Germans, now became convinced that some measure of democratization which allowed for greater popular input—and, consequently, for wider popular support—was essential for the nation. (In fact, as was seen earlier, he had begun to realize this as early as 1910.) But this presented the neoconservative publisher with a difficult dilemma: for while he supported broader popular participation in national affairs, the idealistic cultural principles he preached were inherently elitist. In his eyes, the democratic "mass spirit" was by definition materialistic and mechanistic, while true idealism and spirituality were attainable only by a select few. "One sees," Diederichs lamented, "that the crowd will not be led by *Geist*; they want to see the phantom of material success before them. . . . We cultivated men live in a realm of ideas of which the common man is completely ignorant."[87] As he contemplated political power passing into the hands of the masses, he saw more clearly than ever that "the idealistic spirit is always aristocratic," and that "only a narrow cultivated stratum . . . can transmit cultural progress." A truly idealist culture required a spiritual aristocracy, he realized; democracy, in which the materialistic masses dominated, was capable only of an inferior, superficial type of "civilization."[88] He thus harbored highly ambivalent feelings about democratization: "Right now," he confided to a friend in 1916, "despite a democratic disposition, I have a truly aristocratic stance toward the masses." The central problem of postwar German cultural and political life, he said, would be "the leadership problem—that is, how can the all-too-small minority of excellent people make their impact felt on the larger *Volk*?"[89] This perplexing dilemma of elitism or democratization, he concluded, could be overcome only by means of a new type of spiritual and political elite.

Elitist doctrines played an important role in late nineteenth- and early twentieth-century German thought. As Walter Struve has shown,[90] several theorists before and after World War I preached the need for an "open yet authoritarian elite" as Germany's only hope of escaping mass rule. These thinkers agreed that rule by an elite was both inevitable and desirable, but they felt (at least those before 1918) that imperial Germany's conservative ruling elite of agrarian Junker aristocrats, the state bureaucracy, and the industrial upper middle class had become ossified and incapable of effective leadership. Germany's hereditary, socially exclusive, and often blindly reactionary elite must be replaced by a new elite enjoying greater popular support and inspired by more imaginative policies, these theorists warned, lest a political revolution by the lower classes force mass democracy or (after 1918) bolshevism on the nation. To forestall such a sociopolitical revolution, these writers called for government by a new elite which would be democratically recruited from all sectors of society, and hence more open to popular needs, but which would rule in an authoritarian manner, immune from popular control.

During the war it became increasingly clear to Diederichs that the conservative propertied classes which ruled Germany were too narrowly based and too socially exclusive to accept talented outsiders into their ranks or to inspire broad popular support, and too politically and spiritually bankrupt to carry out the kinds of extensive reforms he envisioned. What the nation needed, he came to believe, was a new elite which would cut horizontally across all social classes and be more open toward individuals and ideas from the lower classes. He had in mind a system like China's mandarin class where talented, dedicated men, no matter how lowly their birth, had an opportunity to rise to the top and enter the elite. "We need," Diederichs proclaimed in 1917, "an aristocracy in public life. Not a hereditary one, but one which rests on personal virtue, a deep sense of responsibility, and on a genuine breadth of vision."[91] Practical, sensitive men who had previously shunned politics would be attracted to this new elite because they would not have to prostitute themselves and their ideals through shabby, democratic electioneering. Once admitted, members of the elite would transcend the narrow material interests of Germany's various social classes and pressure groups because they would see the spirit as the fundamental basis of all economic and political life; they would carry idealism to the masses and thereby create a new, unified national community devoid of political, social, or economic antagonisms.[92]

An "organic people's state (*organischer Volksstaat*) was the term Diederichs chose to describe the new, more popularly based but essentially elitist political order he hoped would arise out of the war. While he never worked out the details, this "people's state" was to be more democratic than the Second Reich, but not a democracy; it was to be led by an open, yet authoritarian elite; and it would somehow combine all the best features of liberal individualism, conservative order, and socialist solidarity. It would also allow for more regional identity and independence than did the Wilhelmian order, and would be less oriented toward Prussia and more rooted in the south German states.[93] Although Diederichs expounded on his plans for a new political order primarily through the pages of *Die Tat*, some of the same general ideas were also expressed in Hugo Preuss's *The German Volk and Politics* (*Das deutsche Volk und die Politik*), which the EDV published in 1915. Through this work, which sold more than nine thousand copies, Preuss became a well-known political and constitutional theorist; after the revolution of 1918 he was asked to draft the constitution for the new Weimar republic.

Diederichs's vision of a new political order, like his utopian wartime plans for a fundamental cultural, social, and economic transformation of the nation, arose from his conviction that World War I presented Germany with a singular opportunity to break with the past and forge that "new Germany" of which he had dreamed since the 1890s. As the "spirit of 1914" seemed to open the door to the neoconservative millennium, visionaries like Diederichs (and Lehmann) became all the more anxious, indeed desperate, to break loose from the Wilhelmian order and enter what they believed to be Germany's dawning new age. But as the initial enthusiasm of August 1914 was soon spent and war weariness set in, as early German successes on the field gave way to military stalemate and then to serious setbacks, and as the entrenched ruling classes and the social, economic, and political realities of the imperial order proved more resistant to change than Diederichs had expected, he gradually became disillusioned and bitter over the effects of the war on Germany. Rather than bringing the dramatic spiritual rebirth he had initially envisioned, he eventually came to suspect that the war was consummating the many noxious modern trends he hated. By 1915 Diederichs was complaining that "the craving for material pleasure and the selfish concerns which characterized our life before the war are still ascendant," and within a year he was denouncing the annexationist greed and vulgar chauvinism of many of his countrymen. He soon realized, moreover, that a modern nation at war, with its regulated production, shortages, and rationing becomes more rather than less subordinated to material interests. To Diederichs, while the war had unleashed some new spiritual forces, it was at the same time transforming Germany into "a single large factory," an "interest-society" with the "naked rule of the mammonistic masses looming in the background."[94]

He placed a large share of blame for this clearly on the shoulders of the Reich's conservative leaders: intimidated by the ravings of the chauvinist demagogues, captive to the calculating *realpolitische* policies and decisions of their predecessors, concerned with trivialities and with narrow material questions rather than with the larger, more important idealist goals of German policy, and—worst of all—utterly lacking in any ideals themselves, they were unable to grasp the unique opportunity for idealistic renewal which the war had offered. Hoping merely that conditions would return to the prewar state so that they might preserve their own position, Germany's ruling class had squandered the nation's chances for a general spiritual and social rebirth.[95]

As with Lehmann, Diederichs's professional position as publisher brought him into conflict with government censors during the war (*Die Tat* was briefly banned several times). These encounters served to heighten his neoconservative consciousness and further embitter him toward the system. He expressed his dismay that the government was not only unwilling to carry through a spiritual revolution of its own, but also suppressed those creative voices (like his own) which might lead the nation out of its materialistic morass; this, he complained, left only petty bureaucrats, unscrupulous politicians, and self-interested parvenus to fill the vacuum. "After the war," Diederichs warned in 1917, "there will be a lot more to say when the blinders and muzzles fall off and when our range of vision expands in the light of our bitter experiences."[96]

By the spring and summer of 1918 (that is, before Germany's loss of the war had become fully apparent to the German public), Diederichs was openly condemning Wilhelm II and the Reich leadership as bungling, indecisive, politically naive dilettantes who had inadequately prepared the nation for the ordeal of war, had mismanaged both the conduct of the war and the nation's domestic opportunities for reform, and had brought the nation to the brink of disaster. The war made it apparent, he said, that "our ruling class is totally bankrupt, and with it, our entire system of government."[97] Worst of all, he realized that "everything which used to be called authority and which could hold sway over the masses is now tottering. . . . The war has shattered our old traditions; it is a destroyer not only on the battlefield, but at home as well." Diederichs charged that the war had in fact dissolved all the bonds of German cultural and social life and had created "an anarchism of values"; "our entire culture," he lamented, "appears to me to be disintegrating." He foresaw a violent, anarchistic "social catastrophe" looming in the future, a convulsion which would shake all of human society.[98]

Like Lehmann, Diederichs projected his disillusionment and the bitterness of his dashed utopian hopes into the past, rejecting the entire Bismarckian Reich as a cruel mistake for Germany. Ever since its founding in 1871, he declared, the centralized, Prussian-dominated Reich had led the German *Volk* down a false path, destroying its honored traditions, violating its rich regional diversity, and stifling its cultural creativity. He deeply regretted that there had not been more cultural and political opposition to the Byzantine, soulless Wilhelmian order in the years before the war.[99] Thus, even before the November revolution swept away the old imperial order, neoconservatives like Diederichs and Lehmann had become convinced that the Second Reich was not only culturally, but politically disastrous for the nation and had to be replaced by a radically different order.

The Legacy of the War

Despite their growing disillusionment over the war, Germany's defeat in 1918 came as a traumatic shock not only to the neoconservative publishers, but also to nearly all Germans. The psychological legacy of the lost war lingered throughout the Weimar republic; long after the material consequences of the war had been surmounted, Germans were still struggling to assimilate the meaning of the 1914–18 experience. For, as James McRandle has noted,

> In a normal society, grief would have lost its edge, the memories
> of the war would have been stilled by the many concerns and
> opportunities of peace. But in [postwar] Germany all things
> conspired to turn men's minds back towards the war. The harshness
> of the peace treaty, the enforced weakness of the state, the continuing
> vexation of reparations, all kept before the veterans the fact that
> their efforts had been in vain. It proved difficult under these
> conditions for many of them to grow out of the mood of 1918. . . .
> The instability of the Weimar republic opened to them an avenue of
> salvation. The *Frontkämpfer* [front-line warriors] did not have to
> perish with the peace because the society itself was a battlefield. . . .
> The image of the warrior [became] the symbol of all that was good
> and valuable in German life, the carrier of important political
> concepts and an ideal figure worthy of emulation.[100]

Through the voluminous and extremely successful war literature they produced after 1918, the neoconservative publishing houses played a central role in this often bitter controversy over the significance of World War I for Germany. By presenting a highly idealized popular image of the recent war experience and by mythologizing Germany's defeat, the publishers' postwar books on this topic fueled the militaristic and antidemocratic sentiments which ultimately destroyed the Weimar republic.

One interpretation of the war popularized after 1918 by several of the neoconservative publishers was the myth that Germany had lost the war not through military defeat, but because the military had been betrayed on the home front by pacifists and leftists whose democratic revolution in 1918 had pulled the rug out from under the victorious German army. This "Stab-in-the-Back" legend (*Dolchstosslegende*), which became one of the most powerful political slogans of the antidemocratic Right and did so much to undermine public support for the Weimar republic, was originated by Hindenburg, Ludendorff, and other high military leaders in 1918. It did not become popular among the wider public, however, until the early 1920s, when publicists like Paul Cossmann and J. F. Lehmann began actively to promote it.[101]

Lehmann was personally convinced that Germany did not lose the war militarily. In late 1918 he stated: "Who broke the backbone of the German *Volk*? The Jews and the all-Jewish press. They betrayed us at home by destroying belief in the Fatherland, and then they crushed the front lines." And soon thereafter he reiterated: "Unbeaten at the front, our *Volk* was destroyed internally by the Jewish spirit; when we collapsed at home, the military front was dragged down as well."[102] After consulting with General Ludendorff in 1920,[103] Lehmann commissioned General Dickhuth-Harrach to serve as editor for a series of books which would demonstrate that German and Austrian military forces had never been defeated in the war. This tripartite series, *Undefeated on the Field* (*Im Felde unbesiegt*), *Undefeated in the Air* (*Im Luft unbesiegt*), and *Undefeated at Sea* (*Auf See unbesiegt*) appeared between 1920 and 1928 and sold more than one hundred sixty thousand copies by 1932. As booksellers across Germany reported to the publisher, the series broke a postwar trend of declining interest in the recent war and was "directly responsible for reversing public opinion [about the outcome of the war]."[104] To supplement the *Undefeated* series, the JFLV published some nine additional titles, such as A. Krauss's *The Causes of Our Defeat* (*Die Ursachen unserer Niederlage*, 1920) or L. Freiwald's *The Betrayed Fleet* (*Die verrattene Flotte: Aus den letzten Tagen des deutschen Kriegsmarine*, 1931), which idealized the German military leaders of World War I or demonstrated that the German-Austrian military machine had been invincible until finally betrayed by its domestic enemies.

The Gerhard Stalling house, one of the most prolific producers of war literature in the 1920s, also helped glorify Germany's military performance in the world war by publishing two massive series. Stalling's thirty-nine-volume *The Great War* (*Der Grosse Krieg in Einzeldarstellungen*, 1918–19), was produced at Hindenburg's request and in close cooperation with the German General Staff.[105] The thirty-six-volume *Battles of the World War* (*Schlachten des Weltkrieges*, 1921–30), on the other hand, was published by the GSV in conjunction with the National Military Archive, and proved highly popular: one title, *Douaumont* (1923), sold one hundred thirty-five thousand copies by 1940. And the HVA, too, did its part by issuing such apologies for the military as A. von Tirpitz's *Germany's Policy of Weakness in the World War* (*Deutsche Ohnmachtspolitik im Weltkriege*, 1926).

However much conservative Germans sought to deny that the nation had been defeated militarily in the world war, they could still not cite ultimate victory as a justification for the human suffering, enormous loss of life, and massive destruction of resources the conflict had incurred. Instead, they had to look elsewhere for a vindication of the lost war. In what was either a conscious or unconscious attempt to rationalize Germany's crippling sacrifices and extract some positive gain from the lost war, those like the neoconservatives who had enthusiastically supported Germany's involvement in the war now claimed that the ultimate good of the undertaking lay in the momentous experience of war itself. In their eyes, war—the most extreme of human conditions—called forth many noble qualities in man which are stifled in normal times of peace and security: social unity; the near-mystical comradeship of battle; heroic dedication and self-sacrifice; the "natural" hierarchy, strong leadership, and intense personal loyalty which emerges within a group of warriors; a rediscovery of the primal instincts of survival; the existential ability to impose one's own meaning and values on a brutal, chaotic world whose old values have been destroyed. (It was no accident that these were precisely the values and certainties which many Germans yearned for in the chaotic, anxiety-ridden postwar era.) The ennobling experience of war alone justified German involvement in the world war, neoconservatives believed, and the "front generation" whose character had been transformed and hardened in the trenches would, it was hoped, in turn transform and rejuvenate the entire nation. Thus Eugen Diederichs, whose house had issued one of the first idealized studies of the new psyche of the front-line soldier, E. Everth's *On the Soul of the Soldiers in the Field* (*Von der Seele des Soldaten im Felde*, 1915), consoled his countrymen in 1918: "the new spirit of Germany will arise not in the academic parlors and studies, but from the feeling of comradeship out on the front lines, where all are dedicated to the same single task, where 'authority' is based on the fact that the leader shares the same sorrows and hardships as the communal group he leads. This experience of comradeship will be the kernel of a new spirit, will usher in a new era."[106]

Neoconservatives reacted vehemently to any interpretation of the war experience which challenged their own idealized image. The appearance in 1928 of E. M. Remarque's classic antiwar novel *All Quiet on the Western Front* (*Im Westen Nichts Neues*), for example, provoked a bitter response that transformed the entire realm of belletristic war literature into a volatile political battlefield. Remarque's book, published by the liberal, Jewish-owned Ullstein Verlag, was one of those "egocentric" novels which emphasized the negative impact of the war on the individual psyche; it portrayed World War I as a futile, senseless slaughter which psychically and physically destroyed an entire generation of German youth.[107] Moreover, the novel suggested none too subtly that the German military had indeed lost the war at the front, not through some fictitious stab in the back. The liberal, pacifistic spirit of Remarque's book corresponded closely to the peaceful, conciliatory policies of the Weimar republic and became an overnight best-seller. The work also polarized the nation politically and emotionally. The nationalist Right was enraged over the novel's antiwar, antimilitary message and alarmed over its popularity. Some extremists like the Nazis staged riots which prevented the 1930 film version of the book from being shown. Others responded by producing a flood of prowar "ethnocentric" novels after 1928 which, by stressing the positive, reintegrating, and solidifying effect of the war on the national community, were intended as direct refutations of Remarque's book. Many of these works, which blatantly glorified the German war experience, were written less for artistic or personal reasons than as thinly veiled political statements which called for the kind of order, authority, and blind certainty which Germans had felt during the war. By idealizing those values and experiences which the Weimar democrats and pacifists condemned, and by contrasting the supposed heroism and fervid nationalism of the war years with the weak, cowardly policies of the new republic, most of this prowar literature of the late 1920s and early 1930s was really an attack on the liberal values and institutions of the Weimar republic. In this way, during the latter years of the Weimar era "the experience of the war was politicized and made the basis for a powerful anti-Republican ideology. Disillusionment with the Republic led to an idealization of the period immediately preceding it, and the experience of the trenches was seen in retrospect as embodying those virtues of the ideal future state that were lacking in the present one."[108]

The neoconservative publishers were personally responsible for generating some of the most influential works of this post-1928 flood of war novels. For example, when Remarque's book appeared, Heinrich Stalling of the GSV suggested to the young author Werner Beumelburg that he write a popular account of the war experience from a nationalist viewpoint.[109] The result, *Barrage Around Germany* (*Sperrfeuer um Deutschland*, 1929), sold one hundred twenty thousand copies its first year on the market and a total of one hundred sixty-six thousand by 1933. Beumelburg soon followed this work with *The Tempering Years* (*Die stählenden Jahre*, 1929), and with *Group Bosemüller* (*Gruppe Bosemüller*, 1930), a novel which idealized the comradeship of war and of the larger *Volk* during the war years; this latter sold ninety thousand copies by 1935. As one scholar of the Weimar era noted, it was from these GSV books by Beumelburg "that a whole generation of young and not so young Germans got its inspiration and ideals."[110]

Lehmann, too, was deeply disturbed by the success of *All Quiet on the Western Front* and took immediate action to counter it. The publisher, who had lost his own son Arnold in the war, warned his readers that the ideas of pacifism, goodwill, the League of Nations, and pan-Europeanism which Remarque's book conveyed were dangerous illusions, for a people which refused to go to war for its interests would soon perish. In contrast to the Ullstein house, which published pacifistic books like Remarque's, Lehmann proclaimed that his firm was dedicated to the urgent task of "awakening and preserving Germany's will to defend itself. . . . Our books affirm war as a life necessity for the *Volk*. . . . [Our books] affirm the spirit of manliness, of hardness toward one's self, and the spirit of sacrifice and comradeship which war brings."[111] To demonstrate his commitment to these values, Lehmann soon published *We of the Infantry* (*Wir von der Infanterie*, 1929), a book hastily composed by his nephew Friedrich Lehmann, who helped manage the JFLV. This volume, which was intended as a direct refutation of Remarque,[112] was written because the author felt it his "duty" to inform German youth of the joys of war: "Our youth must know that there is something far greater than merely 'escaping the grenades of war,' something greater than one's own life and one's own meager personal insights. [The youth of our day] should imitate the front-line soldiers; our youth should, in fact, surpass them and do it all even better."[113] The Lehmann volume, which the author frankly admitted was to "help prepare for the time when we shall fight again,"[114] sold some ninety thousand copies the first year alone. It was soon joined in the JFLV catalog by other prowar works such as H. Stellrecht's *Despite All! A Book of the Front* (*Trotz Allem! Ein Buch der Front*, 1931), another attempt to refute Remarque. Only he has truly experienced war, Stellrecht argued, "who can see above all the [war's] personal suffering the greater struggle of his *Volk*, the fight for living space, for light, for the land of his children, for the ethnic heritage, for the eternal idea of his *Volk* . . . to which the heart can better respond than the mind."[115]

In the waning years of the republic, the Hanseatic and Diederichs houses also produced a number of best-selling volumes on the glories of warfare. HVA titles such as Witkop's *War Letters of Fallen Students* (*Kriegsbriefe gefallener Studenten*, 1929), or Euringer's *Flying School 4* (*Fliegerschule 4*, 1929) sold, respectively, seventy thousand and fifteen thousand copies by 1933, while the DHB offering *Seven Before Verdun* (*Sieben vor Verdun*, 1932) by J. Wehner was able to market one hundred thirty thousand copies by 1940. One subgenre of antiliberal war literature especially cultivated by the EDV and the DHB was the so-called return (*Heimkehr*) novel. These stories portrayed the bitter disappointment experienced by idealistic young soldiers who returned from the front to find a postwar Germany still wracked by decadence, materialism, and disunity. Like most other prowar books of these years, the *Heimkehr* novels, too, were often intended as thinly veiled protests against the liberal Weimar state and as ringing calls for a neoconservative national revolution. Thus the DHB advertised H. Stegwert's *The Young Man in the Fiery Furnace* (*Der Jüngling im Feuerofen: Ein Heimkehr Roman*, 1932) as "a novel about a returning soldier who undergoes peril under fire, who remains loyal during the collapse of the Fatherland, and who bravely helps to rejuvenate his homeland."[116] The Diederichs house contributed a trilogy of books in this category: E. E. Dwinger's *The Army Behind Barbed Wire* (*Die Armee hinter Stacheldraht*, 1929), *Between White and Red* (*Zwischen Weiss und Rot*, 1930), and *We Call Germany* (*Wir rufen Deutschland: Heimkehr und Vermächtnis*, 1932). Of this triology, one literary critic has said:

> No other work dealing with the experience of soldiers has focused more clearly—from a nationalist and ethnocentric viewpoint—upon the War of 1914–1918 as the crisis in the history of Western civilization. In this war, according to [Dwinger's] view, the foundations of a modern, degenerated society were tried, judged, and condemned by the peoples, and a new meaning of existence had to arise: the ethnic community, an ideal not to be found in the collectivism of the masses, but in the national and social war experiences of the people.[117]

By vindicating the military for the loss of the war and by idealizing the war experience after 1918, the publishers preserved and heightened the militaristic sentiments of many Germans. Nostalgically contrasting the war's euphoric atmosphere of national rebirth, *völkisch* solidarity, and antiliberal jihad with the disunity, despair, and defeatist foreign policies of the liberal Weimar republic, the widely read books of the neoconservative firms encouraged the nation to reject the democratic postwar order and recapture the martial spirit of the war, if not actually relive the war experience itself.

Six

A Bitter Harvest: The Political Consequences of World War I

Revolution

The Second Reich, weakened and discredited by World War I, was finally swept away by revolution in November 1918. Neoconservative publishers greeted the passing of the imperial order with relief rather than with regret, for they believed the revolution—like the outbreak of war four years earlier—threw everything into flux and presented a new opportunity to radically transform German life. Speaking for the authors and readers of *Die Tat*, Eugen Diederichs declared in December 1918: "All of us who felt like outsiders [in the Second Reich] feel compelled to shout a joyful 'Yea' to the revolution, for we feel that true German *Geist* was stifled by the narrow, bureaucratic perspectives of the old regime."[1] In the early days of the revolution, the Jena publisher remained confident that out of the political and military collapse of the German state, a spiritually rejuvenated and more united *Volk* would arise and would channel its energies in new, more productive directions than it had before the war. A new day was dawning, he believed, and a glorious "organic," forward-looking, creative, and idealistic Third Reich was drawing near to replace the defunct, mechanistic, backward-looking, calculating, materialistic Second.[2] J. F. Lehmann, too, was initially hopeful that the demise of the old imperial state and the misery of defeat might fuse a newer, more intense German national consciousness and open up for the *Volk* exciting new avenues of development which had been blocked in the old Reich.[3]

To insure that this revolutionary opportunity was not again squandered, both Diederichs and Lehmann immediately set about soliciting plans for reform, laying out neoconservative goals for the revolution, and educating the public through their journals and house publications. "The seriousness of the hour requires action," Diederichs told his readers in November; "I consider it the duty of *Die Tat* to expedite a powerful breakthrough of a new German spirit within our *Volk*."[4] Lehmann quickly wrote several essays and proclamations, held lectures, and distributed thousands of brochures during the early days of the revolution. He felt it "a pure joy to be a publisher during such times, for in few other callings can one have such an effect."[5]

When it soon became apparent that the revolution was taking quite a different direction than they had envisioned and was not destined to ring in the neoconservative millennium, the publishers' elation gave way to pessimism, despair, and bitterness, much as it had during the war. Within days of the Kaiser's abdication on 9 November, Diederichs was warning that the wrong forces were assuming control of the revolution: the spontaneous soldiers' and workers' councils which held power during the winter months of 1918–19 appeared to Diederichs as "elements of disorder which clearly demonstrate that the crowd by itself cannot rule; . . . the councils are atomistic manifestations of disintegration."[6] Nor were the left-wing journalists and bohemian intellectuals who emerged as revolutionary spokesmen any more capable in Diederichs's mind of bringing about national regeneration, for these "theoretical fanatics" advocated all manner of reckless experiments which would bring certain disaster: "What else can one expect from Berlin except the babble of literati?" he complained; "the new spirit which must emerge now stands in danger of perishing through incompetence, vulgarity, and perhaps through Judaism and the nonsense of the theoreticians."[7] He bitterly berated the middle class for standing passively by while the proletarian masses and the literati seized control of events. The spineless German burgher, he concluded, was too politically immature, too apathetic, and too concerned with protecting his property to play a formidable role in the momentous struggle being waged over the nation's future.[8]

The communist uprisings, mass strikes, and street terror which erupted after January 1919 only heightened Diederichs's fear that the uprooted masses were gaining control of Germany. He attributed the nation's revolutionary chaos to the basic forces of the liberal age: "Through our modern industry," he lamented,

> we have unfortunately reached the point in Germany where we
> have ten million rootless proletarians who now terrorize the majority
> of the populace. They have no sense of *Gemeinschaft*, no feeling for
> the whole, but only for one-sided class warfare. As a means of liber-
> ating themselves . . . they demand equality, but mean by it only
> a general proletarianization; they demand freedom, but mean
> the destruction of all those barriers which protect the rights of

individuality. . . . [One] cannot protest loudly enough against the proletariat's presumption that the rootless are called to lead those [of us] who still have roots.[9]

As mass violence and sporadic civil war spread during the winter and spring of 1919, the Jena publisher became increasingly pessimistic. He saw "chaos, terror, plunder, and famine" radiating outward from revolutionary Berlin, and predicted the nation would soon be plagued by anarchism, nihilism, unemployment, class warfare, and invasion by the Asiatic Bolsheviks. Germany stood "on the brink of a catastrophe," Diederichs moaned, and "the future lies black before us"; "I have the feeling, he presaged, "that Germany will not find peace for another generation."[10]

As Diederichs's assessment of the revolution and of Germany's future blackened during the early months of 1919, he began exhibiting traces of the same kind of anti-Semitism which he had condemned during the war. In January and March, for example, he complained that one of the greatest dangers facing Germany was that of excessive intellectualism, a trait he believed was closely linked to the large metropolis and to the Jewish race, and he voiced the common complaint that the Jewish intellect was capable at best of transmitting, but not of creating new spiritual values. Revolutionary Germany, he mourned, seemed to be increasingly controlled by Jews; "I would hope," he confided to one of his authors, "that we can one day be finished with the Jewish spirit (*mit dem jüdischen Geist einmal fertig werden*)."[11]

While Diederichs confined his revulsion over the course of the revolution to journalistic outbursts, J. F. Lehmann chose more concrete counterrevolutionary action. Traditional Bavarian particularism and conservative Bavarian hostility toward the new Socialist-dominated national regime combined to make the publisher's native Munich a center of radical, antirepublican activities throughout the postwar era.[12] Lehmann, who blamed not only Germany's defeat, but all the postwar revolutionary turmoil on "Jewish elements,"[13] became a central figure in the maze of underground counterrevolutionary anti-Semitic organizations which sprang up in Munich in 1918–19. Because he feared that Jews and Socialists might gain power in Bavaria when the tottering Wittelsbach monarchy finally collapsed, on 24 October 1918 he called a joint meeting between the Munich chapter of the Pan-German League, of which he was chairman, and the recently founded, radically anti-Semitic Thule Society (Thule Gesellschaft), of which he was also a leading official.[14] Lehmann proposed to the two groups that they cooperate in a preemptive rightist coup to prevent a socialist takeover. He then organized an ad hoc "Committee of National Defense" to solicit money and support for the putsch from other radical right-wing organizations.[15] Before the Committee could act, however, the Bavarian Socialists under their (Jewish) leader Kurt Eisner seized power on 7 November. In hopes of overthrowing the new Jewish-socialist regime, Lehmann on 10 November persuaded the Thule Society to create a clandestine counterrevolutionary paramilitary organization, the Fighting League Thule (Kampfbund Thule). This group, composed of representatives from virtually every nationalist organization in Munich, including the local chapter of the DHV, became a crystallization point for the entire Bavarian *völkisch* movement and was soon the province's most important center of counterrevolutionary resistance.[16] Working with the *Bund Oberland* (a paramilitary league of war veterans in which Lehmann's son-in-law Friedrich Weber was active), the Fighting League secretly procured arms from the Army Command and stored them on the premises of Lehmann's publishing house in preparation for a coup against Eisner's government.[17] The plot was discovered late in December, however, and Lehmann and other Thule leaders were briefly imprisoned. Upon his release in February, the publisher helped found and direct another counterrevolutionary, militantly anti-Semitic organization, the German-*Völkisch* Defense and Offense League (Deutsch-völkischer Schutz- und Trutzbund).[18] The League's statement of principles, which Lehmann helped draft, read: "We must overcome the international forces of homeless people [i.e., Judaism]. . . . Our name tells all: Defense of everything German, genuine, and indigenous; . . . offensive attack on everything which is un-German, on all the destructive and demoralizing demons which try to pull down nationalistic life. . . . We reject domination by any foreign, non-German minority. . . . Germans can be aided only by Germans."[19] This League, which confined itself primarily to propaganda rather than underground conspiracy, became one of the most extreme and most powerful right-wing organizations of the immediate postwar years. Lehmann remained active in it until it was banned by the Weimar republic in 1922 and went underground.

When an associate of the Thule Society succeeded in assassinating Eisner on 21 February 1919, Lehmann and other Thule leaders were again arrested. Eisner's death allowed communists to gain power in Bavaria and to establish a soviet republic, which in turn unleashed a bloody civil war between Left and Right. Amidst the confusion Lehmann managed to escape to neighboring Württemberg, shortly before his less fortunate prisonmates were executed; there he and his son-in-law joined the Epp Free Corps, a volunteer group of armed veterans dedicated to crushing the Bavarian soviet republic. He assisted the corps as it fought its way into Bavaria, and was an active combatant during the brutal conquest of Munich from 30 April to 2 May, and in the "White terror" which followed.[20]

The neoconservative publishers' animosity toward the outcome of the November revolution was reflected in their postwar publications. After 1919, attacking the revolution and its leading participants became a standard means also of denouncing its child, the democratic Weimar republic. Through such titles as H. von Liebig's *The Swindle of the German Volk* (*Der Betrug am deutschen Volke*, 1919); K. von Müller's *The Hoodwinked German Volk* (*Das betörte deutsche Volk: Mahnworte für die Wahlen zur Nationalversammlung*, 1919); *For 9 November, the National Day of Mourning and Repentance for the German Volk* (*Zum 9. November, dem nationales Trauer- und Busstag des deutschen Volkes*, 1928); or *Peace, Freedom, Bread? How Low We Have Sunk!* (*Friede, Freiheit, Brot? Wie Tief sind wir gesunken!*, 1926), the Lehmann and Beenken houses portrayed the revolution as high treason to the nation and sought to arouse public opinion against the new republican order. Even books on revolution in the abstract became antirepublican tools in the hands of the publishers. At the height of the revolutionary turmoil in 1919, for example, Lehmann decided to publish Freytag-Loringhoven's history of the Russian Revolution in order to make the public aware of the dangers of a leftist revolution and to induce Germans to turn theirs into a right-wing, *völkisch* revolution.[21] In 1928 he issued P. Sorokin's *Sociology of Revolution* (*Soziologie der Revolution*) because, as he told his readers, this book demonstrated "how terrible the changes are which a revolution calls forth in a people: an unbounded degeneracy and brutalization of morality; . . . an uprooting and downfall of exactly those social groups which have always been the bearers of culture; an upswarm of the masses, who have hitherto been hostile toward and destructive of culture. [Revolution] brings the rule of the subhumans."[22]

An Unwelcome Peace

It was not only the liberal domestic results of the revolution which embittered neoconservatives. Because they believed it had weakened the nation internally and had produced a fainthearted democratic regime unwilling to resist the demands of the Western Allies, neoconservatives also blamed the revolution for the harsh terms of the Versailles peace settlement imposed on Germany in 1919. Although many Germans during the early days of the armistice entertained unrealistic hopes that the Allies would agree to a moderate peace settlement, more astute observers like Diederichs suspected that any kind of just peace for Germany was a "phantom" and that the nation would be "raped and desecrated" by the Anglo-Saxons who hoped to destroy the competitive threat of the German economy.[23] Believing that the new republican order would not withstand Allied terms, in January 1919 Diederichs called upon the Germans to organize a "moral resistance" against their coming "enslavement" by the victorious Allies.[24] When the new republic signed the humiliating Versailles treaty on 28 June 1919 as expected, thereby committing the nation to fulfillment of its harsh terms, the entire nationalist Right erupted in outrage. Throughout the Weimar era, the vitriolic campaign by the Right against the treaty became at the same time an attack upon the Weimar republic which had signed it. The calls for "liberation" from the treaty's provisions or for a foreign policy of "resistance"[25] came increasingly to be understood as a summons to resist or even overthrow Germany's new democratic order as well.

The neoconservative publishing houses sought to arouse public wrath against the treaty by emphasizing how unjust, humiliating, and disastrous its terms were for Germany. As soon as the settlement was signed, Heinrich Beenken issued *The Treaty of Versailles: The Root Cause of Germany's Distress* (*Der Vertrag von Versailles: Die Grundursache der deutschen Not*, 1919), an inexpensive "people's edition" of the treaty. Article 231, the famous "war guilt clause" which attributed total responsibility for the war to Germany, was printed in red ink. By 1932, 4.5 million copies of this publication had been printed and distributed by the Beenken house. The publisher wanted every German to own a copy of the "infamous document" so that "shame will continually burn in every [German] heart and will give rise to the longing: Liberation from Versailles!"[26] Besides inducing H. von Zobelitz to write *What the Enemy Has Done to Us: A Book on the Plunder-Peace* (*Und was der Feind uns angetan! Das Buch von Raubfrieden*, 1921) for his firm, Beenken himself composed two works, *What We Have Lost* (*Was wir verloren haben: Entrissenes, doch nie vergessenes deutsches Land*, 1920) and *Land in Chains* (*Land in Ketten: geraubtes deutsches Land*, 1932) to keep alive the bitter memory of the territories Germany had lost through the treaty, and to arouse the nation's desire to recover that land. In these volumes (the former of which sold one hundred thousand copies), Beenken claimed that by robbing Germany of its land and resources, the dictated treaty had condemned the German *Volk* to misery and hunger. The Versailles settlement was, therefore, an international crime against humanity. "It is absolutely necessary," the publisher told his public,

> that every German—man, woman, and child—get to know this
> shame. Only with a full realization of this outrage and injustice
> which has been perpetrated upon us can we hope to awaken
> the desire for its abolition. Think of it always, talk about it always.
> . . . The purpose of this book is to sharpen German *Volk* conscious-
> ness of the native lands and old German culture which the Versailles

treaty has robbed from us, to show our brothers and sisters in these stolen lands that we have not and cannot forget them. . . . [This book is] to assist the *Volk* in finally asserting its will to make German again that which used to be German.[27]

The Hanseatic, J. F. Lehmann, and Gerhard Stalling houses all supplemented Beenken's efforts by issuing such inflammatory titles as: *The German Misfortune: Versailles* (*Das deutsche Unglück: Versailles*); L. Benninghoff's *Free From Our Chains* (*Vom Ketten frei*, 1921); W. Beumbelburg's *Germany in Chains* (*Deutschland im Ketten*, 1931); F. W. Oertzen's *Such is 'Disarmament'! The Mockery of the Disarmament Article of Versailles* (*Das ist die Abrüstung! Der Hohn der Abrüstungsartikel von Versailles*, 1931); and F. Grimm's *The Enemy Dictates* (*Der Feind diktiert*, 1932). Lehmann, who in 1919 believed he might himself be tried by the Allies as a "war criminal" under the provisions of the treaty,[28] issued a work by Ernst Zahn which sought "to make clear the true reason for the enemy's demand that war criminals be extradited: namely, to completely destroy us by rendering harmless our best people, who served the Fatherland loyally during the war."[29] Another JFLV offering, O. Fritsch's *Germany's Bondage and Liberation* (*Deutschlands Knechtschaft und Befreiung: Das Zeitalter der Befreiungskriege im Lichte der Gegenwart*, 1927), urged a new war of national liberation to free Germany, just as Germany had freed herself from Napoleonic bondage a century earlier.

Many of the works appearing in the neoconservative houses specifically attacked the burdensome reparations payments imposed on Germany by the Allies and called for national resistance against this "tribute slavery." When one of his authors had completed a manuscript on the reparations problem, Lehmann (who of course believed the treaty of Versailles was the work of international Judaism)[30] wrote to him: "I have just read your essay 'Reparations Slavery.' It is a uniquely excellent work. When reading it, one's bile simply boils over so that one must really exercise great self-control to keep from lashing out and smashing everything. I shall have it printed immediately. . . . I will apply my utmost energies to insure that this excellent work achieves the greatest possible distribution." The publisher then added: "You speak of international world capital. Will you permit me to substitute 'Jewish world capital' for 'international world capital'? That way, everyone knows what is at stake."[31]

Publicistic attempts by neoconservative publishers to stop reparations payments proved less effective than the postwar economic inflation, which in 1922–23 forced Germany to suspend its payments to France. When French troops occupied the Rhineland and Ruhr area in retaliation, the entire nation raised a campaign of active and passive resistance against the French. During these months and in subsequent years, the HVA and the other neoconservative publishing houses produced a steady stream of propaganda literature characterizing the French occupation as a policy of terror and injustice. Diederichs not only prompted authors to write articles about the Ruhr invasion which would show how Germany's "inherent" rights were being violated, but he also worked closely with big business to send nationalistic speakers into the area in hopes of arousing popular resistance to the French.[32] Lehmann—whose inflammatory journal *Deutschlands Erneuerung* was banned from the areas under French occupation—issued an anonymous manifesto, *Let Us Play Our Game on the Rhine! Documents on the History of the French Annexationist and Separatist Policies in the Rhineland* (*Spielen wir unserer Spiel am Rhein! Dokumente zur Geschichte der französischen Annexations- und Separationspolitik am Rhein*, 1922), which sought to arouse anti-French resistance by "exposing" French plans to annex the entire Rhine region. This work was so provocative that the usually bold publisher dared not issue it under his house's imprint; rather, he produced it under the fictitious label of the "Süddeutscher Verlag München-Passing." When no theater would perform W. Meyer-Erlach's *The German Sorrow* (*Das deutsches Leid*), an intensely anti-French drama about the Rhine occupation which the JFLV published in 1923, the publisher organized a theatrical company of his own to present the play in various Bavarian cities.[33] The radical Munich bookman supported violent action against the French occupiers as well: after two extreme German nationalists attempted to assassinate a pro-French Rhineland official in 1923, Lehmann hid the fugitives in his home for six weeks.[34] Even after the occupation ended—through what many radical nationalists regarded as capitulation to the French—the Hanseatic house sought to keep its bitter memory alive by issuing such works as F. Grimm's *France on the Rhine* (*Frankreich am Rhein*, 1931) or L. Schrickel's *Blood for Blood* (*Blut zum Blut: Ein Roman aus Deutschlands Notzeit*, 1927), a novel set during Louis XIV's seventeenth-century occupation of the Rhineland. This latter work was advertised as "an uncommonly exciting picture of terrible German peril; it is at the same time a grim but true mirror of our own times."[35] From the HVA also came two highly idealized studies of the "martyr" Albert Leo Schlageter, an extreme nationalist with Nazi connections who was executed by the French in 1923 for his resistance to the occupation. With the help of these two best-selling works—R. Brandt's *Albert Leo Schlageter: Life and Death of a German Hero* (*Albert Leo Schlageter: Leben und Sterben eines Deutschen Helden*, 1926), which sold twenty-five thousand copies in four years, and H. Johst's *Schlageter* (1933), which reached its thirtieth printing after one year—the Nazis succeeded in making Schlageter into a popular national hero who represented resistance not only to the Versailles settlement, but to the capitulatory policies of the Weimar republic as well.

After the French occupation inflamed the reparations problem and the German government persistently demanded a revision of Germany's payment schedule, the Allies eventually drew up the so-called Young Plan in 1929 to formalize Germany's reparations obligations. When Lehmann learned the terms of the Young Plan, he helped organize the "Reich Commission for the Popular Will" (Reichsausschuss für ein Volksbegehren), a right-wing coalition of conservative Nationalists and Nazis which mounted a national plebiscite campaign against the reparations plan. He called the founding of the plebiscite commission "the greatest day of my life; one felt that one was present at the hour of birth of a new era."[36] Although the campaign was ultimately unsuccessful at the polls, it indeed proved significant in other ways: for it first gained the Nazis entrance to the national political arena and access to important political contributors.

Five Against the Republic

It was not merely the Weimar republic's acquiescent acceptance of the Versailles treaty which the neoconservative publishers found intolerable, but the very existence of the republic itself. To their minds, this new democratic state was an alien, un-German political system imposed upon the nation by foreign-inspired revolutionaries and the victorious Western Allies. Because it symbolized the ultimate political triumph of Western liberalism in Germany, the postwar republican order became a convenient focal point for all neoconservative antiliberal hatred. Radicalized and politicized by the war, the revolution, and the peace settlement, neoconservatives became convinced that overturning the new liberal political system was the necessary first step of that larger conservative revolution which would rid the nation of liberal influences in cultural, social, and economic life and usher in that long-overdue rejuvenation of the nation. During the postwar era, therefore, the neoconservative publishers waged a relentless campaign against the institutions, leading personalities, and policies of the Weimar republic.

Attacks on the Weimar constitution were one means by which the publishers sought to discredit the new state. The Lehmann house issued what it called "the first description of the republican constitution from a *völkisch* standpoint," Freytag-Loringhoven's *The Weimar Constitution in Theory and Practice (Die Weimarer Verfassung in Lehre und Wirklichkeit*, 1924). According to the firm, this work "is a description in which the empty talk [of the constitution] is pitilessly contrasted with the reality. It shows that a totally different kind of 'justice' exists than that which the Weimar constitution describes."[37] In a similar vein, the Hanseatic house advertised Stapel's *The Fictions of the Weimar Constitution* (*Die Fiktionen der Weimarer Verfassung*, 1928) as an analysis which "confronts liberal political theory with the theory of a *Volk*-conservative state. . . . [Stapel] unmasks the fundamental ideas of the liberal Weimar constitution as being empty juristic fictions."[38]

The republic's parliamentary system and leaders were also condemned by the neoconservative bookmen. The HVA published two works by the rightist Reichstag delegate Walter Lambach, *Something On the Reichstag* (*Etwas vom Reichstag der Republik*, 1922) and *The Rule of the 500* (*Die Herrschaft der Fünfhundert: Ein Bild des parlamentarischen Lebens im neuen Deutschland*, 1926) exposing and denigrating parliamentary life in the new state, and the house did not shrink from advertising other offerings as works which openly called for "the overturn of parliamentary democracy."[39] The Gerhard Stalling firm added its voice by issuing F. Meier's *The Democratic Idea and the Power of the State* (*Der demokratische Gedanke und der Machtcharakter des Staates*, 1926), which argued that parliamentary democracy weakened the state. Throughout the 1920s, Eugen Diederichs also raised a litany of charges against parliamentarism. The republic's first Constituent Assembly, he charged, was a "nil-assembly" (*Nullversammlung*) and elections and party squabbling exacerbated national divisions. Political party life was dominated by capitalistic interest groups, with the Reichstag serving as another stock exchange where private rather than the nation's public business was conducted. The clique of mediocre political hacks, party bosses, and pedantic bureaucrats who rose to the top governmental posts under parliamentarism were incapable of understanding, much less of solving Germany's pressing spiritual problems. The system's excessive emphasis on rational laws and rigid administrative procedures stifled imagination and ignored the vitalistic rhythm of life on which all true justice was founded. In short, Diederichs regarded parliamentarism as an unstable, materialistic, and mechanistic system which was killing the German spirit.[40] By 1922 the publisher was convinced that "because of parliamentarism, the German state has become the destroyer of all the creative forces of the German essence. . . . I personally wouldn't shed the slightest tear over parliamentarism if it were to be brought to its much-deserved end."[41]

Leading Weimar parliamentarians such as Matthias Erzberger and Walter Rathenau were also favorite objects for neoconservative wrath. The HVA, JFLV, and HBV, for example, issued such libelous attacks on these men as W. Lambach's *Dictator Rathenau* (1919), H. von Liebig's *Erzberger as Statesman and Puppet* (*Erzberger als Staatsmann und Werkzeug*, 1919), and

M. von Taube's *Erzberger: the Gravedigger of the German Reich* (*Erzberger: Totengräber des deutschen Reiches*, 1919). Such polemics contributed to the atmosphere of hatred which culminated in the assassination of these two leaders in 1921–22.

A coalition of three parties shared power throughout most of the republic's existence: the Social Democrats, the Catholic Center party, and the Democratic party (Deutsche Demokratische Partei). This "Weimar coalition" controlled both the national government and the strong republican bastion of Prussia. Lehmann regarded the Weimar coalition as a gang of "racketeers" who, in league with international Jewish finance and world Masonry, were bent on destroying the nation's morals, German Protestantism, and nationalist sentiment.[42] The publisher used a number of indirect means to vilify the coalition, and through it, the republic. For example, he sought out an author to write an attack on Ludwig Kaas, leader of the Center party, whom Lehmann regarded as "one of our worst evils" because his cultural and school policies were inculcating the younger generation with a "black-red" (i.e., Catholic-Marxist) viewpoint.[43] On another occasion, the Munich bookman launched a sensational attack on the administration of justice under the Weimar coalition in Prussia. Although the courts of the Weimar republic were surprisingly lenient toward the nationalist Right and excessively harsh toward offenses by the Left,[44] some extremists like Lehmann objected vehemently to the "unfairness" of the 1922 Law for the Protection of the Republic, which facilitated prosecution of certain antirepublican activities. When, under this law, the JFLV's inflammatory *Deutschlands Erneuerung* was briefly suppressed or banned in certain regions such as the Prussian Rhineland, Lehmann felt he was being harassed and developed a deep hatred for one particular official in the Prussian Ministry of Justice.[45] Blending personal and professional resentments with his animosity toward the Weimar coalition, Lehmann developed the plan for a book which, by exposing the supposed politicization of justice in Prussia, would force the government of this republican stronghold to resign. Could he but "liberate Prussia from this regime," even if it meant personal imprisonment, Lehmann felt he would have "served [his] Fatherland in no small way. . . . If God would only grant that I could topple the Red Prussian government," he said, "I would gladly make my exit."[46]

The publisher found a willing author for this project in M. E. Moritz, a hack journalist who was familiar with the Prussian judicial administration and had personal grievances of his own against it. Using the pseudonym "Gottfried Zarnow," he began work on the book for the JFLV in 1930. Lehmann informed Zarnow he wanted a work which would demonstrate how the republican government of Prussia had bent or broken the laws,

166 · ENTREPRENEURS OF IDEOLOGY

dragged sacred values through the mud, and turned the entire judicial process into a "prostitute of politics." The book should not only expose existing conditions, the publisher explained, "but also show exactly where the rotting abscess is, how to prick it open and cauterize it, and how things must be changed if we hope to reestablish justice."[47] Lehmann continually prodded his author to expand the work from an account of specific judicial cases into a sweeping indictment of the entire system. At one point the exasperated author retorted: "You set . . . ever higher and broader tasks for the planned book; . . . our working agreement constantly suffers because you always dream up a high goal, but never know much about the means which will lead us to that goal."[48]

Zarnow's completed draft for the first volume of the projected two-volume work still did not meet the publisher's satisfaction. Lehmann wrote to his author that:

> We must make sure the style is so simple and direct that the man
> in the street will be gripped by the brutality of the facts and
> say: "These incredible conditions, which violate law and justice,
> . . . must cease." When I write for the *Volk*, I always represent the
> situation in such a way that everything immediately becomes obvious
> and convincing. One must not ask, the way you do: "Has a common
> murder been committed here?" Rather, I would say quite clearly:
> "A common murder has been committed!" Or again, I wouldn't say:
> "Has Herr Severing [Social-Democratic Prussian Minister of
> Interior] thwarted the investigation?" I'd say rather: "The judicial
> investigation has been thwarted by Minister Severing.". . . In this
> vein I have made a few alterations [in your manuscript], and
> I hope you will feel that I, as your squire, have acted correctly. I have
> used these kinds of tactics for over forty years, and they have always
> served me well.[49]

After boasting about the success of other JFLV books which he personally rewrote, Lehmann requested that in the second volume of his work, Zarnow dwell more on the fact that such a high percentage of Prussian judges were Jewish.

Lehmann knew publication of this vituperative exposé would provoke a rash of libel suits and perhaps even government confiscation. Before releasing the book, therefore, the publisher consulted closely with his lawyer and laid careful plans to insure a large number of copies would be distributed before the police could sequester the remaining stock.[50] When volume one of Zarnow's *Fettered Justice* (*Gefesselte Justiz: Politische Bilder aus deutschen Gegenwart*) finally appeared in December 1930, the JFLV announced it as "a book which every German is simply duty-bound to read.

[From it] the reader will draw the logical conclusions and will not rest until the situation in Germany is changed from top to bottom, until the guilty, regardless of their high titles and offices, are brought to their just punishment."[51] Lehmann sent the first copy to President Hindenburg and distributed complimentary copies to the leaders of all important nationalistic leagues, parties, and unions. He also wrote to more than a thousand newspapers, asking them to publicize the work.[52]

As expected, Zarnow's polemic provoked a spate of lawsuits against both its author and its publisher, who under German law could be held responsible for the content of any of his house's publications. During 1931, Lehmann incurred nearly eight thousand marks in court costs; he anticipated the total legal costs to run as high as twenty-five thousand marks for volume one alone, and foresaw equal or greater legal expenses when volume two was published.[53] Yet this did not deter the publisher. He not only proceeded with the second volume of Fettered Justice (which appeared in 1932), but also paid several thousand marks to Zarnow to assist him with his legal costs. "For me," Lehmann declared, "it is not a matter of making money, but rather of defying all the authorities in order to distribute to the German Volk as many copies as possible of this mighty indictment."[54]

Using deceptive printing techniques to circumvent the censorship and libel decisions levied against the work, Lehmann managed to sell 53,400 copies of volume one by the end of 1931; volume two, expected to do equally well, enjoyed an unusually large first printing of 18,000 copies in 1932.[55] One of the largest markets for the book was the Nazi party. Not only were excerpts from Zarnow's book serialized in the party newspaper, but Hitler—who reportedly read the book himself—ordered 10,000 copies of volume one and 8,000 copies of volume two so that each local Nazi cell might have one.[56] This wide dissemination of Fettered Justice may have helped harden public opinion against the Socialist government of Prussia. For when Chancellor von Papen, acting on very dubious constitutional authority, deposed the Prussian government on 20 July 1932 and placed this last republican stronghold directly under his new semidictatorial national regime on the grounds that the old Prussian government was not capable of preserving law and order, the daring coup raised little more than a ripple of public protest.

Few things did more to undermine public confidence in the Weimar republic than the dire economic conditions of the postwar years. Many middle-class Germans, whose support was crucial to the republic, blamed the rampant inflation of the 1920s and the economic collapse and massive unemployment of the early 1930s on the nation's weak, ineffectual new republican order and on the burdensome reparations payments to which it had committed itself. Some, like Diederichs, believed the economic naïveté of the republic's leaders was pushing Germany into "a purgatory of poverty, unemployment, hunger, unrest, and inner collapse."[57] Others, like Lehmann, charged that the left-wing republic was intentionally ruining the nation's economy in order to socialize and proletarianize it: "We must show the government," he thundered, "that we will no longer tolerate such abominable economic conditions."[58]

Precisely because the new state was so vulnerable in this area, the neoconservative publishers issued a number of works like P. Bang's *State Bankruptcy or Renewal* (*Staatsbankrott oder Erneuerung*, 1920), R. Huch's *1922: A Novel From the Inflation* (*Anno 1922: Ein Roman aus der Inflationszeit*, 1930), and Engel & Eisenberg's *Millions Accuse: Marxist Mismanagement of Social Insurance* (*Millionen Klagen an: Marxistische Misswirtschaft in der Sozialversicherung*, 1932) to publicize Germany's economic plight under the Weimar system. The HVA-owned Georg Müller Verlag even announced a prize of twenty thousand marks in 1931 for the best manuscript on the German economic situation which could refute the work of a pro-Weimar liberal.[59] The alarming rise of unemployment after 1930, especially, called forth several mawkish works such as R. Euringer's *The Unemployed* (*Die Arbeitslosen*), published by the HVA in 1930, which sought to arouse public indignation over the sufferings of the unemployed. The civil servant and part-time author B. N. Haken specialized in books of this type, which he published with the Diederichs, Hanseatic, and Stalling houses. The HVA, for example, portrayed his *Rubber-Stamp Chronicle* (*Stempelchronik: 261 Arbeitslosenschicksale*, 1932) as a "ruthless representation" and "alarmingly frank and terrifyingly vivid illumination of the psychic and material plight of Germany's 7 million unemployed"; according to the HVA, this work would "shake up every last German and make them fully conscious of the extent and danger of the unemployment problem."[60] After Diederichs published Haken's *The Case of Bundhund* (*Der Fall Bundhund*, 1930), a thinly fictionalized exposé of municipal unemployment policy, the author was dismissed from his bureaucratic post in Hamburg. His publisher immediately rallied to his defense, however, and wrote to all the EDV authors informing them of Haken's case. "Political forces are at work here," the publisher said, "which are trying to suppress the book and make life impossible for a writer who accurately portrays the social plight [of the unemployed] and who seeks justice for them." Diederichs asked his house's authors to help make the public aware of the government's harassment of Haken and to do everything in their power personally to assist the author.[61]

Through their books on the economic situation and through other anti-republican titles such as von Müffling's *Ten Years of Republic* (*Zehn Jahre*

Republik, 1924), P. Bang's *An Interim Statement on German Politics* (*Ein Zwischenbilanz deutscher Politik*, 1927), and L. Dingräve's *Where is Germany Headed?* (*Wohin treibt Deutschland?*, 1932), the publishers hoped to convince Germans that the Weimar regime had inflicted misery and foreign bondage upon the nation. To encourage their countrymen to throw off the republican order which oppressed them, the neoconservative houses sought inspiration from the German past. Thus an HVA advertisement for Stapel's *German Freedom Songs* (*Deutsche Freiheitslieder*, 1922), an anthology of defiant old patriotic ballads, declared: "For us today the question is posed: Is the moral tone of these freedom songs correct? That is, is freedom a *Volk*'s highest good? May the happiness and life of individuals be sacrificed for the freedom of the *Volk*? May one lead a war to achieve freedom? May one kill for his *Volk*? Should a *Volk*, for the sake of its freedom, demand solidarity and tolerate no traitors? The old German poets of freedom, the angry as well as the moderate, answer with one loud YES. One is not only permitted [to do all this]—one should and must do it."[62] The Heinrich Beenken house produced an *Images of German Misery* (*Spiegelbilder deutscher Not*, 1919–25) series portraying previous periods of national distress and crisis. This series, the house stressed, was not merely a group of historical novels, but was intended to show the *Volk* "where German disunity has brought us in the past and to demonstrate that only unity and strict leadership can lift us out of our misery." By examining the heroic protagonists who rescued the nation from its earlier tribulations, the novels of this series (according to the HBV) would assure Germans that strong leaders will again arise to lead the *Volk* out of its present perils of revolution and Socialist rule.[63] And a JFLV publication, Kaibel's *The Sands and the Kotzebues* (*Die Sands und die Kotzebues*, 1919), made reference to an 1819 assassination in which the patriotic student Karl Sand murdered the "traitor" Kotzebue in order to free Germany from an oppressive regime; new Sands must arise, the book implied, to deal with the new Kotzebues of the Weimar republic.

While some neoconservative publishers merely hinted at violent insurrectionary action against Germany's republican order, Lehmann openly sanctioned it. For the Munich publisher believed that "those in power yield only to force; that means: oppose force with force."[64] Thus he was not only active in counterrevolutionary organizations during 1918–19, but throughout the 1920s he provided secret financial support to such antirepublican paramilitary groups as the *Bund Oberland*, of which his son-in-law Friedrich Weber was leader.[65] When he learned of Kapp's attempted putsch against the republic in 1920, Lehmann "rejoiced from the bottom of [his] heart"; after the coup failed, he hid one participant in his house until a general amnesty was granted.[66]

Lehmann was also peripherally involved in Hitler's ill-fated "beer hall putsch" of 1923. By that year, a semidictatorial emergency regime under Gustav von Kahr had gained control of the Bavarian state government. From his base there, Kahr hoped to initiate a nationalist uprising which would topple the Weimar republic and establish a right-wing dictatorship over the entire nation. Lehmann not only supported Kahr's undertaking but also took an active role in preparing for it. He sought to organize military supplies for the planned "march on Berlin" and, because of his connections with all the right-wing extremist groups in Bavaria, tried during October and early November to convince the leaders of these groups, including Hitler, to unite behind Kahr's uprising.[67] Lehmann was present at the Bürgerbräu beer hall on the night of 8 November when, in hopes of preempting leadership of the nationalist uprising from Kahr, Hitler's Nazi party and the *Bund Oberland* staged a surprise putsch of their own. The six members of Kahr's government taken hostage by the Nazis during the putsch were transferred to Lehmann's country house in Grosselohe, where they were guarded by a thirty-man contingent of stormtroopers under Rudolf Hess. When Hitler's coup collapsed the next day, Lehmann persuaded the Nazi guards to flee rather than to execute the hostages as they had been ordered.[68] (Perhaps because of his role in saving the hostage's lives, no legal action was taken against the publisher after the attempted putsch was crushed.)

Although Lehmann did not personally believe Hitler and his movement were ready to assume leadership of the nation, the publisher would have liked to have seen Hitler gain control of Bavaria, "to see how well he did running [the province] before attempting larger things." Even though the putsch failed, the publisher reflected that "because of Hitler's act, we have made a great leap forward, and I have written to him in prison that he must by no means consider his activities and his usefulness at an end. I told him he has achieved about 25 percent of his goal; now the rest depends on his enlightening the broader public [about his goals]."[69] When the putschists were brought to trial in 1924, Lehmann undertook an energetic campaign on their behalf. To arouse national sympathy for their cause, he devoted the entire April 1924 issue of *Deutschlands Erneuerung* to the putsch and invited Hitler and Ludendorff to write ringing justifications of their actions. Some of these articles, such as Hitler's *Why a 9 November Had to Come* (*Warum ein 9. November kommen musste*, 1924) were reprinted as pamphlets and distributed on a mass scale.

During the late 1920s, Lehmann also became involved with what was perhaps the most violent of all underground antirepublican movements, the notorious *Feme*. The *Feme* were vigilante proceedings in which fanatic nationalists and paramilitary groups administered "*völkisch* justice"—that is, assassination—on civilians and republican officials who were considered traitors to the German cause. Hundreds of these brutal political murders, including assassinations of Foreign Minister Walter Rathenau and former Finance Minister Matthias Erzberger, were perpetrated throughout the 1920s.[70] Lehmann took a special interest in the case of a Lieutenant Paul Schultz who was imprisoned in 1928 for a *Feme* murder. Although unable to persuade Schultz to write his memoirs for publication with the JFLV, the publisher decided to take charge of Schultz's legal defense, and to "conduct a glorious campaign of public enlightenment" on his behalf. "We must be in a position," Lehmann felt, "to counter the clever and insidious attempts being made by the government to incite the masses [against Schultz]. We must somehow bring about a swing of public opinion . . . [so that] a German who dares fight for his Fatherland is not viewed as a despicable criminal."[71] Lehmann retained the lawyers F. Grimm, W. Luetgebrune, and F. Felgen for Schultz and commissioned them to write some eight books and pamphlets justifying the *Feme* assassinations on the grounds that any action which arises out of an overpowering patriotic motive absolves the perpetrator from all guilt. Some of these works, such as Felgen's *The Feme Lies* (*Die Femelüge*, 1928) and *What the Volk Doesn't Know* (*Was das Volk nicht weisst*, 1930), were personally rewritten by Lehmann before being published. Copies of these books were sent to prominent journalists, politicians, and jurists, and proceeds from public sales went to pay Schultz's court costs.[72] Through this propaganda blitz, Lehmann succeeded in persuading much of the conservative German press to refer to the *Feme* activities as "*Feme* judgments" rather than "*Feme* murders." In an audacious turnabout the Lehmann house even sought to convince the public that "*Feme* murders" was a term invented by Jews who hoped to slander the brave men protecting the nation from traitors; the *real* crime here, Lehmann claimed, was in calling the *Feme* actions murders.[73] The JFLV campaign on Schlutz's behalf was successful, for not only was he released unpunished, but sentences for several other *Feme* murderers were reduced by half during 1928–29. Indeed, Lehmann eventually claimed that because of his house's activities, a total of twenty-five antirepublican *Feme* "judges" were partially or fully acquitted.[74] This service was but one of many the neoconservative publishers contributed to the forces seeking to undermine the Weimar republic and open the way for a new, radical right-wing order.

Seven

Culture and the *Volk* in the Postwar Era

The neoconservative publishers' postwar opposition to the new Weimar republic and their calls for a nationalist uprising to liberate Germany from Western fetters were, of course, direct outgrowths of that more general critique of Western culture and campaign of radical nationalism which men like Diederichs and Lehmann had been waging since the 1890s. Indeed, during the Weimar era the publishing programs of all five neoconservative firms revolved around the basic tenets which Diederichs and Lehmann had hammered out before the war. But as a result of the powerful catalysts of war, defeat, and revolution, the vague antimodern anxiety and the frustrated nationalistic dreams these two had preached in the Wilhelmian era now assumed a much sharper focus and a greater sense of urgency. After 1918, the prewar cultural pessimism of the Eugen Diederichs Verlag and the radical nationalism of the J. F. Lehmanns Verlag crystallized into a fairly coherent neoconservative cultural and political program, a program which centered on the principles of irrationalism, anti-Westernism, and *völkisch* militancy and which came to be increasingly shared by firms such as the Hanseatic, Beenken, and Stalling houses.

The Culture of Antimodern Revolt

The pessimism and alienation which characterized so many of the cultural opponents of the Second Reich did not dissipate when the imperial order collapsed. Rather, the revolution of 1918—which seemed to shatter society's last conservative bulwarks, to sweep into power a modern, pluralistic, liberal system, and to imperil the nation with mass rule—merely heightened the antimodern cultural despair of many Germans, especially those members of the anxious middle classes who now felt increasingly threatened by industrial capitalism and a restive mass proletariat.

After the shattering outcome of the war and revolution, J. F. Lehmann for example—a man who before 1918 had identified with Germany's confident industrial bourgeoisie and had therefore hardly been touched by cultural pessimism—suddenly developed a new appreciation for angry cultural critics such as Paul de Lagarde. Although a decade earlier he had briefly considered publishing a new edition of Lagarde's essays or a Lagarde biography, it was not until 1918–19, as he reread Lagarde while imprisoned by the Munich revolutionaries, that the radical Munich publisher took to heart the message of this German Jeremiah and resolved to add Lagarde's name to the JFLV list of authors.[1] To that end he contacted Karl Ludwig Schemann, Lagarde's most renowned biographer, asking his advice. Schemann replied that he had been planning himself to issue a new edition of Lagarde's *German Writings* (*Deutsche Schriften*); for he was disturbed that the original edition had gone out of print and that the only other edition available—the 1913 EDV volume—had too many distracting illustrations. Lehmann seized the opportunity and offered to publish the *Writings* if Schemann would serve as editor. To sweeten the offer, he also promised to acclaim Schemann's biography of Lagarde in the JFLV journal *Deutschlands Erneuerung* "so that it may achieve the widest possible dissemination."[2] Schemann accepted the arrangement, and in 1924 the JFLV issued a two-volume anthology, *Writings for the German Volk* (*Schriften für das deutsche Volk*), followed shortly by F. Krog's *Lagarde and the German State* (*Lagarde und der deutsche Staat*, 1929). The JFLV's edition of Lagarde is generally credited with sparking a "Lagardian renaissance" among the members of Bavaria's radical Right in the late 1920s.[3]

The men around the DHV and the Hanseatic house also displayed a vague, generalized Lagardian mistrust of modern civilization. But because they spoke for a constituency of commercial clerks and white-collar employees who were partly dependent on and yet partly threatened by modern industrial developments, it is not surprising that they exhibited a certain ambivalence about modernity. On the one hand, the DHV and HVA complained that the modern forces of materialism, specialization, and liberal individualism had destroyed traditional values and undermined human security, thus "opening up an abyss before man." On the other hand, however, they contended that:

> We don't indict the age of [modern] civilization because it poses
> new and difficult tasks for us; rather, we want to master it. Large
> economic enterprises, the technologization of life, social stratification

—these can't be undone through romantic ideas. We have no choice but to spiritually surmount these things, so that we do not lose the best segments of our *Volk* [i.e., the *Mittelstand*] to them. We must come to grips with modern economics, the modern metropolis, the modern mass state—but in a *German*, not an American way.[4]

While such sentiments seem to indicate a progressive, realistic outlook, many of the subsequent activities of the HVA, as shall be seen, hint that the "German way" of dealing with modernity was indeed to attempt to undo it through romantic ideas.

But of the neoconservative publishers, it was of course Eugen Diederichs who most clearly and consistently articulated the antimodern cultural despair which was so pervasive during the Weimar era. Voicing the anxieties of that small, preindustrial mandarin elite of cultivated middle-class Germans who felt their status and very existence endangered by the emergence of modern mass society, Diederichs throughout the 1920s lamented the rapid "cultural disintegration," the universal "uprootedness," and the sense of "spiritual chaos" which afflicted modern man. The "cultural and spiritual crisis" he detected around him he attributed to the dissolution of social and intellectual bonds and the triumph of technology over the spirit, processes which he believed had been endemic to Western civilization at least since the eighteenth century, perhaps since the Renaissance. As the spiritual ground disappeared from under man's feet, he believed, human life became increasingly materialistic and forlorn. In his eyes not only the German soul but all of European culture was "sick," and Europeans faced an imminent ruin if an entirely new set of values were not created to fill the modern spiritual vacuum.[5]

The intrinsic evils of modernity which seemed to weigh most heavily on Diederichs after 1918 were much the same as those he had condemned in more general terms before the war: intellectual fragmentation, excessive rationalization, and vulgar materialism. He maintained that modernist culture, with its stress upon logical scientific analysis and specialized learning, had lost sight of the overall unity of life. For the rational, objective approach to modern learning, because it was incapable of grasping the irrational elements of existence, could comprehend only a part, but never the whole of life. The realm of the spirit had therefore become "splintered" and man was left with an anarchy of values. The materialist assumptions of modern science, moreover, denied the primacy of the spirit and failed to recognize that the material world was merely one of appearances. For these reasons, Diederichs preached that modern man's overreliance on the rational intellect and on the materialistic methods of modern science had fragmented spiritual life, atomized human existence, and estranged man from the irrational life-forces of the cosmos: "the one-sided development of technology and natural science," he declared in 1924, "has driven our feeling for the totality of life into a dead end of individual isolation and alienation (*Vereinzelung*)."[6] The gloomy Jena publisher blamed the splintered, mechanistic outlook which arises out of modern rationalism for the catastrophic history of the twentieth century. "Life cannot be mechanized indefinitely," he warned in 1927, "as it has been for the last two generations under the reign of applied scientific thought. The ultimate result of this was the world war, which was merely an external expression of the inner spiritual chaos of humanity."[7]

Diederichs also traced the nation's social problems back to the flawed materialistic outlook of modern man. The mechanistic spirit, he charged, was intimately linked to the urban proletarian masses who spent their lives working at machines. That spirit led the working masses and many other Germans as well to practice an uninhibited greed and mammonism which, during the war and after, had undermined national solidarity by unleashing a system of naked-interest politics, ruthless economic exploitation, and class antagonism. And since materialism robbed them of that inner spiritual realm which alone could provide direction and true freedom, the modern masses existed as mindless automatons, ready victims for depersonalized mass collectivization. But above all, Diederichs lamented that modern materialism was destroying that small but crucial stratum of idealistic, culture-bearing middle-class Germans to which men like him belonged.[8] Diederichs's negative assessment of modern materialism was echoed by one of the JFLV's postwar books, M. Wundt's *On the Spirit of Our Times* (*Vom Geist unserer Zeit*, 1920), which Lehmann proclaimed as a work which identified "the spirit of mammonism which rules Germany" as the source of all the German *Volk*'s postwar distress.[9]

If, as Diederichs maintained, rational scientific analysis and specialized learning fragmented the modern spirit, then man's spiritual crisis could only be overcome by a comprehensive new outlook which stressed the larger coherence of things and which could grasp the essential interrelated unity of all existence. This "organic world view," as Diederichs called it, must be rooted in the "subsoil" (*Untergrund*) of man's unconscious and in his irrational intuition. In contrast to the sundering dissection of modern reason, it would be capable of conceptually ordering and integrating life's various elements into an organic whole.[10] To promote this "biocentric weltanschauung," the EDV issued such works as A. Schmieder's *Biology of Consciousness* (*Biologie des Bewusstseins*, 1929), which explored the organic basis of all human thought, and two studies by the renowned German life-philosopher and former intimate of the Stefan George circle, Ludwig Klages. The J. F. Lehmann house, too, contributed a theoretical work to the campaign for an organic weltanschauung: R. von Engelhardt's *Organic Culture* (*Organische Kultur: Deutsche Lebensfragen im Lichte der Biologie*, 1925). According to Lehmann, this work demonstrated that "not reason, but only our inner, Life-related intuition . . . and organic thinking can liberate us from the oppression of deterministic philosophical systems."[11]

Diederichs's postwar efforts for a new organic mode of thought—in many ways but a continuation of his earlier activities in the areas of life-philosophy and vitalism—were clearly based on his long-standing conviction that humanity must be freed from the tyranny of reason. After 1918 the pernicious effects of rational intellectualism became clearer to him than ever before. Rationalism not only deadened everything to which it was applied, but it was sadly incapable of grasping the whole complexity of life. Rational deliberation led ultimately to fatalism, vacillation, and ethical relativism, and thus paralyzed the human will and destroyed man's capacity for decisive action.[12] And the overdevelopment of the rational faculty was associated in Diederichs's mind with undesirable social effects, such as artificial urbanism and estrangement from the living forces of rural nature, impersonal collectivization, and the proletarianization of society. Ultimately, the rationalization of political life meant mass democracy, where majorities were mechanistically tallied up and handed power—a system the publisher found "almost unbearable."[13]

After the war Diederichs, still under the influence of the "Ideas of 1914," defined the German character as "in essence irrational."[14] By embracing the irrational, elemental forces of life such as intuition, fantasy, the unconscious, and primal myths, the publisher believed Germans could liberate themselves from the spiritual and political influence of the hyper-rationalized West, where mechanization and impersonal mass organization were closing down on man, circumscribing his freedom and spiritual autonomy. Irrationalism, he hoped, would allow the German *Volk* to recover that spiritual and cultural ascendancy of which the war and revolution had robbed it. Equally important, however, Diederichs believed that through the dark powers of the unconscious, man could once again grasp the totality of life and regain his sense of spiritual wholeness. By means of irrationalism, modern man might also transcend the relativism and fatalistic determinism which the rational intellect imposes, and replace sterile theorizing with a will to action.[15] Anxious to hasten man's liberation from Western rationalism, the Jena publisher proclaimed in 1924 the coming of a new antirational era founded on intuition and the domination of Dionysus over Apollo, an age "in which we must think irrationally, and above all, act irrationally." Shortly thereafter, the Hanseatic house and its Langen-Müller subsidiary joined the struggle against Western rationalism by pledging to serve as "fulcrums in the overthrow of Voltaire."[16]

The same element of anti-Western resentment was evident in Diederichs's postwar campaign against materialism and its more vulgar manifestation, mammonism. For him, "true" German culture was by nature metaphysical; mammonism and mechanization, as well as the modern rational order out of which they grew, were therefore inherently un-German.[17] Germans might still salvage their cultural essence, Diederichs believed, by turning away from materialism and rooting out its vile effects. To help inspire an antimaterialist reaction among his countrymen and thus rescue the German soul from the clutches of Western modernity, Diederichs held up a materialistic bogey: America. At least since 1917, when the United States entered the war against Germany, many German idealists viewed America as materialism incarnate and regarded Americanism, with its uninhibited capitalism, robber barons, and inhuman technological mechanization, as the symbol of modernity's worst evils. American culture—or rather, lack of it—served as a grim warning for Germany, indicating what befalls a nation where materialism reigns. As Diederichs explained to his readers in the 1920s, "Americanism means collective mass thinking, it means the death of all independent thought and action which arises from inner spiritual impulses. . . . Americanism is: a material view of life which lacks any higher perspective. It means overvaluing the present and a disregard for one's heritage. . . . It is Mammonism with its corresponding love of mere pleasure, . . . the leveling shallowness of the large city, with its directionless, manipulated masses."[18] Allowing liberal, democratic American principles to triumph in German life, the Jena publisher warned, would be to negate Germany's rich idealist heritage and to accept the rule of money and machines.[19] To warn Germans of the dangers of Americanization and of a materialist future, the EDV issued works such as A. Halfeld's *America and Americanism* (*Amerika und der Amerikanismus*, 1927). When the book met with some criticism in the press, the publisher counteracted by inducing his house's most famous authors to issue public encomiums on its behalf.[20]

The same rejection of modern rationalism and materialism which prompted Diederichs to scorn America and the West induced him to turn his attentions toward eastern Europe, and to Russia in particular. For to many Germans, the Slavic East represented not only the geographical, but the ideological antithesis of the liberal Anglo-Saxon West. The further Western Europeans progressed down the road of rationalization and modernization, the more attractive the "backward," antiliberal culture of eastern Europe became for those, like Diederichs, who scorned Western values; a new Eastern orientation for the German *Volk*, they hoped, might divert German culture from the disastrous path of Western materialist decadence.[21]

Shortly before the war Diederichs had visited eastern Europe, Russia, and the Balkans. Although afterward he confessed a certain fear of the "chaotic" Slavic spirit, he nevertheless became convinced that a mysterious spiritual marriage existed between Slavs and Germans and that "only through a new contact with Eastern Europe can Germandom truly realize its most idealistic essence."[22] Thus, already before 1918 the EDV issued the collected works of such Russian authors as Tolstoy, Chekov, Gorki, and Solovyev, as well as some seven monographs on the enigmatic "Slavic soul" and what Westerners might learn from it. After the harsh peace settlement and the formation of the pro-Western Weimar republic in 1918–19 soured Diederichs once and for all on Western liberalism, he took a renewed interest in Slavic culture. Indeed, at this time many Germans began to look at Russia, particularly the old pre-Bolshevik Russia, in a new way and began to emphasize the anti-Western traditions of Russian culture and its affinity with Germany's. The ideas of Dostoevski—that prophetic Russian writer who in the mid-nineteenth century had warned against the rationalism and scientific "progress" of Western culture and had predicted the spiritual nihilism to which it would lead—became especially popular with cultural pessimists in Germany. For "Dostoevski, above all, passed as *the* interpreter of Russia. . . . Through him, many of the ideas of the Russian nineteenth century made their way into Germany shortly after the First World War where, in turn, they became rerooted in German Romanticism and German Idealism."[23] Diederichs contributed to this postwar Dostoevski fad by issuing P. Natorp's *Fëdor Dostoevski's Significance for the Current Cultural Crisis (Fjedor Dostojewskis Bedeutung für die gegenwärtige Kulturkrisis*, 1923).

Diederichs also found much in the new, Bolshevik Russia which was a welcome alternative to the bankrupt values of the West. In 1922, for example, he praised the deeply rooted religious, mystical spirit of the Russian people, their close-knit sense of local community, and the new, less materialistic attitudes toward private property which seemed to be emerging in the Soviet Union; at the same time he chided the West for not moving in a similar direction.[24] To better inform German readers on the alternative system of values which the new Russia represented, the EDV issued several sympathetic travel reports on the Soviet Union, including A. Paquet's *In Communist Russia (Im kommunistischen Russland*, 1919) and Lou Andreas-Salomé's *Rodinka (Rodinka: Eine russische Erinnerung*, 1923).

When the collapse of the Western economy in 1929 exposed the precariousness of the liberal system and dealt a near fatal blow to faith in Western values, the neoconservative publishers looked with even more interest to the anti-Western, socialist East; there they perceived a solution to Germany's own crisis. Some ideologues dusted off the old wartime notion of a central European economic and political hegemony for Germany. German expansion eastward, they believed, would bring the nation the new resources, markets, and "living space" it needed to surmount the world depression. Thus, one Hanseatic publication, K. Krüger's *German Extraterritorial Economics* (*Deutsche Grossraumwirtschaft*, 1932), was heralded as a work which preached "the salvation of Germany through economic union with the peoples of *Mitteleuropa* and the intensification of German production, the markets of which lie in southeastern Europe."[25] Others around the Diederichs and Hanseatic houses, however, idealized a new pro-Russian orientation as the means by which Germany could escape the downfall of the West and overcome her own spiritual and cultural crisis. The EDV's *Tat* Circle, for example, used *Die Tat* after 1929 to preach that a "turning away from the West" (*Abwendung vom Westen*) and a closer association with the Soviet Union would help Germany recover her inner and her international strength;[26] these same ideas were disseminated in a book-length monograph, G. Wirsing's *Middle Europe and the German Future* (*Zwischeneuropa und die deutsche Zukunft*), which the EDV issued as a *Tatschrift* in 1932. Likewise, the HVA—which in 1932 proclaimed a program of "conservative-revolutionary renewal of Germany through an East-European orientation"—issued F. Mariaux's *The Rubble Heap: Mutiny of a World* (*Der Schutthaufen: Aufruhr einer Welt*, 1931). This work, the firm declared, "comprehends the convulsion of our times as an elementary rebellion by the peoples of the world against the political and social life-styles of the mechanistic age. It's goal: victory over parliamentary democracy and creation of a new economic solidarity in Central Europe. [Mariaux's tract is] an overwhelming appeal for a German foreign policy directed toward the Southeast in light of the collapse of the Western, capitalistic, mechanistic world."[27]

One of the aspects of east European culture which pessimists like Diederichs found most appealing was the simple, almost mystical religious faith of the Slavic peoples, a faith which the rationalized, secularized West had long since lost. The yearning for a new religious mystique played a central role in Diederichs's postwar activities, as it had before 1914. But as a result of the nationalistic fervor of the war and the trauma of class and civil war at home, by the 1920s religion had assumed a dual function in the publisher's mind: he continued to view religious faith as a means of overcoming rationalism, but he now also regarded it as a tool for forging a deeper sense of communal solidarity for the German *Volk*.

Diederichs believed the coming age of irrationalism would take a religious form: "If, after an epoch of spiritual death a counterepoch of spirituality is to arise," he told the new editor of *Die Tat* in 1929, "then I can only conceive of this spirituality as being founded on the feeling for Life, which arises out of the irrational—and that can only be religion. *Die Tat*, there-fore, must above all promote the irrational—that is, religion."[28] Modern man desperately needed some new faith, Diederichs believed, a new reli-gious mystique to fill life's spiritual vacuum; this mystique, which would "touch the dark secrets behind Life" that were closed to modern reason and science, must of necessity be rooted in the irrational human conscious-ness. Only religion could call forth the new system of values and provide the cosmic rootedness which Germans needed if they were ever to rise above the modern cultural crisis.[29] Indeed, in the 1920s Diederichs not only foresaw religion as a force which could create "a new German man," but (and here he was reviving ideas he had first developed during the war) he came to idealize religious consciousness and a system of universally shared religious beliefs as the key to attaining a more compelling sense of national unity and social solidarity. For this reason he considered religion and the *Volkstum* movement of the Weimar era to be closely linked. This notion was also echoed by J. F. Lehmann, who identified religious service with service to the social whole, and proximity to God with promotion of the interests of the German *Volk*.[30]

Most of the EDV's postwar publications on religion (which numbered nearly twoscore) were simply continuations of the firm's earlier programs in this area. Thus, Diederichs issued C. Schrempf's two-volume study of Kierkegaard (1927–28). New works by A. Drews, H. Raschke, and others who attacked or radically revised orthodox Christian dogmas continued to appear from the firm. Titles such as Feiler's *The Birth of Christianity From Magical Thought* (*Die Entstehung des Christentums aus dem Geiste des magischen Denkens*, 1927) emphasized the mystical and occult origins of modern reli-gious mythology. Earlier house series on pantheism, theosophy, or Eastern spiritualism were also continued or brought to completion after 1918. The firm's earlier exploration of mysticism was supplemented by a new 1924 biography of Jakob Böhme by W. Peuckert. The Hanseatic house, like-wise, was active on behalf of mysticism, for it issued H. Leisegang's *Foundations of Anthroposophy* (*Grundlagen der Anthroposophie*, 1922), a multi-volume series on *Mystics of the Occident* (*Mystiker des Abendlandes*, 1931), and a new edition of Böhme's *On the Threefold Life of Man* (*Vom dreifachen Leben des Menschen*, 1924). The HVA produced works like Böhme's, it said, because it believed that medieval mysticism represented "the longing of our age."[31]

Some titles on Diederichs's religious list, however, represented initia-tives in new directions. He succeeded, for example, in signing on the young theologian Friedrich Gogarten. Gogarten, who drew heavily from pantheism and life-philosophy, was one of the foremost disciples of Karl Barth and of his antiliberal "crisis theology" which rejected any accommodation with modern secular culture and preached the return to a simple faith as the fundamental core of religious experience. Four of Gogarten's theological tracts, including his seminal *The Religious Decision* (*Die religiöse Entscheidung*, 1921) and *On Faith and Revelation* (*Vom Glauben und Offenbarung*, 1922) appeared in the EDV catalog, as did G. Weiser's 1930 intellectual biography of Gogarten.

Since the war, Diederichs had also taken a renewed interest in Martin Luther and this, too, was reflected in the EDV catalog. Because the four hundredth anniversary of the Reformation fell in 1917, at the zenith of Germany's anti-Western patriotic fervor, Diederichs and many of his countrymen began at that time to see Luther in a new light: as a valiant German hero who had cast off an alien, Western-Romanic religious system and established a new, independent, more "German" brand of Christianity.[32] To honor the "German Luther," Diederichs had published G. Kutzke's *From Luthers Home* (*Aus Luthers Heimat*, 1914) and K. König's *On the Spirit of Luther the German* (*Vom Geiste Luthers des Deutschen*, 1917). The appearance of these volumes was in fact part of a general "Luther renaissance" which took place during and immediately after the war. This phenomenon, originally merely a theological movement, became linked to the political struggle between liberals and conservatives. For after the war, pro-Weimar liberals attacked traditional German Protestantism, and Luther in particular, for having fostered an attitude of authoritarianism and political subservience in Germans, and for contributing significantly to the fateful divergence between Germany and the rest of western Europe. Anti-Weimar conservatives replied by seeking to rehabilitate Luther's image, portraying him as a world historical hero and a defender of the unique German religious and spiritual identity. This postwar Luther renaissance, to which Diederichs contributed in 1926 by issuing a new edition of Luther's sermons, thus took on a political character and ultimately merged into the larger campaign against Western culture which neoconservatives were waging. In the opinion of one religious scholar, "the neoconservative tendencies which had been undermining social and political life since the foundation of the republic possessed a moral ally in Lutheranism. . . . There is no doubt that the Luther renaissance, with its decidedly conservative tendency, converged with similar movements anxious to safeguard Germany's true political and cultural heritage."[33]

As in the imperial period, neoconservative publishers like Diederichs continued to see art as a close ally of religion in the struggle against Western rationalism. He held to his conviction that the process of artistic creation bordered on a mystical experience; the artist, because he experienced life directly rather than rationally analyzing it, was able "to catch a glimpse of a second eternity when his intuition blows away the clouds of the unknown."[34] Since he was in contact with the irrational forces of the cosmos and could grasp reality in its totality rather than in fragmented pieces, in Diederichs's mind the artist had a crucial role to play in generating that new set of values so desperately needed in postwar Germany. "It is my firm conviction," he proclaimed in 1920, "that the guidelines for a new order in Germany will be forged not by the politician or the economist, but rather by the artist."[35]

To promote the development of artistic consciousness and help art gain its rightful place in national affairs, he issued an anthology of artists' *Writings on Cultural Politics* (*Schriften zur Kulturpolitik*, 1920), in which there were repeated calls for a new and closer communion between the artist and the broader *Volk*. Diederichs added a personal postscript in which he argued that Germany's political and economic problems could be more easily overcome if only the public would take heed of the artists' message. Besides issuing some thirteen monographs on dance, music, and the philosophy of art, the EDV also published works by visionary young architects such as Hans Kampffmeyer and Bruno Taut who, in their *City of Peace* (*Friedensstadt*, 1918) and *The City Crown* (*Die Stadtkrone*, 1919), respectively, advocated an idealistic, semiexpressionistic new style of "social architecture" which was both to raise man's inner spirit and promote a deeper sense of social unity.[36]

If Diederichs, by idealizing art and assigning it ambitious new national functions, honored the memory of Wagner and Langbehn indirectly, then Lehmann did so more openly. After being invited by his author H. S. Chamberlain to attend the Wagnerian festival in Bayreuth in 1925, the Munich publisher became a devoted Wagnerite and pledged "to do everything in my power to work for Bayreuth and its powerful legacy."[37] This he soon did: after Chamberlain, leader of the Bayreuth circle, died in 1927, Lehmann published two laudatory studies of him by G. Schott. And in 1930, the JFLV brought out R. Eichenhauer's *Music and Race* (*Musik und Rasse*), a monograph which explored a relationship first posited by Chamberlain's father-in-law Richard Wagner.

Romanticism, too, continued to play a central role in the neoconservative publishers' postwar cultural program; and like the other elements of that program, it was embraced largely for its antirational content. Eugen Diederichs identified the loss of the romantic appreciation for the irrational and the fundamental organic unity of life as one of the foremost causes of the modern spiritual crisis.[38] To help Germans recover that romantic weltanschauung, his firm issued W. Michel's and K. Obenauer's scholarly studies of the romantic poets Hölderlin and Novalis, as well as other titles such as K. Eberlein's *German Romantic Painters* (*Deutsche Maler der Romantik*, 1920) and R. Benz's *Fable Literature of the Romantics* (*Märchendichtung der*

Romantiker, 1926). Likewise, the HVA sought to revive public interest in romanticism through L. Benninghoff's *Romantic Land: A Part of Us* (*Romantikland: Ein Stück von uns*, 1921). In an effusive advertisement for this popularized account of the German romantic era, the HVA reminded readers that

> over one hundred years ago during Germany's greatest degradation, a new Spring suddenly blossomed forth. At that time the German found his way out of the intellect's transparent, threadbare edifice, out of the superficial pseudoculture [of the Enlightenment], and rediscovered the sources of power and energy, the secrets of the earth, of nature, and of his own being. But [romanticism] should not be for us something bygone, some merely literary phenomenon which has been put to rest. For it was our greatest achievement and continues to live on in us. Today more than ever we need its power. So through this book, *Romantic Land*—the land of the German soul—will spread itself before us in all its sincerity and yearning, in its joy and its mysterious darkness.[39]

A revival of romanticism was further cultivated when the EDV and HVA published the works of leading lyricists and novelists of the Neoromantic literary school. Between 1918 and 1933, for example, Diederichs issued some twenty titles by or about such Neoromantic authors as Carl Spitteler, Agnes Miegel, Ina Seidel, and Lulu von Strauss und Torney, while the collected works of Wilhelm Schäfer and Paul Ernst, as well as Börries von Münchhausen's *Idyllics* (*Idyllen*) were all acquired by the HVA when the firm gained control of the Langen and Müller houses in the late 1920s.

Finally, the neoconservative houses strongly supported the postwar German Youth Movement. After 1918 the movement entered a *"bündisch"* phase which was more radical, more politicized, and which stood further to the right than had the vaguely utopian prewar *Wandervögel* and Free German youth groups. German youth now tended to organize themselves into elite paramilitary orders (*Bünde*). These cells, each of which consisted of a strong, charismatic leader (*Führer*) and his close-knit band of blindly loyal followers, professed a romantic idealism and a deep sense of comradeship, and most also adhered to some vague but radically activistic social and political ideology, usually antirepublican in nature. To those who rejected the "Weimar system" of political parties and interest groups, these youth groups represented a fresh, alternative form of social and political expression.[40]

Eugen Diederichs, a prominent mentor of the prewar Youth Movement, was at first suspicious of the new, postwar *bündisch* trend. He felt a certain generational alienation from Germany's radicalized youngsters, and perhaps also a trace of jealousy that German youth were now following a different set of younger, more activistic leaders.[41] Yet he soon overcame his reservations and again placed his firm's wholehearted support behind the German youth cause. For he saw in the postwar Youth Movement that same romantic spirit, the same rejection of intellectualism and urban alienation, the same urge to recover man's contact with nature, and the same sense of the unity of life which he had found so appealing in the earlier *Wandervögel* and Free German youth groups. The youth *Bünde*, which he believed worked for social reconciliation by uniting the youth of all social classes, were to him evidence of Germany's recovery and represented the hope of a new age; it was therefore the duty of the older generation, he declared, to assist youth with all the means at their disposal.[42]

Thus in the 1920s Diederichs rededicated his journal *Die Tat* to the Youth Movement and joined enthusiastically in the activities of the youth orders, attending youth congresses in 1919, 1920, and 1921, and seeking to organize a second Hohe Meissner festival in 1923 to commemorate the tenth anniversary of the first.[43] The EDV published several volumes of Meyer-Steineg's folksongs for use within the youth groups, issued the antirepublican political manifesto of the 1920 Hofgeismar youth festival, and brought out other important Youth Movement statements. These included works such as P. Natorp's *Hopes of the Youth Movement* (*Hoffnungen der Jugendbewegung*, 1920), E. Busse-Wilson's *Phases of the Youth Movement* (*Stufen der Jugendbewegung*, 1925), and L. Dingräve's *Where Does the Younger Generation Stand?* (*Wo steht die junge Generation?*, 1931), which sold nearly fifty-five hundred copies in two years. Diederichs also used his extensive connections to help establish a national treasury which could provide support for Youth Movement activities, and served as a respected authority to those seeking information about the movement.[44]

Of most interest. however, was Diederichs's service as a paternal protector of youth elements during the Weimar years. In 1920, an eccentric young *Wandervögel* preacher named Friedrich Muck-Lamberty began an unusual odyssey across Germany. Like a modern Pied Piper, Muck roamed the countryside playing folksongs and calling upon German youth to cast off their temporal bonds and "push into the blue." Contemporary reports claimed that Muck's audience was often suddenly seized by a wild abandon and would break into frenzied dance. Adolescents viewed him as a new religious prophet and left their homes to join his "new flock" (Neue Schar).[45] As Thuringian officials grew alarmed at Muck's Dionysiac cult during the winter of 1920–21, Diederichs intervened on his behalf. To fend off police suppression of the movement, which he viewed as a positive manifestation of Germany's spiritual rebirth, the publisher helped Muck procure a local castle where, it was hoped, the clan would confine their unusual activities. The EDV also issued A. Ritzhaupt's sympathetic *The 'New Flock' of Thuringia* (*Die 'Neue Schar' in Thüringen*, 1921). But reports of free love in the Muck cult soon shocked officials, who moved to expel the group from the province. In several press articles, Diederichs used his position as a respected authority on Youth Movement affairs to urge toleration of the "flock's" antics. As suppression appeared imminent in February 1921, the publisher wrote to the Thuringian minister of culture to plead Muck's case and give it his personal sanction. Praising Muck as a sincere religious enthusiast and an exponent of youth's chaotic inner strug-gle for meaning, Diederichs urged the government to tolerate rather than repress spirits like Muck because they were leading the way to an internal regeneration of the nation.[46] (While Diederichs's eloquent defense man-aged to win a brief reprieve for Muck, the "new flock" was eventually expelled from Thuringia the following year.)

J. F. Lehmann and the Hanseatic house were also active supporters of various postwar youth orders, especially radically antirepublican organ-izations such as Frank Glatzel's Young German Order (Jungdeutscher Bund) or the Young Nationalist Order (Jungnationaler Bund). Lehmann, for example, after losing his Burg Persen in Tyrol to Italy in 1919, ac-quired another castle in Franconia, Burg Hoheneck. After renovating the castle, he regularly turned it over to right-wing youth and student groups such as the Young German Order, the German Circle of University Stu-dents (Hochschulring deutscher Art), or the Hitler Youth for use as a meeting and festival site.[47] The HVA aided the Young German Order by issuing two of Glatzel's manifestos, *Young German Will* (*Jungdeutsches Wollen: Vorträge gehalten auf den Grüdungstag des Jungdeutschen Bundes*, 1920) and *German Youth* (*Deutsche Jugend*, 1922), and by serving as publisher for his journal *Jungdeutsche Stimmen* (*Young German Voices*) between 1919 and 1921. In addition, the Hanseatic firm brought out such works as W. Stählin's *The New Life-style: Ideals of German Youth* (*Der neue Lebensstil: Ideale deutscher Jugend*, 1923) and *Fever and Cure in the Youth Movement* (*Fieber und Heil in der Jugendbewegung*, 1932). Another HVA offering, M. Strach-witz's novel *The Standard-bearer* (*Der Fahnenträger*, 1925), succeeded in capturing the entire antirepublican, neoconservative ideology of the post-war German Youth Movement. This book, according to the HVA, "is a treatise about Nature and the Fatherland. In clear opposition to the democratic age, with Strachwitz—the modern Romantic—one hears the armour clatter, the sea thunder, the wind roar. His standard is: Youth! Youth! Youth!"[48]

Cultural Revolt and *Völkisch* Militancy

It was not only the publishers' antimodern cultural resentments which were aggravated and magnified by the war and its traumatic aftermath. Their sense of German cultural identity, their concepts of German nationhood, and their gnawing fears over the fate of Germandom in the modern world also took on a grave new significance after 1918 and came increasingly to dominate their publishing programs. As one scholar has noted, the German notion of *"Volk"* underwent a postwar inflation no less dramatic and no less portentous than that of the German currency;[49] just as the frantic printing of money was intended to help the nation surmount its postwar economic crisis, so too the forging of a new *Volk* consciousness was seen as a means of overcoming the general crisis of modern life. Thus neoconservatives, who believed the identity and the future of the German *Volk* was endangered by the postwar acceleration of general modern Western trends on the one hand, and by the domestic and international political settlements "imposed" on Germany by the West on the other, developed a militant new national consciousness aimed at defining, protecting, and asserting the identity and interests of the German *Volk*. In this way the earlier ideas both of cultural pessimists like Diederichs and of radical nationalists like Lehmann became fused after 1918 into a radically anti-liberal *völkisch* ideology which, in its most extreme forms, took expression as vulgar racism and virulent anti-Semitism.

The new postwar *völkisch* consciousness of the publishers is perhaps best illustrated by the men around the Hanseatic Publishing Institute, especially Wilhelm Stapel, whose 1917 book had done so much to clarify the difference between a *Volk*-oriented and a state-oriented patriotism. As editor of the HVA's *Deutsches Volkstum*, Stapel in 1923 reaffirmed his conviction that

> it is not "humanity" which shapes and elevates man; rather, it
> is the *Volk* which, as a political, economic, and spiritual entity, forms
> man's ethical powers. In recognition of this fact we must always be
> unconditionally rooted in our Germanic *Volk* character. . . . Our
> state, economy, society, art, literature, and religion are all
> manifestations of a certain spiritual type, a type which can only
> be designated by the word "German" because they are all of a special
> German kind. [It is therefore our task] to explore the eternal, the
> pure, the genuine essence of the German *Volk*, that which one
> can call "the German ideal."[50]

When Stapel drew up a set of programmatic guidelines for the HVA's cultural division (of which he was director) in 1926, he transferred this new *völkisch* orientation to the Hanseatic house at large. Thus, the HVA announced to its readers that henceforth

> [the HVA] is duty-bound to promote the values of *Volkstum*, especially in the areas of academic learning, art, religion, education, and social life. Within the area of academic learning, special emphasis will be placed on the German world view, German history, and German folklore—that is, on the cultivation of our *Volk* consciousness. In the area of art, we will promote only *Volk*-rooted artists. We are less concerned with the purely aesthetic aspects of any artwork than we are with its meaning for our *Volk*. . . . [The major goal of the HVA will therefore be] the self-recognition of our own *Volkstum*. The work of the HVA thus assumes a mediating role between the world of learning and the life of the *Volk*, and we will attempt to explore and to link the two.[51]

The HVA-related German Home Library declared similar goals in the 1920s when it pledged to help "truly German books, which explore and reflect the essence of our Germanic *Volk* character, find their way into the homes and hearts of our subscribers."[52]

To implement this program the HVA issued two new editions of Stapel's *Volksbürgerliche Erziehung* and distributed them through the Home Library, and in 1921 issued two new books by him, *Volkstum* and *Volkstum or Human Rights? (Volkstum oder Menschenrechte?)*. Another HVA offering in its *Volkstum* program, K. Weidel's *The German World View (Deutsche Weltanschauung*, 1925), was proclaimed by the firm as "a portrayal of the *German* way of seeing and evaluating the world. . . . Whoever has German blood in his veins will discover his own inner spiritual relation to this German outlook; he will become clearer about his own dark, obscure dreams and visions, and will joyfully and actively acknowledge his own Germandom."[53]

The other neoconservative houses likewise began a new intensive exploration of the essential bases of *Volk* identity. When the Heinrich Beenken Verlag acquired the journal *Der Türmer (The Watchman)* in 1930, Beenken pledged that under his control the organ would "cultivate only what is German and genuine [in order to] strengthen the body and spirit of our Germanic *Volk*."[54] Many of the postwar publications of the JFLV, such as H. Meyer's *German Man (Der deutsche Mensch*, vol. 1: *Völkische Weltanschauung*, vol. 2: *Deutsche Volksgemeinschaft*, 1925) or M. Wundt's *German World View: Characteristics of Völkisch Thought (Deutsche Weltanschauung: Grundzüge völkischer Denkens*, 1926) explored the essence of Germanic *Volk* character and its essential differences from the liberal outlook of the West. Wundt's work, for example, purported to "take the ideas handed down by all the pioneers of the German spirit—the Eckehardts, the Böhmes, the Luthers, the Leibnitzes, the Kants, the Fichtes, and the other great German Idealists—and relate them to that weltanschauung which is the common property of the German *Volk*. By means of that weltanschauung, the German *Volk* shall again find the strength to resist foreign influences."[55] Eugen Diederichs, too, consciously steered his EDV closer to *völkisch* circles and the general *Volkstum* movement in the years after the war because he hoped to transcend the individualistic psychology of liberalism.[56] Thus the Jena publisher subsidized indigent authors to write on the great "What is German?" question,[57] and issued such treatises on the nature of the German *Volk* as K. Obenauer's *Faustian Man* (*Der faustische Mensch*, 1922). Several of the EDV volumes on the Germanic *Volk* character, as well as many from the JFLV, were highly regarded by the directors of the German Home Library and were recommended to DHB subscribers.[58]

The publishers made it clear that their postwar *völkisch* efforts grew out of a strong antiliberal reaction, but at the same time were to be considered distinct from traditional German conservatism. Stapel, for example, while laying out his *völkisch* program for the HVA, sought to define a new type of *Volk*-oriented conservatism distinct from the more traditional conservatism of right-wing parties such as the DNVP, the DVP, or the Bavarian Peoples party (BVP). The traditional Weimar Right, he argued, represented the interests of the conservative propertied elites which had controlled the old prewar Reich. They remained psychologically rooted in the vanished imperial era and their ultimate goal was, if not the outright restoration of the monarchy, then at least the reestablishment of its essential political and social features under a pseudomonarchical order. In contrast to this reactionary, backward-looking, "state conservatism" of the old Right, Stapel (and other neoconservatives) preached a forward-looking "*Volk* conservatism" which would defend not the social and political interests of a narrow elite, but the interests of the entire *Volk*.[59] Thus, his guidelines for the HVA stated that "the HVA serves *Volk*-conservative ideas—that is, ideas which preserve or conserve the *Volk*. The ultimate goal of our publishing activity is the health, the power, and the honor of our German *Volk* as a whole, without regard to the arbitrary divisions of state boundaries or to the excessive egotistical claims of certain national subgroups."[60] Likewise, the HVA heralded one of its works on Germanic *Volk* character, H. Ullmann's *The Evolving Volk: Against Liberalism and Reaction* (*Das werdende Volk: Gegen Liberalismus und Reaktion*, 1928) as a work which, because it interpreted all of life in terms of the *Volk*, was necessarily critical of the traditional right-wing parties and their social exclusiveness; "out of such criticism [Ullmann] then posits the image of a new, living, *Volk*-rooted conservatism which must arise as a counterweight against the forces of liberalism."[61]

Eugen Diederichs, like Stapel, desired a forward-looking new conservative outlook firmly rooted in a consciousness of the needs of the *Volk* as a whole.[62] One of his firm's most famous and influential postwar publications, H. Freyer's *Revolution from the Right* (*Revolution von Rechts*, 1931), defined the essence of Germanic *Volk* character as inherently antagonistic to the principles of modern Western industrial society, and concluded by calling for a new type of radical conservatism, a "revolution from the Right" by the *Volk* against modern liberalism.[63] In much the same way Beenken, after exploring the concept and meaning of the *Volk*, concluded that a *völkisch* orientation must inevitably lead one to reject liberalism. For liberalism, "in place of the old German concept of true freedom, preaches the uninhibited, unbounded freedom of the individual, the right of unrestricted private profiteering and hedonism, and the spreading, whenever and wherever one pleases, of any views or ideas, regardless of their effect on the state and on the *Volk*."[64] And finally, the Gerhard Stalling house conceived of Germany's new postwar national consciousness as being intimately bound up with a new, more popular brand of conservatism. When inaugurating the GSV's *Writings to the Nation* (*Schriften an die Nation*) series in 1931, editor Martin Venzky (son-in-law of Heinrich Stalling) proclaimed the firm's series would be national in orientation:

> This word "national" . . . is therefore to be understood in the sense it is used by [the leading neoconservative theorist] Moeller van den Bruck—that is, "conservative." This type of conservative viewpoint is national because it emanates from the organic conditions which are essential for national life; it is also social, because it recognizes the totality of the nation. . . . In this way the new Stalling series will make an impact on the nation as a whole, especially on the "anonymous" but responsible, nationally minded individual. For it will help him find direction in a world where everything seems to have been thrown into question, and will help direct him so that he can become historically and organically anchored in his times.[65]

In calling for a more historically rooted national consciousness, the GSV was utilizing Diederichs's prewar strategy of emphasizing Germans' shared historical traditions and folklore as a means of strengthening their national identity and common sense of *Volk* belonging. Indeed, the deliberate revival of historical tradition to raise *völkisch* consciousness was a tool utilized by all the neoconservative houses after 1918. Thus Diederichs reiterated in the 1920s that because a *Volk* was a "community of fate" (*Schicksalgemeinschaft*), awareness of the community's common traditions served as a powerful bond between its members. "The future of our *Volk*," he declared, "depends on our listening to the voices of our past"; a new appreciation for German history, especially for the irrational forces which have shaped German destiny, could help overcome the mechanization and sense of uprootedness which plagued his modern countrymen.[66] The Hanseatic house was even more candid about the ideological intent of its activities in the area of history: "It is important that in our works on history, the *Volk* be seen as one living whole so that the unity of our political and cultural life . . . will become clear. We share Fichte's opinion that history is not merely a pursuit for scholars, but that it must be written for the *Volk*. Through its history, the German *Volk* should become aware of its own unique essence, its own unique path, its own unique value. We must never lose sight of this didactic task of history."[67]

Revival of a *Volk*'s legends and folklore could similarly aid in the search for national identity. For according to Diederichs, folktales "most clearly mirror the true German *Volk* soul." Since it was grounded in the fantasies, magical beliefs, and superstitions of premodern man, folklore might also offer the irrational new mystique which Diederichs and those at the HVA were convinced postwar Germans needed to overthrow modern intellectualism. To Diederichs, folktales were thus "living forces for the present and the future," traditions whose revival could lead Germans to a deeper awareness of their common *Volk* character.[68]

During the Weimar era, therefore, the neoconservative firms issued a number of monographs treating German history and folklore. The EDV, for example, supplemented its prewar series of folktale publications with two new multivolume series, *German Tribal Customs* (*Deutsche Stammeskunde*, later changed to *Stammeskunde deutscher Landschaften*, 12 vols., 1924–29) and *The Folktales of German Authors* (*Die Märchen deutscher Dichter*, 5 vols., 1931). In announcing one of his firm's new folktale series, Diederichs expressed the hope that these tales "will make clear what creative forces a rootedness in the blood and soil can produce, and will reveal the very essence and the primal roots of our German *Volk* spirit."[69] For similar reasons, the HVA, DHB, and JFLV published such titles as F. Heyden's *On the Beauty of German Folktales* (*Von deutschen Märchenschönheit*, 1921) or *55 Forgotten Grimm Folktales* (*55 Vergessene Grimmische Märchen*, 1922). Most impressive of all, however, was Diederichs's monumental *Germanic Volk Identity* (*Deutsche Volkheit*) series which appeared in seventy-five volumes between 1925 and 1930. He was quite frank about the antimodern intent of this massive project. Besides helping to revive an interest in the German past and giving Germans a new appreciation of the eternally valid traditions of their *Volk* heritage, Diederichs believed the series would lead the nation out of the "dead end" of modern science, technology, and individual alienation by directing the *Volk* back to the primal, irrational sources which formed the bedrock of the *Volk* spirit.[70] To carry out the undertaking, which involved collecting volumes of old Germanic myths and folktales, biographies of German heroes, and accounts of significant episodes in the *Volk*'s history, the Diederichs house curtailed much of its other publishing activity in the late 1920s. The *Germanic Volk Identity* series was greeted not only by neoconservatives like Stapel, who claimed it corresponded perfectly to the *Volk* conservatism of his own *Deutsches Volkstum* journal, but also by respected intellectuals such as Thomas Mann.[71] Through an energetic publicity campaign which included prizes for book-dealers who developed the most imaginative window displays for the books, the EDV managed to sell nearly three hundred twenty thousand volumes from the series between 1925 and 1933, although this figure fell far short of Diederichs's expectations. To complement the project, the firm also issued a seven-volume series of historical source materials, *The Old Reich* (*Das alte Reich*, 1922–32), which, however, was even less successful, selling barely six thousand individual copies.

Neoconservative interest in German history and mythology naturally extended also to ancient, pre-Christian Germanic culture. Those qualities of the primitive Nordic tribes which had been praised before the war as models for the *Volk* underwent an even more noticeable romanticization after 1918. As the directors of the HVA proclaimed in 1923 when they initiated the *Peasants and Heroes* (*Bauern und Helden*) series of old Nordic tales: "when the German *Volk* of the present day, because of its internal crises and weakness, seeks consolation and strength, . . . [then] it can drink deeply from the ancient Icelandic sagas of vitality. For those sagas reach up to us from the depths and roots of our *Volk* and reveal to us the German soul."[72]

Eugen Diederichs, who had been one of the first to till the Nordic field with his prewar *Thule* series, continued to be the most active and prolific publisher of Nordic literature in the Weimar era. Other neoconservative houses like the LMV rather jealously observed that "Diederichs has almost a monopoly over the literature on Nordic man and Nordic culture, and also has the largest and most receptive public for it."[73] The cornerstone of the EDV's postwar efforts remained the *Thule* series, which he brought to completion in 1930. But he added to this another multivolume series of early Germanic culture, *Early Germandom* (*Frühgermanentum*, 1928–29), which he advertised as an endeavor "which seeks to make the inner experience of our early *Volk* community fruitful for the present and for the future."[74] Diederichs also produced a new mass edition of the classic eleventh-century Icelandic "Edda" saga; by making this epic available to the public, Diederichs hoped to spark a spiritual rebirth of the *Volk*, just as the rediscovery of classic Greek texts had sparked the Renaissance in Italy.[75] Finally, the EDV saturated the Nordic market with a serial entitled *Deutsch-Nordisches Jahrbuch für Kulturaustausch und Volkskunde* (*German-Nordic Yearbook for Cultural Exchange and Folklore*, 1921–30), with a number of individual monographs on old Nordic sagas, myths, and religious practices, and with three heroic Icelandic novels by the young author H. F. Blunck: *Battle of the Heavens* (*Kampf der Gestirne*, 1926), *Conflict with the Gods* (*Streit mit den Göttern*, 1926), and *Dominion Over Fire* (*Gewalt über das Feuer*, 1928).

Despite the EDV's predominance in the field, the Hanseatic and Lehmann houses were also active in Nordic publications. The HVA's *Peasants and Heroes* series (1923–32) consisted of gripping novels set in the dim Nordic past. Like W. Vesper's separately published *The Stern Race* (*Das harte Geschlecht*, 1931), these were "tale[s] of blood vengeance, loyalty unto death, courageous sea voyages, and of the ancient heritage of our *Volk*"; their purpose, the HVA declared, was to revive the often forgotten "deep ethical powers" of the Nordic-Germanic legacy.[76] Since these novels were distributed to DHB subscribers in abridged form, they reached a large audience; Vesper's work, written especially for the book club, sold sixty-five thousand copies in four years. Both the HVA and JFLV also issued several semischolarly studies of ancient Nordic-Germanic folklore, including K. Strasser's *The North Germanic Tribes* (*Die Nordgermanen*, 1932) and W. Meyer-Erlach's *Nordic Prophets and Heroes* (*Nordische Seher und Helden*, 1927). One such JFLV publication, E. Jung's *Germanic Gods and Heroes in the Christian Era: Contributions on the Development of the German Spirit* (*Germanische Göttern und Helden in der christlichen Zeit: Beiträge zur Entwicklungsgeschichte der deutsche Geistesform*, 1922), was announced by the firm as a book which demonstrated that despite the church's attempts to suppress Germanic paganism, "our primal heathen-Germanic memories have consciously or unconsciously remained alive and active to the present day."[77]

In its cultivation of the Nordic ideology, the JFLV added a new element. Two important JFLV books, H. F. K. Günther's *The Nordic Idea Among the Germans* (*Der nordische Gedanke unter den Deutschen*, 1925) and Ludwig Clauss's *The Nordic Soul* (*Die nordische Seele*, 1932), introduced the notion that old Nordic culture and the original Germanic *Volk* spirit it represented were racial phenomena based on a unique, irreplaceable Nordic genetic determinant. This Nordic racial type, which alone was considered capable of the heroic, communal values admired by neoconservatives, had all but perished in modern civilization. To prevent the extinction of Nordic man, these authors urged, Nordic racial types must be selected out from others and energetically cultivated; only then could Germans recaptu :e the communal solidarity and idealistic values of the ancient Nordic age.[78] Clauss's book on this theme was especially popular, selling thirty thousand copies in five years. It was in fact one of the most important and widely read treatises of the entire racial movement in pre-Nazi Germany. Since racial thought in Germany first became widely accepted in the form of Nordic ideology,[79] not only Lehmann's publications in this area, but all neo-conservative attempts to idealize and revive the Germanic-Nordic heritage of the *Volk* had fateful consequences.

The popularity of Nordic ideology in the Weimar period was in part a disguised manifestation of Germans' fear that they were losing or had lost their rural heritage. Because of the rapid growth of German cities and the metropolitan and cosmopolitan nature of liberal Weimar culture, anti-urban resentment was widespread in the Weimar republic.[80] To those like Diederichs who had voiced deep reservations about urbanization before the war, the large metropolises of postwar Germany represented cancerous concentrations of modernity's worst evils, and their rapid growth betokened cultural doom. He saw in urbanism (which he now called simply "the Berlin spirit") a "chaotic and unnatural" accumulation of people and buildings. The frenzied pace of urban life, he believed, made spiritual peace impossible and resulted in rampant mammonism, a frivolous and hedonistic pursuit of senseless amusements, general moral depravity, and cynical manipulation of public opinion by the overintellectualized "asphalt literati" around the large liberal press empires of Mosse and Ullstein. Large cities like Berlin, he concluded, represented "a real sickness of the *Volk* psyche" which threatened to infect the entire nation.[81] This blight of urban life, with its spiritual dissipation, fragmentation, and social atomization, followed inevitably once contact with the rural traditions of the *Volk* was lost. "The more we collect into the cities," Diederichs lamented, "and the more we become separated from nature in all its totality, the more we lose our feeling for the totality of human existence and thought and the more we dissolve into isolation." Urban dwellers, especially the modern proletariat, had lost their natural roots and ancient *völkisch* heritage, and thus had become alienated, directionless, self-centered creatures who felt no sense of communal solidarity with the larger *Volk*.[82] The solution to the spiritual and social malaise of modern urbanism seemed evident to the neoconservative publishers: as Diederichs explained, "the German spirit must again root itself firmly . . . in the natural German soil."[83] (Both Lehmann and Diederichs, for example, suggested that factories and the urban work force be relocated to the rural countryside.)[84]

Through their publishing programs, the neoconservative houses sought to awaken a new interest in nature which would somehow reverse the tide of German urbanization and bring to an end "big city civilization"

(*Grossstadtzivilisation*). The Stalling and Diederichs firms, for example, issued works like E. Schmahl's *Men in the Big City* (*Menschen in der grossen Stadt*, 1932) or H. Ullmann's *Flight from Berlin* (*Flucht aus Berlin*, 1932) deprecating urban life. The HVA, JFLV, and EDV each produced a number of idealized studies on German regional geography and native ecology, including L. Schreyer's *The German Countryside* (*Deutsche Landschaft*, 1932); A. E. Günther's *Totem, Animal, and Man in Living Interdependence* (*Totem, Tier, und Mensch in Lebenszusammenhang*, 1927); and R. Mielke's *Settlement Patterns of the German Volk and Their Relation to Man and Landscape* (*Siedlungskunde des deutschen Volkes und ihre Beziehung zu Mensch und Landschaft*, 1927). The HBV, on the other hand, specialized in idyllic serial publications such as *The German Hometown* (*Die deutsche Heimat*, 1926). New editions of works by the early agrarian ideologue W. H. Riehl or studies of his ideas also appeared under the EDV and HVA imprints.

Continuing a tradition Diederichs began before the war, the publishers issued the fictional works of the major "hearth and homeland" writers (*Heimatskünstler*) as another means of turning Germans back to nature. Hans F. Blunck, a prolific and extremely popular "hearth and homeland" author of the 1920s, was signed on by the EDV in 1923; Diederichs published six of his "homeland" works and helped him make an early name for himself. When other publishing firms such as the Hanseatic house later sought to lure Blunck away from the EDV, Blunck felt compelled (at least initially) to remain with Diederichs not only because the Jena publisher had influenced him deeply, but because he had, as Blunck gratefully acknowledged, "backed me at a time when the prospect of commercial success [for my books] was quite small."[85] Diederichs, in return, displayed deep affection for Blunck, whom he regarded as one of his "publishing house sons." In the late 1920s, he used his extensive influence and personal contacts in an attempt to have Blunck appointed to the Prussian Academy of Writers and nominated for the Nobel prize for literature.[86] Likewise the Langen-Müller subsidiary of the HVA, which boasted of its antiurban, anti-Berlin orientation and its preference for works on the rural cosmos,[87] became one of the leading publishers of "hearth and homeland" writers in postwar Germany. Five of Blunck's works eventually appeared on the LMV list, as did eleven by Hanns Johst, ten by Emil Strauss, and the collected works of Ludwig Thoma. Even the small Beenken house published Hermann Löns's autobiography, *From East to West* (*Von Ost nach West*, 1921), and Beenken personally convinced Hans Rosegger to write a sympathetic study of the popular homeland author Peter Rosegger, which the HBV published in 1925.

As it had with Diederichs before 1914, the neoconservative publishers' antiurban fascination with the *Volk*'s rural heritage led ultimately to an idealization of the German peasant. Diederichs now praised the peasantry as "an ovum of aristocratic spirituality" and the origin of all true German cultural traditions. Indeed, he agreed with Riehl that the peasant was the source and essence of Germanic *Volk* character, and for that reason had a unique contribution to make to the *Volk*'s spiritual regeneration.[88] Lehmann regarded the life of the peasantry as so crucial in the shaping of the nation's character that he believed all Germans should be required to work for two years in agriculture before entering their chosen careers.[89]

The publishers' romantic peasant image was diffused to a wider audience through their publication of "peasant novels" such as H. Graedener's *Utz Urbach* (*Utz Urbach: Ein Bauernkriegsroman*), issued by the EDV in 1924, or the DHB's 1919 reissue of W. von Polenz's influential *The Peasant From Büttner* (*Der Büttnerbauer*), a work which joined the peasant motif with antiurbanism and a viscious anti-Semitism. Political tracts such as Karsthans's *The Peasants March* (*Die Bauern marschieren*, 1931), J. Schimmelreiter's *Beneath the Black Peasant Flag* (*Unter den schwarzen Bauernfahne: Die Landbevölkerung im Kampfe für Deutschlands Befreiung*, 1929), or W. Luetgebrune's *Modern Prussia's Peasant War* (*Neu-Preussens Bauernkrieg*, 1931) were issued by the GSV, JFLV, and the HVA, respectively; these works all demanded greater recognition of the peasant estate's political, social, and economic contributions to the nation. But it was Lehmann's house which became the outlet for the most extreme wing of the peasant movement. For the JFLV published the works of R. Walter Darré, the Nazi agrarian ideologue whose "Blood and Soil" (*Blut und Boden*) ideology viewed the peasantry as the primary agent for the *Volk*'s racial rejuvenation. Lehmann, who shared nearly all Darré's ideas,[90] published his two most important works on the peasantry, *The Peasantry as Lifespring of the Nordic Race* (*Das Bauerntum als Lebensquelle der nordischen Rasse*, 1929) and *New Nobility From Blood and Soil* (*Neuadel aus Blut und Boden*, 1930). By exhorting JFLV authors to praise Darré's books,[91] in the 1930s Lehmann was able to sell forty-four thousand copies of Darré's first work, and more than sixty thousand copies of his second. After Darré achieved the post of minister of agriculture and "peasant leader" (Reichsbauernführer) in the Third Reich, he expressed his deepest gratitude to his publisher Lehmann who, he claimed, "first enabled me to initiate my struggle on behalf of the German peasantry."[92]

As the authors of the JFLV demonstrated, many of those who immersed themselves after World War I in theories about the unique character, historical and mythological traditions, and rural Nordic heritage of the German *Volk* were unable to resist the temptation to interpret Germanic *Volk* character in racial terms. For it was through race and blood that the native qualities and unique identity of the *Volk* seemed to be transmitted from generation to generation. Thus surveys of German history were susceptible to the attractions of racism as an interpretive device. W. Classen's three-volume *The Evolution of the German Volk* (*Das Werden des deutschen Volkes*), issued by the HVA in 1921–24, was advertised for example as "the first work in all German historiography to recognize and emphasize the racial community (*Blutsgemeinschaft*) as an elemental historical factor. The epochs of our history are presented here, for the first time, as racial transformations."[93] To be sure, not all the neoconservative firms adopted a racial outlook. Eugen Diederichs, after his brief flirtation with racial anthropology at the turn of the century, progressively distanced his house from racism, while the Beenken and Stalling houses never demonstrated any interest at all in racial theory. But those houses, like the J. F. Lehmanns Verlag, which did embrace racism did so with a vengeance, and their subsequent activities in this area during the Weimar era proved most consequential.

As indicated above, it was through his firm's medical program that Lehmann had become active in racial publications before 1914. As a confirmed social Darwinist and publisher of scientific texts, moreover, he was sympathetic to such works as H. Holle's *General Biology as a Basis of World View, the Conduct of Life, and Politics* (*Allgemeine Biologie als Grundlage für Weltanschauung, Lebensführung, und Politik*), which his firm published in 1919 and which he claimed "demonstrates the possibility and necessity of applying biological thinking to all spheres of life."[94] By the 1920s, the JFLV was Germany's foremost champion of "racial science," and it was in large part through his house's efforts that racial theory gained a mass audience and widespread popularity before 1933.

The notion of race was hardly new in European thought, and one of Lehmann's publishing strategies was to revive earlier racial literature, much as Diederichs sought to revive romanticism. In the mid-nineteenth century, for example, Arthur de Gobineau had developed a fairly sophisticated theory which saw race as a fundamental factor in history and regarded racial mixing as the inevitable cause of a civilization's decline and fall. A Gobineau Society had flourished in Germany since 1894 under the direction of Karl Ludwig Schemann, Gobineau's German biographer, translator, and a pioneering racial scholar in his own right. When a young researcher uncovered a new Gobineau manuscript in 1924 and submitted it to the Lehmann house, the publisher therefore contacted Schemann (now a professor at the University of Freiburg) to verify the manuscript's authenticity and the accuracy of the German translation. He then made the published edition, *The Importance of Race in the Life of Nations* (*Die Bedeutung der Rasse im Leben der Völker*, 1926), available to the members of the Gobineau Society at a 25 percent discount in hopes they would distribute the work to wider circles.[95]

The most important racial author associated with Lehmann's firm, however, was Hans F. K. Günther. This relationship proved extremely beneficial for both men. The publisher's discovery and energetic promotion of Günther transformed the author into Germany's leading racial theorist, while the enormous success of Günther's works raised the JFLV to undisputed leadership in the racial field.

Lehmann first encountered Günther in 1920. In that year the publisher was laying plans for a definitive illustrated handbook on the German race which would be "a human guidebook through Germany in which general racial characteristics will be stressed and represented predominantly through ideal types." This scientific racial ethnology (*Rassenkunde*), he hoped, would serve as a basis for all future work in racial science.[96] Deeply impressed by a manuscript on modern decadence which Günther, then a young school teacher, had submitted to the JFLV,[97] Lehmann decided this author was just the man to execute the racial handbook. The publisher called Günther to Munich, interviewed him intensely for two days, and finally commissioned him for the undertaking. So committed was Lehmann to this project that he persuaded Günther to resign his teaching post; for the next two years the JFLV supported the author financially while he researched and wrote.[98] Günther's *Racial Ethnology of the German Volk* (*Rassenkunde des deutschen Volkes*) appeared in 1922. Lehmann, although slightly offended that Günther had not mentioned in the foreword that the book had been written at the publisher's instigation, nevertheless greeted the volume as "a salvation" for Germans and was convinced that because of it, "in the future the racial question will be of the greatest possible importance to our *Volk*."[99] The work proved a great success, for unlike most popular racial tracts, it was grounded in an impressive amount of scholarly research, had the appearance of scientific objectivity, and won acclaim from some respected university scholars. The first printing was exhausted after six weeks and by 1932 some thirty-two thousand copies had been sold; a decade later the original edition and an abridgment (*Kleine Rassenkunde des deutschen Volkes*, 1929) had combined sales of more than three hundred twenty-two thousand copies.[100]

The *Rassenkunde* volume began a lustrous career for Günther as Germany's leading racial authority. During the later 1920s, he produced six more works on racial science for the Lehmann house, all of which he claimed (possibly with some prompting from Lehmann) had been written "with the greatest personal participation and support" of his publisher. In the case of his *Nobility and Race* (*Adel und Rasse*, 1926) and the extremely influential *Race and Style* (*Rasse und Stil: Gedanken über die Beziehung von Rasse und Stil im Leben und in der Geistesgeschichte*, 1926), for example, Günther had originally intended to write only short essays, but was persuaded by Lehmann to expand them into full-length volumes.[101] By 1926, Günther was earning twelve thousand marks annually in royalties; he earned more yet in subsequent years, for an estimated five hundred thousand copies of his works had been sold by 1945.[102] His pseudoscientific racial works and his book *The Nordic Idea* were among the earliest expressions of a coherent racial outlook acceptable to educated Germans. When the Nazi-controlled Thuringian state government created Germany's first chair of racial science at the University of Jena in 1930, it appointed Günther to the post. That event marked a significant victory for the racial movement and demonstrated the extent to which racial thought had penetrated German culture. It testified also to the success of the Lehmann house, which had first catapulted Günther into the public eye and which rode the tide of his subsequent fame.

Lehmann's commitment and service to the racial cause is equally evident in his dealings with K. L. Schemann. While planning a multivolume historical series which would "prove how race has been a determining factor in the development of nations," Lehmann wrote to Schemann in 1925 soliciting his advice on scholars who might contribute works for the project. When Lehmann learned that Schemann himself was writing a comprehensive history of racial thought in the social sciences, the publisher asked him to publish it as part of the projected JFLV series. As inducement, he promised to furnish Schemann with some two thousand racial illustrations he had collected and which, he claimed, were otherwise unobtainable. Lehmann made it clear that if Schemann did not accept this offer, then the JFLV would be forced to duplicate Schemann's topic in its own series. Giving the valuable illustrations to another author, the publisher pointed out, would surely place Schemann's book in a poor competitive position.[103] Schemann was forced to acknowledge that the JFLV "has achieved a virtual monopoly on racial works," and he agreed to publish his study with the house.[104] After the first volume of Schemann's projected three-volume *Race in the Liberal Arts* (*Die Rasse in den Geisteswissenschaften*) appeared in 1927, Lehmann sought to popularize it by requesting a score of prominent public figures to send in favorable reviews of the book to newspapers and journals.[105]

Meanwhile, a minor episode briefly disturbed Schemann's relation with his publisher. Skeptical of Günther's journalistic treatment of the racial issue and perhaps jealous of his sudden popularity, the more academically inclined Schemann questioned the validity of Günther's scholarship in critical reviews. When Lehmann learned of Schemann's remarks, he was infuriated. Schemann's attacks on Günther, the publisher thundered, not only cast doubts on one of the great path breakers of racial science and encouraged the "Jewish press," but also had a highly unfavorable effect on the entire market for racial literature at a time when the general economic situation was especially grim. The financial resources of his house were not unlimited, Lehmann pointed out to Schemann; since the JFLV was already taking a large financial loss on Schemann's first volume, Schemann should not be so ungrateful as to attack other authors of the house.[106]

Pressured by his benefactor, Schemann ceased his public criticisms of Günther and the matter quickly passed. And none too soon, for that same year Schemann himself came under attack in an episode that once again demonstrated Lehmann's loyalty toward his authors. Schemann had been completing his work under a grant from the Prussian Emergency Association for German Scholarship (Notgemeinschaft für deutsche Wissenschaft). When the second volume of his work, *Major Epochs and Major Peoples of History and Their Relation to Race* (*Hauptepochen und Hauptvölker der Geschichte und ihre Stellung zur Rasse*), appeared in 1929, the outcry of liberals was so great that the Socialist minister of interior in Prussia was forced to withdraw the Association's grant to Schemann. Lehmann immediately took up his author's cause and sent ringing protests to several newspapers. He undertook this campaign, he later admitted, partly to advertise for the book; he was duly pleased that the "Jewish press," by publicizing the controversy, had helped make Schemann's books more widely known.[107] At the same time, the publisher sought other means of support for his author by requesting a stipend for Schemann from another scientific academy so that the final volume of the trilogy could appear.[108] When the academy rejected Lehmann's request, he wrote to Schemann: "Under these circumstances I consider it my compelling duty, despite the present economic crisis, to enable you to complete the third volume of your work. . . . I bid you proceed with peace of mind. It is a matter of proving that in Germany today, works of pure scholarship which represent solely German interests are still possible. Therefore I will make it possible for you to finish your study even without the help of the Emergency Association."[109] Lehmann himself thereupon supplied the subsidies previously provided by the Association.

When the third and final volume, *The Racial Question in Recent Literature* (*Die Rassenfrage im Schrifttum der Neuzeit*), of his magnum opus appeared in 1931, Schemann thanked Lehmann for making the entire undertaking possible, adding that it was "a special fortune that my last work, which is also my most important, appeared in your house."[110] Indeed, Lehmann had sacrificed much to produce Schemann's books: by 1929, the publisher claimed to have lost more than seven thousand marks on volume 1 and expected a similar loss for each of the two successive volumes.[111] That he remained committed to the publication of works like Schemann's despite such financial sacrifice attests strongly to Lehmann's ideological devotion to the racial cause.

In order to "systematically till the whole field of racial literature,"[112] the JFLV produced nearly twenty additional books, by both prominent academics and lesser-known authors, examining all aspects of racial theory. These included such monographs as M. Grant, *The Decline of the Great Races: Race as the Basis of European History* (*Der Untergang der grossen Rassen: Die Rasse als Grundlagen der Geschichte Europas*, 1925); L. Clauss, *Race and Soul* (*Rasse und Seele*, 1926); the photographic collections *Archive of Racial Portraits* (*Archiv für Rassenbilder: Einzeldarstellungen aus dem Gebiet der Rassenkunde*, 1926–27); and *German Heads of the Nordic Race* (*Deutsche Köpfe nordischer Rasse*, 1927); and three works by the Hamburg anthropologist Walter Scheidt. Lehmann believed that "it is necessary today, now that the importance of race for general culture is universally acknowledged, to treat all the specific disciplines from the standpoint of the race question."[113] Thus he published such discourses as P. Schultze-Naumburg's *Art and Race* (*Kunst und Rasse*, 1927) and S. Radner's *Race and Humor* (*Rasse und Humor*, 1930).

To complement its extensive book publications, the Lehmann house also acquired three racial journals. As a member of the German Society for Racial Hygiene (Deutsche Gesellschaft für Rassenhygiene), Lehmann had long been acquainted with that organization's journal, *Archiv für Rassen- und Gesellschaftsbiologie* (*Archive for Racial and Social Biology*). As the *Archive* encountered severe financial difficulties in 1921–22 and was in danger of folding, Lehmann, who was better able to absorb the losses, took over publication from the B. G. Teubner Verlag. Under its new publisher, the organ began addressing

> all those who are interested in the questions of demographic policy
> and renewal of the *Volk*. We appeal especially to those who hold
> the fate of our *Volk* in their hands: teachers, politicians, physicians,
> clerics. Besides examining general problems of racial biology
> (heredity, selection, adaptation), of social biology (social selection,
> the rise and fall of peoples and cultures, the biological bases of socially
> important phenomena), and of racial hygiene (research into the
> conditions of biological survival and development of races, etc.),
> the *Archiv* will henceforth attempt to resist . . . the danger of a
> declining pool of "young blood."[114]

In 1926 the Munich publisher founded a separate new racial journal of his own, *Volk und Rasse* (*Volk and Race*), which soon attained a circulation of nearly three thousand. As the title implied, *Volk und Rasse* represented a conscious attempt to fuse the traditional concept of *Volk* with that of race and thus win adherents from the larger *völkisch* movement. Lehmann and the journal's editor Börries von Münchhausen hoped to unify folklore, the social sciences, and racial science into one endeavor which would serve the racial needs of the *Volk*.[115] In cooperation with the German Society for Research into Bloodgroups (Deutsche Gesellschaft für Blutgruppenforschung), the JFLV founded a final racial journal in 1928, *Zeitschrift für Rassenphysiologie* (*Journal of Racial Physiology*).

To further the racial movement in Germany, the publisher used other imaginative means. Convinced that "the stubborn activity of a few can create a general shift of opinion among the *Volk*," in the early 1920s he founded the Association for Germanic *Volk* Character and Racial Research (Werkbund für deutsches Volkstum und Rassenforschung). The Association directed racial agitation through mass petitions, press activity, and public lectures (for which the JFLV produced the racial wall charts, photographs, and other aids).[116] To encourage racial research, it cosponsored contests with the Nordic Ring (Nordischer Ring) and the Young Nordic League (Jungnordischer Bund) in which cash prizes as high as 500 marks were awarded to individuals who assembled pictorial family trees demonstrating how Nordic racial features were passed down from generation to generation.[117] And the first issue of *Volk und Rasse* announced that "in order to support *völkisch* and racial research, the editors and the Lehmann Verlag have formed an agreement to apply certain of this journal's revenues directly to research work. We thank the publishing house that even before the appearance of this [first] issue, it designated a large sum to be used in initiating racial research."[118]

Whether neoconservative publishers conceived of the German *Volk* in racial terms or not, they were generally agreed that the *Volk*'s survival hung on the successful discharge of three pressing tasks. First, the collapse of the Austro-Hungarian empire and the territorial and colonial losses imposed on Germany by the Treaty of Versailles had multiplied the number of Germans in Europe and elsewhere who now lived beyond the boundaries of the German Reich. With the international insecurities and nationalist passions of the postwar era, it was feared now more than ever that the loss of these endangered fellow Germans, many of whom were systematically persecuted by the non-German governments under which they found themselves after 1918, would seriously threaten the future of the *Volk* as a whole. Solidarity with these imperiled German minorities abroad was thus considered imperative until such time as the entire *Volk* could be united under the protection of a single German state. Second, with the loss of seventy thousand square kilometers of the prewar Reich (not to mention the vast areas of its colonial empire), and with the continuing postwar growth of the German population, many feared that the need for new "living space" (*Lebensraum*) for the *Volk* was even more urgent and essential for the nation's long-term survival than before the war. And third, as we have seen above, there was in the postwar years a growing concern over the Westernization of German culture and a corresponding anti-Western reaction. This, however, was merely one part of a larger and more gnawing fear that the increasing domination of the *Volk* by non-German, "alien" elements and forces was rapidly destroying the *Volk*'s identity, vitality, and very existence. Many neoconservatives therefore came to believe that only a general purification and the elimination of undesirable non-German influences from within the *Volk* could assure its survival.

After 1918 nearly all the neoconservative publishers actively supported the various organizations which worked for the interests of endangered German minorities abroad. Lehmann, of course, continued to play a powerful role within the Pan-German League and sat on its national executive committee until the mid 1920s. In 1919 he personally helped League President Class draft the League's Bamberg declaration which outlined the stubbornly antirepublican, revanchist, irredentist course the organization pursued throughout the Weimar era.[119] The DHV, which had been closely associated with the Pan-German League since the turn of the century, joined the German Protective League for Border Germans and Germandom Abroad (Deutschen Schutzbund für Grenz- und Auslandsdeutschtum) in 1919, and in 1930 the DHV's newly acquired subsidiary, the Georg Müller Verlag, applied for membership in the Society for Germandom Abroad (Verein für das Deutschtum im Ausland)—although, as the GMV admitted, the application was at least partly motivated by the hope of "gaining access to the [reading market of] Germans living abroad."[120] As indicated above (see pp. 47–48), the journals of the major neoconservative houses all held membership in Rudolf Pechel's Workgroup of German Journals for the Interests of Border Germans and Germandom Abroad. When the Workgroup supplied *Die Tat* with propaganda material on the German minorities in Denmark, Diederichs eagerly incorporated it into the March 1925 *Tat-Sonderheft*, which was dedicated entirely to the problems of Schleswig-Holstein.[121]

The publishers, through their publications, continually drew attention to the plight of German minorities abroad, especially in the east. Diederichs for example, who feared that German communities in mixed border areas such as Poland were being overrun by foreign cultural influences, personally commissioned H. Hauser to investigate the problems of Germans in East Prussia who were cut off from the Reich by the new Polish corridor. The subsequent book in which Hauser reported his findings, *Storm in the East* (*Wetter im Osten*, 1932) was then advertised by the EDV as a volume which hoped "to awaken Germans to the decisive task of rescuing the East Prussian provinces from Polish domination."[122] Lehmann, too, considered it "completely necessary and appropriate to present to our *Volk* the terrible peril [which minority Germans face] in the East. We must make clear to the entire nation and to the government that this heinous situation can and must no longer be allowed to continue."[123] After discussing with authors how they might best treat the "eastern problem" and suggest appropriate solutions, Lehmann issued such inflammatory pan-German tracts as H. Krieger's *Mass Murder in the Romanian Prison Hell of Sipote* (*Der Massenmord in der rumänischen Gefangenhölle Sipote*, 1920), E. von Stackelberg-Sutlem's *A Life in Struggle for the Baltic* (*Ein Leben im baltischen Kampf*, 1927), and Manteuffel-Katzdangen's *Germany and the East* (*Deutschland und der Osten*, 1926), of which some two hundred fifty thousand copies were distributed. Likewise, the Stalling house and the GMV demonstrated solidarity with the Germans of Poland and Alsace by publishing F. von Oertzen's *This is Poland* (*Das ist Poland*, 1931) and A. Mayer's *The Alsace* (*Das Elsass: Volks- und Kulturfragen: Die natürliche Einheit und der kulturellen Zusammenhang der oberrheinischen und süddeutschen Länder*, 1919). Nor were the Germans in the Reich's lost colonies forgotten: the HVA issued novels like H. Grimm's *The Oil Prospector of Duala* (*Der Ölsucher von Duala*, 1918), which portrayed the mistreatment and death of a German in Africa at the hands of the French who assumed control of the German Cameroons after 1914. This passionate work, which reached its thirtieth printing by 1933, called for violent revenge against the French oppressors of German-Africans. Another HVA novel, H. Reepen's *Children of the Steppes: A Novel from the German Colony of East Africa* (*Kinder der Steppe: Ein Roman aus der deutschen Kolonie Ostafrika*, 1927) claimed to prove "that the [African] land we peacefully conquered with our hot and heavy labors has not been lost forever. German yearning still embraces it, and these 'children of the steppes' [German settlers in Africa] will one day return to the womb of their unforgotten German Motherland."[124]

But it was not merely the larger unity of the *Volk* with its scattered members which concerned the *völkisch* nationalists around the neoconservative houses. Many of them believed the future of the *Volk* could be assured only if there were also adequate living space, especially new rural land, where Germany's own excess population could settle and where the world's endangered German minorities could find refuge and reunion with their fellow Germans. Lehmann, for example, after working closely with the author on the manuscript, issued R. Böhmer's *The Heritage of the Disinherited* (*Das Erbe der Enterbten*, 1928) which argued that the workers and lower middle-class Germans who had been "disinherited" of their rural heritage by industrialization and urbanization should each be given a plot of land to farm. This would allow the German masses to recover their premodern roots in the natural landscape. Distribution of land on such a vast scale, however, required acquisition of vast expanses of new territory for Germany. With new resources at its disposal, moreover, Germany could achieve complete economic autarky and thus gain independence from foreign influence. In Lehmann's mind, therefore, new living space for the German *Volk* was as much a "life-necessity" after the war as before it. The men behind the Hanseatic publishing empire shared these convictions, for in the late 1920s the HVA and its subsidiaries published works such as W. Sombart's *Volk and Space* (*Volk und Raum*, 1928) or G. Schröer's *Land Crisis* (*Land Not*, 1928), a work which demanded more land for German peasants and workers and which sold more than sixty thousand copies. By far the most famous and influential of these expansionist books, however, was Hans Grimm's 1,300-page *Volk Without Space* (*Volk Ohne Raum*), which reached a huge audience in the early 1930s, in part because of the unusual commercial predicament of the HVA's Langen-Müller house. Grimm's militant fictionalized manifesto on the need for more German *Lebensraum* originally appeared in the Albert Langen Verlag catalogue in 1926.[125] Although the cumbersome, two-volume work was priced at a nearly prohibitive 25 marks, it had already sold some sixty thousand copies and made Grimm wealthy by 1931, when the ALV was acquired by the DHV and GMV. At that time Gustav Pezold, director of the financially troubled new Langen-Müller house, was locked in a bitter struggle with the book industry and the liberal press over the Krause affair (see pp. 53–56), and he desperately needed both new capital and a public relations victory. Pezold decided he might gain both by issuing an inexpensive new one-volume edition of *Volk Without Space*. Although the high production costs of such an undertaking and the low retail price of 8.5 marks might mean a long-term financial loss for the house, he believed the edition's high sales would dramatically increase the LMV's turnover and provide the firm with an immediate source of badly needed cash, not to mention the favorable publicity. After persuading a reluctant Grimm to agree to the gamble by promising him a handsome 1 mark royalty for each copy and guaranteeing his nearly total independence in future dealings with the house, Pezold was able to issue a "mass edition" (*Volksausgabe*) of Grimm's classic work in time for the 1931 Christmas season. While the house ultimately lost as much as 1.53 marks on each copy sold, a sensational two hundred twenty-five thousand copies of this edition of *Volk Without Space* were sold by 1934, and its call for more *Lebensraum* for Germany became deeply anchored in the public consciousness. By issuing several more of Grimm's works, including paperbound excerpts from *Volk Without Space*, the LMV was able to more than quintuple its turnover by 1933 and recoup some of its losses, while at the same time disseminate Grimm's ideology of *völkisch* imperialism even more widely.[126]

Finally, postwar neoconservatives were convinced that the future of the German *Volk* stood in extreme jeopardy unless it were able to liberate itself not only from foreign bondage in international affairs (the Versailles Treaty), but from the internal influence of "alien," non-German forces as well. We have seen how, out of a deep-seated hatred for modernity, cultural pessimists frequently sought psychological escape by positing the compensatory ideal of some premodern German *Volk* utopia enjoying heroic values and communal harmony. According to standard *völkisch* theory, this original *Volk* existence had been progressively destroyed by the forces of modernity; the corruption or loss of the "natural," original Germanic essence was thus one effect of modernization. At some point in the chimeric dreamland of *Volk* ideology, however, the relationship between modernity and the loss of the *Volk*'s original purity became twisted and inverted, and one of the supposed effects of modernity (corruption of the *Volk* and a loss of their true German identity) became the cause—that is, some *völkisch* ideologues came to believe that the multifarious evils of the modern age were in fact a direct *result* of the adulteration and dissolution of the ancient Germanic essence by alien, un-German forces. There were thus some who firmly held that, to overthrow modernity and return to those idealized, utopian values and life-styles of the distant past, Germans must free themselves from those alien elements which had obscured pure, genuine Germanic qualities and robbed Germans of their clear identity as a *Volk*. In short, the removal of foreign influence in German life was to remove the hated conditions of modernity.

Eugen Diederichs, for example, attributed a large part of Germany's modern spiritual crisis to the "foreign infiltration" (*Überfremdung*) of the nation's cultural life.[127] Before the war, under the influence of A. Bonus, he had suspected that even Christianity represented an alien force within German life. After 1918 he was certain that the introduction of this Romanic-Hebraic religion had destroyed the healthy natural paganism of the ancient Germanic tribes and thus weakened the original *Volk* spirit. His firm issued books like F. Schaafhausen's *The Entrance of Christianity Into the German Essence* (*Das Eingang des Christentums in das deutsche Wesen*, 1929), he told his readers, because he hoped to demonstrate precisely how Christianity had destroyed the *Volk*'s primal character.[128]

The publishing houses associated with the DHV were also obsessed with alien influence. The DHV bookstore, for example, considered it "a sacred duty to fight for German culture" by "driving back all literature that is alien to the German essence."[129] Even more emphatic on this point were the directors of the German Home Library, who saw an historic struggle being waged over the German soul, a struggle on which hung the fate of the *Volk*. "Over the past two decades," the DHB proclaimed in 1932, "wherever our agonized *Volk* has feverishly and passionately sought to reassert its freedom and regain its power, honor, and *Lebensraum*, the same destructive alien forces have come forward to choke off our national idealism and the sound national instincts from which we draw our strength." Germans must be on guard against the talented, but dangerous forces which use the press and book trade to spread "alien spiritual goods" among the *Volk*: "It is a matter of the being or nonbeing of our German way of life. We call {upon our readers] to join the struggle against dissolution and foreign infiltration, against domination by non-Germans. Each of our books will be like an army fighting for the German idea, the German disposition, the German will." Because the DHB considered itself "a sharp weapon in this struggle against the alien literary domination of our German *Volk*," it pledged to promote only that which was purely German: "[Our firm] is founded on the belief that only German authors have anything to say to us Germans, that only authors who are rooted in the Germanic *Volk* character and whose ideas have arisen out of it can be in a position to offer more than [the usual fare] of divisiveness, agitation, and tension. The works of the DHB are spiritually pure because the corrosive poison which is found in so many contemporary books has no place in ours; . . . {our books] will lead us back to the roots of our power—the Germanic *Volk* character."[130] In keeping with such a philosophy, when the HVA acquired the esteemed Georg Müller Verlag in the late 1930s, the new director Pezold struck from the firm's extensive lists all those works by authors whom he considered alien and un-German (although this move was also related to Pezold's financial retrenchment of the GMV). These stricken authors included: Charles Baudelaire, Denis Diderot, Heinrich Heine, William Shakespeare, Stendhal, R. L. Stevenson, and Henry Fielding.

J. F. Lehmann was equally anxious to prevent non-German forces from dominating the *Volk*. JFLV works such as Wundt's *The German World View* or J. Tillenius's *Racial Soul and Christianity* (*Rassenseele und Christentum: Ein Verusch, die Erkenntnisse der Rassenforschung im religiösen Dienst am Volk zu verwenden*, 1926) were published to help Germans clarify their own unique weltanschauung and develop a Germanized form of Christianity so as better to resist foreign influences.[131] The radical Munich publisher backed up his publicistic work with activity in organizations such as the xenophobic German-*Völkisch* Defense and Offense League, mentioned earlier (see p. 158), and the Fighting League for German Culture (Kampfbund für deutsche Kultur), a Nazi-controlled organization founded in 1928 and dedicated to the overthrow of alien, "anti-*Volk*" forces in German cultural life. Lehmann, indeed, was one of the Fighting League's patron members.[132]

But Lehmann, who after the war saw nearly every issue involving the *Volk* in biological and racial terms, ultimately conceived of *Volk* purification as requiring racial eugenics. Interest in eugenics was widespread in Europe after 1918 and was accepted by many scientists both in Germany and the Soviet Union. While in Russia eugenics was seen as a progressive, left-wing force which could be used to reform society and forge a new socialist order, in Germany the science of eugenics became linked with right-wing, racial values.[133] Lehmann (who like other racists preferred the term 'racial hygiene' to eugenics) believed the Nordic-Germanic race was being fatally endangered by the "upsurge of inferior and decadent sectors of the population" and by pollution from non-German races.[134] In order to safeguard the *Volk* from racial adulteration and decline, Lehmann devoted his house and his journals to "opposing the influence of foreign races in German life."[135] The Munich publisher, who personally advocated the sterilization of "inferiors," issued some eighteen works on racial hygiene which preached the necessity of such measures as premarital racial certification and selective breeding to strengthen German racial stock. These publications included the following: a highly respected two-volume *Outline of Hereditary Theory and Racial Hygiene* (*Grundriss der Erblichkeitslehre und Rassenhygiene*, 1921) by the well-known geneticists and hygenicists E. Bauer, E. Fischer, and F. Lenz; *Hereditary Theory, Racial Hygiene, and Population Policy* (*Vererbungslehre, Rassenhygiene, und Bevölkerungspolitik*, 1926) by H. Siemens; and O. Kankeleit's *Sterilization For Racial-Hygenic and Social Reasons* (*Die Unfruchtbarmachung aus rassenhygienischen und sozialen Gründe*, 1929). Lehmann hoped to produce a clear eugenic program "which, after the creation of a dictatorship, can then be easily transformed into law. I have long worked for this kind of program and am pleased that my work is falling on fertile ground. It must be consciously and deliberately laid out so that the coming dictator will find the ground fully prepared."[136]

Lehmann died just a few months before the Nuremberg racial laws of 1935 were promulgated. Before his death, however, Hitler personally commended the Munich publisher for all he had done to spread racial thought and the desire for racial eugenics in Germany.[137] The JFLV was perhaps better suited to this task than any other. For the Lehmann house brought together, as few other institutions of the time, respected geneticists, practicing physicians, university scholars, and lay popularizers of racial and eugenic theory. The prestige of the house's medical publications alone lent much credibility and respectability to its literature on racism and racial hygiene, and probably convinced many lay readers that eugenic measures to preserve the health and purity of the race were indeed a medical necessity. On the other hand, the firm's racial and eugenic publications were often of high enough quality to be taken seriously in medical and scholarly circles.[138]

When neoconservatives like Lehmann warned of the dangers of alien or inferior racial types and of the need to extirpate foreign influence from Germany, they meant above all the Jews. Anti-Semitism was an integral part of the *völkisch* reaction against liberal modernity. For to some Germans, the Jews were a symbol for economic, political, and intellectual liberalism. Legally excluded from landownership and craft guilds until the nineteenth century, Jews had become concentrated in those few urban, bourgeois occupations left open to them: commerce, finance, capitalistic enterprise, journalism, and the liberal professions. They became liberalism's most loyal supporters because the liberal program of civic equality, economic freedom, religious toleration, and popular representation promised to free them from their social, legal, and economic bondage. Indeed, the triumph of liberalism and Jewish emancipation went hand in hand. After Bismarck introduced full civic equality in 1867 along with other liberal measures such as laissez-faire capitalism and a national parliament, Jews began to play an increasingly important and prominent role in German life. Thus Jews became closely associated with liberalism: "they contributed to its establishment, benefited from its institutions, and [came] under fire when it was attacked."[139] In the popular mind, the Jew often personified modernity in general, and his growing influence was often seen less as the by-product than as the root cause of modernization and the ills which it brought. The neoconservative reaction against liberal modernity and the desire to clarify German *Volk* identity therefore frequently took expression as anti-Semitism.

As we have seen, even Eugen Diederichs, the most humane and noble minded of the publishers, became susceptible to anti-Semitic outbursts during the war and its traumatic aftermath. In 1922, however, in a lengthy article on anti-Semitism,[140] he tried to confront head-on his own ambiguous attitudes toward the Jews. Jews, he decided, were spiritually and racially distinct from the "European race" (Germans, Slavs, and the Romance peoples), and were destined forever to remain so; their status as a "guest *Volk*" residing among the "host *Volk*" was a permanent and immutable one. For the "oriental" Jewish ethos was essentially rational and intellectual, while the European ethos was inherently demonic and irrational. Abandoning his earlier wartime belief that assimilation of Jews into the German *Volk* was possible, Diederichs now maintained that Jews, because of their intrinsic rational outlook, could never melt into the European host nations. An assimilated Jew became a rootless, homeless individual hopelessly torn between two fundamentally contradictory outlooks, the intellectual and the instinctual. Although Diederichs thus believed a certain inevitable tension existed and would continue to exist between Jews and Europeans, he nevertheless rejected the vulgar anti-Semitism he saw around him. To be sure, some anti-Semitic hatred was perhaps inevitable and understandable when peoples like the Germans struggled to attain *völkisch* self-consciousness; but eventually this must give way to a coexistence and cooperation between Germans and Jews. For the Jews, in his opinion, performed a valuable and indispensable function as "leavening" or seasoning within European society, and the relation between Jews and Europeans was ultimately a symbiotic one, beneficial to both parties. Vulgar anti-Semitic hatred, he concluded, was un-German and Germans, after finally achieving their self-awareness as a *Volk*, must learn to work with Jews. Such conclusions, he noted at the end of his essay, would probably prove disappointing to many of his *völkisch* readers. But to demonstrate the sincerity of his beliefs, the following year Diederichs devoted an entire issue of *Die Tat* to an objective, and at times quite sympathetic examination of current trends and problems of Judaism; one of the guest contributors to this issue was Leo Baeck.

Had the men of the Hanseatic house been aware of Diederichs's stance on anti-Semitism, they would indeed have been disappointed, while the owner and director of the Lehmann house would have been infuriated. For these two publishing institutions were engaged throughout the postwar era in fighting what they termed the "Jewish problem." Few books published by the HVA and the JFLV were without some trace of anti-Semitism.

The Hanseatic publishing empire's parent organization, the DHV, was after all one of Germany's largest and most influential anti-Semitic organizations. To the DHV, the social struggle of the commercial employees it represented was inseparable from the "Jewish problem." Since its founding in 1893, the union devoted its energies to fighting Jewish influence in German economic life.[141] The DHV's Hanseatic publishing empire, accordingly, published such works as P. Bröcker's *Class Struggle and Racial Struggle (Klassenkampf und Rassenkampf*, 1920). But the HVA also regarded itself as a guardian against the Jewish infiltration of German cultural life. Statements of the DHV bookstore and the DHB, cited above (see pp. 205–6), about "alien literary domination" were merely thinly veiled references to the role of Jewish intellectuals and journalists in Germany. Wilhelm Stapel, a director of the HVA and editor of *Deutsches Volkstum*, was also one of Weimar Germany's leading anti-Semitic spokesmen, and his *Anti-Semitism?*, published by the HVA in 1922, did much to stake out the battlefield on which the postwar Jewish issue was fought. In advertising another of his anti-Semitic tracts, *Anti-Semitism or Anti-Germanism* (*Antisemitismus oder Antigermanismus*, 1928), the HVA declared that Stapel "sees the conflict between the German and Jewish races as arising from the fact that two fundamentally different and separate races live together on the same soil. The immigrant race—the Jews—does not content itself with the role of guest which befits it. Rather, it wants to be assimilated into the *Volk* community of the native race—the Germans—and to become a member of the family. Stapel decisively exposes all the foolish, sentimental objections to anti-Semitism. His books [on the topic] can be heartily recommended."[142] Other anti-Semitic works published by the HVA houses included Hans Blüher's *The Uprising of Israel Against Christian Goods* (*Die Erhebung Israels gegen die christlichen Güter*, 1931), several popular new editions of T. Fritsch's influential nineteenth-century *Handbook of the Jewish Question* (*Handbuch der Judenfrage*, 1887), and a new 1917 mass edition of W. Raabe's widely read novel *Pastor to the Hungry* (*Hungerpastor*, 1862), which contrasted the benevolent, idealistic German with the greedy, ruthless Jews.

The HVA acquired the Albert Langen and Georg Müller houses in the late 1920s the better to carry on its anti-Semitic struggle. These two firms, according to the directors of the HVA, contained some of Germany's finest authors but because of financial difficulties, were in danger of falling into the hands of Jewish businessmen. By purchasing the houses, the HVA claimed it had guarded German national values by "foiling the Jewish manipulators of German cultural life" and by "slamming the door shut on further Jewish infiltration into German publishing."[143] Once under HVA control, Pezold sought to use the Langen-Müller house to break what he believed was a "Jewish artistic monopoly" and "leftist literary dictatorship" being exercised by liberal publishing houses and newspapers whose most prominent authors and critics were usually Jewish. Langen-Müller house publications after 1930, he claimed, had succeeded in routing the "alien, Jewish asphalt literature" which had previously ruled the German literary scene.[144]

The anti-Semitism of the HVA was surpassed only by that of J. F. Lehmann. Lehmann, one of whose earliest publications had been C. Klopfer's *On the Jewish Question* (*Zur Judenfrage*, 1891), was immensely proud of his house's anti-Semitic reputation. To uphold its image, he sometimes found it necessary to rebuke his authors for associating with Jews or retaining Jewish lawyers.[145] By the 1920s, the Munich publisher had come to hold Jews responsible for all the modern ills which plagued the German *Volk*, especially those which affected him personally. He was convinced, for example, that the Jews were not only the cause of the loss of the war, the revolution, the harsh Versailles settlement, and the postwar economic slump, but he also blamed them for the rising cost of paper, the poor sales of some of his house's books, and for the JFLV's commercial setbacks in 1929–30.[146] He was certain that Jews pulled the strings behind the Weimar coalition, for according to him "Jews, through loans, gifts, and favors of all kinds, have made the leaders of the Social Democratic and Catholic Center parties dependent on them. These parties work only in the interest of international Jewish capital." And, leaving no stones unturned, he considered it no accident that the Communists' red star so closely resembled the Star of David; for all the Communist leaders were Jews.[147] Finally, he knew—and so informed his authors who were working on economic topics—that the social problems of German workers and the misery and unemployment of the post-1929 depression were actually a result of Germany's reparations payments (imposed by the Jews), and of Jewish capitalists. He refused to accept any economic manuscripts which would lay these problems at the doorstep of German businessmen; for Germany's social and economic problems could be solved only by publications which took a clear stand on the "Jewish problem."[148] Thus the JFLV issued only economic treatises like W. Lieck's *The Role of Judaism in the Collapse of Germany* (*Der Anteil des Judentums im Zusammenbruch Deutschlands*, 1930), which sold more than one hundred fifty thousand copies. Above all, through works such as S. Passage's *Judaism as a Geographical and Ethnological Problem* (*Das Judentum als landschaftskundlich- und ethnologisches Problem*, 1929) and H. F. K. Günther's *Racial Ethnology of the Jewish Volk* (*Rassenkunde des jüdischen Volkes*, 1930) Lehmann sought to convince the nation that the Jewish problem was fundamentally one of race, and could be solved only by racial hygiene. Indeed, Lehmann's greatest contribution to the anti-Semitic cause in postwar Germany was his firm's general popularization of racial theory. For racism provided anti-Semites with a pseudorespectable, "scientific" means of expressing their hatreds. Many *völkisch* ideologues, encouraged by the racial literature of neoconservative houses like the JFLV, came to believe that the evils of liberal modernity would be overcome only when the German race regained its original pristine quality and reasserted its natural racial ascendancy in national life. Increasingly, this came to mean eradicating the influence of the Jewish race.

Eight
Into the Third Reich
and Beyond

Visions of the New Order

German neoconservatives had been heartened by the war and the collapse of the Second Reich in 1918 because they believed these events finally opened the way for that radically antiliberal order they had envisioned since the 1890s. The actual outcome of the war and revolution, however, proved disastrous for their dreams, and after 1918 they fiercely rejected the cultural, political, and social system which had replaced the old Wilhelmian order.

Unlike the traditional Right during the Weimar era, neoconservatives did not wish to return to the conservative prewar order or to set up some streamlined ersatz for it. For, rooted as they were in the tradition of prewar cultural opposition, neoconservatives regarded the state and culture of the old Reich as too contaminated by liberalism to serve as a vehicle for the rebirth of German values; they were therefore as contemptuous of the Second Reich as they were of the new liberal Weimar republic. Rather, they called for a radically new order which would transcend all conventional political outlooks. They preached a "Third Way" between the old aristocratic conservatism of the Second Reich and the liberal democracy of the Weimar republic, a solution which would overcome the weaknesses of both in order to protect the German nation from the threat of Marxist mass rule and rescue it from the torment of liberal modernity without falling into the reactionary exclusiveness of the old Right. Speaking to the needs of the socially and economically distressed middle and lower classes, neoconservatives demanded a fundamentally new political, social, and economic system more attuned to the concerns of the "little man" and to the needs of the nation as a whole. This new order, by restoring the social solidarity of the German *Volk*, was to lead to a national spiritual rebirth and a revival of those sacred Germanic values which were being endangered by modernization.

As with most revolutionaries, however, the "conservative revolutionaries" who rejected the democratic Weimar republic and the system of liberal Western values on which it was based were far better at identifying and agreeing on that against which they were revolting than they were at defining the nature of the new system with which they hoped to replace it. Indeed, except for a shared hatred of liberal modernity and a general, although by no means complete agreement on certain broad cultural values and *völkisch* goals which the new order would incorporate, neoconservatives differed markedly over the features of the new society they hoped would supplant the hated liberal republic, a regime which they regarded as merely an interregnum. There were thus nearly as many varieties of neoconservative thought in the postwar era ("young conservatives," "national revolutionaries," "national bolsheviks," "Christian nationalists," "national socialists," etc.) as there were neoconservative theorists.

During the energetic debate within the new Right during the 1920s over the precise outlines of the new order which the "conservative revolution" was to install, the neoconservative publishers naturally played a prominent role. They personally put forward, or helped others put forward, a vague design for the new political, social, and economic system they hoped to see displace the Weimar republic. The ideas of the publishers on these matters—and indeed the values of most neoconservative ideologues after 1918—inevitably bore the heavy imprint of the insights they had gained during the war years.

For example, works such as F. Fick's *German Democracy* (*Deutsche Demokratie*), published by the JFLV in 1918, or Moeller van den Bruck's *Conservative* (1922) and H. Gerber's *The German State* (*Deutscher Staat*, 1922) from the HVA, argued that a truly "German state" must be both "democratic"— in the sense of appealing to all social groups and allowing for more popular participation than did the old Reich—and "conservative"—in the sense of rejecting the basic assumptions of Western liberalism. A "German democracy," therefore, would be something quite different from Western democracies such as the Weimar republic. Indeed, Lehmann seemed to believe that a dictatorship and a German-style democracy were not incompatible, and in the early 1920s he sought to make clear to Germans, through the pages of *Deutschlands Erneuerung*, how often in history nations had resorted to dictatorships to solve their problems, and how successful those experiences had been.[1] Diederichs, on the other hand, both in his essays in *Die Tat* and through EDV publications such as S. Marx's *The Organic State Principle* (*Das organische Staatsprinzip*, 1919) continued to push his wartime notion of an "organic state." Whatever the specific form of a state, he argued, it must be "organically structured" if it is not to fall under mass rule. For Diederichs, too, believed that "true democracy"—

which he defined as "the ability of the individual personality to assert itself against the mass spirit"[2]—was incompatible with atomized Western mass society. Democracy in his sense could exist only where there was an "organic" hierarchy of ranks or levels extending from the bottom of society to the top. Thus he envisioned an "organic state" which would be democratic in that it would be based on the widest possible popular participation and would allow for popular influence over legislation and administration, but unlike "Western" democracy would not allow majority (i.e., "mass") rule. Rather than leveling egalitarianism, there would exist in this new "organic state" a social hierarchy, with a responsible spiritual elite at the top.[3]

The notion of an "open yet authoritarian" elite, which he had first articulated during the war, continued to play a central role in Diederichs's political thought after 1918. For he believed modern society had become so complex and unwieldy that no single individual could possibly manage it. Since the alternative of mass rule was equally unacceptable, it seemed that rule by an elite spiritual order, a new aristocracy, was the only practical answer. He pointed to the fact that throughout history, there had always existed a visible elite of specially qualified and unusually dedicated men whose higher calling it was to manage, guide, and spiritually uplift the society: knights and priests in the Middle Ages; urban patricians and the court circles around the absolute princes in early modern times; and the university-trained civil servants of the nineteenth century. Weimar Germany's social, political, and spiritual crisis, he now maintained, was in large part due to the disappearance of the old elite of the nineteenth century and the failure of any modern twentieth-century elite to emerge; without the leadership of an elite, a society inevitably sinks into chaotic mass rule. In the new organic state of the future, therefore, a new spiritual elite must stand at the summit of the hierarchy—he once spoke of a "dictatorship of the intellectuals" (*Diktatur der Geistigen*).[4] It would not be a closed elite based on property or education, but would cut diagonally across class lines. Those called to this select brotherhood would not represent the material interests of the classes from which they came; rather, they would form "a spiritual stratum encompassing all the classes, a stratum which feels a deep sense of responsibility toward the entire *Volk* community and which will create a new set of values to shape the future."[5]

The Jena publisher believed the postwar book trade, as a guardian of German culture, was particularly obligated to assist in the formation of this new spiritual elite by providing forums and points around which Germany's most talented and creative men could crystallize.[6] To help spread elitist theory among Germans, therefore, the EDV announced plans for the first German edition of Vilfredo Pareto's two-volume *Treatise on*

General Sociology (*Trattato di sociologia generale*), one of the twentieth century's most compelling arguments on the need for some social elite.[7] (This EDV translation, however, never appeared, perhaps because of Diederichs's death in 1930.) Carrying on a tradition he had begun in the war years, Diederichs also began planning a new series of organizations and discussion circles which he hoped would serve as nuclei for Germany's new spiritual elite. These groups, which he envisioned as "leagues of virtue," were to be meeting places where interested individuals from all walks of life would meet with contributors to *Die Tat* to discuss the nation's most pressing problems and devise plans for their solution. To deepen solidarity among the members of this select order of men and to demonstrate their common commitment to life's mystical and spiritual forces, the publisher proposed various "cultish rites" for the groups such as the regular performance of medieval mystery plays.[8]

During the runaway inflation of 1922–23, which was especially disastrous for the educated middle class which Diederichs foresaw as the backbone of his new elite, he decided that members of Germany's future spiritual order required material as well as organizational assistance. He thus helped found a series of provincial Cultural Emergency Societies (Kulturelle Notgemeinschaften) whose purpose it was to aid starving writers and artists and other "economically distressed creative forces [which are] working for the renewal of German culture."[9] Diederichs personally assumed responsibility for Thuringia. Through calls in *Die Tat* for reader contributions and through other solicitations, he raised several million marks for the Thuringian Cultural Emergency Society and distributed it to needy authors such as Ricarda Huch and Heinrich Driesmans. He also approached private organizations such as the Zeiss Foundation and tried to persuade them to supply pensions for indigent elderly artists.[10]

Neoconservative publishers called for a new political order, with or without a spiritual elite at its helm, as a means of establishing a new, more just social order. Diederichs and Lehmann especially were deeply disturbed over the bitter interest politics and class conflict which seemed to lacerate postwar German society.[11] In the 1920s, both men committed their houses to the development of a new set of social relationships which would end class conflict by, on the one hand, subordinating all individual and class interests to the larger needs of the social whole, and on the other, by developing a deeper sense of the social responsibilities which the whole owed toward its individual members. Works like M. Habermann's *The New Order of Capital and Labor* (*Die neue Ordnung vom Kapital und Arbeit*), published by the HVA in 1921, or EDV titles such as C. Jatho's *From Society to Community* (*Von der Gesellschaft zur Gemeinschaft*, 1919) or P. Natorp's

Individual and Community (*Individuum und Gemeinschaft*, 1921) recalled to mind Ferdinand Tönnies's classic prewar sociological distinction between a "society," governed by rational calculation and the conflicting interests of its components, and a "community," based on man's subjective "natural will" and the "organic" integration of its individual members through shared values.[12] Diederichs, who after the war continued to characterize himself as "a conservative who is socially committed," preached that the future of Germany depended on cooperative social efforts. Overcoming class divisions and creating a truly united community of brothers, he declared, depended on each individual and group subordinating their own personal material comforts to the welfare of the larger community.[13] Lehmann agreed that a new social solidarity was sorely needed, but believed it could emerge only if the social whole also demonstrated a greater concern for the individual needs of its members, especially the more disadvantaged, by fulfilling their basic, legitimate material needs. This might be accomplished by raising the society's total material production through mandatory labor service and by exercising more state supervision over the social distribution of goods. Such a scheme, which clearly drew its inspiration from Germany's wartime economy and from the 1916 Auxiliary Service Law, was outlined in a 1923 JFLV publication, F. Köhler's *Labor Service and the Rights of the German Volk: The Basis of an Economic and Social Reconstruction* (*Werkpflicht und Lebensrechte des deutschen Volkes: Die Grundlage des wirtschafts- und sozialpolitischen Aufbaus*).[14]

The just, benevolent new social order envisioned by the neoconservatives after the war seemed to them largely incompatible with the laissez-faire capitalism which dominated the Weimar republic. Drawing on a long tradition of conservative anticapitalism in Germany,[15] men like Diederichs condemned the selfish egotism and brutal competition of liberal capitalism in the 1920s, and singled out the entrepreneurial bourgeoisie for its lack of a social conscience. Through his own essays and through publication of such anticapitalist works as C. Haensel's *Zweimann: An Industrial Novel* (*Zweimann: Ein Industrieroman*, 1930), Diederichs charged that the progressive concentration of wealth and power in the hands of a small group of greedy entrepreneurs was ruining Germany's idealistic educated middle class, thus deepening the spiritual crisis. "Through the accumulation of capital," he proclaimed, "our economic freedom is being rapidly eroded. The middle levels of the bourgeoisie which stand between capitalism and the workers—that level which until now has relied on its inherited wealth to gain the leisure and means necessary to pursue the cultivation of the inner man—these middle levels are rapidly shrinking."[16] The capitalistic bourgeoisie, he said, must be forced to develop a new sense of social responsibility, perhaps through some limitation of the rights of private property. In his more extreme moments, he called for "a comprehensive, practical implementation of a socialized order to demonstrate to Western capitalism, which is trying to enslave us, that its role in world history has been played out."[17] Similar anticapitalist sentiments were strong within the HVA, which had been founded to protect white-collar clerks and the German middle classes (*Mittelstände*) against the abuses of their capitalist employers. The DHV's Hanseatic publishing empire consequently became an important outlet for anticapitalist literature in the 1920s.

As an alternative to a capitalist economy, the publishers explored the concept of corporatism in the years after 1918. Diederichs, for example, continued to preach (as he had during the war and revolution) that Germany needed some sort of corporate system centered around the three major estates of the peasantry, the craftsmen, and the professional bourgeoisie, with an economic council (*Rat*) to represent the interests of each occupation. An organization of the state and society along corporate lines (a *Berufsstaat*) would, he believed, provide the organic hierarchy necessary as a bulwark against mass leveling and atomization.[18] To convince his countrymen of the value of corporatism, he devoted the entire January 1919 issue of *Die Tat* to the ideas of Karl C. Planck, and turned the October 1925 issue of the journal over to Heinz Brauweiler, a leading corporatist associated with the HVA. (Brauweiler's *Occupational Estate and the State: Reflections on a Neooccupational Constitution [Berufsstand und Staat: Betrachtungen über eine neuständische Verfassung*, 1925] and his *The Corporate Movement and Agriculture [Die ständische Bewegung und die Landwirtschaft*, 1922] had appeared in the Ring Verlag and later passed to the HVA.) Other publications such as Dursthoff's *Memorandum Regarding the Extension of the Parliamentary System Through Incorporation of Occupational Representation (Denkschrift, betreffend den Ausbau des parlamentarischen Systems durch Eingliederung einer berufsständischen Vertretung*, 1919), F. Behringer's *Extension of the Economic Councils (Fortbildung der wirtschaftlichen Räteverfassung*, 1921), and G. Treuner's *The Law Regarding Labor Cooperatives and Self-Administration in Economics (Das Gesetz betreffend Werkgemeinschaften und Selbstverwaltung der Wirtschaft*, 1929), published by the GSV, HVA, and JFLV respectively, also propagandized for a new corporative system.

In their tireless postwar quest for a new, conflict-free socioeconomic order, the neoconservative publishers became increasingly attracted to the notion of "socialism," a concept which they reinterpreted in a distinctly *völkisch* manner. During the war, for example, Diederichs had come to the realization that "true socialism" was not identical with Marxism; rather, it meant simply the voluntary limitation of one's material interests out of a sense of social responsibility and national solidarity, and was thus fully compatible with patriotism and the *Volk* mystique. Understood in this sense, "socialism" became a central element of his and other neoconservatives' thinking in the 1920s. He was especially attracted to "socialism" after 1918 because it connoted not only anticapitalism, but a rejection of the entire political and philosophical system of the liberal West. Indeed, he maintained that one of the ways Germany could best oppose the capitalistic West was to develop its own new anticapitalistic "socialist" notion of property.[19] And perhaps most importantly, by characterizing their envisioned socioeconomic order as socialistic, neoconservatives hoped to win the support of the German working class, in which socialist sympathies were deeply rooted. For after 1918 the neoconservative publishers explicitly expressed their hope of "deproletarianizing" German socialism in order to win over the working class to *völkisch* values. Diederichs, for example, issued four works by the maverick Belgian socialist Hendrik de Man, including: *On the Psychology of Socialism* (*Zur Psychologie des Sozialismus*, 1925), which sold 4,488 copies; *The Intellectuals and Socialism* (*Die Intellektuellen und der Sozialismus*, 1926); and *The Socialist Idea* (*Die sozialistische Idee*, 1933). The publisher claimed these works, especially de Man's first, "point the way for the overthrow of Marxism within Social Democracy."[20] Likewise, the HVA issued three works by August Winnig, a former revisionist Social Democrat who was expelled by the party in 1920 for his increasingly *völkisch* and anti-Semitic views. Winnig's three books, *The Ever-Greening Tree* (*Die ewig grünende Tanne*, 1927), *From Proletariat to Worker's Estate* (*Vom Proletariat zum Arbeitertum*, 1930), and his popular autobiography *The Long Way* (*Der weite Weg*, 1932), which with the aid of the DHB sold eighty-five thousand copies by 1940, preached a vague, right-wing mixture of corporatism, Christian socialism, and national socialism. Winnig demanded that the proletariat exchange its Marxism for a rootedness in blood and soil in order to become a new "worker estate" which would play an integrated and leading role within the national *Volk* community.[21] Lehmann, impressed by Winnig's chauvinistic brand of socialism, contacted the author and offered to reprint some of his speeches and distribute them on a mass scale. He asked Winnig in turn to distribute nationalistic JFLV books to trade unionists, and, if it would help make workers see the necessity of racial policies, Lehmann even offered to donate free copies 'of his firm's books to the effort.[22]

After 1918, the EDV and HVA issued several volumes on the notion of a "new socialism," including: R. Wilbrandt, *Socialism* (1919), which sold 8,144 copies by 1933; E. Weitsch, *On the Socialization of the Spirit* (*Zur Sozialisierung des Geistes*, 1919); M. Barthel, *Worker Souls* (*Arbeiterseele*, 1920); and F. Brunstäd, *Germany and Socialism* (*Deutschland und der Sozialismus*,

1927). In addition, Diederichs devoted three special issues of *Die Tat* (March 1925, July 1926, and July 1927) to the theme. Germany needed a socialist system, Diederichs believed, but one which worked for the welfare of the entire nation rather than merely that of the working class. Under such a system, brotherly love and social justice would replace greed and exploitation, and a "social peoples' state" with a comprehensive system of social protection would guarantee the welfare of every citizen and social group. The abuses and class antagonisms generated by capitalism would be eliminated because the rights of private property would be tempered by a new sense of social responsibility toward the *Volk*. Central planning would insure that the needs of the social whole always took precedence over particularistic interests, while traditional class barriers would give way to unlimited upward mobility for talented individuals, regardless of social origin.[23]

Neoconservative socialism, as defined by men like Diederichs, would reject the materialist philosophy of Marxism and would be based instead on religious and ethical foundations which incorporated philosophical idealism, vitalism, and irrational life-philosophy. This new German socialism would not abolish private property nor would it "proletarianize" society, although the working class might have an honored position within it. In fact, "organic socialism" would protect the nation against the egalitarianism, collectivism, and mass leveling which posed such a danger to the spirit of modern man. It would permit upward mobility for the talented, but would preserve a social hierarchy in which an elite of the talented few would govern. For Diederichs believed that "socialism without an aristocracy—i.e., a leading role for the 'best'—is pure humbug." In short, his new order would be a utopian fusion of individualism, conservative hierarchy, leadership by an elite, and socialist solidarity.[24]

In their search for a new sociopolitical model in the 1920s, the publishers—like many right-wing Germans—became intrigued by Mussolini's fascist experiment in Italy.[25] Diederichs, for example, was impressed by the way the former socialist Mussolini had managed to instill a new nationalistic consciousness into the workers' movement, and the publisher briefly searched for a "German Mussolini" who might do the same for the German proletariat.[26] Although personally he rejected the notion of a Mussolini-style dictatorship as a solution to Germany's problems, he did admire some of the changes the Italian fascist leader had brought about in Italy and he sought—although unsuccessfully—to have Mussolini write one or two articles for *Die Tat* to acquaint German readers with the new order being implemented south of the Alps.[27] Lehmann, on the other hand, admired the way Mussolini's iron rule had radically transformed Italy and he expressed the belief in 1929–30 that the same would be done in Germany in the near future.[28] The HVA sought to acquaint its readers with Italian fascism by sending the coeditor of *Deutsches Volkstum*, A. E. Günther, to Italy in 1931 to study the fascist system. Günther's reports appeared not only in his own journal, but in other DHV-related publications such as the union's newspaper.[29] In 1932 the HVA also issued *Fascism and Nation: The Spirit of the Corporative Constitution (Faschismus und Nation: Der Geist der korporativen Verfassung)* by G. Bortolotto, an active Italian fascist.

The efforts of the neoconservative publishers in the 1920s to sketch out a utopian order which would combine elitism, nationalism, socialism, and perhaps elements from the Italian fascist state at first had little direct impact. They did, however, have an indirect significance in that they helped create a climate of opinion in postwar Germany which Hitler's National Socialist movement was able to exploit after 1930.

The Coming of the Third Reich

After 1930, as parliamentary government in Germany collapsed under the impact of the Great Depression and was replaced by a series of conservative, authoritarian "presidential chancellors" ruling by emergency decree, neoconservative opponents of the despised Weimar system were certain that its end was finally imminent and that their long-awaited "conservative revolution" would shortly usher in the millennium. Apocalyptic titles from the EDV such as F. Fried's *The End of Capitalism (Das Ende des Kapitalismus*, 1931), which sold nearly twenty-five thousand copies in two short years, confidently announced the end of the liberal era, while others such as H. Freyer's *The Revolution from the Right (Revolution von Rechts*, 1931) laid out the program for the conservative uprising which was to establish the radically new postliberal order. That same year, in an essay confidently entitled "The Coming Conservative Revolution," Stapel claimed that "after the liberal revolution of the eighteenth century the conservative revolution is at hand. When the forms . . . that now obtain are trodden under the feet of the apocalyptic angels, . . . then the conservative revolution will build up not a better world, perhaps, for we do not believe in progress, but a world more approximating to and more in harmony with that which is eternal."[30]

In this pregnant atmosphere, neoconservative theorists redoubled their efforts to define the exact form they hoped the new order would assume. Between 1930 and 1933, the neoconservative publishing houses supported this drive by issuing a flood of visionary works outlining principles, structures, and policies for Germany's impending political and social transformation: H. Bogner's *The Formation of the Political Elite* (*Die Bildung der politischen Elite*) and G. Weippert's *The Principle of Hierarchy* (*Das Prinzip der Hierarchie*), issued in 1932 by the Stalling and Hanseatic houses respectively, sketched the nature of the new elite which, it was hoped, would soon assume direction of the nation. F. Fried's *Autarky* (*Autarkie*, 1932), published by the EDV, and K. Schöpke's *A Year of German Labor Service Instead of Unemployment Chaos* (*Deutsches Arbeitsdienstjahr staat Arbeitslosenwirrwarr*, 1930), issued by the JFLV, argued that for Germany to survive the crisis of Western capitalism, it must become economically self-sufficient by effecting a permanent mobilization of the work force and by establishing a solid economic bloc in central Europe. EDV, HVA, and GSV publications such as G. Wirsing's *Germany in World Politics* (*Deutschland in der Weltpolitik*, 1933), G. Günther's *The Forthcoming Reich* (*Das werdende Reich*, 1932), F. Mariaux's *Nationalist Foreign Policy* (*Nationale Aussenpolitik*, 1932), or E. Banse's *Space and Volk in the World War: Thoughts on a National Defense Policy* (*Raum und Volk im Weltkriege: Gedanken über eine nationale Wehrlehre*, 1932) marked out for the coming polity a nationalistic foreign policy designed to overcome the humiliating legacy of the Versailles settlement.

Numerous manifestos calling for a revolutionary new type of conservative "German socialism" to overcome internal class antagonism were also published with renewed vigor after 1930. In 1932, for example, the HVA brought out W. von Moellendorf's *Conservative Socialism* (*Konservativer Sozialismus*), a work which attempted to resurrect, under a new and more popular label, the author's ideas on a "communal economy" which the EDV had published earlier. As part of its influential *Writings to the Nation* series, the GSV in 1932 issued an excerpt entitled *Every Volk Has Its Own Socialism* (*Jedes Volk hat seiner eigener Sozialismus*) from Moeller van den Bruck's earlier manifesto *The Third Reich*, and an excerpt from O. Spengler's *Prussianism and Socialism* (*Preussentum und Sozialismus*), which argued that German socialism was identical with Prussian discipline and *völkisch* patriotism.

Of all the visions for a new social order which the decomposition of the Weimar republic heaved up, however, one of the most radical was undoubtedly Ernst Jünger's chilling *The Worker: Mastery and Form* (*Der Arbeiter: Herrschaft und Gestalt*), a work which quickly became a literary sensation after its publication by the Hanseatic house in late 1932. Jünger declared the death of bourgeois society and demanded its replacement by an antipodal "workers' state." Like most neoconservatives who spoke of workers, workers' states, and new socialist systems, Jünger's use of these terms was unorthodox in the extreme: he used "worker" to connote heroic, Nietzschean individuals who, in contrast to the orderly, rational, Apollonian burgher, had rediscovered life's primal, irrational forces and acted on these. Like the trench warriors of World War I (in which Jünger had served as a valiant and decorated officer), these Dionysian "workers" of the future would be driven by a romantic yet brutal storm trooper ideology which glorified nihilistic activism, especially war. Jünger's demonic worker-warriors would function as a dictatorial elite and were to keep the masses totally and permanently mobilized for war. For a tightly disciplined society dedicated to the idealistic pursuit of war for its own sake would become a totally integrated, "organic" community in which not only all social distinctions between workers and nonworkers, but even the differences between civilians and warriors would cease to exist.

In their fervid attempts to prepare the way for the impending conservative revolution, the neoconservative publishers were ultimately forced to contend with Germany's National Socialist party (NSDAP). With the rapid decline of the Weimar political system after 1929–30, the size and political influence of the Nazi party rose at a remarkable and alarming rate. An increasing number of conservative groups, including many neoconservatives who until then had remained aloof from the Nazis, if not outright hostile toward them, succumbed to the powerful lure of the National Socialist movement and saw it as the force most capable of carrying out the long-awaited conservative revolution.

This fate befell some of the neoconservative publishers. With the exception of J. F. Lehmann, who had been close to the early Nazi party in 1919–23[31] but drifted away from it after 1924 when the party faded from public view, the publishers showed little interest in Nazism before the party's electoral breakthrough in 1930. Diederichs, for example, never directly discussed either Hitler or Nazism in the 1920s, although he did condemn both vulgar anti-Semitism and the yearning for a messianic political führer. Since he died a mere four days before the Nazis scored their great electoral triumph of 14 September 1930, the Jena publisher was spared the necessity of having to confront squarely the problem of Nazism's proper role in the reshaping of Germany along neoconservative lines. Diederichs's sons Peter and Niels, who took over the EDV in 1930, gave H. Zehrer's *Tat* Circle complete independence over the editorial policies of the house journal. The *Tat* Circle after 1930 criticized Hitler's growing movement as too plebian, too opportunistic, and too closely tied to the interests of the reactionary bourgeoisie; instead, the men around *Die Tat* believed the "socialist general" Chancellor Kurt von Schleicher would be the man to carry out the anticipated "German Revolution." Thus the EDV journal became one of the leading outlets for Schleicher's views and a kind of semiofficial organ for his short-lived cabinet. The *Tat* Circle members were among the strongest supporters of Schleicher's unsuccessful attempt in late 1932 to undercut Hitler and split the Nazi movement by winning over the uncompromisingly socialistic Strasser wing within the party.

Diederichs's successors had become increasingly wary of Nazism after 1930 and explored ways to prevent Hitler from taking control of the conservative revolution. Lehmann's stance was just the opposite. In 1929, after a half-decade of disinterest in Hitler's movement, the Munich publisher happened to attend the Nazi party rally in Nuremberg and discovered it to be a "beautiful" and "totally uplifting experience"; he predicted that Germany would soon turn to a movement like Hitler's, just as Italy had turned to fascism in 1922.[32] In December 1931 he decided formally to place himself and his firm in the service of the Nazi movement. He thus wrote to Hitler:

> Because today the National Socialists alone represent the cutting edge [of the *völkisch* movement], it is completely fitting that my publishing house—which for forty years . . . has always represented the [*völkisch*] vanguard—should join the most energetic *völkisch* elements and fight with them on the most advanced fronts during the present struggle. The majority of my house's authors have already switched from the Nationalist or Pan-German camp over to the National Socialists. . . . I have strongly supported the [goals of the Nazi] movement for the past ten years. . . . Since the greater part of my house's work . . . today stands in the National Socialist camp, I too would like formally to join the party.[33]

Although his house would continue to print some authors of other orientations, Lehmann assured Hitler that these would not conflict with the goals of the Nazi movement. He would use his position as a publisher, he said, to insure that the similarities between National Socialism and the other neoconservative movements were stressed rather than their points of divergence. During the subsequent two years, Lehmann published three works for the Nazi movement: K. Eckehard's *Crest or Historical Turning Point? Reflections on National Socialism* (*Fieberkurve oder Zeitwende? Nachdenkliches über den Nationalsozialismus*, 1931); G. Hartz's *National-Social Revolution: The Solution to the Workers Problem* (*Die national-soziale Revolution: Die Lösung der Arbeiterfrage*, 1932); and the anti-Weimar exposé, *The Great Black-Red Lie* (*Die grosse schwarz-rote Lüge*, 1932), of which some one hundred thousand copies were distributed. In addition, Lehmann actively campaigned for the party and personally wrote a pamphlet in support of Hitler's candidacy for the presidency in 1932.[34]

But the most revealing (and perhaps even symbolic) reaction exhibited by neoconservative publishing houses toward the rising Nazi party after

1930 was neither the aloof disdain of the EDV nor the eager affiliation of the JFLV, but the calculating opportunism of houses like the GSV and the HVA. The Stalling house, for example, sought to capitalize on the "Nazi phenomenom" in 1930 by issuing Czech-Jochberg's sympathetic study *Hitler, A German Movement* (*Hitler, eine deutsche Bewegung*, 1930), a copy of which Heinrich Stalling personally endorsed and sent to Hitler with his compliments. The Hanseatic firm, on the other hand, believed it could use the Nazis for its own ends and important directors of the house such as Stapel came to regard National Socialism as a useful ally in their struggle for the neoconservative revolution. Stapel's personal ambitions and frustrations may have influenced the HVA's policies, for by early 1931—partly out of resentment that Ziegler rather than he had been appointed head of the HVA, and partly because he was disappointed with the way the HVA handled production of his *Deutsches Volkstum*—Stapel had become disillusioned with the DHV and HVA and considered leaving his position there for a post elsewhere, perhaps with the Nazis.[35] But when Rudolf Hess visited Stapel in an attempt to enlist him for the Nazi cause, Stapel declined, claiming that he could better assist the Nazi movement as a respected independent figure than as a party functionary.[36] After speaking with Hess, however, in June 1931 Stapel composed an important memorandum for the leaders of the HVA in which he urged the firm to consider the politically powerful National Socialist movement as a "breakthrough force." Once the Nazis had "broken through" the Weimar republic and opened the way for a new order, Stapel continued, then the genuine "national conservative" front could dispense with the Nazis and reform the nation according to its own neoconservative ideals. Accordingly, Stapel recommended that the DHV and HVA maintain the closest possible contact with the Nazis, but carefully avoid total commitment to them. The Hanseatic house, he believed, should meanwhile concentrate on preparing a national conservative program which could preempt the Nazi program at the decisive moment.[37] As part of his tactical collaboration with the Nazis, Stapel's *Six Chapters on Christianity and National Socialism* (*Sechs Kapitel über Christentum und Nationalsozialismus*) appeared in the HVA in 1931. The following year he began to court Hitler in other ways as well. When Stapel's *The Christian Statesman* (*Der christliche Staatsmann*)—which, like his first book, has been called "one of the most important programmatic works of the neonationalist movement"[38]—was published by the HVA in 1932, the author sent the first copy to Hitler with the personal inscription: "To the German Fighter and Führer, Adolf Hitler."[39]

It was a desire to draw closer to the Nazi movement which also prompted the Hanseatic house to reissue Arthur Moeller van den Bruck's classic manifesto *The Third Reich* (*Das Dritte Reich*), originally published by the Ring Verlag in 1923. For centuries, the concept of the "Third Reich" had served as a mythical reference to a distant future utopia where all contradictions would be perfectly synthesized into a "higher Third," all latent ideals would be fully realized, and all aspirations fulfilled. Because the term reached back to the medieval mysticism of Joachim of Floris and recalled the glory of the universal Christian empire under Germany's first Reich (the Holy Roman Empire), the Third Reich also carried powerful mystical, religious, and imperial overtones. During the heady days of the 1918 revolution as the Second Reich was collapsing and it appeared that a neoconservative state might arise in its place, Diederichs's *Die Tat* had revived the concept of the Third Reich from the depths of national memory by speaking of "a Reich of the future" and of "the coming Third Reich."[40] Thereafter, the neoconservatives borrowed the myth of the Third Reich and made it their own. They increasingly used the notion to designate the utopian new era which a conservative revolution would launch.[41] But it was Arthur Moeller van den Bruck, perhaps the most important postwar neoconservative ideologue, who first popularized the slogan. His *The Third Reich* became one of the gospels of the new Right during the Weimar years. With the collapse of the republic after 1930 and the almost certain prospect that a new order would take its place, the term gained a new significance. Works like F. Everling's *Organic Construction of the Third Reich* (*Organischer Aufbau des Dritten Reiches*), published by the JFLV in 1931, used the slogan to connote the coming post-Weimar era. The Nazis also appropriated the "Third Reich" to designate their program, and succeeded in identifying themselves with the term.

It was against this background that the HVA, having since acquired the Ring Verlag, decided in 1931 to publish a new edition of Moeller van den Bruck's *The Third Reich*. For the Hanseatic house saw the book as "a work written completely in a National Socialist vein"; its reissue, the house believed, would not only further the Nazi cause, but also help the HVA establish its tactical alliance with the Nazi movement.[42] The Ernst Rowohlt Verlag, one of Germany's most influential left-wing publishing houses, moved to counter the HVA action by issuing a book of its own, also titled *The Third Reich*, which would parody the Right's Third Reich concept. The Hanseatic house reacted immediately to the Rowohlt plan by procuring a court order prohibiting Rowohlt from using the title *The Third Reich*. While the Rowohlt house thereupon renamed its book *Is the Third Reich Coming?* (*Kommt das dritte Reich?*, 1930), the firm also appealed for a reversal of the court's decision, claiming the original order had been issued by a prejudiced right-wing judge. A lengthy legal battle soon developed over the title *The Third Reich*. It was a battle not only between two publishing houses but also between two opposing ideologies. This conflict within the publishing industry symbolized the intense polarization of German society during the death throes of the Weimar republic, and at the same time revealed how quickly the ideological motivation behind so much of German publishing could turn the book trade itself into a political battleground.

Indeed, the HVA charged that the Rowohlt firm was working in league with leftist radicals to make the case into a "political sensation." There was much truth to this: for since Rowohlt had already issued its book under the altered title and it seemed unlikely to change its book even if the original court decision were reversed, Rowohlt's appeal for a new court hearing involved more than the original dispute over the use of the title *The Third Reich*. Rowohlt used the proceedings in an attempt to discredit the Nazi movement. For example, Rowohlt lawyers sought to refute neo-conservative and Nazi claims of "idealism" by pointing out in court how petty it was for the HVA to make a legal issue out of a book title in the first place. Rowohlt also attempted to call Hitler and each ranking Nazi into court to have them testify on what the term "the Third Reich" meant to them. In this way the house hoped to show there was no clear consensus on the concept within the Nazi movement, much less was it an exclusive Nazi trademark.

The HVA responded by appealing to the Nazis for support. In a circular letter sent to Nazi party leaders, the firm declared: "The Hanseatic Publishing Institute, as publisher . . . of Moeller van den Bruck's national-socialistic *The Third Reich*, would like to fight shoulder to shoulder with the NSDAP in order to beat back these malicious and dangerous attacks by Jewish and leftist opposition groups."[43] Rowohlt's actions, the house warned, were ultimately directed not against the HVA, but against the Nazi cause. By showing in court that every Nazi understood something different by the concept "Third Reich," Rowohlt would "make the intellectual basis of National Socialism appear ridiculous." If Rowohlt were to win the right to title its book *The Third Reich*, then unsuspecting readers who hoped to learn more about National Socialism would purchase a copy of the volume but would find material in it which ridiculed the Nazi cause; potential Nazi supporters, the HVA cautioned, would be turned away from the movement as a result of Rowohlt's intentionally misleading volume. The Hanseatic letter thus advised that all Nazi party members and sympathizers be made aware of the true nature of the Rowohlt book, whatever its title. Moreover, the publishing house asked for wholehearted

Nazi support during the court battle against Rowohlt. By pointing out that the HVA was, at great expense to itself, conducting a struggle which was actually an affair of the Nazi party, the house none too subtly implied it was interested in more than just moral support from the Nazi party.[44]

The Hanseatic house ultimately won its legal contest for the exclusive right to use *The Third Reich* as a book title. If the firm was correct, then its success in this affair was also an important triumph for the Nazi cause. At any rate, it was not long after the Third Reich triumphed in the German book trade that it triumphed as well in the larger political arena. The episode over the HVA's new edition of *The Third Reich* was in fact strangely symbolic of the fate of the German neoconservative movement. For just as this publishing house portrayed Moeller van den Bruck's classic neoconservative manifesto as a National Socialist work in order to gain the support of the Nazi party, so too was much of the neoconservative movement willing to compromise its unique, independent stance after 1930 in hopes of benefiting from the popularity of the Nazi movement. Unable to put their inherently elitist program into effect without the aid of some politically organized mass movement, many neoconservatives temporarily suspended or abandoned their reservations about National Socialism in hopes of harnessing this powerful new force for their own ends. Once they had used the Nazis to overturn the Weimar system and launch the conservative revolution, neoconservatives like Stapel hoped to abandon them and direct the revolution along neoconservative lines. On their part, the Nazis encouraged such thinking. For just as the Nazi movement had usurped the term "Third Reich" from the neoconservative movement and transformed it into a central slogan of Nazi ideology, so too did it adopt many of the principles of the neoconservatives. National Socialist ideologues made every effort to present their movement as merely a continuation and culmination of neoconservative ideology.

At the crucial moment of victory in 1933, it was the Nazis who used and then discarded their neoconservative allies, rather than vice versa. The publishing houses which had helped generate the neoconservative movement and guide its development to the very verge of triumph soon realized that the Third Reich which the Nazis inaugurated was quite different from the one they had so long envisioned. By then, however, it was too late.

After the Deluge

That [our house's] program [before 1933] fit in with the aims of
National Socialism, and that, for their part, conservative
publishers, in light of the outward radiance and exhilaration of
the national resurgence, refused to admit to themselves that their
best ideals were being butchered before their eyes—this is a bit of
fate and guilt with which the younger generation now directing
the house must somehow come to grips.

—*175 Jahre Stalling*, p. 4

With the exception of J. F. Lehmann, who had long stood at that dark
edge of the movement where radical *völkisch* ideology blurred into Nazism
and who had stepped effortlessly over into the Nazi camp even before
1933 without missing a beat, the publishers and journalists who had earlier
sown the winds of neoconservatism now reaped a whirlwind after Hitler's
seizure of power. If the men around the Diederichs, Hanseatic, Stalling,
or Beenken houses had any illusions in 1933 that the Nazi revolution was
in fact that neoconservative revolution of which they had dreamed, they
were quickly disabused of such notions. For after the public bookburning
of May 1933, the relentless "coordination" (*Gleichschaltung*) of the book
trade and all other communications media, and the "blood purge" of
30 June 1934 when the Nazis either murdered leading neoconservative
theorists such as Edgar Jung and Gregor Strasser or forcibly suppressed
all ideologies and organizations opposing orthodox Nazi doctrine, it became clear that the Third Reich would tolerate critics neither on the Left
nor on the Right. Consolidation of Nazi control over Germany after January 1933 thus meant the end of the neoconservative movement. It also
meant the end of that independent, creative role which publishers like
Diederichs, Lehmann, Pezold, et al. had played within German cultural
life. For book production no less than the press and all other areas of
public life became strictly controlled by a state apparatus which demanded
and received total ideological conformity. Faced with the harsh realities
of the Third Reich, neoconservative publishers (like other Germans) were
forced to choose between collaboration, resistance, or resigned psychological withdrawal vis-à-vis the Nazi system.

Julius F. Lehmann was the only publisher who greeted the coming of
the Third Reich and who remained one of its most enthusiastic supporters. As his widow later boasted, Lehmann "did not need to accommodate his firm [to the new Nazi regime]; everything he had fought for
during his life at last met with approval in the Third Reich."[45] Indeed, the
Munich publisher and his firm attained an honored position under the

Nazis. Before his death in March 1935, Lehmann received a coveted honorary medical degree from the University of Munich in recognition of the JFLV's publication of outstanding medical literature. On his seventieth birthday in 1934 he was awarded a golden Nazi party emblem by Hitler, with the accompanying commendation: "Not only has your publishing activity helped to promote the spread of nationalist ideas—and especially racial perceptions—within the German *Volk*, but at a time when we had few friends you did everything in your power to help bring about the triumph of the idea of National Socialism. You have thereby deserved extraordinarily well of the NSDAP."[46] With such official sanction, the JFLV continued to prosper under Nazi rule, issuing between fifty and one hundred titles annually and enjoying healthy profits from the sale of its racial titles, which found a new market after 1933. Now that all political issues were theoretically settled, however, the house—whether willingly or not is unclear—limited its publications primarily to the areas of medicine, "racial science," and technical military affairs. By 1938–39 the house had opened a branch office in Berlin and had been awarded another high Nazi honor for its "exceptional achievements as a model enterprise." (Thanks to a sixty thousand mark fund established specifically for employee needs by Lehmann's widow and by the new firm director Fritz Schwarz, the more than seventy-five employees of the JFLV enjoyed unusually generous fringe benefits.)[47] During World War II, the JFLV premises in Munich suffered severe bomb and fire damage, which destroyed much of the firm's equipment and commercial records. American military occupation authorities ordered the enterprise suppressed in 1945, and all remaining stocks of books, paper, and plates were confiscated. The firm was allowed to reopen in 1948, but only as a retail bookstore; in 1950 permission was granted for the JFLV to resume its publishing activities as well. Today the J. F. Lehmanns Verlag, under the direction of Lehmann's son-in-law and grand-son, operates as a publisher of medical, political, historical, and artistic literature.

The "coordination" of the Lehmann house to the Nazi system after 1933 was unnecessary, but that of the Hanseatic publishing empire proved a more lengthy and a more difficult task. When Robert Ley's German Labor Front (Deutsche Arbeitsfront) usurped control of all labor unions in the spring of 1933, the HVA's parent organization, the German National Union of Commercial Employees, also fell under Nazi dominion, and top DHV officers such as Hans Bechly, Max Habermann, and Christian Winter were forced to resign. By October 1934 the DHV had been abolished and its functions formally assumed by the Labor Front. As control of HVA stock passed from the DHV into Ley's hands, the position of both the Hanseatic publishing empire and of Stapel's *Deutsches Volkstum* jour-

230 · ENTREPRENEURS OF IDEOLOGY

nal became precarious. HVA director Benno Ziegler, no doubt motivated largely by opportunism, joined the NSDAP in late 1933, a ploy which apparently succeeded in warding off any Nazi intrusion into HVA affairs. Indeed, by 1943 Ziegler was able to detach his firm completely from the Labor Front, and the HVA was reincorporated as the Hanseatische Verlagsanstalt Benno Ziegler Kommanditgesellschaft. Throughout the Third Reich the HVA gradually expanded its activities and published numerous titles in the areas of literature, history, military affairs, law, commerce and economics, and leisure pursuits. The Hamburg firm also became the outlet for all the monographs of Walter Frank's Reich Institute for the History of the New Germany (Reichsinstitut für Geschichte des Neuen Deutschlands).

The HVA's literary subsidiary, the Langen-Müller Verlag, was less successful at maintaining its independence, however. Gustav Pezold, LMV director, with the support of his firm's most prestigious authors, initially sought to steer an independent course after January 1933, for he did not want to see the house's reputation in the field of quality belles lettres tarnished by the publication of partisan fiction written by Nazi hacks. For this reason, the Nazi journal *Der Angriff* launched a series of attacks on the LMV in late 1933, charging that the house and its literary journal served as a haven for "reactionary" anti-Nazi authors. Nazi pressure on the LMV intensified in 1934, and Pezold's publishing policies were characterized as "cultural mutiny" and "spiritual high reason."[48] By 1936–37 the LMV journal *Das innere Reich* was sporadically banned, and LMV stock, acquired by the Labor Front during the 1933 takeover of the DHV, was transferred to a Nazi holding company. Threatened with arrest for financial malfeasance and other assorted charges, Pezold was finally compelled to step down as LMV director in January 1938.[49] After four years under a new pro-Nazi manager, the Langen-Müller house was formally merged into the Nazi party's mammoth publishing concern, the Franz Eher Verlag, in 1942–43.

Stapel's HVA journal, *Deutsches Volkstum*, suffered a similar fate. Like Benno Ziegler, Stapel jumped on the Nazi bandwagon in mid-1933 after the DHV and HVA were taken over by the Labor Front, although he stopped short of joining the party. Motivated partly by a desire to protect the position of his journal, and partly by the sincere hope that he might be able to steer the new Nazi regime closer toward his own concept of "national conservatism," Stapel and his journal struck a moderately pro-Nazi stance during much of 1933. Thus he greeted the May 1933 book burning as "a beautiful and necessary symbol of liberation from an alien [i.e., Jewish] spirit."[50] He became disillusioned with the Third Reich before long, however, and adopted a more reserved position in his journal.

The consequences were not long in coming: in 1935 the ss journal *Schwarze Korps* published a series of highly critical articles about Stapel and his circle, singling out especially their independent "confessional" orientation. Publicistic attacks on Stapel and *Deutsches Volkstum* quickly intensified, and the chief Nazi ideologue, Alfred Rosenberg, labeled him an "enemy of Nazism." Under intense pressure, Stapel finally stepped down from his editorial post in 1938, and the *Deutsches Volkstum* was completely transmuted into a new, pro-Nazi organ, the *Monatsschrift für das deutsche Geistesleben*. Drawing on his reputation as one of pre-Nazi Germany's most prominent anti-Semitic journalists and perhaps also capitalizing on his HVA ties, Stapel eventually managed to procure an obscure position as adviser to Frank's Reich Institute, where his expertise on the "Jewish question" was highly valued.

Although relentless Nazi pressure succeeded in breaking up and absorbing the DHV and a large part of the Hanseatic publishing empire by 1945, not all of the neoconservatives associated with these ill-fated organizations acceded final victory to the Nazis as easily as Stapel or Pezold. After his ouster from the DHV in 1933, for example, Max Habermann eventually joined other labor leaders in the underground resistance movement, and became an intimate of the Leuscher-Leber-Beck circle of anti-Nazi conspirators. Deeply implicated in Stauffenberg's attempt on Hitler's life, Habermann was arrested in July 1944 with the other conspirators, whereupon he committed suicide. Stapel's former coeditor on the *Deutsches Volkstum*, A. E. Günther, also entered the active resistance movement and became a member of the "*Stosstrupp Heinz*," a secret military detachment around Admiral Canaris which also plotted the forcible overthrow of Hitler. And even HVA director Benno Ziegler, although nominally a Nazi member himself, is reported to have used the premises of the HVA in Hamburg to arrange secret meetings between Habermann, Günther, and other resistance figures.[51]

After 1945 both the HVA and LMV, like the JFLV, managed eventually to resume their publishing activities. The HVA, which had been heavily damaged during the destruction of Hamburg and which had lost its director Ziegler in the closing months of the war, became the subject of a bitter and protracted legal dispute between Stapel (who, on the basis of his long association with the HVA demanded that he be appointed director of the firm) and Ziegler's heirs (who rejected Stapel's claims).[52] It was not until Stapel's death in 1954 that the HVA, now completely refounded as the Hanseatische Verlagsanstalt GmbH, resumed its activities, although on a limited scale, and concentrated on the areas of mathematics, technology, geodesics, and law. The Langen-Müller house, on the other hand, having emerged from the Third Reich as a totally owned Nazi enterprise,

232 · ENTREPRENEURS OF IDEOLOGY

faced more serious postwar problems. The firm's building in Nymphen-
burg was seized in 1945 to house officers of the American military occupation government, and the firm itself was liquidated, its lucrative book
rights being distributed to various other publishing houses. In 1952, however, the LMV was suddenly resurrected, and after a lengthy court battle
to recover its copyrights, it soon was reestablished as one of Germany's
leading houses for political and historical monographs, belles lettres, maps,
and art books.

The Heinrich Beenken and Gerhard Stalling houses, which of the five
firms studied here were the most peripherally associated with the neoconservative movement, correspondingly encountered fewer difficulties
after 1933. Beenken's small house survived by dropping much of its political program and concentrating instead on harmless areas such as children's
literature and nostalgic works on the geography, history, and folklore of
Brandenburg province. Both Beenken and his firm vanished after the fall
of Berlin in 1945, and no attempt was made to revive the HBV after the
war. By contrast, the century-and-a-half old Gerhard Stalling house survived the Third Reich and the war with only minimal disruption. Under
Heinrich Stalling, Jr., who died in 1941, the GSV rode out the Nazi years
by publishing almanacs, fiction, technical literature, and Oldenburgiana,
and also by relying more heavily on job work for its large printing facilities. These policies changed little when Hans Zehrer assumed direction of
the house after Stalling's death. After three postwar years of inactivity, in
1948 the firm was finally granted a license by the British occupation
authorities to resume its publishing; thereafter, it became active once
again in the areas of economics, sociology, history, science, and almanacs.

Finally, the entire gamut of responses to Nazism—enthusiastic participation, opportunistic accomodation, resigned retreat into neutral or
noncontroversial areas, and courageous resistance—which were variously
exhibited by the bookmen of the JFLV, HVA, HBV, and GSV, can all be
found in the neoconservatives around the Eugen Diederichs Verlag. In
this regard the EDV, that most prominent and quintessential of all the
neoconservative houses, faithfully reflects the complexity of the neoconservative movement and the different, often contradictory ways in which
individual neoconservatives came to grips with the Third Reich.

Since the independent and unpredictable Diederichs was now deceased
and presented no threat to the Nazi system, commentators after 1933
could afford to be generous in their praise of his persistent antiliberal
campaign even if they felt constrained for ideological reasons to point
out where his neoconservatism had fallen short of orthodox National Socialism. Thus in 1936, on the fortieth anniversary of the founding of the

EDV, one eulogist summarized the Third Reich's assessment of Diederichs (and, one might add, of the entire pre-Hitler neoconservative movement) by writing that the cultivated Jena publisher had failed to see that the struggle against modern, Western, technical civilization had ultimately to be fought and won not in the cultural, but in the political arena: "To be sure, [Diederichs] could not have forseen the solution which was decisively and politically achieved in 1933, a solution which he, in retrospect, believed could be attained solely through his cultural activities. Indeed, he still believed too strongly in the possibility of a [national] renewal through spiritual means to have dared anticipate that renewal through actual deeds which National Socialism has achieved."[53] As if to confirm this judgment, Diederichs's sons carefully steered the EDV away from social and political literature after 1933 and issued instead cautious, nontendentious volumes of poetry, fiction, travelogues, and works on religion and folklore. A large percentage of the EDV lists during the years of the Third Reich were in fact merely reissues of earlier popular house titles or new editions of the works of "classic" German authors such as Luther, Herder, Goethe, or Jahn.

While the circumspect publication policies of the EDV may have convinced the Nazis there was little need to tamper with the firm's offerings, the men around the EDV journal *Die Tat* did not escape Nazi intervention so easily. Although his *Tat* Circle had opposed the Nazis in 1932–33, after Hitler's seizure of power Zehrer steered *Die Tat* along a moderately pro-Nazi line, at least initially. Like Stapel, Zehrer hoped partly to accommodate the new regime, and partly that Hitler would prove to be the vehicle for that "genuine" national revolution of which the *Tat* Circle had dreamed for three years. But Zehrer, too, soon became disillusioned with the direction of the Third Reich, and adopted a more independent stance for his journal. In June 1933, therefore, Nazi leaders informed Peter and Niels Diederichs that Zehrer was no longer acceptable as editor of the EDV journal. Two months later Zehrer stepped aside in favor of Eschmann and Wirsing. He then withdrew from public life altogether to the lonely isle of Stylt, where he remained a virtual recluse until 1938. That year Heinrich Stalling, Jr. convinced him to end his "inner emigration" and to accept a post with the Gerhard Stalling Verlag as literary advisor. In 1939 Zehrer became manager of the GSV's Berlin office, and after Stalling's death in 1941, he assumed directorship of the entire Stalling enterprise. Zehrer's other associates at *Die Tat* followed radically different courses: Fried and Wirsing, for example, both accepted high posts in the Nazi apparatus, and both joined the SS in the late 1930s. On the other hand Adam Kuckhoff, who had briefly coedited *Die Tat* with Diederichs before the publisher

Nine

Conclusion

The Publishers and the Neoconservative Movement

German neoconservatism, which before 1933 laid the cultural and intellectual groundwork for the triumph of Nazism, drew its fundamental principles not from a single source or intellectual tradition, but rather from an extremely diverse potpourri of distinct, and generally autonomous cultural currents which reached well back into the nineteenth century. This disparate collection of ideas contained—especially before 1914—frequently contradictory elements: respectable academic literary or philosophical movements as well as vulgar antiintellectual cults; reactionary or antiindustrial tendencies as well as progressive, avant-garde movements; ideas behind which stood conservative political motives as well as ideas which had no apparent political implications at all.

It was not until August 1914 that this amorphous assortment of cultural currents, which could be loosely grouped under the two general headings of "cultural pessimism" and "radical nationalism," converged and linked, forming a somewhat more well-defined and roughly coherent new ideology on the radical Right. By its very nature, however, neoconservatism even after 1914 remained a splintered, disorganized, even chaotic affair. For the highly independent, rigidly doctrinaire, and often politically inexperienced middle-class intellectuals who were the most prominent exponents of neoconservative ideology were unwilling or unable to forge any kind of larger organizational framework or central authority for the movement. Neoconservatism, consequently, remained at best a loosely knit coalition of individuals and small factions, all tending in the same general direction.

The Diederichs, Lehmann, Hanseatic, Beenken, and Stalling publishing houses provided much of the coherence and direction for the neoconservative movement. For as both publishers and authors have recognized,[1] in the modern age of collectivization the efforts of an individual intellectual are often fragmentary and insufficient. Working alone in isolation, concentrating on a single limited object, and addressing himself to a narrow audience, he becomes self-oriented and too easily loses sight of a nation's broader cultural needs or the larger context within which his own work is situated. For this reason individual writers need the assistance of the publisher, who stands on the one hand between the producers and the consumers of culture, and on the other hand between spiritual and material concerns. This peculiar intermediatory position of the publisher gives him a unique entrepreneurial perspective on cultural life. By the very nature of his profession, he must take a broader view than does the individual author, for he is forced to fit each one of his firm's publications into the larger context of his overall publishing program and the needs of the market. Moreover, his contact with the public at large and his professional overview of the totality of intellectual effort allow him to see, as no single author can, the public's general needs and the means of satisfying them. The publisher can thus serve as a kappelmeister for creative soloists. Functioning as a "director of literature" who can "guide the powers of intellectuals to where they are most needed and effective, . . . using the insight and knowledge which his position affords him, he must unite many [individual] intellectuals into a single, grand literary undertaking in such a way that a useful, well-ordered whole arises from their common efforts."[2]

The neoconservative publishing houses performed precisely these organizational and managerial services for the amorphous neoconservative movement in the years before 1933. Publishers like Diederichs, Lehmann, Beenken, the Stallings, and those in control of the Hanseatic empire used their unique professional positions to synthesize the disparate individual elements and proponents of neoconservative ideology into a more coherent entity, and to direct that movement into fruitful new directions.

By collecting a contingent of like-minded authors and journalists behind their respective firms and organizing them into what Pezold called a "spiritual front," for example, the publishers created important visible focal points or centers of concentration for the nascent neoconservative movement. A journal like *Die Tat* or *Deutsches Volkstum*, or the author list of a house like the JFLV or EDV stood for a more or less distinct and clearly recognizable program or intellectual tendency. Other neoconservative figures often turned to one or another of the houses for ideological orientation, such as the young author who maintained that "it is very clear to me how much my intellectual life is bound up with the Eugen Diederichs Verlag and how indebted I am to [that] house. When I think of my intellectual development ever since my Gymnasium days, and of the influences which determined that development, then I always think primarily of books from [Diederichs's] publishing house, and almost all the men who have influenced me were Diederichs's authors."[3]

The publishers also fostered solidarity within the movement when they explored new ways to heighten the intellectual interchange among individual neoconservative authors and between authors and their audiences. The collaborative multivolume series devoted to a single theme which the houses frequently undertook were one means of encouraging greater interaction among authors, especially those working on common themes. Likewise, the direct exchange of ideas among authors and readers was facilitated by such experiments as the LMV's "Author Evenings" and "Gera Author Congress," or by the Lauenstein Cultural Congresses and the network of local *Tat* Circles which were formed under EDV tutelage.

In order to promote investigation into new areas, the neoconservative publishers sought to direct the efforts of neoconservative intellectuals into promising new territory, thereby broadening and deepening the body of neoconservative thought and filling lacunae within the movement. This was accomplished by suggesting general topics to authors, specifically commissioning authors such as von Liebig, Zarnow, Günther, or Hauser to carry out some preconceived project, soliciting new manuscripts on certain topics or offering prizes for the best new work on a specific subject, and finally, by granting research funds, such as Lehmann did to the Anthropological Society, the Society for Racial Hygiene, and the Association for Germanic *Volk* Character and Racial Research. Even more importantly, the publishers as part of their ongoing program continually expanded the movement by establishing links to numerous distinct cultural groups such as the Monist League, the revisionist socialists, the Free Religious communities, the German Theosophical Society, the *Kunstwart* Circle, the German Evangelical League, and the Bayreuth Circle, or by forging bonds to contemporary intellectual schools such as life-philosophy, Fabianism, *Jugendstil* art, the Youth Movement, Germanic Christianity, or eugenics. Within the publishing houses, these diverse currents were synthesized and fused with one another, sometimes in ways which created entirely new branches of neoconservative thought. Thus the popular new field of "Nordic ideology," which Diederichs almost single-handedly created after the turn of the century, was the result of his merging of the German *Volkstum* movement with folklore and the reissue of ancient literary texts such as *Edda* and *Thule*. Nordic ideology eventually became one of the more important subcurrents within the neoconservative movement and was further explored by firms like the JFLV and the HVA after the war. Diederichs also linked prewar currents of moderate, reformist socialism with elitism, the "Ideas of 1914," and corporative theories to yield the important new concept of a "German socialism" after 1914. In a similar manner, the JFLV became Germany's leading proponent of "racial science" after Lehmann linked radical nationalism with his house's long-standing activities in the area of medicine and biology; and by bringing together racial thought with his firm's work in genetics and eugenics, he opened up the fateful area of "racial hygiene."

The publishers applied their entrepreneurial skills to assist in the unfolding of neoconservatism in other ways as well. By creating new journals, by founding ad hoc theatrical companies (as Lehmann did in 1923), by developing the area of book graphics, and by turning their house catalogs into cultural manifestos which frequently contained original contributions by house authors, the publishers provided the movement with a number of innovative forums for neoconservative activity. And of course, men like Diederichs or Lehmann were inveterate organizers of groups and societies where neoconservative theorists and activists could find outlets for their energies. These two publishers, for example, personally founded or helped cofound over a dozen neoconservative organizations, including such diverse groups as the Sera Circle, the German Werkbund, the Hohe Meissner festival, the Patriotic Society 1914 in Thuringia, the Cultural Emergency Associations, the Fighting League Thule, the German-*Völkisch* Defense and Offense League, the Reich Commission for the Popular Will, the Association for Germanic *Volk* Character and Racial Research, and the Fighting League for German Culture.

Their organizational support for the neoconservative movement was frequently supplemented by financial support. Able to draw on the broad commercial basis of their firms, the publishers could apply revenues from their more successful, nonideological enterprises to the less remunerative neoconservative cause. Thus, besides direct contributions to such groups as the "endangered" Baltic Germans, the Anthropological Society, or Burg Persen, the publishers also used their financial resources to shore up or rescue bankrupt outlets for neoconservative ideas. Thus their acquisition of the ailing *Die Tat*, *Bühne und Welt*, the *Archiv für Rassen- und Gesellschaftsbiologie*, the *Münchener Abendzeitung*, the Ring Verlag, the Albert Langen Verlag, or the Georg Müller Verlag may well have saved these publicistic organs from extinction. Drawing on their commercial expertise and extensive professional contacts, Diederichs and Lehmann also helped establish various funds and foundations (the *Tat* War Fund, a "war chest" for the Pan-German League, the Cultural Emergency Associations, etc.) which were used to support a variety of neoconservative causes and activities.

Perhaps most important for the development and dissemination of neoconservatism, however, was the way in which these bookmen combined publishing with other forms of personal activity. This was significant because, as research in mass communications has revealed, "mass media prove most effective in conjunction with . . . centers of organized face-to-face contact."[4] New ideas and values are actually disseminated within a society through a complex network of media and interpersonal relations. Certain "opinion leaders" help shape opinion by picking up new ideas from the media and then diffusing them to the broader public by means of personal and group contact. And within each of these groups, certain members serve as information "gatekeepers" who transmit information from outside to within the group, information which they most often obtain from the media.[5]

The neoconservative publishers, besides founding the groups of their own mentioned above, were active in a wide variety of other cultural and political organizations. Diederichs, for example, belonged to the Dürer League and the Friends of Iceland. Lehmann was active in the Pan-German League, the Fatherland party, the Thule Society, *Bund Oberland*, the German Society for Racial Hygiene, the German Society for Research into Blood Groups, the German National Peoples party, and the Nazi party. The HVA was closely associated to the DHV, the Fichte Society, and the Society for Germandom Abroad. Beenken had ties to the German Employers League and the League Against Social Democracy. Because of their membership in these organizations, the publishers were able to make maximum effective use of both the publishing medium and of personal and organizational influence. They energetically diffused neoconservatism through the publishing medium, of course, but as cultural and political actors, they also served as opinion leaders and information gatekeepers for the many groups to which they belonged. In this capacity they were able to spread neoconservative ideology within those groups. (Lehmann, to cite but one example, sought to push the Pan-German League toward the Break-With-Rome movement and toward racism, two movements in which his firm was active.) Conversely, the publishers absorbed neoconservative ideas from the groups to which they belonged and disseminated those to the broader public through the publishing medium. Their singular professional position thus enabled them to coordinate and combine personal, group, and publishing activities in ways unavailable to other neoconservative ideologues. As entrepreneurs operating on a broad scale, the Diederichs, Lehmann, Hanseatic, Beenken, and Stalling houses served as managers or directors of the neoconservative movement in Germany, and they helped to determine the character of the movement and direct its development in significant ways.

These publishers also became effective agents for the dissemination of neoconservative thought to the society at large. Besides their energetic personal espousal of the neoconservative cause, their organizational services on its behalf, and the sheer volume of their neoconservative publications, these bookmen employed a variety of imaginative marketing techniques to maximize public awareness of and receptivity toward neo-conservative publications. For example, on their own initiative the publishers often sent complimentary copies of important neoconservative tracts to key figures in public life and journalism. In other instances, to insure that their publications would be favorably reviewed in the press, they encouraged or even requested their house authors to endorse each other's works or to write flattering critiques of specific books, which were then sent to major newspapers and journals. Pezold, to circumvent what he considered liberal and Jewish monopolization over the nation's feuilleton, even founded a neoconservative periodical for book reviews, the *Kritische Gänge*. To attract more attention to their publications, publishers like Diederichs employed innovative book graphics (sometimes, as in Hesse's case, as a way of counteracting the limited appeal of the text), or sponsored well-publicized contests among bookdealers. Diederichs's Lauenstein Summer Academies for young bookdealers was no doubt another way he intended to win over a segment of the retail book trade and create an atmosphere within the industry which would be more favorably disposed toward the general goals of the EDV. Diederichs, Pezold, and Lehmann knew how useful litigation and court trials could be in publicizing their houses' publications, and after 1914 Lehmann seemed intentionally to court confiscation, libel suits, and other legal actions against his firm as a means of gaining public sympathy for his causes.

Perhaps the greatest service which these bookmen provided to the dissemination of neoconservative literature, however, was the respectability and aura of legitimacy which they bestowed upon the movement. The EDV was a house of international repute which claimed several authors with Nobel prizes; the GSV was one of Germany's oldest publishing houses; the Hanseatic house was associated with one of the nation's largest and most important labor organizations, and the JFLV was a leading purveyor of quality academic medical and scientific literature. Diederichs, Lehmann, and eventually Heinrich Stalling received honorary university degrees, and all the houses could boast of several respected academics among their authors. When firms such as these embraced neoconservative ideas, much of their prestige inevitably rubbed off onto the movement, lending a certain status and legitimacy to even the crudest neoconservative tract.

Just how successful were the publishers in their efforts to disseminate neoconservative ideas? How wide an audience did their books reach, what was the nature of that audience, and what impact did the firms' products have upon the reading public? These, alas, are questions which are virtually impossible to answer. Complete sales figures for the books published by these houses are no longer extant, nor are the subscription lists of the houses' journals. There is thus no way of establishing, with even minimal accuracy, precisely how many publications of these five houses found their way into the hands of readers, much less which readers. Even if such information were available, it would reveal little, for a book purchased or a periodical received in the mail is not necessarily one which is read, and a volume or issue read may or may not have any effect upon the reader—indeed, he may completely disagree with what he finds printed there. Thus the fate of neoconservative books once they left the possession of these five firms will probably forever remain an impenetrable terra incognita.

As indicated throughout this study, however, some data has survived on the sales of certain titles. The value of such spotty information is limited. With it one might compare the sales of one book relative to another, for example, but not the total or average sales of all neoconservative books, the volume of turnover for a particular house, or the average sales of any given type of neoconservative publication. Nevertheless, keeping in mind the fragmentary nature of the extant sales data, a few cautious generalizations seem warranted.

It was unusual for a work produced by one of these publishing houses to sell more than 30,000 copies. Indeed, figures for the Diederichs house (which are most complete) indicate that the vast majority of the EDV's neoconservative publications sold fewer than 4,000 copies. Of the works produced by these firms, the type which most frequently enjoyed spectacular sales (100,000 copies or more) was the politically tendentious novel, especially novels which dealt with the experience of World War I. Thus, the two most successful titles to be published by the five houses between 1890 and 1933 appear to have been H. Löns's brutal peasant paean *Der Wehrwolf*, which sold some 565,000 copies for the EDV by 1939 (375,000 of these by 1933), and Hans Grimm's *Volk Ohne Raum*, which in its initial and its subsequent "popular" edition reached combined sales of more than 290,000 copies by 1935 and 480,000 copies by 1940. (Next to Hitler's *Mein Kampf*, of which some 10 million copies were distributed by 1945, the two all-time best-selling single titles in Germany between 1915 and 1940 were Thomas Mann's *Buddenbrooks*, which had sold more than 1.3 million by 1936, and Remarque's *Im Westen Nichts Neues*, which sold more than 900,000 during its first year alone.)[6] The HVA empire could boast of at least three other best-selling novels which, like Grimm's, topped 100,000 copies sold: A. Bartels's *völkisch* tale of *The Dithmarshers* (*Die Dithmarscher*; 208,000 copies by 1928); G. Fock's "hearth and homeland" novel of North German fishermen, *Seafaring is Vital* (*Seefahrt ist Not*; 218,000 copies sold by 1936); and J. Wehner's gripping war tale *Sieben vor Verdun* (130,000 copies by 1940). Werner Beumelburg's two war novels *Sperrfeuer um Deutschland* (328,000 copies sold by 1940, of which 166,000 before 1933) and *Gruppe Bosemüller* (90,000 by 1935) proved to be, respectively, the most and the third most popular titles on the GSV list. On the other hand, E. Dwinger's two war novels *Zwischen Weiss und Rot* and *Wir Rufen Deutschland*, each of which eventually sold more than 200,000 copies, were among the top five or six best-selling titles ever produced by the EDV.

If fiction, especially war novels, appeared to enjoy the greatest success with readers, then the nonfictional works which seemed to achieve the most dramatic sales were books which also dealt with the war or with racial themes. After Löns's and Grimm's novels the most widely sold title to be issued by the neoconservative houses was Günther's *Kleine Rassenkunde des deutschen Volkes*, of which some 272,000 copies had been sold by 1943. If one also considers Günther's original *Rassenkunde des deutschen Volkes*, then the combined sales of both the complete and the abridged versions of this racial handbook reached some 322,000 copies by 1943. The next most widely distributed titles of the JFLV (excluding short reprints from *Deutschlands Erneuerung*, which were often distributed gratis and might reach printings of 250,000 copies or more) were: Lehmann's own wartime tract *Deutschland bei einem guten und einem schlechten Frieden* (225,000 copies); Dickhuth-Harrach's *Im Felde Unbesiegt* (160,000 copies); F. Lehmann's autobiographical *Wir von der Infanterie* (90,000 copies in only one year); and Darré's *Neuadel aus Blut und Boden* (60,000 by 1940). The two best-selling nonfiction titles from the HVA were T. Fritsch's *Handbuch der Judenfrage* (93,000 copies by 1933) and P. Witkop's *Kriegsbriefe gefallener Studenten* (90,000 copies by 1934). Likewise, two of the EDV's most successful multivolume series were *Kriegslieder* (127,000 copies by 1923) and *Kriegsflugblätter* (over 50,000 copies by 1923). The only title published by the Heinrich Beenken Verlag ever to sell more than 100,000 copies was Beenken's own anti-Versailles *Was Wir verloren haben*. Finally, the most widely disseminated nonfictional volumes from the GSV were the account of the World War I battle *Douaumont* (135,000 copies sold by 1940), Chamberlain's *Deutsche Kriegsziele* (43,000), and H. Schacht's *Das Ende der Reparationen* (which sold more than 40,000 copies its first year).

Thus, tendentious, politically charged novels, fictional and nonfictional works treating World War I and its immediate after effects, and to a somewhat lesser extent racial literature, fictional or not, appear to have been the kinds of neoconservative publications most likely to find a large market in Germany.[7] Certainly titles from these categories accounted for most of the dramatic commercial successes of the neoconservative publishing firms. The popularity of novels is hardly surprising, as fiction has been the mainstay of the German book trade since the early eighteenth century.[8] But the thriving market for books treating World War I and racial matters may suggest that the experience of the war and racial anxieties were among the most deep-seated, persistent concerns of the German public in the early twentieth century. Indeed, even the popular films of the Weimar era reveal a collective obsession with the loss of the world war and contain frequent unconscious images which suggest that Germans attributed their defeat primarily to betrayal by alien, non-German elements within the nation.[9] Was it any wonder, then, that someone like Hitler[10]—whose "program" consisted almost entirely of two fundamental aims: to reverse the outcome of World War I and to find a solution to the "Jewish problem"—could find a broad basis of support among Germans?

The Publisher as Patron and Cultural Entrepreneur

The most important patronage actually arises from dilettantism— that is, from that condition of artistic impotence where one longs for deliverance through art, where one seeks some artistic form of expression, but can't yet find it.

—Leo Berg[11]

The position and role of the publisher equals (*gleicht*) that of a Louis XIV, of the Medicis, of a Maecenas—in short, all the famous figures whom history recognizes as protectors of literature. Discovering meritorious emerging talent, helping it along in its earliest stages, encouraging it, supporting it, often providing it with the means it needs for its self-development, strengthening it and if necessary protecting it against its adversaries, insuring in general a carefree existence for the muses—do we not do this every day?

—Ferdinand Brunetière,
in a speech to the 1901
Congress of Publishers,
Leipzig.[12]

However offensive one might find these firms' ideological orientation, the activities of the Eugen Diederichs Verlag, the J. F. Lehmanns Verlag, the Hanseatische Verlagsanstalt and its related enterprises, the Heinrich Beenken Verlag, and of the Gerhard Stalling Verlag reveal much about the modern publisher's sociocultural role. The case of the neoconservative publishers illustrates above all the peculiar dual nature of the publisher's profession, for he is simultaneously a commercial entrepreneur and an agent of culture.

A complex, interdependent relation existed between the neoconservative publishers and their authors. It was through their authors, for example, that these bookmen seemed to find vicarious fulfillment for their own frustrated aspirations. As one observer of the German book trade has noted, publishers are like mutes who can speak only through others. Many publishers long to be culturally creative, but often lack the ability to express themselves directly. Instead, they find release by mobilizing and supporting artists who do possess the gift of self-expression.[13] Such was the case with men like Diederichs, Lehmann, Beenken, or Gustav Pezold. Semi- or self-educated and often keenly aware of their own intellectual limitations, they were stirred by strong opinions and creative urges but were unable to articulate fully their ideas. Through their house's authors, however, they achieved that degree of self-expression and public recognition which they were incapable of achieving on their own. Like so many other bookmen—including Samuel Fischer, Germany's foremost literary publisher during the Wilhelmian and Weimar eras[14]—the neoconservative publishers satisfied their own personal creative needs by nurturing and promoting the talents of others; they attained social prominence through contact with other prominent personalities. Their situation reflects both the essence and the irony of the publisher's calling; for as one bookman has stated, "the talent of a publisher lies in his ability to recognize the nascent talents of others. . . . He has the ability to sense what is timely and what is eternal, he discovers men and truths. But personally, he remains in the background and is hardly ever seen. He is more than his calling allows him to appear."[15]

In the process of finding vicarious expression, neoconservative publishers established a relationship with their authors which bears a striking resemblance to that which existed between an aristocratic patron and his protégés. Traditional patrons of the premodern era provided material assistance or total support to an artist, thereby allowing him to devote his full energies to intellectual work. By placing the prestige of his own name or court behind an intellectual, a patron conferred greater respectability to and influence on his protégé. Occasionally, a powerful patron helped secure a public office for his protégé, which served to increase the intellectual's income, influence, and social standing. Patrons traditionally functioned as spokesmen and protectors for their protégés, shielding them from attacks by public authorities or artistic rivals. And by bringing protégés to their court or putting them in contact with educated urban audiences, patrons helped writers gain new opportunities for self-expression and assisted in breaking down the intelligentsia's social isolation. In return for the services they rendered, patrons expected loyalty, endorsement, and acquiescence. They frequently exercised some control over the material their protégés produced, and often used this material for their own ends. Indeed, many patrons sought out intellectuals precisely because their talents could be useful in furthering the political, ideological, or social concerns of the patron. A patron usually viewed his patronage as an investment which would be repaid when a successful artist's work brought him recognition, political advantage, or social prestige. Patrons thus received as much from a patronage relationship as did the protégés; few patrons acted out of pure altruism.[16]

These features of traditional patronage were all present in the relationships between the neoconservative publishers and their authors. These publishers sought to alleviate the material cares of their authors. Lehmann, for example, considered it "the honorable duty of every publisher . . . to see to it that writers receive whatever is necessary for their creative work."[17] Besides commissioning writers and artists for various undertakings, the bookmen tried to assist needy authors and neoconservative groups by procuring monetary aid for them from private and public institutions (as Diederichs did through the Cultural Emergency Associations, for example, and as Lehmann sought to do for Schemann). When this failed, the publishers personally provided destitute authors (like Löns, Wirth, and Schemann) with grants, gifts, or donations. The neoconservative publishers also served as financial patrons when they willingly incurred monetary losses in order to publish books and journals which had little prospect of commercial success, but which they considered politically or culturally necessary.

Furthermore, these publishers provided their protégés with intangible benefits such as social opportunities and respectability. Diederichs, for example, sought public posts, awards, and access to prestigious academies for his authors (Hesse, Blunck), while professorships or ministerial portfolios were awarded to writers like Günther and Darré, whom Lehmann's firm had helped make famous. The publisher created a number of new forums for neoconservative activity, and preserved other neoconservative publicistic outlets from extinction. Lending their prestigious house imprints to neoconservative literature, they conferred a measure of respectability on individual authors, especially nonacademic popularizers of neoconservative ideas, and bestowed the appearance of legitimacy on the causes they championed. And, like traditional patrons, the neoconservative publishers frequently assumed the role of public spokesman for their authors and guardian of their interests. When house protégés such as Zarnow, Haken, Lt. Schulz, Muck, or Günther were challenged by authorities, sued by adversaries, or attacked by artistic competitors, these publishers intervened on their behalf and (as in Lehmann's case), even assumed their authors' legal costs if necessary.

As patrons received reciprocal services from their protégés, so too did the neoconservative publishers from their authors. By commissioning books directly, suggesting themes or topics to writers, or in some cases even personally rewriting manuscripts, the publishers brought their influence to bear on the artistic products of their clients. In this way, the personal concerns and opinions of the publishers received due consideration not only in the houses' general publishing programs, but in many of the specific books issued as well. These publishers expected—and usually received—a certain degree of loyalty from the authors whom they patronized. Finally, the neoconservative publishers hoped their patronage would be repaid when the future success of their author protégés brought financial, ideological, and other benefits to their houses.

What the neoconservative publishers did to aid, support, and protect individual writers, they did also on a larger scale for neoconservatism as a whole. From their unique entrepreneurial position, they functioned not only as managers and directors, but also as true patrons of the entire neoconservative movement, placing the considerable influence, prestige, and resources of their houses behind the neoconservative cause and helping it to gain recognition, respectability, and influence.

Diederichs, for one, was conscious of the similarity of publishers to patrons: "Every new development," he declared, "needs helpful solicitude, and without patrons, no cultural flowering is possible. Thus the publisher, who with an eye to the future makes sacrifices to aid new forces, is a patron too."[18] The kind of broad patronage which he and the other four publishing houses exercised on behalf of the neoconservative movement was by no means uncommon within the German book industry. Throughout the nineteenth and early twentieth centuries—when small, highly personalized, and strongly programmatic houses comprised a larger share of the German publishing industry than under today's large-scale business conditions—numerous publishers closely identified their houses with a specific cultural or political cause and tirelessly championed its development. What the EDV, JFLV, HVA, HBV, and GSV did for neoconservatism, for example, the publishing firms of Wilhelm Fleischer, Friedrich Nicolai, and J. H. Campe did for the German Enlightenment.[19] In much the same way, the houses of J. C. Mohr, Mohr & Zimmermann, and G. A. Reimer served the romantic movement. The Hoffmann & Campe, Löwenthal & Hoff, and Sauerländer houses patronized the so-called Young Germany movement, while the Otto Wigand and Duncker & Humblot houses sponsored the Young Hegelian authors.[20] Samuel Fischer and his famous S. Fischer Verlag served as a patron for the German naturalist and impressionist writers. Similarly, Georg Bondi's house performed the same service for the Stefan George Circle, as did Wieldand Herzfelde's Malik Verlag and the Paul Steegman house for the Dada movement.[21] Likewise, Kurt Wolff—who believed a publisher should "represent and promote not books, but authors"—and Ernst Rowohlt both used their houses to direct and support the expressionist movement.[22] By the early twentieth century, then, it had become clear to many in Germany that modern publishers had assumed most of the functions previously exercised by aristocratic patrons.

This role arose not so much from the publishers' personal inclinations as it did from the nation's peculiar social and legal development. Beginning in the eighteenth century, a large reading public and comprehensive copyright laws in Europe first made it possible for a writer to live solely from the proceeds of his writing. This freed writers from their traditional dependence on some conventional occupation or their reliance on wealthy patrons for a stable income, and permitted the emergence of the independent, professional writer. As writers passed from dependence on patrons to dependence on the impersonal book market, however, they fell under the new authority of the publisher, whose function it was to mediate between the writer and the reading public by providing a commercial mechanism with which to exploit the market.

Because of Germany's long-standing political fragmentation, these developments occurred later there than in other Western European nations. A nationwide copyright law protecting German authors was first established in 1837; not until it was further strengthened and extended in the 1870s and 1880s, however, was the threat of literary piracy completely eliminated in Germany.[23] Likewise, a truly unified national book market large enough to support a class of professional authors did not emerge until the establishment of the Second Reich in 1871.[24] Thus, during the greater part of the nineteenth century the process by which publishers supplanted patrons was still taking place in Germany, and forms of the traditional patronage relationship survived well into the twentieth century. This explains why, on the eve of World War I, one might hear disgruntled writers such as Erich Eckertz lamenting that "the dependent relationship of a writer to a patron which was so common during the Renaissance and even in Goethe's day appears today to be changing into a dependency of authors toward publishers. A publisher behaves toward his authors as the princely patron did in those days. Before long, we shall probably see an epic poem in which the hero is not one of the Medicis, but rather a modern publisher."[25]

While authors realized that under the conditions of the modern economic market many of the functions of premodern cultural patronage had devolved to publishers, they failed to see that this was only part of a transition toward the ultimate elimination of patronage. As writers in Germany became more self-conscious and, after 1840, began organizing their own interest groups to reform copyright laws, fight for higher honoraria and royalties, and generally to press their interests vis-à-vis publishers, writers were able to gain greater independence even from publishers.[26] More importantly, however, publishers served merely as transitional patrons because they were economically dependent on the success of their authors. As with impressarios and other types of managers who handle the commercial aspects of art, a publisher's ultimate goal is the public success of his author-clients; the greater that success, with its correspondingly higher royalty income for the author, the more financially and socially independent the author becomes and the less he must rely on patronage of any sort.

In contrast to the relatively sterile and often demeaning relationship between artists and traditional patrons, then, that which has developed between the modern artist and his publisher or manager is more dynamic and mutually gratifying. Because the publishing industry makes it possible for an artist to earn his own means of support directly rather than to receive it as an allowance from some benefactor, publishers help overcome the isolation which often exists between art and the intelligentsia on the one hand and the practical workaday world on the other. And, as some German writers have realized, the fact that the interests of a publisher converge with those of his authors means that the publisher-manager has become the modern artist's most natural and powerful ally in the ongoing competition of new cultural movements for public success and recognition.[27]

The role of the modern publisher is thus complex and multifarious. The book trade forms an important segment of that modern "culture industry" which has arisen between the producers and the consumers of intellectual goods. As managers of the marketplace which lies between authors and the reading public, bookmen must mediate between author and public; in doing so, they are alternately the masters and servants of each party. A publisher must follow public taste to survive economically, but at the same time he often seeks to lead the public in new directions. He serves authors by distributing their products, yet he is also something of an employer or patron of authors in that writers are partially dependent on him for their income and he often directs and influences their artistic production.[28] Moreover, the book industry represents a unique juncture between the material and the spiritual realms; personal disposition, material self-interest, and altruistic service (whether intentional or not) to larger cultural ends all converge in the publisher's profession. Because of the unique spiritual nature of the products in which they deal and because of their unusual intermediate position between cultural producers and cultural consumers, bookmen must unite and harmonize the often conflicting demands of commerce and culture. They are, consequently, far more than mere businessmen. They are cultural entrepreneurs.

Notes

CHAPTER I

1. Schiller to Cotta, 1 Sept. 1794, as quoted in Schottenloher, *Bücher bewegten die Welt*, 2:451.

2. Schücking, *Soziologie der Geschmacksbildung*, p. 62.

3. The most active German scholar in this area is Helmut Hiller. See his "Buch und Verlagswesen," and *Sozialgeschichte von Buch*. Robert Darnton's studies of prerevolutionary French publishers have provided not only a more precise picture of how deeply Enlightenment ideas penetrated into French society, but have also demonstrated that the dissemination of the Enlightenment and of antimonarchical literature was due in part to the structure and peculiarities of the French publishing industry. See his "Reading, Writing, and Publishing," "Encyclopédie War," and his masterful *Business of the Enlightenment*. Byrnes's "French Publishing Industry" argues, less convincingly, that the economic collapse of the book industry in France drove an entire generation of intellectuals into radical, antirepublican activities. Morris's "German Nationalist Fiction" is an attempt to examine the production of anti-Semitic fiction within the structural and economic context of the German book industry.

4. I have borrowed this phrase from von Klemperer, "Austrofascism," p. 316.

5. The major general works on the neoconservative movement in the Weimar republic include: Gerhard, *Reiches Zukunft*; Vermeil, *Doctrinaires révolution allemande*; Rauschning, *Conservative Revolution*; Mohler, *Konservative Revolution*; Theisen, *Nihilistischen Nationalismus*; Neurohr, *Mythos vom Dritten Reich*; von Klemperer, *Germany's New Conservatism*; Schüddekopf, *Linke Leute*; Sontheimer, *Antidemokratisches Denken*; Lepsius, *Extremer Nationalismus*; Lebovics, *Social Conservatism*; Gerstenberger, *Revolutionäre Konservatismus*; and Petzold, *Konservative Theoretiker*.

6. On the general problem of conservatism and the traditional Right in modern German history, see: von Martin, "Altkonservativen Denken"; Mannheim, "Konservative Denken"; Neumann, *Stufen des preussischen Konservatismus*; Schüddekopf, *Deutsche Innenpolitik*; Romein, "Über Konservatismus"; Epstein, *Genesis of German Conservatism*; Glum, *Konservatismus*; Kaltenbrunner, *Rekonstruktion des Konservatismus*; and Nolte, "Germany." On specific conservative political parties in Germany between 1871 and 1933, see: Stolberg-Wernigerode, *Unentschiedene Generation*; Booms, *Deutschkonservative Parteien*; Viebig, *Freikonservativen*; Kaufman, *Monarchism in the Weimar Republic*; Hartenstein, *Deutschnationalen Volkspartei*; Hertzman, *DNVP*; Thimm, *Flucht in der Mythos*; Liebe, *Deutschnationale Volkspartei*; and Schönhoven, *Bayerische Volkspartei*.

7. Turner, "Fascism and Modernization," pp. 123–24.

8. Ibid., p. 120.

9. Boris Nikol'ski's statement of 1905, as quoted in Rogger, "Russian Fascism," p. 400.

10. Wilhelm Stapel, "Zwanzig Jahre Deutsches Volkstum," *Deutsches Volkstum* 40 (1938): 798.

11. "Every totalitarian government starts from a new image of man; this, by definition, is what distinguishes it from the classical forms of coercive government. Its revolutionary claims are not aimed solely at the reconstruction of the state; it not only prescribes new laws, demands new principles of order or new forms of mutual relationships, but also calls for a 'new man.' Unlike the great revolutions of past ages, it sets out to change not things but people, not structures but life itself: this is precisely what identifies it as totalitarian." (Fest, *Face of the Third Reich*, pp. 424–25.)

12. See for example Gerhard, *Reiches Zukunft*, p. 211; Mohler, *Konservative Revolution*, pp. 99–100; von Klemperer, *Germany's New Conservatism*, p. 238; Ketelsen, *Völkisch-nationale Literatur*, pp. 56, 78; and Epstien, "Review," p. 660.

13. On the Hugenberg Concern, see: Guratzsch, *Macht durch Organisation*; Oschilewski, *Zeitungen in Berlin*, pp. 97ff., 163ff., 216ff.; Ecksteins, *Limits of Reason*; and Leopold, *Hugenberg*.

14. The Ring Verlag, for example, issued the works of Arthur Moeller van den Bruck and Max Boehm's *Ruf der Jungen* (1921); the Deutsche Rundschau Verlag brought out Edgar Jung's important *Die Herrschaft der Minderwertigen* (1927), while Niekisch's Widerstand Verlag published books by F. C. Jünger, Othmar Spann, Hermann Ullmann, and August Winnig.

15. Kratzsch, *Kunstwart und Dürerbund*, and Mauersberger, *Pechel und die 'Rundschau'* are good examples.

CHAPTER 2

1. Eugen Diederichs, *Aus meinem Leben* (Jena, 1938), p. 10 (hereafter cited as *AmL*). Captivated by Langbehn's *Rembrandt als Erzieher*, which portrayed the *Niederdeutsch* tribes as the true spiritual ancestors for all that was most authentic in the German nation, Diederichs convinced himself that he, too, was "three-quarters heavy-blooded *Niederdeutsch*." (Ulf Diederichs, ed., *Eugen Diederichs: Selbstzeugnisse und Briefe von Zeitgenossen*. Düsseldorf, 1967, p. 27, hereafter cited as *SBZ*. Eugen Diederichs, *Leben und Werk: Ausgewählte Briefe und Aufzeichnungen*. Edited by Lulu von Strauss und Torney-Diederichs. Jena, 1936, p. 464, hereafter cited as *LW*.)

2. *AmL*, p. 9.

3. Ibid., p. 12.

4. He came to know authors from Ferdinand Avenarius's literary circle (the Kunstwartkreis) and the Wilhelm Bölsche-Friedrichshagen circle of German naturalists. All these early acquaintances eventually published with the EDV and helped establish the firm's reputation in belles lettres.

5. The *Monographien zur deutschen Kulturgeschichte* (1899–1905) burdened the house for years. Hans Blum's popular history of the 1848 revolution, Bölsche's *Die Liebesleben in der Natur*, and Maurice Maeterlinck's early poetry and prose sold phenomenally well. Reports differ as to the size of Diederichs's inheritance from the death of his mother in 1902; Menz, *Deutsche Buchhandel*, p. 287 gives the sum as 70,000 marks, while Diederichs's grandson Ulf ("Marketing um die Jahrhundertwende," p. 98) maintains it was only 30,000 marks.

6. See Diederichs, "Marketing um die Jahrundertwende," pp. 93–103.

7. *LW*, pp. 109–10.

8. Diederichs boasted that "no other German publishing house can offer in its report of the year's activity as comprehensive an insight into the driving forces of our times as does my house" (*SBZ*, p. 41). One admirer called the Diederichs house catalogs "reports from the

workshop, personal confessions, cultural-political communiqués, pedagogical manifestos, reflections of his creative personality, and autobiographies-in-the-making" (Oschilewski, "Charakterköpfe," p. 561).

9. Zweig, "Lob deutschen Verleger," p. 574. For additional public praise of the EDV see Hesse, "Verlag Diederichs," p. 318 and *Protestanten Blatt*, 9 April 1913.

10. *SBZ*, p. 288; *LW*, p. 297; and Diederichs to H. Löns, 17 Aug. 1914, in Deimann Nachlass.

11. *SBZ*, pp. 225, 266, 320.

12. Melanie Lehmann, ed., *Verleger J. F. Lehmann, Ein Leben im Kampf für Deutschland: Lebenslauf und Briefe* (Munich, 1935), pp. 9–10 (hereafter cited as *LKD*). Lehmann also briefly joined Eugen Richter's *Freisinnige Partei*, but soon became "disgusted" with it (*Fünfzig Jahre JFLV*, p. 56).

13. *LKD*, p. 238.

14. Ibid., p. 17.

15. Lehmann to H. S. Chamberlain, 26 Feb. 1904, Chamberlain Nachlass.

16. *LKD*, pp. 152–53, 157–58, 178; Lehmann to M. E. Moritz, 29 Jan. 1931, Zarnow Nachlass.

17. *LKD*, p. 36; Lehmann, *Zum 25. jährigen Gründungstag*, pp. 12–13.

18. Lehmann to F. Curtius, 21 Jan. 1905, Lehmann Archive.

19. On the social and economic situation of *Angestellten* and *Gehilfen* in imperial Germany, see Gewerkschaftsbund, *Lage der Angestellten*; Lederer, *Privatangestellten*; Hamel, *Völkischer Verband*, pp. 9–20; Kocka, *Unternehmensverwaltung und Angestelltenschaft*, and "Vorindustrielle Faktoren."

20. Quoted in Hamel, *Völkischer Verband*, p. 10, and Bechly, *Handlungsgehilfenbewegung und Parteien*, p. 7. To date, Hamel's is the only comprehensive study of the DHV, although Walter Struve is currently at work on another.

21. For the socioeconomic situation of white-collar employees after 1914 see: Croner, "Angestelltenbewegung nach der Währungsstabilisierung"; Fischer, *Die Angestellten*; Engelhard, "Die Angestellten"; Dreyfuss, *Beruf und Ideologie*; Kocka, "First World War and *Mittelstand*," *Klassengesellschaft im Krieg*, pp. 65–82, and "Problematik der Angestellten"; Krause, "Rolle der Mittelschichten"; Coyner, "Class Consciousness and Consumption"; and Speier, *Angestellten vor dem Nationalsozialismus*.

22. For the political alliances and dilemmas of the DHV, see Krebs, *Tendenzen und Gestalten*, chap. 1; Hamel, *Völkischer Verband*, pp. 190ff.; Jones, "Between the Fronts," and "Crisis of White-Collar Politics."

23. Entries for 12 Dec. 1904, 26 Feb. 1906, and 20 Aug. 1909 in "Die Verwaltung. Verwaltungssitzungsberichten 1893–1930," in DHV Archive; *Deutsche Handelswacht* 24 (1917): 57–58 (hereafter cited as *Handelswacht*); Hamel, *Völkischer Verband*, pp. 140–41. An additional 100,000 marks was loaned to the firm by the DHV in November 1919 through the purchase of stocks.

24. *Bericht DHV für 1909–10*, p. 26.

25. As quoted in Hamel, *Völkischer Verband*, p. 140.

26. Ibid.

27. "Verwaltungssitzungsberichten," entries for 10 Dec. 1918 and 28 Apr. 1920, DHV Archive; "Bericht des Aussichtsrats am 4. Dec. 1932 in Hamburg," DHV Archive; *Rechenschaftsbericht für 1930; Rechenschaftsbericht für 1931*. In 1925 a branch of the HVA was opened in Berlin under Otto Rippel and given the task of cultivating political literature, especially works dealing with the Reichstag.

28. "Verwaltungssitzungsberichten," entry for 9 Nov. 1928, DHV Archive; *Handelswacht* 38 (1931): 229–30; "Tagebuch," entry for 24 June 1943, Stapel Nachlass; "Zum Bericht der

Deutschen Allgemeinen Treuhänder AG über die im Albert Langen-Georg Müller Verlag vorgenommene Statuserstellung per 30. 6. 1934. Stellungsnahme des Geschäftsführers und allein verantwortlichen Verlagsleiter Gustav Pezold," pp. 9, 16, in Pezold Nachlass.

29. On the Ring Movement and the Ring Verlag, see von Klemperer, *Germany's New Conservatism*, pp. 102–11, and Schwierskott, *Moeller van den Bruck*.

30. "Verwaltungssitzungsberichten," entries for 12 Jan. 1928 and 5 June 1928, DHV Archive; "Tagebuch," 24 June 1943, Stapel Nachlass; *Handelswacht* 38 (1931): 229–30.

31. After a ten-year career as a naval officer, Pezold joined the free corps and engaged in antirevolutionary battle against Sparticists in Wilhelmshaven and in Tübingen in 1918–19. As a member of the Brigade Ehrhardt, he participated also in the 1920 Kapp putsch. He was active in the Nazi party during 1922–23 and was arrested twice by the Weimar republic: after the assassination of Rathenau and again after Hitler's abortive putsch in 1923. Although he then left active political life to enter the book trade, he claimed that even "my house and my bookstore in Tübingen were for a long time at first the secret, later the known but not provable center of an active, all-out political struggle against the [Weimar] system." (Pezold, "Schrifttum und Buchhandel und ihre Bedeutung im Leben der Nation. Ein Denkschrift," mimeographed manuscript dated April 1933, Box 2, Pezold Nachlass; also Morris, "German Nationalist Fiction," chap. 5.)

32. Pezold, "Bericht über den Verlag Albert Langen—Georg Müller AG, München, von verantwortlichen Leiter seit 1930," Box 1, Pezold Nachlass.

33. Morris, "German Nationalist Fiction," chap. 5.

34. "Once this great loss was incurred, it seemed best to me not to give up our cultural goal as well, but rather to put additional, but more limited resources on the line for the acquisition of the ALV so as to be able to carry on our national cultural work that much more intensively." (Pezold, "Zum Bericht Treuhänder per 30. 6. 1934," p. 2, and "Bericht über den Verlag," Pezold Nachlass.) Stapel's reasons for advocating purchase of the ALV were equally ideological. He told the DHV leadership that the failing ALV must be acquired to prevent valuable German works from falling into Jewish hands, and that having the house would strengthen the DHV-HVA publishing empire's ability to spread its propaganda and to silence its opponents. (Undated Stapel letter to Verwaltungsrate des DHV, Box 2, Pezold Nachlass.) On a more practical level, Pezold hoped that by acquiring the ALV, he could force bookdealers who wanted to carry the more popular ALV books to carry the less popular GMV authors as well.

35. Hanns Floerke, "Verlagsgeschichte der Albert Langen Verlag," (undated typescript in Box 4, Pezold Nachlass), pp. 248–49. ALV losses for the year 1930 alone totaled 52,300 marks, and total debts stood at 800,000 marks. Merger of the two houses occurred on 7 March 1932 but was not publicly announced until 1 April. Max Habermann, Chairman of the Board for the new LMV, told the stockholders that "This enterprise serves German spiritual life, above all German belles lettres; it has created a commercially more secure cradle [for German literature] through the merger of the previous Albert Langen and Georg Müller publishing houses."

36. Max Habermann, "Der Deutschnationale Handlungsgehilfen-Verband im Kampf um das Reich, 1918–1933" (unpublished manuscript in DHV Archive), p. 30.

37. "This willingness to grant great latitude to enterprises like Stapel's *Deutsches Volkstum* . . . and the great Munich concern [the LMV] goes far to explain why the DHV succeeded in collecting under one roof most of the leading lights of nationalist literature, the majority of whom, viewing themselves as voices of the *Volk* as a whole, were fiercely jealous of their freedom from party-political control. The DHV had achieved something beyond the capacity of Hugenberg's great industrial wing of the DNVP with its Scherl concern or of the NSDAP with its Eher, Boepple, and other houses. Scherl and the Nazi (and other *völkisch*) firms never suc-

ceeded in enlisting anything more than authors of lowgrade *Tendenz-* or *Unterhaltungsliteratur*. Langen-Müller continued to set the pace for literature in the Third Reich even after the DHV itself ceased to exist." (Morris, "German Nationalist Fiction," chap. 5.)

38. See Fullerton, "German Book Markets."

39. Coyner, "Class Consciousness and Consumption," pp. 320–21, 331 n. 38. Coyner concludes (p. 325) that this demonstrates a distinct white-collar identity.

40. Neven du Mont, *Kollektivierung des literarischen Konsums*, pp. 46–60.

41. The HVA's link with the DHB proved a boon for HVA writers, several of whom were employed in the late 1920s at rather high fees simply to turn out novels for the DHB. Authors of the GMV were also drawn into this lucrative trade after 1928. (Pezold, "Die deutsche Hausbücherei," typescript dated 1 Feb. 1934, Box 1, Pezold Nachlass.) Morris believes Pezold used the DHB commissions to pacify GMV authors who were displeased over the DHV's takeover of the firm ("German Nationalist Fiction," chap. 5).

42. DHB advertisements always stressed that the selection committee contained prominent cultural authorities. The committee had a strong neoconservative orientation; among those serving on it in the 1920s were Stapel, Eugen Class, Adolf Bartels, Hans Grimm, Ernst Jünger, Kolbenheyer, General von Lettow-Vorbeck, Wilhelm Schäfer, Hermann Ullmann, and August Winnig.

43. The periodical, *Der Hansische Bücherbote*, was inaugurated in 1923 and edited by Stapel. Each issue was devoted to works on one particular theme or by one author. The first issue (Jan./Feb. 1923) stated: "These pages are devoted to our most precious cultural goods: to German literature and scholarship, to the striving toward light and clarity as represented and preserved in the immortal works of German geniuses past and present. We must uphold the desire for good books even in this time of economic distress—for it is the desire for spiritual self-reliance and freedom. By means of reviews of good books of enduring value, our pages hope to help and advise book lovers." As the DHB grew, the *Bücherbote* proved "too narrow for the tasks of the Home Library," and in 1929 the DHB acquired another periodical for its subscribers, *Das Herdefeuer*.

44. Pezold, "Bericht über den Verlag," Pezold Nachlass.

45. *Handelswacht* 23 (1916): 179.

46. *Rechenschaftsbericht 1929*, p. 260.

47. The initial success of the DHB may be partly due to the fact that white-collar commercial employees were turning away from public libraries precisely at the time the DHB was created. As reported in *Blätter für Volksbibliotheken und Lesehalle* 17 (1916): 4, library use by all other occupational groups increased during World War I, while a sharp decrease in library use occurred among "Gehilfen des Handels und Gewerbes."

48. *SBZ*, p. 33; *AmL*, p. 17. Diederichs's decision to enter publishing came during a visit to a dimly lit Italian temple, an experience he later described in semimystical terms.

49. *AmL*, p. 22.

50. *LW*, p. 130; *AmL*, p. 39; *SBZ*, p. 204.

51. Reported in Unseld, *Autor und Verleger*, p. 75. The young author was Hermann Hesse.

52. *LW*, p. 275.

53. *LW*, pp. 197, 411; Diederichs to Blunck, 9 Nov. 1926, in Blunck Nachlass; Blunck, *Licht auf den Zügeln*, p. 482. Diederichs's frequent use of the term "marriage" in relation to his authors can be seen especially in his correspondence with Blunck. The publisher stressed that this relationship should be a "regular marriage," by which he meant a monogamous one; for he believed an author should be associated with only one publishing house and should remain loyal to it. Diederichs did, in fact, marry two of his authors, Helene Voigt and Lulu von Strauss und Torney.

54. *SBZ*, p. 66; also Menz, *Deutsche Buchhandel*, p. 280.

55. Lehmann to Chamberlain, 15 Mar. 1904, Chamberlain Nachlass.

56. *Handelswacht* 31 (1924): 441; *SBZ*, p. 41. See also *Deutsches Volkstum* 24 (1922): 369ff.

57. "Im Kampf um das deutsche Schrifttum," 1931 flyer in Box 561: DHV, Forschungsstelle für die Geschichte des Nationalsozialismus in Hamburg (hereafter cited as Forschungsstelle).

58. Diederichs, "Über Sommerakademien für den Buchhandel" (1925), p. 11; Pezold, "Nachkriegssortimentererfahrungen," p. 34 and "Schrifttum und Buchhandel," pp. 11, 17, Pezold Nachlass. See also *Handelswacht* 26 (1919): 229 and *Deutsches Volkstum* 28 (1926): 911. Lehmann expressed a similar outlook; he realized that publishing was his calling because "although I am unable to create any new values myself, as a publisher I can help bring ideas to the nation" (*LKD*, p. 99).

59. Beenken, "Nachwort," in Lehmann, *Ein deutscher Verlag*, p. 310.

60. Diederichs, "Aufmarsch der Interessenverbände" (1927), p. 243; *Handelswacht* 31 (1924): 441 and 26 (1919): 229; *LW*, p. 94. See also Max Habermann's comments on the HVA and LMV in "Der DHV im Kampf," p. 30, DHV Archive.

61. Pezold, "Nachkriegssortimentererfahrungen," p. 54.

62. *LW*, p. 218.

63. Ibid., p. 40; *SBZ*, pp. 38, 152, 155; Diederichs, "Verlegerische Aufgaben" (1912) pp. 193–94.

64. Diederichs, "Buchhändler und Idealismus" (1914), p. 109.

65. *LKD*, p. 143.

66. Stapel, "Sechs Sätze zur Entwicklung der Verlagsunternehmungen des DHV (18 Juni 1931)," in Box 2, Pezold Nachlass; Habermann, "Der DHV im Kampf," p. 31, DHV Archive.

67. Diederichs to Ziegler, 20 May 1904, Ziegler Nachlass; Diederichs to Tönnies, 29 Oct. 1907, Tönnies Nachlass.

68. Pezold, "Schrifttum und Buchhandel," pp. 14–15, Pezold Nachlass. He also sought to win over retail bookdealers, who in Germany exercised great influence over what customers purchased. Pezold believed that negative reviews of conservative books by influential leftist newspapers discouraged booksellers from stocking and promoting conservative literature, and hence hindered the dissemination of conservative ideas. To counter this leftist influence and to predispose dealers more favorably toward neoconservative books and authors, Pezold founded the *Kritische Gänge*, a weekly which sent recommendations of conservative and nationalist books to over 1,200 bookdealers and newspapers. Although financed solely by the LMV, the weekly review promoted the nationalist books of several publishing houses.

69. Lehmann to Chamberlain, 15 Mar. 1904, Chamberlain Nachlass.

70. Diederichs to Paul Natorp, 7 Sept. 1911, Natorp Nachlass; *LW*, p. 196.

71. *AmL*, p. 102; *LW*, pp. 196, 203; *SBZ*, p. 201; Diederichs, "Buchhändler und Idealismus" (1914), pp. 109–10.

72. Stapel, "Literarische Diktatur?" pp. 219.

73. Pezold, "Schrifttum und Buchhandel," pp. 14–15, Pezold Nachlass.

74. HVA to Blunck, 10 Jan. 1924, Blunck Nachlass.

75. Diederichs, "Vom Verlegerberuf" (1926), pp. 4–8.

76. See Dietze, *Diederichs und seine Zeitschriften*, pp. 36–38.

77. *LW*, p. 188.

78. *SBZ*, pp. 37–38, 47; Diederichs, "Buchhändler und Idealismus" (1914), p. 110; Diederichs, "Zur inneren Krise" (1924), p. 36; Diederichs, "Gründung eines 'Kulturamtes'" (1925), p. 9736. See also Diederichs's "Verlegerische Aufgaben" (1912), pp. 193–94 and "Erzieht der Buchhandel Charaktere?" (1894), pp. 175–76.

79. Stapel, "Die Grosse Aufregung"; *Handelswacht* 23 (1916): 180, 27 (1920): 146, 29 (1922): 151, and 38 (1931): 326. Also *Jahrbuch für Handlungsgehilfen*, p. 254.

80. *Handelswacht* 19 (1912): 169.

81. Habermann, "Der DHV im Kampf," p. 30, DHV Archive; Habermann, *Erziehung zum deutschen Menschen*, pp. 10ff.; *Handelswacht* 32 (1925): 4–6, 411 and 38 (1931): 375–76.

82. *Handelswacht* 9 (1904): 398. The Advisory Center drew up a recommended list of nationalist books, called the "German Library," which was intended to help DHV members "become useful, virtuous, and healthy men." The list contained several books from the other neoconservative firms like the JFLV and the EDV. See *Handelswacht* 16 (1909): 168, 19 (1912): 170, and 20 (1913): 170.

83. *Rechenschaftsbericht 1929*, p. 260; Pezold, "Die Deutsche Hausbücherei," Pezold Nachlass.

84. Box 561: DHV, Forschungsstelle. The DHV liked to boast that subscribers made relatively little use of their opportunity to choose books from the optional list because they preferred the guidance exercised by the DHB through its mandatory list (*Herdefeuer* 6 [1931]: 3).

85. Stapel to K. Bott, 15 Jan. 1931, Box 5, Pezold Nachlass; Pezold, "Schrifttum und Buchhandel," p. 13, Pezold Nachlass. Pezold confessed that during his years as a Tübingen bookdealer, he had deliberately suppressed the books of leftist *Literaten*.

86. *Deutschlands Erneuerung* 6 (1922): 14.

87. "20 Jahre für deutsches Schrifttum," *Herdefeuer* 10 (1935). Those who directed the HVA regarded the house as "a means of gaining intellectual power," as a "political and cultural weapon," and as a means of establishing the ideas of the DHV among the wider public. (Stapel, "Sechs Sätze," Pezold Nachlass; Zimmermann, *Der* DHV, p. 131.)

88. *SBZ*, pp. 38, 171. See also Diederichs, "Gegenwart und Zukunft" (1926), p. 30. Lehmann to Chamberlain, 15 Mar. 1904, Chamberlain Nachlass.

89. For example, in 1931 the GMV offered a 20,000 mark prize for any manuscript which would refute K. P. Morgan's leftist book *Nicht warten–wirken!* and the EDV offered a 10,000 mark prize in the late 1920s for the best novel submitted to the firm. The director of the Stalling house, impressed by one of Cäsar Fläischen's public lectures, wrote to the author later and asked him to submit a new manuscript to the GSV. (GSV to Fläischen, 29 Sept. 1916, Deutsches Literaturarchiv.) On another occasion, Diederichs solicited from Gustav Frenssen some sort of manuscript, "even if only a brochure," which would deal with current religious issues (Diederichs to Frenssen, 28 Nov. 1902, Frenssen Nachlass).

90. For three examples of Diederichs approaching authors to carry out ideas which he himself had conceived, see Diederichs to Dr. Preuss, 25 May 1903 and Diederichs to H. Potthoff, 3 Nov. 1910, Diederichs Archive; and *LW*, p. 21. Additional examples from the EDV and the other neoconservative houses will be cited in subsequent chapters.

91. Lehmann to A. Chamberlain, 25 June 1906, Lehmann Archive.

92. *Fünfzig Jahre JFLV*, p. 7; also *LKD*, p. 143.

93. Menz, *Deutsche Buchhandel*, p. 281.

94. *SBZ*, p. 66.

95. Ibid., pp. 38, 50; Hesse, "Der Verlag Diederichs," p. 319.

96. *Fünfzig Jahre JFLV*, p. 9; also F. Lehmann, "Mein Oheim," p. 270 and Lehmann to Chamberlain, 15 Mar. 1904, Chamberlain Nachlass.

97. Lehmann to A. zu Hohenlohe, 4 Feb. 1905, Lehmann Archive.

98. "Bericht über den Verlag" and "Bericht der Deutschen Allgemeinen Treuhänder AG über die bei der Firma Albert Langen—Georg Müller Verlag GmbH, München, vorgenommene neuerliche Statuserstellung per 30. April 1934," p. 9, in Box 3, Pezold Nachlass. See also Scholten, "Deutsche Verleger," p. 3 and Stapel, "Sechs Sätze," Pezold Nachlass.

99. Subsequent chapters will reveal several instances of neoconservative publishing undertakings on which the publishers willingly took financial losses. The most persuasive evidence for the publishers' sacrifices, however, is the fact that the journals which each house pub-

lished were great financial burdens, but burdens each publisher was willing to bear so that the message of their journals could continue to be heard. For the depressing story of the Langen-Müller house's finances (nearly 500,000 marks annual losses in the early 1930s), see "Bericht der Deutschen Allgemeinen Treuhänder AG über die bei der Firma Albert Langen—Georg Müller Verlag GmbH, München, vorgenommene neuerliche Statuserstellung per 30. Juni 1934," in Box 3, Pezold Nachlass. The LMV subsidized the unprofitable Eduard Avenarius Verlag at the rate of 10,000 marks per year, and by 1933 was pouring 25,000 marks into the Avenarius literary review *Die neue Literatur*. Of this journal Pezold said: "The journal was founded for cultural, not financial reasons. The small subsidies which have been necessary to maintain it in the past can and must be carried [by the LMV]. For Will Vesper's critical literary review *Die neue Literatur* is the only one of its kind in Germany. Besides, this journal accomplishes valuable propaganda work for us, in that it fights against every kind of inferior literature and for precisely that kind of literature that our house publishes. . . . I am of the opinion that the journal *must* be continued even if, in the worst case, it must be financed completely by [the LMV] house." ("Bericht Deutschen Treuhänder 30. Juni 1934," Pezold Nachlass.)

100. In a survey he conducted in 1914–15, Diederichs found that more of his customers (approximately 30 percent) were prompted to purchase books because of references to or reviews of them appearing in periodicals than for any other reason. (See *Die Tat* 7 [1915/16]: 798–800, hereafter cited as *Tat*.) This survey, probably the first empirical market survey conducted in Germany, revealed that after reviews, customers learned of books through the following means, in order of importance: publishers' catalogs (20 percent of purchases); personal recommendations from friends (17 percent); recommendations or window displays by book dealers (17 percent); customers' acquaintance with other works by the same author (10 percent); public lectures (2 percent); advertisements in other books (1 percent); from one's own studies in the field (1 percent); purchases after having read the book (1 percent); customers' personal acquaintance with the author (0.7 percent); and aesthetic beauty of the book's graphics (0.3 percent).

101. In the 1920s and 1930s, 49.1 percent of all German journals were associated with publishing houses, 36.5 percent with an independent society or organization, 11.7 percent with some official institution or agency, and only 2.7 percent were run by private individuals (Menz, *Kulturwirtscraft*, pp. 96–98, 101–3).

102. Pross, *Literatur und Politik*, pp. 10–11.

103. Lehmann, who knew Kiefer, reported in 1916 that the DHV gave Kiefer a total of only 100 marks for honoraria per issue. (Lehmann to Chamberlain, 11 Aug. 1916, Chamberlain Nachlass.) Other journals, such as Diederichs's *Die Tat*, paid nearly that amount to an individual author for a major essay.

104. The publisher received the support of the *Ostpreussenhilfe* by promising to donate to that organization 50 percent of the net proceeds from the journal's first issue (of which 200,000 copies were printed); in return, the group promised to propagandize for the new journal with all the means at its disposal. (Lehmann to Chamberlain, 20 July 1916, Chamberlain Nachlass.) Lehmann had been planning to found a journal entitled *Unser Vaterland* and had lined up an editor for it, but dropped the plans when approached with the idea for *Deutschlands Erneuerung*.

105. *Tat* 6 (1914/15): 113; *Die Neuerscheinungen im 1912*, p. 6.

106. EDV Rundschreiben, 28 Sept. 1930, Blunck Nachlass.

107. Diederichs to Arno Steglich, 3 Aug. and 2 Sept. 1916, in EDV Mappe, Archiv der deutschen Jugendbewegung.

108. Fifty marks per printer's sheet, representing sixteen printed pages. By 1925, *Die Tat* was paying 80 marks per printer's sheet for major essays, and 100 marks per printer's sheet for the journal's special issues (*SBZ*, p. 215).

109. Before becoming editor of *Die Tat*, Zehrer (1899–1966) was foreign affairs editor for the influential liberal Ullstein newspaper *Vossische Zeitung*. Although Zehrer began serving unofficially as *Tat* editor in the fall of 1929, his ties to the Ullstein house prevented him from making his new position public until the fall of 1931. The *Tat* Circle collected by Zehrer included Horst Grüneberg, E. W. Eschmann, Friedrich Zimmermann (who is better known by his pseudonym, "Ferdinand Fried"), and Giselher Wirsing. Zehrer also established close contact with the DHV after 1932. After Eugen Diederichs's death in September 1930, the new EDV owners Peter and Niels Diederichs gave Zehrer a free hand with *Die Tat*. The personalities, ideology, activities, and impact of the *Tat* Circle have been the subject of numerous studies. See Barker, "Sociological Function of Intellectuals"; Vermeil, *Doctrinaires révolution allemande*, pp. 188–220; Brunzel, "Die Tat"; Neurohr, *Mythos vom Dritten Reich*, pp. 130–37; von Klemperer, *Germany's New Conservatism*, pp. 129–33; Sontheimer, "Der Tatkreis"; Struve, "Hans Zehrer"; Koszyk & Pruys, *Wörterbuch zur Publizistik*, pp. 353–54; Lebovics, *Social Conservatism*, chap. 6; Demant, *Von Schleicher zu Springer*; Schmidt, "Die Tat"; Hecker, *'Die Tat' und Osteuropabild*; and Fritzsche, *Politische Romantik*.

110. Lehmann to Chamberlain, 11 Aug. 1916, Chamberlain Nachlass. The initial board of editors consisted of H. S. Chamberlain, Heinrich Class, Friedrich Kapp, Max von Gruber, Georg von Below, Dietrich Schäfer, Georg Schiele, Bavarian Minister-President von Schwerin, Karl Seeburg, and K. Geyer. Erich Jung was added in 1919, and Max Wundt, H. F. K. Günther, Alfred Krauss, and Paul Bang (all four of whom were JFLV authors) in 1927. Kühn, who was an early member of the German Workers Party (Deutsche Arbeiterpartei, DAP) and of its successor the Nazi Party (NSDAP), was replaced as managing editor in 1925 by Freiherr Walther von Müffling.

111. *Fünfzig Jahre JFLV*, p. 43.

112. Lehmann to Kühn, 1 July 1921, as quoted in Sippell, *Lehmann als Zeitschriftenverleger*, p. 52.

113. For examples of Lehmann's meddling, see ibid., p. 53, and *Fünfzig Jahre JFLV*, p. 78. Lehmann paid as much as 300 marks per printer's sheet for essays in the journal's first issue, and paid authors 20 percent of the retail price for any journal reprints which were sold individually (Lehmann to Chamberlain, 20 July 1916, Chamberlain Nachlass).

114. For a comprehensive treatment of Stapel and his neoconservative ideology, see Kessler, *Stapel*.

115. The *Dürerbund: Bund von Vereinen und Einzelnen zur Pflege ästhetischen Lebens* was founded by F. Avenarius in 1902 as a parallel organization to his journal *Kunstwart*. After joining the staff of *Kunstwart*, Stapel also became active in the *Dürerbund* and served for many years as one of its highest officers. Eugen Diederichs was a member, as was the DHV. On the program and activities of the *Dürerbund*, see Kratzsch, *Kunstwart und Dürerbund*. The *Fichtegesellschaft* was founded in 1916 to counteract the onset of war weariness; the founders included *Bühne und Welt* editor Kiefer, several *völkisch* writers from the journal, members of the Wagnerian *Bayreuthkreis*, and leading officers of the DHV. A regular newsletter of the society, *Mitteilungen der Fichtegesellschaft*, appeared in the pages of *Bühne und Welt* and later in *Deutsches Volkstum*. The society propagated a strong Christian nationalism in the tradition of Luther and Fichte. Early financial support came exclusively from the DHV, although after 1920 private contributions from wealthy landowners became a second important source of income. By 1930 the society had 3,200 members and stood quite close to the DNVP. Stapel continued to be one of the most important officers of the society, and the *Deutsches Volkstum* was seen by many as the organ of the *Fichtegesellschaft*. See Edmundson, "The Fichte Society"; Sieh, *Hamburger Nationalistenklub*, pp. 26ff.; Hamel, *Völkischer Verband*, pp. 128ff.; and Kessler, *Stapel*, pp. 36ff. In 1917 the *Fichtegesellschaft* founded the *Fichtehochschule* and the *Hamburger Volksheim* to counter the Social Democratic *Volkshochschule* movement; again, Stapel was a leading figure in both these organizations.

116. It was this desire for independence which prompted the creation of the short-lived Verlag des Deutschen Volkstums in 1918. In 1931, Stapel reflected that "from 1919 on it was my main worry not to let the *Deutsches Volkstum* appear as an organ of an association or of a society, but to found it on the great conscience and responsibility of the editor, exactly as the other great journals are spiritually independent." (Stapel to Habermann, 5 July 1931, as quoted in Morris, "German Nationalist Fiction," chap. 5.)

117. *Deutsches Volkstum* 28 (1926): 909. Through his post as editor of *Der Hansische Bücherbote* Stapel was also active in the DHB. He received a salary of 1,000 marks per month as editor of *Deutsches Volkstum*, but nothing for his work with the HVA. Stapel's ultimate ambition was to become actual director of the HVA and its extensive publishing empire. Although he managed to have two HVA directors removed in the 1920s, he was never able to capture the post for himself and had to remain content with the title of HVA *geistige Leiter*. From that position, however, he was able to exert a great deal of influence over the types of material the HVA empire published. The extension of the HVA empire was closely linked to Stapel's internal political ambitions. For by serving as middleman in the acquisition of the GMV and ALV, Stapel hoped his chances of gaining the top HVA post would be enhanced. By 1931, however, after Pezold had been appointed to head the LMV and Ziegler named to direct the HVA, Stapel's relations with the HVA became increasingly strained. He complained that no one in the HVA was interested any longer in the *Deutsches Volkstum* and that he was no longer consulted by the HVA on the publication of important political works. Stapel complained that the *Deutsches Volkstum*'s special relation to the HVA put the journal at a disadvantage, for the publishing house's early press deadlines meant *Deutsches Volkstum* issues had to be submitted early; by the time the issue appeared, many articles were already outdated. This made the *Deutsches Volkstum* less competitive than other journals. Yet the journal was not free to seek another publisher. Some of these problems were resolved in April 1932 when *Deutsches Volkstum* went from a monthly to a biweekly format. (See "Tagebuch," entry for 24 June 1943, and Stapel's letters to the HVA, 14 Feb. 1949 and to Schleicher, 6 Apr. 1949 in the "HAVA Auseinandersetzung" file, Stapel Nachlass. Also Morris, "German Nationalist Fiction," chap. 5.)

118. See HVA to Blunck, 17 Mar. and 25 Mar. 1933, Blunck Nachlass; and HVA to Paul Ernst, 27 Mar. 1933, Deutsches Literaturarchiv.

119. *Deutsches Volkstum* 24 (1922): 369.

120. *Tat* 14 (1922/23): 474.

121. By founding or conducting the journal, Diederichs hoped "to create a circle of readers [*Lesergemeinde*]." See his comments in the first issue of *Das deutsche Gesicht* 1 (1927): 2.

122. *Tat* 23 (1931/32): 1032ff., and Demant, *Von Schleicher zu Springer*, pp. 73ff. The total membership of the local *Tat* circles has been estimated at 800 to 900. The weekly communiqué, *Nachrichtendienst Tat-Kreis*, was sent not only to each local circle, but also to prominent public figures.

123. HVA to Paul Ernst, 27 Mar. 1933, Deutsches Literaturarchiv.

124. Sippell, *Lehmann als Zeitschriftenverleger*, pp. 48–49.

125. Pechel as quoted in Mauersberger, *Pechel und die "Rundschau,"* pp. 161–62.

126. For a complete account of the *Arbeitsgemeinschaft*, see ibid., pp. 160–204.

127. Ibid., p. 170 n. 35.

128. Müffling to Pechel, 9 July 1925, Pechel to Müffling, 13 July 1925, and Lehmann to Pechel, 8 Oct. 1925, Pechel Nachlass.

129. Over 85 percent of all literary and cultural journals, and some 67 percent of all German political journals had circulations of between 500 and 5,000 copies, and most of these were actually within the 500 to 2,000 range (Menz, *Die Zeitschrift*, pp. 49–50, 53).

130. Dietze, *Diederichs und seine Zeitschriften*, pp. 150, 159. He never indicated on what he based this estimate.

131. Ibid., pp. 139, 142, 151; *LW*, pp. 321, 441.

132. Lehmann to Chamberlain, 22 Mar. 1917, Chamberlain Nachlass.

133. Lehmann to K. L. Schemann, 17 July 1929, Schemann Nachlass.

134. *Deutschlands Erneuerung* 7 (1920): 454 and 15 (1931): 754.

135. Pechel's *Deutsche Rundschau*, one of the foremost and influential of such journals, had a circulation of 3,500 to 4,000 during the period 1920–32. A neoconservative journal such as *Das Gewissen*, which had a circulation of about 30,000 in the 1920s, was extremely rare.

136. *Deutsches Volkstum* 26 (1924): 85.

137. Hüttig, *Politische Zeitschriften*, p. 14.

138. The small *Neue Merkur* was unable to survive independently in the 1920s, but was continually at loggerheads with the different publishers who controlled it. The journal's first publisher forced its editors to abandon their controversial stances and to function more as an ongoing advertisement for the publishing house. (Stern, *War, Weimar, and Literature*, pp. 97ff.) The important *Deutsche Rundschau*, after policy disagreements with its first publisher, attempted to survive as its own publishing house but because of serious financial problems in the later 1920s was forced to turn to wealthy industrial patrons for support. These, in turn, pressured the journal into dropping much of its support for cultural radicalism. Mauersberger, *Pechel und die "Rundschau,"* pp. 204–21.

139. For a complete list of the major contributors to each journal and a more detailed analysis of these authors, see Stark, "Entrepreneurs of Ideology," pp. 174–76, 605–10.

140. Eugen Diederichs, for example, read the *Deutsches Volkstum* regularly (and envied its wider circulation). (*LW*, pp. 425, 437.) The *Deutsches Volkstum* often contained advertisements for books published by the EDV and JFLV; one issue (Sept. 1920) contained a JFLV prospectus and added: "The books announced in this [JFLV] prospectus . . . pursue in essence the same goals and the same idealistic philosophy as does this journal and the *Fichtegesellschaft*."

141. I owe these observations on the function of a journal to Pascal, *From Naturalism to Expressionism*, pp. 280–81.

142. Lehmann, *Ein deutscher Verlag*, pp. 17, 38–48.

143. Hamel, *Völkischer Verband*, p. 160.

144. *Deutschlands Erneuerung* 3 (1920): 454–55 and 6 (1922): 97; *LKD*, pp. 180–81.

145. *Deutsches Volkstum* 29 (1927): 609–15.

146. *SBZ*, p. 181.

147. Diederichs, "Aufmarsch der Interessenverbände" (1927), pp. 242–43 and "Organische Gesetze" (1927), pp. 269–72; *Tat* 18 (1926/27): 951–52.

148. This was a reference to the Ullstein Verlag, a publishing house and newspaper chain which concentrated on the production of inexpensive paperbacks and which provided severe competition to houses like the EDV. On the book publishing activities of the Ullstein Verlag and the related Propyläen-Verlag, see Ecksteins, *Limits of Reason*, pp. 104–22, esp. 112.

149. *SBZ*, pp. 37–38, 49, 53–54; *Tat* 6 (1914/15): 74ff.; *Das deutsche Gesicht* 1 (1927): 2; *Der Diederichs Löwe* 2 (1928): 60; Diederichs, "Eine sachliche Beschwerde" (1930), pp. 6–7.

150. On the liberal Jewish press companies in Weimar Germany, see Ecksteins, *Limits of Reason*, pp. 104–37.

151. "Schrifttum und Buchhandel," and "Bericht über den Verlag Langen-Müller," Pezold Nachlass.

152. Richter, "Die literarische Diktatur des Deutsch-nationalen Handlungsgehilfen-Verbandes," *Berliner Tageblatt*, 19 June 1931.

153. *Regensberger Echo*, 19 June 1931. Among the newspapers which either reprinted the *Berliner Tageblatt* article verbatim or published similar anti-DHV pieces were: *Münchener

Post, 16 June and 23 June; *Frankfurter Zeitung*, 17 June; *Neue Leipziger Zeitung*, 17 June; *Neue Badische Zeitung*, 17 June; *La-République* (Strasbourg), 18 June; and *Der Staat seid Ihr*, 29 June.

154. Public statement of the Georg Müller Verlag, 16 June 1931, in Box 5, Pezold Nachlass. According to Pezold, Krause had made several improper advances on his secretary and had a long history of alcoholism which prevented him from fulfilling his duties. Pezold never made public the exact reasons for Krause's dismissal—out of consideration to the Krause family, he claimed. But the GMV director did present the information in court at the subsequent libel hearings. Whether Krause was in fact dismissed for political reasons or for moral causes is a question which the documents do not clarify and which, therefore, must remain open.

155. *Münchener-Augsburger-Abendzeitung*, 20/21 June 1931. One of the directors of this newspaper was none other than J. F. Lehmann. The JFLV and an organization known as "VERA" (Finanzgesellschaft für gefährdete Provinzialblätter, Verlagsanstalt GmbH) secretly acquired this paper in April 1920 for a price of 3.2 million marks. "VERA" had been founded in 1917 by the right-wing press magnate Alfred Hugenberg to advise and to financially aid hard-pressed provincial newspapers; during the 1920s it was generously financed by the huge Hugenberg concern. (See Ecksteins, *Limits of Reason*, pp. 75, 78–81; Leopold, *Hugenberg*, pp. 10–14, 96; Koszyk, *Deutsche Presse*, p. 185.) Lehmann participated in the acquisition of the *Abendzeitung* partly as a front man. But he did so because he believed a public forum was needed in south Germany to represent "nationalist and economic interests," and because he wanted to help create "a unified front against Social Democracy." Lehmann sat on the board of directors until 1931, by which time the paper had become a mouthpiece for Hugenberg and the DNVP. (Sippell, *Lehmann als Zeitschriftenverleger*, pp. 28ff.; *LKD*, p. 178.) Other papers publishing pro-GMV articles were: *Deutsche Zeitung*, 20 June; *Tägliche Rundschau*, 21 June; *Völkischer Beobachter*, 23 June; *Deutscher Handelswacht*, 25 June; and *Hamburger Korrespondenz*, 27 June.

156. Borchardt, *Deutsche Literatur im Kampf*.

157. Pezold, "Bericht über den Verlag Langen-Müller," Pezold Nachlass.

158. Lehmann made such a motion at the *Deutscher Verlegerverein* meeting in Leipzig. (Lehmann to A. Lehr, 27 Sept. 1898, Lehmann Archive.)

159. Diederichs, "Es muss anders werden" (1922), pp. 576–78 and "Lauensteiner Winterlager" (1923), pp. 118–20. Also *AmL*, p. 84.

160. Diederichs, "Sommerakademien für den Jungbuchhandel" (1923), pp. 323–33, "Jungbuchhandel und Sommerakademie" (1925), pp. 1–6, and "Schlusswort" (1925), p. 85.

161. *Der Zopfabschneider*, which appeared from Nov. 1923 to May 1924, had a circulation of about 600, while *Der Ochs von Lauenstein*, published from Apr. 1925 to May 1927, reached approximately 1,000 readers.

162. See for example the testimony of Hans Köster in his "Jugendbewegung— Lauensteiner Kreis," p. 758.

CHAPTER 3

1. Nietzsche, *The Will to Power*, p. 3.

2. *AmL*, p. 3.

3. *Die Kulturbewegung Deutschlands 1913*, p. 1; *Tat* 5 (1913/14): 39.

4. *LW*, pp. 142, 220; *SBZ*, pp. 37–38; Diederichs to Tönnies, 29 Oct. 1907, Tönnies Nachlass.

5. *Der Verlag Diederichs in Jena*, p. 88.

6. Diederichs to O. Jimmisch, 23 Sept. 1910, Diederichs Archive; and Diederichs as quoted in *Eugen Diederichs: Verleger, Buchgestalter, Publizist*, p. 12.

7. Interview with Niels Diederichs, 6 Nov. 1972, Cologne; see also Diederichs to M. Lechter, 31 Aug. 1906, Diederichs Archive.

8. Diederichs to O. Jimmisch, 23 Sept. 1910, Diederichs Archive; U. Diederichs, "Marketing um die Jahrhundertwende," p. 100.

9. See Anstett, "Lagarde"; Stern, *Politics of Cultural Despair*, pp. 25–128; and Lougee, *Lagarde*.

10. *LW*, pp. 232, 383; Diederichs to Frau Anna Lagarde, 21 Sept. 1915, Diederichs Archive.

11. *LW*, pp. 233–34.

12. Ibid., p. 232; *AmL*, p. 50.

13. Dietrich, "Verleger Eugen Diederichs," p. 559.

14. Diederichs to Ziegler, 26 Oct. 1903, Ziegler Nachlass; EDV prospectus for *Erzieher zu Deutscher Bildung* series, undated, Diederichs Archive; *Der Verlag Diederichs in Jena* (partly reprinted in *SBZ*, pp. 41, 190).

15. Inner cover of *Der Verlag Diederichs in Jena*.

16. *LW*, p. 80.

17. Nietzsche, *Unzeitgemässe Betrachtungen*, sect. 1, 2.

18. The phrase is Ralf Dahrendorf's (*Society and Democracy*, pp. 129–41, 200–203).

19. Gay, *Weimar Culture*, pp. 70ff.

20. Personalities and groups as diverse as Hegel, the romantics, Wagner, Ranke, Marx, heavy industrialists, Pan-Germans, and leading academics of the 1920s have all been susceptible to it.

21. Ringer, *Decline of the German Mandarins*, p. 403.

22. *Der Verlag Diederichs in Jena*, pp. 41, 28. See also *Tat* 6 (1914/15): 77.

23. *LW*, p. 134.

24. *Neuerscheinungen Politik*, p. ii; *Die Neuerscheinungen im 1912*, p. 9.

25. Diederichs to Tönnies, 29 Oct. 1907, Tönnies Nachlass.

26. *LW*, pp. 40, 164; *AmL*, p. 26; *Die Kulturbewegung Deutschlands 1913*, p. 1.

27. *SBZ*, pp. 41, 204; Diederichs to H. Scholz, 8 Dec. 1911, Diederichs Archive. See also Diederichs, "Buchhändler Beruf und Kulturentwicklung" (1914), p. 6.

28. *LW*, p. 140.

29. *Jena und Weimar*, p. 176.

30. Diederichs to Ziegler, 9 Nov. 1904, Ziegler Nachlass.

31. Haeckel, *Monism*, pp. 3–4.

32. See Holt, "Haeckel's Monistic Religion," pp. 267–68, 279–80, and "German Monist Movement." Gasman's *Scientific Origins of National Socialism* is a less reliable account which sees monism as a radical, antiliberal, antirational, and racist philosophy which was a direct forerunner of the conservative revolutionary, *völkisch*, and Nazi movements.

33. *LW*, p. 95.

34. Bruno Wille, another monist, once wrote to Bölsche that Darwinism "also fits into our idealistic view of nature. Both of us, friend Bölsche, are idealists in that we attribute to the totality of nature a psychic, spiritual character." (As quoted in Bolle, "Darwinismus und Zeitgeist," p. 265.) Bolle describes how "Wille and Bölsche propagated their unique mixture of Darwinism and pan-psychic nature-idealism not only through their numerous essays and books, but also through the many free-spirited, free-religious, monist organizations which sprang up at the turn of the century like mushrooms." (Ibid., p. 266.)

35. Weber, *The Protestant Ethic*, pp. 15–27, 76–78, 182–83; *From Max Weber*, pp. 138–39, 155.

36. *SBZ*, p. 35; *Neuerscheinungen Politik*, p. ii; Diederichs, "Jugendentwicklung oder Jugendkultur?" (1913), p. 94.

37. *LW*, pp. 74, 95–96, 107, 180.

38. Ibid., pp. 68, 163; *SBZ*, p. 220; *AmL*, p. 26.

39. *LW*, p. 140.

40. EDV advertisement in Oct. 1926 issue of *Deutsches Volkstum*.

41. EDV advertisement in July 1927 issue of *Deutsches Volkstum*.

42. *LW*, p. 154.

43. *AmL*, p. 55.

44. *LW*, p. 162.

45. *Stirb und Werde*, p. 73; *Die Kulturbewegung Deutschlands 1913*, p. 3.

46. See Lersch, *Lebensphilosophie*, p. 9, and Bollnow, *Lebensphilosophie*, pp. 7, 21.

47. *SBZ*, p. 305; Bergson to Diederichs, 19 Oct. 1929, Diederichs Archive.

48. *AmL*, p. 55.

49. See Rosteutscher, *Wiederkunft des Dionysos*, p. 258.

50. *LW*, pp. 92, 186.

51. Ibid., pp. 61, 181; *SBZ*, pp. 189–91.

52. *LW*, p. 62; also *Tat* 19 (1927/28): 651–53.

53. *SBZ*, p. 190; *LW*, pp. 62, 257; Diederichs to Frenssen, 28 Nov. 1902, Frenssen Nachlass.

54. *LW*, p. 255; Diederichs to Pastor Lipsius, 4 Oct. 1910, Diederichs Archive.

55. *LW*, p. 61; *SBZ*, p. 200.

56. Craig, *Germany*, pp. 182–83.

57. For a brief survey of religion and the churches in the Second Reich, see ibid., pp. 181–86; Pascal, *From Naturalism to Expressionism*, pp. 161–97; and Latourette, *Christianity in Revolutionary Age*, 2:9–130.

58. *SBZ*, pp. 33–34, 118–19; *LW*, pp. 83, 179, 334. See also *Tat* 10 (1918/19): 642.

59. *LW*, p. 143; *SBZ*, p. 190.

60. See Diederichs's letter of 28 Nov. 1902 to Frenssen in Frenssen Nachlass, and his letter to Carl Jatho in *LW*, pp. 200–201 for examples of how the publisher sought out new religious manuscripts. Also ibid., pp. 59–60.

61. Ibid., p. 84.

62. Ibid., pp. 153–54.

63. Ibid., pp. 16, 164; *SBZ*, pp. 200–201; Diederichs to Frenssen, 28 Nov. 1902, Frenssen Nachlass; and *Stirb und Werde*, p. 4.

64. *LW*, p. 73.

65. Diederichs to Frenssen, 28 Nov. 1902, Frenssen Nachlass; *LW*, pp. 59–60, 83.

66. *SBZ*, pp. 132, 330. Another of Tolstoy's works published by the EDV, "Du sollst nicht töten," was confiscated by the German authorities on grounds of *lèse majesté*.

67. *SBZ*, pp. 145–46.

68. *LW*, p. 267.

69. Ibid., pp. 136, 159, 219, 263, 297; Kindt, *Wandervogelzeit*, pp. 469–71. Diederichs invited leading monists such as Bruno Wille to these festivals.

70. Diederichs to H. von Scholz, 9 Dec. 1911, Diederichs Archive.

71. *LW*, pp. 40, 83, 300, 381; *SBZ*, pp. 118, 328.

72. *LW*, p. 84.

73. *SBZ*, p. 144.

74. Diederichs confessed that his publication of Eckehardt's works in 1903 was of "decisive importance" for his own personal development (*LW*, p. 15). It was Buber who approached Diederichs in 1907 with the idea for an anthology of Jewish mystical texts, which he

promised would contain the statements of "visionary, truly blessed men about their innermost lives. . . . It seems to me that such a work belongs in *your* publishing house" (*SBZ*, pp. 166–67).

75. Diederichs first requested Leopold Ziegler, then the Swiss philosopher Walter Haeser to edit the Böhme volume. When Haeser completed his lengthy introduction to the Böhme anthology, however, Diederichs finally rejected it because Haeser had not sufficiently pointed out the uniqueness of Böhme's personality and his importance as a model for modern Germans. (Diederichs to Ziegler, 2/3 Dec. 1902, Ziegler Nachlass; *SBZ*, pp. 142–44.)

76. Wagner, "Art and Religion," as quoted in Anchor, *Germany Confronts Modernization*, p. 121.

77. *LW*, p. 52.

78. For a more detailed treatment of Langbehn's ideas, see Stern, *Politics of Cultural Despair*, pp. 131–227.

79. *LW*, p. 205.

80. Diederichs, "Verlegerische Aufgaben" (1912), pp. 193–94; Eugen Diederichs, *Politik des Geistes* (Jena, 1920), p. 32 (hereafter cited as *PdG*); Diederichs, *Die geistigen Aufgaben der Zukunft* (1920), pp. 7–8.

81. *LW*, p. 205.

82. Surprisingly little has been written about Avenarius or *Der Kunstwart*. The best treatment is Kratzsch, *Kunstwart und Dürerbund*; Broermann's *Kunstwart in seiner Eigenart* is also helpful.

83. *LW*, pp. 380–83; also *Tat* 8 (1916/17): 837.

84. *PdG*, p. 131.

85. *Tat* 6 (1914/15): 332. On Diederichs's theories about book graphics and his firm's extensive and pioneering activities in this area, see: Grauthoff, *Entwicklung der modernen Buchkunst*, pp. 127–41; Schauer, *Deutsche Buchkunst*, 1:57–58, 76–80; Oschilewski, "Diederichs und die deutsche Buchkunst," and "Diederichs: Beitrag zur Geschichte der Buchkunst."

86. Emil Rudolf Weiss, a close friend of Diederichs and one of the EDV's first authors, was the firm's chief artist for several years. Melchoir Lechter, a member of the Stefan George Circle, sought to express aspects of medieval mysticism in his style. His first important work was the illustrations for Maeterlinck's *Der Schatz der Armen*, which Diederichs published in 1898. Fidus (pseudonym for Karl Höppner) liked to portray Aryan youth in touch with transcendent cosmic forces; his art was a varying mixture of theosophy, mystical symbolism, and the occult, and it stressed the value of the *Volk*, the emotions, and intuition. In later years, his works appeared in nearly all German *völkisch* publications. Other *Jugendstil* artists who created for the EDV included J. Cissarz, Heinrich Vogeler, and B. Pankok. For the many ways in which Diederichs's patronage benefitted the careers of these artists, see Ehmcke's comments in his "Erinnerungen an Diederichs."

87. *SBZ*, p. 191.

88. The best account of the *Werkbund* is Campbell, *German Werkbund*.

89. Muthesius, *Der Werkbund*, pp. 36–48.

90. *Tat* 5 (1913/14): 41–44.

91. *LW*, p. 217; Campbell, *German Werkbund*, pp. 12, 35–37.

92. Diederichs, "Kampf um die Fraktur" (1911), pp. 12260–62. See also his "Sollen wir die Fraktur abschaffen?" (1912), pp. 66–70.

93. Diederichs, "Kampf um die Fraktur" (1911), p. 12261.

94. See Anderson, "German Romanticism"; Brunschwig, *La crise de l'état prussien*; Kohn, "Romanticism and German Nationalism," and *Mind of Germany*, pp. 49–68; Schenk, *Mind of the European Romantics*; and Halsted, *Romanticism*, pp. 1–42.

95. Anchor, *Germany Confronts Modernization*, p. 40–41.

96. Ibid., p. 40.

97. *LW*, pp. 40, 80, 89.

98. *Nicht Lesebücher*, p. 42.

99. *Zu Neuer Renaissance*.

100. *SBZ*, pp. 148–49.

101. Diederichs to E. Ackerknecht, 17 Feb. 1905, Deutsches Literaturarchiv; *LW*, p. 14.

102. Ibid., pp. 62, 84.

103. Diederichs boasted that his house introduced Hölderlin and Novalis to the modern German public (*AmL*, pp. 30–33). In the opinion of one scholar, "the real breakthrough in the recognition and veneration of Hölderlin occurred first in our century. It was connected with the name of Norbert von Hellingrath, a young Munich student [and member of the Stefan George Circle] who—following a suggestion of Friedrich von der Leyen—first published in 1910 Hölderlin's Pindar translations." (Ryan, *Friedrich Hölderlin*, p. 2; see also von Pigenot, "Gleitwort," in von Hellingrath, *Hölderlin-Vermächtnis*, p. 10.) Von Hellingrath's *Pindarübertragungen von Hölderlin* was published by the EDV in 1911; von der Leyen was at the time closely associated with the firm as well. When von Hellingrath's work appeared, the EDV had already completed its four-volume edition of Hölderlin's works.

104. *Der Verlag Diederichs in Jena*, p. 36.

105. Diederichs to Ziegler, 19 Oct. 1903, Ziegler Nachlass.

106. See for example Mosse, *Crisis of German Ideology*, pp. 52ff.

107. Soergel, *Dichtung und Dichter*, p. 365; Martini, *Deutsche Literaturgeschichte*, pp. 473–76; Friederich, *History of German Literature*, pp. 228ff.; Coellen, *Neuromantik*; Bieber, "Neuromantik"; and Prang, "Neuromantik."

108. Steinhausen, *Deutsche Geistes- und Kulturgeschichte*, pp. 213–14.

109. Bieber, "Neuromantik," p. 496.

110. *SBZ*, pp. 106–9. How Diederichs came to be associated with Hesse and why Hesse sent literary manifestos to the EDV is an intriguing story. In the late 1890s the young Hesse had been corresponding regularly with the poetess Helene Voigt, and the two became close friends. After Voigt married Diederichs in 1898, she convinced the publisher to issue Hesse's first genuine book, *Eine Stunde hinter Mitternacht* (1899). Diederichs had grave doubts about the commercial success of this book, but reluctantly published it as a personal favor to his new wife. To help sales and to overcome the work's forbidding esoteric content, Diederichs applied the most imaginative graphics and decorative work to the volume. Diederichs wrote to Hesse in 1899: "So if, quite frankly, I have little faith in the commercial success of the book, I am all the more convinced of its literary merit. . . . Even I don't believe that I'll sell 600 copies; but I hope to make it striking by means of the layout alone, and thereby neutralize the unknown name of the author." (Cited in Unseld, *Autor und Verleger*, p. 72, and *SBZ*, p. 327.) The EDV sold only fifty-three copies of Hesse's book the first year. But partly because of its avant-garde graphics, the book attracted attention to the young author. During the next two or three years, perhaps out of guilt over the losses he had caused Diederichs or perhaps because he wished to remain on good terms with the publisher so he could publish with the EDV again in the future, Hesse kept up contact with Diederichs, sending him numerous unsolicited manuscripts, prospecti, suggestions, etc., most of which Diederichs politely brushed off. Hesse also began to write favorable reviews of EDV books, "in order to lessen the loss which my first book has caused him." (See Unseld, *Autor und Verleger*, p. 73 and Freedman, *Hesse*, pp. 80, 95.)

111. *AmL*, pp. 25, 27–29; *LW*, p. 52; *SBZ*, p. 190.

112. Coellen, *Neuromantik*, pp. 1–39.

113. *LW*, p. 113.

114. Diederichs to Hesse, 28 Jan. 1902, Hesse Nachlass. Hesse apparently expressed interest in the post, for Diederichs sent another letter on 8 Feb. 1902 providing additional information.

115. *SBZ*, pp. 35, 51; *LW*, p. 195; *Tat* 6 (1914/15): 75, 77. See also *Der Verlag Diederichs in Jena*, pp. 28, 41.

116. *SBZ*, p. 40.

117. *LW*, p. 195; *Tat* 6 (1914/15): 77.

118. *LW*, p. 98.

119. *SBZ*, pp. 140, 35.

120. *LW*, pp. 17, 90, 129; *SBZ*, p. 11.

121. *AmL*, p. 77; Diederichs to F. Kuh, 2 Dec. 1912, Diederichs Archive.

122. *SBZ*, pp. 99–100, 327; Steinhausen in *Im Zeichen des Löwen*, p. 99.

123. Münchhausen's statement in "40 deutsche Gelehrte, Politiker, Schriftsteller und Künstlers urteilen über die Buchorganisation 'Deutsche Volkheit,'" Diederichs Archive.

124. *LW*, p. 57.

125. Diederichs to L. Kuhlenbeck, 11 Mar. 1904, Diederichs Archive.

126. See Field, "Nordic Racism," p. 524, and Poliakov, *Aryan Myth*, pp. 295ff.

127. Diederichs to Hoffmann-Kutsch, 28 Mar. 1912, Diederichs Archive; *Die Kulturbewegung Deutschlands 1913*, p. 2.

128. Friedrich Jahn, *Deutsches Volkstum* (1810), as quoted in Emmerich, *Kritik der Volkstumsideologie*, p. 47.

129. Mosse, *Crisis of German Ideology*, p. 4.

130. Novalis, *Schriften* (1960), as quoted in Emmerich, *Kritik der Volkstumsideologie*, p. 41.

131. Lagarde, as quoted in ibid., p. 78.

132. Diederichs to Gustav Rössler, 14 Dec. 1912, and undated letter to the editors of the journal *Bücherwurm*, in Diederichs Archive; *AmL*, p. 76; *LW*, pp. 215, 225. See also Diederichs to F. Kuh, 2 Dec. 1912, Diederichs Archive.

133. *LW*, pp. 214–15.

134. W. Grimm, *Kleine Schriften*, as quoted in Emmerich, *Kritik der Volkstumsideologie*, p. 42.

135. See for example Diederichs to W. Hertz, 20 Dec. 1901, Wilhelm Hertz Nachlass.

136. Advertisement in *Von Wissenschaft zur Lebensgestaltung*, p. 24.

137. *LW*, pp. 207–8.

138. Advertisement for *Thule* series in *Tat* 14 (1922/23): 135.

139. Mosse, *Crisis of German Ideology*, pp. 92–93.

140. Diederichs to L. Ziegler, 27 Sept. 1904, Diederichs Archive. On Chamberlain, see Réal, "Religious Conception of Race"; Schüler, *Bayreuther Kreis*; and Field, "H. S. Chamberlain."

141. *LW*, pp. 117–18, 132.

142. *Der Verlag Diederichs in Jena*, p. 55.

143. *In Zeichen des Löwen*, p. 120.

144. Mosse, *Crisis of German Ideology*, p. 15.

145. See ibid., pp. 19–24, and Emmerich, *Kritik der Volkstumsideologie*, pp. 56–66.

146. See Köllmann, "Process of Urbanization in Germany"; Lees, "Debates About the Big City"; and Bergmann, *Agrarromantik*.

147. *SBZ*, p. 44.

148. *LW*, p. 148; also p. 104.

149. Ibid., p. 148.

150. Diederichs hoped eventually that the Garden City movement would reinforce and fuse with the attempts by Muthesius's *Werkbund* to bring a new aesthetic dimension to daily life (*SBZ*, p. 35, *LW*, p. 236).

151. On the *Heimatskunstbewegung*, see Jenny, *Die Heimatskunstbewegung*; Fischli, "Monsieur la Capital"; and Rossbacher, "Programm und Romane der Heimatskunstbewegung."

152. See the correspondence between Diederichs and Löns, and especially Diederichs's letter of 20 Dec. 1911, in the Deimann Nachlass.

153. Riehl, *Die bürgerliche Gesellschaft*, as quoted in Emmerich, *Kritik der Volkstumsideologie*, p. 61.

154. *SBZ*, p. 42.

155. Ibid., pp. 183–84; *AmL*, p. 95. On the ideological function of peasant novels in general, see Zimmermann, *Der Bauernroman*.

156. *Die Kulturbewegung Deutschlands 1913*, p. 15.

157. See Struve, *Elites Against Democracy*, pp. 53ff. On the progressive movement in the late Wilhelmian era, see Heckart, *From Bassermann to Bebel*.

158. *LW*, pp. 99, 128; advertisement quoted in U. Diederichs, "Marketing um die Jahrhundertwende," p. 99.

159. *SBZ*, pp. 205–6.

160. Ibid., pp. 40–41, 205–6; *LW*, pp. 140, 195.

161. For an example of this questionnaire, see *SBZ*, pp. 205–6.

162. *LW*, pp. 195, 199, 244. When he was planning these two series in 1908, he decided he would have to cut back on his other publishing ventures in the future so as to concentrate his resources on "these two great undertakings." (Diederichs to Tönnies, 30 Nov. 1908, Tönnies Nachlass.)

163. *SBZ*, p. 193; Diederichs to H. Potthoff, 3 Nov. 1910, Diederichs Archive.

164. *SBZ*, p. 40.

165. *LW*, p. 191; Diederichs to R. Bosch, 8 Oct. 1912, Diederichs Archive.

166. Bernstein, *Die Voraussetzungen des Sozialismus*, p. 158. On Bernstein and revisionism see Gay, *Dilemma of Democratic Socialism*; Johannsen, *Der Revisionismus*; Labedz, *Revisionism*; and Hirsch, *Der 'Fabier' Eduard Bernstein*.

167. Diederichs to Göhre, 1905, Diederichs Archive.

168. Diederichs to P. Harm, 15 Apr. 1912, Diederichs Archive; *Die Neuerscheinungen im 1912*, p. 39; *Zur Neuorientierung deutscher Kultur*, p. 61.

169. See for example Diederichs to F. Naumann, 22 Oct. 1912, Diederichs Archive; *SBZ*, pp. 216–17; and Diederichs, "Verlegerische Aufgaben" (1912), pp. 193–94.

170. *SBZ*, pp. 216, 341.

171. Schulze, *Deutsche Buchhandel und geistige Strömungen*, p. 230.

172. *LW*, p. 215; *SBZ*, p. 46.

173. The literature on the German Youth Movement is immense. Among the most recent and valuable studies are: Domandi, "The German Youth Movement"; Paetel, *Jugendbewegung und Politik*; Ziemer & Wolf, *Wandervögel und Freideutsche Jugend*; Laqueur, *Young Germany*; Pross, *Jugend, Eros, Politik*; Seidelmann, *Die deutsche Jugendbewegung*; Nasarski, *Deutsche Jugendbewegung*; and Müller, *Die Jugendbewegung*.

174. *AmL*, pp. 70–72; *LW*, pp. 171–74, 220; Diederichs, "Jugendentwicklung oder Jugendkultur?" (1913), p. 94.

175. *Tat* 7 (1915/16): 101.

176. On the Sera Circle, see *AmL*, pp. 41–43; *LW*, pp. 19, 159, 171–73; *Tat* 20 (1928/29): 816–17; Oschilewski, *Eugen Diederichs und sein Werk*, pp. 17ff.; and Kühn, "Ein königlicher Verleger," p. 30. Diederichs later claimed that it was the Sera Circle's activities which sparked the folk dance revival within the German Youth Movement.

177. Circular of 17 July 1913, in Eugen Diederichs Mappe, Archiv der deutschen Jugendbewegung. For Diederichs's role in planning the Hohe Meissner festival, see *LW*, pp. 220–25, and his "Bericht über die Besprechung einer Jahrhundertfeier," Diederichs Archive. His important *Aufruf* is reprinted in Kindt, *Grundschriften der Jugendbewegung*, pp. 93ff.
178. Schierer, *Zeitschriftenwesen der Jugendbewegung*, p. 90.
179. Blüher, *Werke und Tage*, pp. 342–43.
180. Diederichs to Altenburgische Kultusminister, 10 Feb. 1921, in Stadtbibliothek Dortmund and in Diederichs Archive.
181. Blunck, *Licht auf den Zügeln*, p. 251.
182. Wilhelm Flitner's eulogy in *In Memoriam: Eugen Diederichs*, unpaged; and Schmidt, "Diederichs und die Jugendbewegung," p. v.
183. See Ringer, *Decline of the German Mandarins*; Stern, *Politics of Cultural Despair*, pp. 1–255; Mitzman, *Sociology and Estrangement*; Struve, *Elites Against Democracy*, especially pp. 41–46, 53–185; Vondung, *Das wilhelminische Bildungsbürgertum*, and "Zur Lage der Gebildeten"; Schoeps, *Wilhelminische Zeitalter*; Rüschemeyer, "Modernisierung und Gebildeten"; Pascal, *From Naturalism to Expressionism*; Kratzsch, *Kunstwart und Dürerbund*; and Rosenhaupt, *Deutsche Dichter um die Jahrhundertwende*.
184. Frecot, "Lebensreformbewegung," p. 139. See also Krabbe, *Gesellschaftsveränderung durch Lebensreform* and Laubenthal, *Gedanke einer geistigen Erneuerung*.
185. Frecot, "Lebensreformbewegung," p. 139.

CHAPTER 4

1. On the radical nationalist opposition in the Second Reich, see: Rapp, *Der deutsche Gedanke*; Westphal, *Feinde Bismarcks*; Class, *Wider den Strom*; Gerstenhauer, *Der völkische Gedanke*; von Westarp, *Konservative Politik*; von Metnitz, *Die deutsche Nationalbewegung*; Vermeil, "Origin, Nature, and Development of German Nationalist Ideology"; Bronder, *Bevor Hitler Kam*; Nolte, "Germany"; Lepsius, *Extremer Nationalismus*; Schilling, *Geschichte des radikalen Nationalismus*; and Wehler, "Sozialdarwinismus." See also Höfele, "Selbstverständnis und Zeitkritik des deutschen Bürgertums"; and Hampe, "Hintergründe der bildungsbürgerlichen Imperialbegeisterung." Geoff Eley's *Reshaping the German Right. Radical Nationalism and Political Change After Bismarck* (New Haven, 1980) appeared too late to be considered for this study.
2. *Werbe- und Merkbüchlein des Alldeutschen Verbandes*, p. 49.
3. See Dahn's letter of 1 Dec. 1908 in *Fünfzig Jahre JFLV*.
4. The most comprehensive studies of the Pan-German League are Kruck's *Alldeutschen Verbandes* and von Seggern's "The Alldeutscher Verband." See also the older works of Andler, *Le Pangermanisme*; Bonhard, *Alldeutschen Verbandes*; Wertheimer, *The Pan-German League*; and Werner, *Alldeutsche Verband*.
5. *Vierzig Jahre Dienst*, p. 8.
6. Lehmann to E. Hasse, 27 Sept. 1901, Lehmann Archive; Lehmann as quoted in Werner, *Alldeutsche Verband*, pp. 79–80; also Class, "Lehmann und der Alldeutsche Verband," p. 259.
7. Class, *Wider den Strom*, p. 282; *LKD*, pp. 32–34, 156.
8. See Lehmann to von Liebert, 11 Jan. 1905, Lehmann Archive, regarding pamphlet no. 20; and Lehmann to G. C. Petzet, 28 Nov. 1897, Petzet Nachlass.
9. *LKD*, p. 20; Werner, *Alldeutsche Verband*, p. 76; Kruck, *Alldeutschen Verbandes*, p. 23.
10. Advertisement in *Werbe- und Merkbüchlein des Alldeutschen Verbandes*, p. 45.
11. Lehmann to Petzet, 28 Nov. 1897, Petzet Nachlass.

12. *Vierzig Jahre Dienst*, p. 9. Lehmann also boasted that the maps and artwork in Defregger's book provided lucrative commissions for German-Austrian artists.

13. *Zum 25. jährigen Gründungstag JFLV*, p. 26.

14. On the history and significance of the *Los-von-Rom* movement, see Albertin, *Nationalismus und Protestantismus*, and Whiteside, *Socialism of Fools*, chap. 10.

15. Class, "Lehmann und der Alldeutsche Verband," p. 258; Bonhard, *Alldeutschen Verbandes*, pp. 17, 21, 58, 94.

16. Wahrmund, a Protestant professor in Innsbruck, charged that Austrian Catholics and academic freedom were incompatible. Infuriated Catholic officials dismissed Wahrmund from his post, and had his books confiscated. This in turn sparked violent clashes between Catholic and Protestant students at a number of universities. The affair ultimately reached the Austrian parliament, where ministers, delegates, and church officials were quick to choose sides. See May, *Hapsburg Monarchy*, p. 340. Lehmann expressed pleasure that the papal nuncio's denunciations of Wahrmund's books had given them much free publicity and boosted their sales considerably. (Lehmann to Chamberlain, 23 Mar. 1908, Chamberlain Nachlass; also *Zum 25. jährigen Gründungstag JFLV*, p. 28.)

17. *Zum 25. jährigen Gründungstag JFLV*, pp. 27–28.

18. Pulzer, *Rise of Political Anti-Semitism*, p. 207; May, *Hapsburg Monarchy*, pp. 188–89. On the impact of the campaign upon Hitler see his *Mein Kampf*, pp. 108–16.

19. Since 1961, literature on navalism, colonialism, and social imperialism in the Second Reich has grown exponentially. Among the most important recent works are: Steinberg, *Yesterday's Deterrent*; Jerussalemski, *Der deutsche Imperialismus*; Wernecke, *Wille zur Weltgeltung*; Berghahn, *Der Tirpitz-Plan*, *Rüstung und Machtpolitik*, and *Germany and the Approach of War*; Schottelius & Diest, *Marine und Marinepolitik*; Böhm, *Überseehandel und Flottenbau*; Smith, *German Colonial Empire*; and Winzen, *Bülows Weltmacht politik*.

20. Lehmann to Dernburg, 8 Jan. 1906, Lehmann Archive.

21. Lehmann to Lehr, 29 Aug. 1897, Lehmann Archive.

22. Lehmann to Lehr, 27 Jan. 1900, Lehmann Archive.

23. *LKD*, p. 233.

24. Ibid., p. 27.

25. *Vierzig Jahre Dienst*, p. 9.

26. *Fünfzig Jahre JFLV*, pp. 63–64; *LKD*, p. 36. On the general intellectual background of social Darwinistic and racial eugenic thought in Germany, see Conrad-Martius, *Utopien der Menschenzüchtung*.

27. Lehmann to Chamberlain, 24 Dec. 1904, Chamberlain Nachlass.

28. Advertisement in K. Kynast, *Apollon und Dionysius: Nordisches und Unnordisches innerhalb der Religion der Griechen* (JFLV, 1927).

29. *LKD*, pp. 73–74. The habit frequently caused heated confrontations between the publisher and his authors.

30. Lehmann to Chamberlain, 26 Feb. 1904, Chamberlain Nachlass.

31. Ibid. This important letter is partially reprinted in *LKD*, pp. 101–2.

32. Ibid., and Lehmann to Chamberlain, 4 Feb. 1904, Chamberlain Nachlass.

33. *LKD*, p. 25.

34. Lehmann to Chamberlain, 4 Feb. 1904 and 12 Feb. 1905, Chamberlain Nachlass.

35. Lehmann to Chamberlain, 26 Feb. 1904, Chamberlain Nachlass.

36. Ibid.; Lehmann to Chamberlain, 23 Mar. 1904, Chamberlain Nachlass.

37. This correspondence is preserved in the Lehmann and Chamberlain archives. Parts are also reprinted in Chamberlain, *Briefe*, 1:102–18, 127–38, 152ff.

38. Lehmann to Chamberlain, 12 Feb. 1905 and 9 Nov. 1905, Chamberlain Nachlass; Lehmann to Chamberlain, 11 Dec. 1905, Lehmann Archive.

39. Chamberlain, *Briefe*, 2:30.
40. See for example Lehmann to Chamberlain, 4 Oct. 1905, Chamberlain Nachlass.
41. For examples, see Lehmann to Chamberlain, 25 Apr. 1906, 15 Oct. 1907, 14 July 1911, and 26 May 1915, Chamberlain Nachlass.
42. Lehmann to Chamberlain, 15 Oct. 1907, Chamberlain Nachlass.
43. Lehmann to Chamberlain, 24 May 1907, Chamberlain Nachlass.
44. *LKD*, p. 108.

CHAPTER 5

1. See Diederichs to H. Löns, 12 Aug. 1914, Deimann Nachlass, and Diederichs to Blunck, 21 Sept. 1914, Blunck Nachlass, in which the publisher asks these writers to contribute to a new anthology of patriotic war literature he is planning.
2. *LW*, p. 254.
3. *Handelswacht* 23 (1916): 93.
4. Ibid., and 22 (1915): 182.
5. *LKD*, pp. 46, 146.
6. *Blätter für Volksbibliotheken und Lesehallen* 16 (1915): 75–77, and 17 (1916): 124.
7. See advertisement in *Handelswacht* 22 (1915): 20.
8. See Fischer's classic *Griff nach der Weltmacht*, especially chap. 5. In this connection see also Gatzke, *Germany's Drive to the West*.
9. EDV prospectus "Schriften zur Kriege von Gustav Steffen," in Diederichs Archive.
10. *LW*, pp. 259–60; *Tat* 7 (1915/16): 15, and 10 (1918/19): 77. On *Die Tat*'s general program of eastern expansion during the war, see Hecker, *'Tat' und Osteuropabild*, pp. 34–37. For the development of the German *Mitteleuropa* plans, see Meyer, *Mitteleuropa in German Thought*.
11. *LKD*, pp. 144–45; Lehmann, *Deutschlands Zukunft*, p. 6.
12. *Zum 25. jährigen Gründungstag JFLV*, p. 15.
13. On the significance of this Pan-German manifesto, see Fischer, *Griff nach der Weltmacht*, pp. 120–21. Bethmann Hollweg regarded confiscation as "necessary for the protection of important imperial interests connected with the conduct of the war." (Jarausch, *The Enigmatic Chancellor*, p. 355.)
14. *LKD*, pp. 75, 131–32; Lehmann to Bavarian War Minister, 25 Aug. 1917, reprinted in *Deutschlands Erneuerung* 6 (1922): 9–17.
15. Lehmann as quoted in Jarausch, *The Enigmatic Chancellor*, pp. 529 n. 19, and 360.
16. *Vierzig Jahre Dienst*, p. 18; *LKD*, p. 42.
17. *LKD*, pp. 40–42.
18. Ibid., pp. 252–53.
19. The tract was secretly printed on onionskin paper. To circumvent censorship yet still remain within the letter of the law, Lehmann waited until 12:00 noon on the day of the book's release before submitting a copy—printed on especially heavy-grade paper—to the censorship office. Because of the traditional long German lunch hour, the office did not reopen until 3:30 P.M.; it was thus several hours before the censor actually reviewed the work. Meanwhile, the JFLV had mailed out most of the 3,000 onionskin copies as personal first-class letters. When the censors finally realized the inflammatory nature of the book, they immediately ordered all copies confiscated. Because they believed the work was printed on bulky paper, however, the authorities failed to detect the onionskin copies in the mails and even overlooked those few copies remaining on the JFLV premises. (*LKD*, pp. 252–53; *Vierzig Jahre Dienst*, p. 19.)

20. *Deutschlands Erneuerung* 1 (1917): 1–5.

21. *LKD*, p. 138.

22. Ibid., pp. 143–45.

23. As quoted in Sippell, *Lehmann als Zeitschriftenverleger*, p. 19.

24. *LKD*, p. 143; Lohalm, *Völkischer Radikalismus*, pp. 54, 348.

25. Lehmann to Chamberlain, 12 Oct. 1917, Chamberlain Nachlass. Chamberlain received an honorarium of 20 percent of the selling price of 25 pfennig. During the postwar inflation, this was reduced to 10 percent. (See Chamberlain's royalty statements in the Chamberlain Nachlass.)

26. During 1916 Lehmann had laid plans for another patriotic house journal, *Unser Vaterland*, and had lined up Graf Bothmer to serve as editor. When the publisher eventually canceled the journal, however, the cantankerous Bothmer demanded 37,000 marks from the JFLV in damages and threatened that if he did not receive it, he would inform the authorities of Lehmann's clandestine publications and censorship evasions. (Lehmann to Chamberlain, 13 Dec. 1916, Chamberlain Nachlass.) The outcome of this unusual situation is, unfortunately, unknown.

27. Jarausch, *The Enigmatic Chancellor*, pp. 360ff.

28. A JFLV advertisement for the 1919 public edition of Liebig's book, printed on the inside cover of J. Alter, *Das deutsche Reich auf dem Wege zur geschichtlichen Episoden* (3rd ed., 1919), stated for example that upon reading Liebig's tract, Bethmann Hollweg declared: "It is as if someone hit me on the head with a hammer. It was the most terrible blow ever struck against me." After Liebig's pamphlet appeared, Lehmann claimed, the chancellor knew that he was "politically demolished."

29. The previously censored excerpts in Adolf Bollinger's *Deutschlands letzte und grösste Not* were underlined in the new edition, for example. In announcing the new edition of J. Alter's *Das deutsche Reich auf dem Wege zur geschichtlichen Episoden*, Lehmann declared that "the mistakes which are exposed [by this work] can never be allowed to happen again." (See JFLV prospectus in the Paul Ernst Nachlass.)

30. *Osteuropäische Zukunft* was apparently a cover journal for the War Ministry, as the journal's editorial board was located there. Lehmann's consultations with these War Ministry functionaries convinced him that the military was "nationally minded" and desired more extensive war aims, but was being held back by the Foreign Ministry. (Lehmann to Chamberlain, 5 Feb. 1916, Chamberlain Nachlass.)

31. Lehmann, *Deutschlands Zukunft*, pp. 2–5.

32. Fischer, *Griff nach der Weltmacht*, p. 444.

33. *LW*, p. 260; *SBZ*, p. 227; Diederichs to R. Buchwald, 11 Oct. 1917, and Diederichs to H. Schultz, 17 Dec. 1918, Diederichs Archive; *Tat* 7 (1915/16): 417; *PdG*, pp. 25–27, 31–32, 66–67, 69–74.

34. See Vondung's insightful essay "Deutsche Apokalypse 1914."

35. *LW*, pp. 282–83; *PdG*, pp. 15, 117.

36. *PdG*, p. 29. Vondung makes a convincing case that the war provoked a typically ideological reaction from the Wilhelmian *Bildungsbürgertum*—that is, members of this threatened class greeted and idealized the war and the sense of national unity which it created because they saw it as a means of rescuing themselves from social decline: "It was hoped that the war would serve as a factor for social integration, and initially this hope seemed justified. However, if one views this hope for integration against the background of the concrete situation of the educated middle classes, then serious doubts arise as to whether these educated middle-class authors were really so concerned over the fate of the national whole. For the social and political polarization of the prewar era worked especially unfavorably toward the educated *Mittelstand*: it saw itself sinking vis-à-vis the rising industrial bourgeoi-

sie, and felt increasingly threatened by the lower social classes. But since the educated middle class was not interested in a one-sided nullification of this polarization (from a social revolution it could expect nothing at all, and from a 'revolution from above' only very little), the transformation of their splintered society into a 'new community,' the reconstitution of a new, 'inner unity of the nation,' must have appeared especially desirable. . . . The German apocalypse of 1914 was one of the last great attempts by the spiritually and socially insecure circles of the established, educated middle class to express, in a programmatic and visionary way, their imaginary goal of a reconstitution of the bourgeois spirit, whereby the goal of a spiritual reconstitution necessarily, although only implicitly, presupposed the social reconstitution of society's cultural elite as well." (Vondung, "Deutsche Apokalypse 1914," pp. 162, 168.)

37. *LW*, pp. 243, 275–76, 299; *PdG*, p. 25; *Tat* 6 (1914/15): 547–48.

38. German thinkers have long distinguished between *Kultur* and *Zivilisation*. "Culture" has strongly positive connotations of profound spirituality, philosophical introspection, and idealism, while "civilization" is largely a negative term connoting external manners and customs, superficial knowledge, and mere technical virtuosity.

39. The "Ideas of 1914" were articulated primarily by Rudolf Kjellen, Friedrich Meinecke, Johann Plenge, Werner Sombart, Thomas Mann, and Paul Natorp. For an account and analysis of these ideas, see Fuller, "War of 1914"; Lübbe, *Politische Philosophie*, pp. 171–235; von Klemperer, *Germany's New Conservatism*, pp. 47–55; Ringer, *Decline of the German Mandarins*, pp. 180ff.; Schwabe, *Wissenschaft und Kriegsmoral*; and von See, *Die Ideen von 1789 und 1914*.

40. *Tat* 7 (1915/16): 13; 9 (1917/18): 976–80, 1026–27, 1054–56.

41. Natorp, *Deutscher Weltberuf*, p. 2; Bischoff, *Deutsche Gesinnung*, p. 111.

42. Diederichs to Crusius, 20 Nov. 1914, Crusius Nachlass; *LW*, p. 278; *Tat* 6 (1914/15): 547–48.

43. *Tat* 7 (1915/16): 103–6; 10 (1918/19): 84.

44. *PdG*, pp. 24, 94; *LW*, pp. 247–49.

45. *LW*, pp. 20–21, 270–71, 284, 289, 305; "Denkschrift der gemeinnützigen 'Vaterländischen Gesellschaft 1914' zu Jena," Diederichs Archive. Audiences for the society's lectures averaged 100 to 150.

46. *LW*, p. 307.

47. Two *Kulturtagungen* were held in 1917, one in 1918, and another in 1925. Other participants included: Otto Crusius, Werner Sombart, Ferdinand Tönnies, Richard Dehml, Wilhelm Vershofen, Gertrud Bäumer, Max Mauernbrecher, Josef Winkler, Ernst Krieck, and Hermann Wirth. On the Lauenstein Congresses, see *LW*, pp. 21, 271, 293, 302–3, 307, 331–32; *SBZ*, pp. 242–43, 245–47, 344; Dietze, *Diederichs und seine Zeitschriften*, p. 33; "Einladung zu einer vertraulichen geschlossenen Besprechung über Sinn und Aufgaben unserer Zeit," Diederichs Archive; Diederichs, "Gründung eines 'Kulturamtes'" (1925), pp. 9735–37; Diederichs to Weber, 24 May 1917 (with accompanying list of participants), Max Weber Nachlass.

48. See for example *Eugen Diederichs: Verleger, Buchgestalter, Publizist*, p. 49; *SBZ*, pp. 246–47; Weber, *Weber: Ein Lebensbild*, pp. 608–10; Mitzman, *The Iron Cage*, p. 293. Theodor Heuss, in his *Erinnerungen*, p. 215, described one such congress: "These few days in the picturesque old castle received their significance from the force of the accusations which Max Weber hurled against the Kaiser and his milieu. He openly challenged the latter to indict him for *lèse majesté* so that he could then invite [leading civilian and military members of the imperial regime] to testify under oath. It was a genuine explosion, which frightened and unsettled some in the audience."

49. *SBZ*, pp. 241, 244; *Tat* 11 (1919/20): 103. See also *LW*, pp. 263, 280–81.

50. *Tat* 6 (1914/15): 547; Diederichs, "Praktischer Vorschlag zu einer Schulung für Volks-werdung," (undated typescript, ca. 1917–18), and "Ansprache am 3. März 1917 in den Räumen der Deutschen Gesellschaft," Diederichs Archive.

51. *Drei Jahre Kulturarbeit*, as quoted in *AmL*, pp. 70–72.

52. *LW*, p. 208; *Tat* 10 (1918/19): 643–45.

53. *PdG*, p. 32.

54. Diederichs to R. von Delius, 19 July 1917, Diederichs Archive (partially reprinted in *LW*, p. 287). See also his comments in *LW*, p. 298, and *Die geistigen Aufgaben der Zukunft* (1920), p. 11.

55. "Zur Aufführung von Georg Kaisers *Koralle*," typescript in Diederichs Archive; also *SBZ*, p. 344.

56. Kaiser thanked him for his support and declared that "you saw clearly what the essence of *Die Koralle* was"; the author then sent the publisher a manuscript copy of his *Gas*, the sequel to *Koralle*, with the hope of being able to "devote" the published version to Diederichs at a later date. (*SBZ*, p. 344.) *Gas*, however, was eventually published by another firm. Baader approached the EDV a few years later with the plan for a multivolume series which he hoped to edit (*SBZ*, p. 279).

57. Diederichs to E. Wietsch, 15 Apr. 1918, as quoted in Dietze, *Diederichs und seine Zeitschriften*, p. 169.

58. On the Nyland Circle, which consisted of the authors Jakob Kneip, Josef Winkler, Gerrit Engelke, and Wilhelm Vershofen, see Hoyer, *Die Werkleute auf Haus Nyland*, and Stappenbacher, *Deutschen literarischen Zeitschriften*, p. 153.

59. *LW*, pp. 269–70, 272, 279; *Tat* 7 (1915/16): 100; *Drei Jahre Kulturarbeit*, in *AmL*, pp. 70–72.

60. Diederichs to A. Steglich, 3 Aug. 1916, in Archiv der Jugendbewegung.

61. *PdG*, p. 69.

62. *Tat* 10 (1918/19): 642; *LW*, pp. 251–52, 267, 334; *PdG*, p. 90.

63. *LW*, pp. 267, 329; Diederichs to S. Lublinski, 19 Oct. 1910, Diederichs Archive.

64. Diederichs, "Brief des Verlegers" (1913), p. 1161; Diederichs, "Krieg und Ewigkeits-glaube" (1915), p. 5; *Tat* 10 (1918/19): 454.

65. *Tat* 7 (1915/16): 100; 10 (1918/19): 454.

66. This manifesto, which originally appeared in *Die Tat*, is reprinted in *LW*, pp. 261–63.

67. Nietzsche, *Beyond Good and Evil*, p. 176.

68. Walter Gerhard, critic and observer of the neoconservative movement, considered Stapel's book one of the most important programmatic tracts of the entire neonationalist movement in the Weimar republic. (*Um Reiches Zukunft*, p. 209.) That same year (1932), the DHV declared that its nationalist educational activities were grounded essentially on Stapel's book. (Quoted in Kessler, *Stapel*, p. 36 n. 3.)

69. Kessler, *Stapel*, p. 30 n. 4.

70. *Deutsches Volkstum* 19 (1917): v.

71. *Handelswacht* 23 (1916): 180; advertisement for R. Benz, *Die Renaissance, das Verhängnis der deutschen Kultur*, in *Zur Neuorientierung deutschen Kultur*, p. 8.

72. On Diederichs's plans for *Die Brücke*, a journal which was to promote Nordic con-sciousness and build a solid bloc of Germanic-Nordic nations such as Denmark, Switzerland, and the Scandinavian nations against the Anglo-Saxon alliance, see *LW*, pp. 309–12 and Dietze, *Diederichs und seine Zeitschriften*, p. 163.

73. *Tat* 7 (1915/16): 992; Diederichs to E. Lissauer, 21 Dec. 1918, Diederichs Archive.

74. *SBZ*, p. 231; *PdG*, pp. 14, 28–29.

75. *Zur Neuorientierung deutschen Kultur*, p. 19.

76. *LW*, p. 268; Diederichs to G. Hildebrand, as quoted in Dietze, *Diederichs und seine Zeitschriften*, p. 81; *Tat* 6 (1914/15): 17. See also *LW*, p. 80, and *Tat* 7 (1915/16): 99.

77. See Bowen, *German Theories of the Corporate State*, and Mosse, "Corporate State and Conservative Revolution."

78. *Tat* 10 (1918/19): 83.

79. See Sontheimer, *Antidemokratisches Denken*, p. 252.

80. *Tat* 10 (1918/19): 83.

81. *Die Tätigkeit des Verlages 1914–1924*, p. 26; *Die geistigen Aufgaben von heute*, p. 70.

82. *Die Tätigkeit des Verlages 1914–1924*, p. 40.

83. *Tat* 10 (1918/19): 85–86.

84. Ibid., 724, 773–74, 857, and the *Tat-Sonderhefte* for January 1919, July 1920, and October 1925. See also Bowen, *German Theories of Corporate State*, p. 9.

85. *PdG*, p. 14; *LW*, p. 283; "Ansprache am 3. März," Diederichs Archive.

86. von Klemperer, *Germany's New Conservatism*, pp. 83, 85–88; Barclay, "A Prussian Socialism?"; Maier, *Recasting Bourgeois Europe*, pp. 65–66, 141ff.

87. *LW*, pp. 328, 353.

88. Ibid., p. 337; *Tat* 7 (1915/16): 101; 10 (1918/19): 83.

89. *LW*, p. 273; Diederichs, "Wirklichkeit und Förderung," newspaper article of 31 March 191?, from *Leipziger Abendzeitung*, in Diederichs Archive.

90. Struve, *Elites Against Democracy*.

91. *PdG*, p. 51.

92. Diederichs, "Praktischer Vorschlag," Diederichs Archive; *SBZ*, p. 244; *Tat* 10 (1918/19): 77.

93. *LW*, pp. 284, 319; *PdG*, pp. 47, 59; *Tat* 7 (1915/16): 98, 101, 106 and 10 (1918/19): 77, 81–88, 555, 637, 773–74.

94. *PdG*, pp. 23, 32; *Tat* 7 (1915/16): 519; 10 (1918/19): 532.

95. *LW*, pp. 288–89; *Tat* 7 (1915/16): 102; 10 (1918/19): 76, 532, 615. Diederichs thundered: "The nation demands of Conservatives that they place the national interest above their class interests," but he had little hope they would (*Tat* 10 [1918/19]: 614).

96. *PdG*, pp. 27–28, 130; *LW*, p. 318.

97. Ibid., p. 322; *Tat* 10 (1918/19): 532, 555–57, 688; Diederichs to F. von der Leyen, 1 Sept. 1918, Diederichs Archive.

98. *LW*, pp. 286, 307–8, 318–19; *Tat* 10 (1918/19): 532.

99. *LW*, p. 322; *PdG*, p. 48; *Tat* 10 (1918/19): 612–15, 686.

100. McRandle, *Track of the Wolf*, pp. 77–78.

101. On the origins and significance of this legend, see Petzold, *Die Dolchstosslegende*, p. 46; Koszyk & Pruys, *Wörterbuch zur Publizistik*, pp. 82–83. It is possible that Cossmann, a Munich journalist who is perhaps more responsible than any other individual for popularizing the *Dolchstosslegende*, first became interested in it through the work of the JFLV. See Betz, "Cossmann und die Münchener Publizistik."

102. *LKD*, pp. 149–50, 163.

103. Ibid., p. 60.

104. *Vierzig Jahre Dienst*, p. 25.

105. Roth, *Einhundertfünfzig Jahre Verlag Stalling*, p. 139.

106. *PdG*, p. 29.

107. For a perceptive discussion of the differences between antiwar "egocentric" novels and prowar "ethnocentric" works, see Pfeiler, *War and the German Mind*, pp. 193ff. This work serves as an excellent introduction to the postwar war literature of Germany.

108. Diehl, *Paramilitary Politics*, p. 211. See also Sontheimer, *Antidemokratisches Denken*,

pp. 136–37; Cysarz, *Geistesgeschichte des Weltkrieges*; Osteraas, "The New Nationalists"; Pruemm, *Literatur des Soldatischen Nationalismus*, and "Das Erbe der Front"; and Schwarz, *War and the Mind of Germany*.

109. See Beumelburg's comments in *Heinrich Stalling*, p. 11, and Roth, *Einhundertfünfzig Jahre Verlag Stalling*, p. 155.

110. Laqueur, "Role of the Intelligentsia," p. 217.

111. *Vierzig Jahre Dienst*, pp. 24–25.

112. *Fünfzig Jahre JFLV*, pp. 94–96.

113. Lehmann, *Wir von der Infanterie*, p. 8.

114. Ibid., p. 94. J. F. Lehmann, too, hoped to prepare Germany for the "final war" against the West, the "Second Punic War in which the German *Volk* will finally triumph" (*LKD*, p. 150).

115. Stellrecht, *Trotz Allem*, p. 5.

116. 1932 DHB prospectus, in DHV Archive.

117. Pfeiler, *War and the German Mind*, p. 285.

CHAPTER 6

1. *Tat* 10 (1918/19): 726. The revolution, however, did not make Diederichs an "insider" to the new republic; rather, it was a different group of prewar outsiders—socialists, democrats, Catholics, Jews—who became the postwar insiders. See Gay, *Weimar Culture*.

2. *LW*, pp. 319, 320, 323; *Tat* 10 (1918/19): 642, 875.

3. *LKD*, pp. 153, 155, 160.

4. *Tat* 10 (1918/19): 612–13; also *LW*, p. 327, and Diederichs to Lt. Adelmann, 13 Dec. 1918, Diederichs Archive.

5. *LKD*, pp. 151–52.

6. *LW*, p. 323; *Tat* 10 (1918/19): 723.

7. *LW*, pp. 328, 331, 333.

8. Ibid., pp. 323, 328; *Tat* 10 (1918/19): 722, 726 and 11 (1919/20): 50–51, 472.

9. Ibid., 11 (1919/20): 208.

10. *LW*, pp. 327, 339, 341; *SBZ*, p. 267; *Tat* 10 (1918/19): 642, 856; Diederichs to Ernst, 12 Feb. 1919, Ernst Nachlass; Diederichs to E. Michel, 17 Feb. 1920, Diederichs Archive.

11. *Tat* 10 (1918/19): 726, 958; *LW*, p. 341.

12. See Landauer, "Bavarian Problem in the Weimar Republic"; Zimmermann, *Bayern und das Reich*; Mennekes, *Republik als Herausforderung*; and Fenske, *Konservatismus und Rechtsradikalismus*. David C. Large's *The Politics of Law and Order. A History of the Bavarian Einwohnerwehr, 1918–1921* (Philadelphia, 1980) appeared too late to be considered for this study.

13. *LKD*, pp. 152–53.

14. The *Thule Gesellschaft* was a conspiratorial group founded in August 1918 by members of the *Germanen Orden*. It eventually grew to some 1,500 members in Bavaria, 250 of which were in Munich. (See Phelps, "Before Hitler Came"; Franz-Willing, *Die Hitlerbewegung*, pp. 29–34; Fenske, *Konservatismus und Rechtsradikalismus*, pp. 53–54; and Maser, *Frühgeschichte der NSDAP*, p. 25.) Although the nominal leader of the *Thule Gesellschaft* was Rudolf Freiherr von Sebetendorff, scholars generally agree that J. F. Lehmann was the organization's most prominent and active member. (Franz-Willing, *Die Hitlerbewegung*, p. 30; Deuerlein, *Der Hitler-Putsch*, p. 25.)

15. *LKD*, pp. 148–49, 151; Lehmann's "Aufruf Brief" of 28 Oct. 1918 in Lehmann Ar-

chive; Phelps, "Before Hitler Came," pp. 252–53. During late October and early November Lehmann completely merged the activities of the local *Alldeutscher Verband* and the *Thule Gesellschaft*.

16. The *Kampfbund* attracted such men as Anton Drexler, Dietrich Eckart, Gottfried Feder, Hans Frank, Rudolf Hess, and Alfred Rosenberg, all of whom later became active in the early Nazi party. For this reason, the *Kampfbund Thule* has been called "one of the most important roots of the National Socialist German Workers Party." (Franz-Willing, *Die Hitlerbewegung*, p. 34.)

17. *LKD*, pp. 47–50.

18. This League was also closely associated with the Pan-German League, and its director (Alfred Roth) was a leading official in the DHV. Lehmann served on the *Schutz-* und *Trutzbund*'s advisory committee. Membership in the organization numbered some 30,000 by the end of 1919, and rose to an estimated 200,000 or 300,000 by 1922. (Lohalm, *Völkischer Radikalismus*; Kruck, *Alldeutschen Verbandes*, pp. 132ff.; Franz-Willing, *Die Hitlerbewegung*, pp. 49ff.)

19. Quoted in Franz-Willing, *Die Hitlerbewegung*, p. 49.

20. Initially Lehmann served as a propagandist on the staff of battalion commander Schmidt. As the group neared Munich, however, Lehmann took up arms himself and was made commander of the *Sturmkompanie Isny*, which fought its way into the city down Lindenwurmstrasse. During the fighting, Lehmann participated in an on-the-spot court-martial and execution of fifty-six "Russian" captives. (See *LKD*, pp. 50–55, 173–76, and Lehmann to Chamberlain, 7 June 1919, Chamberlain Nachlass.)

21. *LKD*, p. 166.

22. Advertisement in cover of P. Bang, *Der Deutsche als Landesknecht*, 2nd ed. (JFLV, 1928).

23. *LW*, pp. 321, 331.

24. *Tat* 10 (1918/19): 725.

25. As late as 1932, the HVA proudly proclaimed that its conservative-revolutionary program was based on a "Will to Resistance" in foreign affairs. (Bücherbrief der HVA, April 1932, in Box 561, Forschungsstelle.)

26. Lehmann, *Ein deutscher Verlag*, p. 72.

27. Beenken, *Land in Ketten*, pp. 4, 156, 159.

28. *LKD*, p. 176.

29. Advertisement prospectus for Ernst Zahn's *Warum ich auf den Auslieferungsliste stehe* (1922), in Lehmann Archive.

30. *LKD*, p. 176.

31. Ibid., pp. 235, 237.

32. Diederichs to E. Schmitt, 24 Mar. 1923, Diederichs Archive; *LW*, pp. 391–92.

33. *LKD*, p. 61; *Vierzig Jahre Dienst*, p. 24.

34. *LKD*, p. 72.

35. *Handelswacht* 35 (1928): 458.

36. Lehmann to Eva Chamberlain, 23 July 1929, Chamberlain Nachlass. Lehmann participated in the preparatory meetings with Hugenberg of the German Nationalist Party in June/July 1929, and it was apparently Lehmann and one of his authors, Paul Bang, who convinced Hitler to join the anti-Young campaign. (See Lehmann to Schemann, 17 June 1929, Schemann Nachlass, and Lehmann to Melanie Lehmann, 9 Dec. 1929, Lehmann Archive.)

37. Advertisement in cover of P. Bang's *Ein Zwischenbilanz deutscher Politik* (JFLV, 1927).

38. Advertisement in 1928 edition of Stapel's *Volksbürgerliche Erziehung* (HVA), p. 191.

39. *Handelswacht* 38 (1931): 376 and 39 (1932): 233.

40. Diederichs to Ernst, 12 Feb. 1919, Ernst Nachlass; *LW*, pp. 343–44; *Tat* 10 (1918/19): 856, 958, 12 (1920/21): 53–54, 14 (1922/23): 84–85, 156, 472, 15 (1923/24): 475, 17 (1925/26): 50, 206, and 18 (1926/27): 790.

41. *Tat* 14 (1922/23): 85, 156.

42. *LKD*, pp. 149, 216, 244, 267–69.

43. Lehmann to H. Schmid, 11 Jan. 1932, Zarnow Nachlass.

44. See Gumbel, *Acht Jahre politischer Justiz*; Kreiler, *Traditionen deutscher Justiz*; Hannover, *Politische Justiz*; Sinzheimer & Fraenkel, *Justiz in der Weimarer Republik*; and Jasper, *Der Schutz der Republik*.

45. Lehmann to M. E. Moritz [pseudonym: "Gottfried Zarnow"], 11 Nov. 1930, Zarnow Nachlass. The publisher said he hoped "to see this rascal hang."

46. *LKD*, pp. 234, 242, 257.

47. Lehmann to Moritz, 25 June 1930, Zarnow Nachlass.

48. Lehmann to Moritz, 31 July 1930, and Moritz to Lehmann, 26 Oct. 1930, Zarnow Nachlass.

49. Lehmann to Moritz, 24 Oct. 1930, Zarnow Nachlass.

50. Lehmann to Moritz, 15 Oct. 1930, Zarnow Nachlass. Lehmann dispersed copies of the printed work to several different distribution points, and in this way was able to disseminate several thousand copies of the book before the government could seize the remaining stock.

51. *Deutschlands Erneuerung* 15 (1931): 114.

52. Lehmann to Moritz, 17 Oct. 1930 and 27 Nov. 1930, Zarnow Nachlass. Lehmann was personally acquainted with Hindenburg's daughter and hoped she would persuade her father to read the book.

53. Lehmann to Schmid, 11 Jan. 1932 and Lehmann to Moritz, 3 Feb. 1932, Zarnow Nachlass.

54. *LKD*, pp. 254–55; Lehmann to Schmid, 11 Jan. 1932 and Lehmann to Moritz, 18 May 1932, Zarnow Nachlass. It is not clear whether Lehmann reckoned the money he sent to Zarnow as part of his total legal costs, or whether it was above and beyond the figures of 8,000 and 25,000 marks he mentioned. At any rate, by the end of 1931, Lehmann had paid some 5,000 marks of Zarnow's costs.

55. After the government confiscated the fourth printing of volume 1, the JFLV drew up an expurgated version which the censors passed. Once the ban on the new edition was lifted, however, Lehmann quickly distributed several thousand more copies of the original, unexpurgated version. By the time the confusing tangle of confiscated, expurgated, and unexpurgated releases was finally resolved, the firm had managed to disseminate the book, largely in its original uncensored form, to a wide readership. (*LKD*, pp. 254–55.) On sales figures for the work, see Lehmann to Moritz, 3 Feb. 1932 and 15 Feb. 1932, Zarnow Nachlass. Volume 1 sold 14,934 copies during its first month on the market.

56. Lehmann to Moritz, 24 Oct. 1930, 29 Nov. 1930, 4 Dec. 1930, and 13 Dec. 1930, Zarnow Nachlass; *LKD*, p. 250.

57. *LW*, p. 401; *Tat* 10 (1918/19): 724, 14 (1922/23): 628 and 15 (1923/24): 209–10, 475; Diederichs to H. Hefele, 13 Oct. 1922, Diederichs Archive.

58. See his comments in *Deutschlands Erneuerung* 3 (1920): 454–55 and 6 (1922): 97–99; *LKD*, pp. 176, 180–81, 220.

59. Announcement in *Börsenblatt für den deutschen Buchhandel* 98 (3 Nov. 1931): 964. The GMV promised to publish the manuscript in a forthcoming anthology, *Deutsche über Deutschland*.

60. HVA to Ernst, 7 Dec. 1932, Ernst Nachlass.

61. EDV Rundschreiben of 22 Oct. 1930, in Blunck Nachlass. The EDV admitted that the

scandal over Haken had in fact been good for his book's sales and was the best form of publicity for it. (See Niels Diederichs to Blunck, 23 Oct. 1930 and 17 Nov. 1930, Blunck Nachlass.)

62. *Handelswacht* 30 (1923): 151.

63. Lehmann, *Ein deutscher Verlag*, pp. 75–76.

64. *LKD*, p. 229.

65. See ibid., p. 201. On the *Bund Oberland*, consult Diehl, *Paramilitary Politics*, p. 230.

66. *LKD*, pp. 58–59. The refugee was Gottfried Traub, a prewar author of the EDV.

67. See Gordon, *Hitler and the Beer Hall Putsch*, p. 398. Lehmann sought to unite Kahr, Munich's Police President Ernst Pöhner, General Ludendorff, and Hitler's Nazi party into one *völkisch*-national front, for "then it will be possible to defeat Bolshevism from the Alps to the North Sea and to establish a national dictatorship. I hope," the publisher said, "that a new epoch in German history will begin and spread from Munich outward." (*LKD*, pp. 187–96.) During the early 1920s, Lehmann had been associated with the forerunner of the Nazi party, the German Workers Party (DAP), which grew out of the *Thule Gesellschaft*. He may also have been one of the earliest members of the NSDAP after its founding in February 1920. (See Maser, *Frühgeschichte der NSDAP*, p. 177.) At any rate, Lehmann knew Hitler personally and considered him "a genuinely honorable man" who would soon rise to national prominence. "I don't know how long it will be before Hitler finally seizes power," the publisher said during his negotiations in October 1923, "but in any case he will play a great role in the new times." (Lehmann to A. Gildmeister, 10 Oct. 1923, Lehmann Archive; also *LKD*, pp. 187–96.)

68. *LKD*, pp. 188–96; *Fünfzig Jahre JFLV*, p. 167; Schwend, *Bayern zwischen Monarchie und Diktatur*, p. 246; Hoffmann, *Der Hitler-Putsch*. It was Friedrich Weber, Lehmann's son-in-law, who suggested that the hostages be kept at Lehmann's villa. Later the publisher remarked: "This cuckoo's egg was laid in my nest by my dear son-in-law." (Lehmann to von Epp, 20 Nov. 1923, as quoted in Gordon, *Hitler and the Beer Hall Putsch*, p. 290 n. 66.)

69. Lehmann to Chamberlain, 4 Dec. 1923, Chamberlain Nachlass.

70. On the *Feme*, see Gumbel, "*Verräter verfallen der Feme*," and *Fememord zur Reichskanzlei*; Mertens, *Verschwörer und Fememörder*; Stern, "Organisation 'Consul'"; and Waite, *Vanguard of Nazism*, pp. 212–27.

71. *LKD*, p. 274; *Deutschlands Erneuerung* 9 (1928): 542; *Vierzig Jahre Dienst*, p. 27.

72. Sippell, *Lehmann als Zeitschriftenverleger*, p. 26; also Lehmann to Moritz, 24 Oct. 1930, Zarnow Nachlass. In addition, Lehmann sent detailed instructions to one JFLV author (Freiherr von Müffling) urging him to write a journal article on the Feme (*Fünfzig Jahre JFLV*, p. 78).

73. *LKD*, p. 236; Theisen, *Nihilistischen Nationalismus*, p. 100.

74. *Vierzig Jahre Dienst*, p. 28.

CHAPTER 7

1. *LKD*, pp. 34, 111.

2. Ibid., pp. 159, 162; Lehmann to Schemann, 16 June 1919, 18 July 1919, and Schemann to Lehmann, 22 June 1919, Schemann Nachlass.

3. Fenske, *Konservatismus und Rechtsradikalismus*, p. 264.

4. Habermann, *Erziehung zum deutschen Menschen*, pp. 5–6; *Deutsches Volkstum* 28 (1926): 909–10; *Handelswacht* 34 (1927): 129–30.

5. *LW*, p. 384; *Tat* 15 (1923/24): 559 and 18 (1926/27): 790; Diederichs to R. Wilbrandt, 17 July 1919, Diederichs Archive; Diederichs, "Eine sachliche Beschwerde" (1930), p. 7 and

Die geistigen Aufgaben der Zukunft (1920), pp. 7–8; *Die Tätigkeit des Verlages 1914–1924*, p. v; Diederichs, "Die Idee 'Lauenstein'" (1924), p. 24; Diederichs, "Zukunft des Buches" (1925), pp. 2–3; Diederichs, "Geistige Krisis und Buch" (1929), pp. 209–10.

6. *LW*, pp. 307, 344, 407–8, 452, 460; *Tat* 14 (1922/23): 86, 15 (1923/24): 475, 17 (1925/26): 609 and 19 (1927/28): 651–52; Diederichs, "Zukunft des Buches" (1925), p. 3 and "Geistige Krisis und Buch" (1929), p. 210; *Die Tätigkeit des Verlages 1914–1924*, p. 5; Diederichs, "Prognosse literarischen Entwicklungen" (1929), p. 3.

7. *Tat* 19 (1927/28): 648; also *Die geistigen Aufgaben von heute*, p. 4.

8. *Tat* 10 (1918/19): 855, 11 (1919/20): 313, 14 (1922/23): 82–83, 15 (1923/24): 472, 559 and 19 (1927/28): 80; Diederichs, "Echo der Lauensteiner Tagung" (1922), p. 1550.

9. Advertisement on cover of H. Günther, *Ritter, Tod und Teufel* (JFLV, 1920).

10. EDV prospectus for "Mythisches und Magisches Denken (1927–28)"; *Volkswerdung durch Mythos*, p. 52; Diederichs, *Die geistigen Aufgaben der Zukunft* (1920), p. 10; *Tat* 19 (1927/28): 648.

11. Advertisement in F. Haiser, *Das Gastmahl des Freiherrn von Artaria* (JFLV, 1920).

12. *LW*, pp. 203, 407; *AmL*, pp. 70–72; Diederichs, "Prognosse literarischen Entwicklungen" (1929), p. 13; *Tat* 19 (1927/28): 651 and 20 (1928/29): 855.

13. *Tat* 10 (1918/19): 76 and 11 (1919/20): 932; Diederichs, "Inneren Krise aller Buchhändlerorganisationen" (1924), p. 34.

14. Diederichs to Lissauer, 30 Apr. 1919, Diederichs Archive.

15. *Tat* 10 (1918/19): 855, 11 (1919/20): 934, 17 (1925/26): 50, 19 (1927/28): 648, 651, 654 and 20 (1928/29): 45; *LW*, p. 397; *AmL*, pp. 70–72.

16. Diederichs, "Inneren Krise aller Buchhändlerorganisationen" (1924), p. 34; *Tat* 12 (1920/21): 136; *Handelswacht* 38 (1931): 326.

17. *Tat* 11 (1919/20): 313; 17 (1925/26): 451.

18. Ibid., 19 (1927/28): 652; Diederichs, "Gegenwart und Zukunft" (1926), p. 29 and "Gedanken zur Buchkrisis" (1927), p. 8. On the symbolic role of America in German conservative thought, see Basler, "Amerikanismus," and Schwabe, "Anti-Americanism With the German Right."

19. *Tat* 19 (1927/28): 652; *SBZ*, pp. 301, 306.

20. See the advertisement for Halfeld's book and for H. G. Wells's *Die Zukunft in Amerika* (1911) in *Die geistigen Aufgaben von heute*, pp. 64–65; letter of EDV to Blunck, 1 Sept. 1927, and Blunck's statement of 6 Sept. 1927 praising Halfeld's book, Blunck Nachlass.

21. See Groh, *Russland und das Selbstverständnis Europas* and Stöckel, *Osteuropa und die Deutschen*.

22. *Tat* 7 (1915/16): 15; *LW*, p. 206; Diederichs to H. Ullmann, 13 Jan. 1917, Ullmann Nachlass.

23. Hecker, *'Tat' und Osteuropabild*, p. 92. See also Löwenthal, "Die Auffassung Dostojewskis."

24. *Tat* 14 (1922/23): 85–86.

25. *Handelswacht* 39 (1932): 233.

26. See Hecker, *'Tat' und Osteuropabild*, pp. 131ff.

27. Advertisement in "Bücherbrief der HVA (April 1932)," p. 3, Forschungsstelle; *Handelswacht* 38 (1931): 376.

28. *SBZ*, p. 311; *Tat* 12 (1920/21): 136.

29. *Tat* 19 (1927/28): 649, 651–53; Diederichs, "Zukunft des Buches" (1925), p. 3.

30. *Tat* 14 (1922/23): 85; *AmL*, p. 76; *LKD*, p. 225.

31. *Handelswacht* 32 (1925): 151.

32. See Diederichs's comments on the 400th anniversary of the Reformation, in the October 1917 issue of *Die Tat* (reprinted in *PdG*, p. 90).

33. Kupisch, "The 'Luther Renaissance,'" pp. 45–46.

34. *Tat* 14 (1922/23): 87 and 19 (1927/28): 648; *SBZ*, p. 311.

35. Diederichs, *Die geistigen Aufgaben der Zukunft* (1920), p. 16 and "Zukunft des Buches" (1925), p. 3.

36. For a discussion of this general movement of visionary architects, see Lane, *Architecture and Politics*, chap. 2.

37. *LKD*, pp. 202–3.

38. Diederichs, "Geistige Krisis und Buch" (1929), pp. 209–12.

39. *Handelswacht* 28 (1921): 75.

40. On Germany's postwar Youth Movement, see: Jovy, *Deutsche Jugendbewegung und Nationalsozialismus*; Seidelmann, *Bund und Gruppe*; Raabe, *Die bündische Jugend*; Siefert, *Entstehung und Frühgeschichte der bündische Jugend*, and *Der bündische Aufbruch*; Leisen, *Ausbreitung des völkischen Gedankes*; Bleuel & Klinnert, *Deutsche Studenten auf Weg ins Dritten Reich*; and Steinberg, *Sabers and Brown Shirts*.

41. *LW*, pp. 348–49; *Tat* 19 (1927/28): 647.

42. *Tat* 13 (1921/22): 962 and 20 (1928/29): 44; Diederichs, "Am Scheideweg" (1923), p. 5; "Plan zur Schaffung von Geldmitteln für die Jugendbewegung sämtlicher Stände" (1921), typescript in Diederichs Archive; see also *LW*, p. 392, and *Tat* 14 (1922/23): 237.

43. *LW*, pp. 348–49, 393–94; *Tat* 11 (1919/20): 238ff. and 21 (1929/30): 486.

44. "Plan zur Schaffung von Geldmitteln," and T. Chappey to Diederichs, 5 Oct. 1922, Diederichs Archive.

45. See Borinski & Milch, *Jugendbewegung*, pp. 21–22; Muck-Lamberty file in Archiv der deutschen Jugendbewegung; and file of Muck newspaper clippings in Diederichs Archive.

46. Diederichs to Altenburgische Kultusminister, 10 Feb. 1921, in Stadtbibliothek Dortmund and in Diederichs Archive; Diederichs to K. Sprengel, 1 Mar. 1921, Stadtbibliothek Dortmund.

47. *LKD*, pp. 67–69. The *Bund Oberland, Tannenburgbund, Verein deutscher Studenten, Jungnationaler Bund*, and Stählin's *Kirche- und Jugendbewegung* also used Hoheneck.

48. *Handelswacht* 32 (1925): 593.

49. Sontheimer, *Antidemokratisches Denken*, p. 244.

50. Advertisement for *Deutsches Volkstum* in *Handelswacht* 30 (1923): 185.

51. Ibid., 34 (1927): 129–30.

52. Ibid., 31 (1924): 439 and 30 (1923): 378.

53. Ibid., 32 (1925): 151.

54. *Der Türmer* 33 (1930): 1–2.

55. Advertisement on dust jacket of B. von Münchhausen, *Deutsche Gedenk- und Weihstätten* (JFLV, 1926).

56. *AmL*, p. 76; *LW*, p. 456; *Tat* 18 (1926/27): 549.

57. One EDV author, Hermann Wirth, came "to the edge of financial disaster" while working on a manuscript entitled *Was heisst Deutsch?* Diederichs felt morally obligated to him and believed that a patriot like Wirth, who had sacrificed so much for his research and writing, should not have to starve. Thus the publisher subsidized the author while he completed his book. Diederichs claimed he treated Wirth's book like his own "delicate problem child" and that in supporting Wirth, he had gone "to the furthest limits of the possible—and actually beyond them." (Diederichs letter of 9 July 1928, Diederichs Archive.) Wirth's book was eventually published by the EDV in 1930 and sold 6,000 copies.

58. *Hansische Bücherbote* 4 (1924).

59. On Stapel's conception of *Volkskonservatismus*, see Hamel, *Völkischer Verband*, pp. 142ff., and Kessler, *Stapel*, pp. 112ff. His ideas eventually led to the formation of a DHV-supported *Volkskonservative Partei* in 1928. See Jonas, *Die Volkskonservativen*.

60. *Handelswacht* 34 (1927): 129.

61. Ibid., 36 (1929): 258, and advertisement in *Der Ring* 2 (1928): inside cover of no. 26.

62. *LW*, pp. 366, 369; *Tat* 17 (1925/26): 206.

63. Freyer, *Revolution von Rechts*, pp. 36, 44, 60–61.

64. Beenken as quoted in Lehmann, *Ein deutscher Verlag*, p. 16.

65. As quoted in Roth, *Einhundertfünfzig Jahre Verlag Stalling*, pp. 162–63.

66. *AmL*, p. 77; *LW*, p. 466; Diederichs, *Die Tätigkeit des Verlages 1914–1924*, Introduction and *Die geistigen Aufgaben von heute*, pp. 4–6; *Tat* 17 (1925/26): 604; 19 (1927/28): 650.

67. *Handelswacht* 34 (1927): 128; and *Deutsches Volkstum* 28 (1926): 909–10.

68. *Volkswerdung durch Mythos*, p. 24; *Tat* 18 (1926/27): 548 and 20 (1928/29): 45. See also HVA advertisement for *Aus alten Bücherschranken* series of folktales, on cover of March 1922 issue of *Deutsches Volkstum*.

69. *Volkswerdung durch Mythos*, p. 22.

70. Diederichs, "Eine sachliche Beschwerde" (1930), pp. 6–7; *Nicht Lesebücher*, pp. 4, 6; *Tat* 17 (1925/26): 609; undated memorandum in Diederichs Archive.

71. *SBZ*, p. 300; "40 deutsche Gelehrte, Politiker, Schriftsteller und Künstler urteilen über die Buchproduktion 'Deutsche Volkheit,'" p. 4, prospectus in Diederichs Archive.

72. *Handelswacht* 30 (1923): 375.

73. Dr. Floerke (of LMV) to Blunck, 9 Jan. 1932, Blunck Nachlass.

74. EDV prospectus in Diederichs Archive.

75. *SBZ*, p. 289.

76. *Handelswacht* 38 (1931): 22; advertisement in *Deutsches Volkstum* 26 (1924): 356.

77. JFLV prospectus in Lehmann Archive.

78. Lutzhöft, *Der nordische Gedanke*, p. 7; also Field, "Nordic Racism."

79. Lutzhöft, *Der nordische Gedanke*, pp. 25, 47.

80. See Poor, "City versus Country."

81. *LW*, pp. 341, 347, 459; *SBZ*, pp. 44, 49; *Tat* 10 (1918/19): 614, 18 (1926/27): 549, 789–90 and 19 (1927/28): 78.

82. *Tat* 20 (1928/29): 44.

83. *LW*, p. 466. See also *Tat* 14 (1922/23): 86, 19 (1927/28): 649–50 and 21 (1929/30): 3; *Die geistigen Aufgaben von heute*, pp. 4, 6; Diederichs, "Prognose literarischen Entwicklungen" (1929), p. 14.

84. *Tat* 11 (1919/20): 208; *LKD*, p. 44.

85. Blunck to HVA, 12 Jan. 1924, Blunck Nachlass; also Blunck, *Licht auf den Zügeln*, p. 371.

86. Diederichs to Blunck, undated [1926], 9 Nov. 1926, and 13 Dec. 1928, Blunck Nachlass. Apparently it was Blunck who pressed his publishers to undertake this campaign on his behalf.

87. Stapel, "Grosse Aufregung."

88. *Tat* 11 (1919/20): 207 and 15 (1923/24): 767; Diederichs, *Die geistigen Aufgaben der Zukunft* (1920), p. 13 and *Volkswerdung durch Mythos*, p. 43.

89. *LKD*, p. 269.

90. Ibid., pp. 225–26.

91. Lehmann sent copies of the books to his house's authors and requested them to write favorable reviews and to distribute the reviews to various newspapers. (Lehmann to Schemann, 10 Sept. 1930, Schemann Nachlass.)

92. Darré's comments are reprinted in *Deutschlands Erneuerung* 19 (1935): 45.

93. *Handelswacht* 35 (1928): 458.

94. Advertisement printed in F. Haiser, *Das Gastmahl des Freiherrn von Artaria* (JFLV, 1920).

95. Lehmann to Schemann, 9 Nov. 1926, Schemann Nachlass.

96. Lehmann to Günther, 11 Oct. 1920, as quoted in Sippell, *Lehmann als Zeitschriftenverleger*, p. 20.

97. *Ritter, Tod und Teufel: Der heldnische Gedanke*, published by the JFLV in 1920 and advertised as "a polemic against the thieving, sensualistic, money-enslaved spirit of our times." (Advertisement on back cover of F. Haiser, *Im Anfang war der Streit* [JFLV, 1920].)

98. *LKD*, p. 60; *Vierzig Jahre Dienst*, p. 40; *Fünfzig Jahre JFLV*, pp. 99–104; Lutzhöft, *Der nordische Gedanke*, pp. 30–31.

99. *LKD*, pp. 183–84; Lehmann to Günther, 19 Oct. 1922, as quoted in Sippell, *Lehmann als Zeitschriftenverleger*, p. 21. The publisher confided to his author: "I would have liked you to have mentioned in the foreword that the book was written at my prompting. That is perhaps a bit of publisher's vanity for which you will have to excuse me; but I consider it important to show that I am not merely a merchant, but can also be an intellectual instigator."

100. Field, "Nordic Racism," pp. 523–24.

101. Günther, "Erinnerungen an J. F. Lehmann," p. 278; Lehmann to Schemann, 31 Mar. 1927, Schemann Nachlass. *Rasse und Stil* played an important role in later Weimar cultural life, for its publication began a popular belief that racial characteristics were reflected in art. The Nazis capitalized on that belief in their attacks on modern "non-Aryan" art and architecture, attacks which they mounted with increasing intensity after Günther's book appeared in 1926. (See Lane, *Architecture and Politics*, pp. 137ff.)

102. Lehmann to Schemann, 31 Mar. 1927, Schemann Nachlass; Zmarzlick, "Social Darwinism in Germany," p. 474.

103. Lehmann to Schemann, 25 Feb. and 4 Mar. 1925, and 10 Mar. 1926, Schemann Nachlass.

104. Schemann to Lehmann, 21 Mar. 1925, Schemann Nachlass.

105. Lehmann to Schemann, 28 Jan. 1928, Schemann Nachlass.

106. Lehmann to Schemann, 6 June and 9 Oct. 1929; Schemann to Lehmann, 17 Oct. 1929, Schemann Nachlass.

107. Lehmann to Schemann, 16 Dec. 1929, 24 Jan. 1930, Schemann Nachlass.

108. Copy of Lehmann's letter to Dr. F. Thierfelder of the *Akademie zur wissenschaftliche Erforschungen und zur Pflege des Deutschtums*, 21 Aug. 1929, Schemann Nachlass.

109. Lehmann to Schemann, 16 Dec. 1929, Schemann Nachlass.

110. Schemann to Lehmann, no date [late June 1931], Schemann Nachlass.

111. Lehmann spent 11,606 marks to produce volume 1, but earned only 4,364 marks during 1927–29. Copy of Lehmann's letter to *Akademie zur wissenschaftliche Erforschungen*, 7 Sept. 1929, Schemann Nachlass.

112. Lehmann to Schemann, 4 Mar. 1925, Schemann Nachlass.

113. Advertisement in Kynast, *Apollon und Dionysius. Nordisches und unnordisches innerhalb der Religion der Griechen* (JFLV, 1927).

114. *Archiv für Rassen- und Gesellschaftsbiologie* 14, no. 1 (1922).

115. *Volk und Rasse* 1 (1926): 1–5. Other members of the editorial board included Walter Scheidt, Otto Reche, and Hans Zeiss. Lehmann admitted that he hoped the journal, like the *Archiv*, would not only provide the racial movement with a new outlet, but would also "help me disperse my books to wider circles." (Lehmann to Schemann, 4 Mar. 1925, Schemann Nachlass.)

116. *LKD*, p. 221.

117. *Volk und Rasse*, 2 (1927): 239. This collection may have been the same that Lehmann offered to Schemann in 1926.

118. Ibid., 1 (1926): 1.

119. Class, "Lehmann und der Alldeutsche Verband," p. 261.

120. GMV to Ernst, 30 Dec. 1930, Ernst Nachlass.

121. Diederichs to Pechel, 19 Feb. 1924, Pechel Nachlass.

122. *Diederichs Löwe* 4 (1932): 111. On Diederichs's concern over German minorities in Poland and elsewhere, see *Tat* 11 (1919/20): 878–79 and 14 (1922/23): 794.

123. *LKD*, pp. 260–63.

124. *Handelswacht* 35 (1928): 457.

125. On the content and significance of Grimm's novel, see Carsten, "Volk ohne Raum."

126. See "Bericht der Deutschen Allgemeinen Treuhänder . . . 30. April 1934"; Pezold, "Zum Bericht . . . 30. Juni 1934" and "Bericht über den Verlag," Pezold Nachlass; and the extensive account in Morris, "German Nationalist Fiction," chap. 5. According to Pezold, the LMV at that time "stood completely alone in the struggle against the entire *Zeitgeist*, against the book trade and the press; it was the book *Volk ohne Raum* which, singlehandedly, helped us win this struggle." ("Zum Bericht . . . 30. Juni 1934," p. 12.) By the mid-1930s, Grimm had become one of the LMV's mainstay authors: eleven of his works were on the LMV list, and most of these had reached at least ten printings, with some as many as forty printings.

127. *Tat* 21 (1929/30): 3.

128. *Stirb und Werde*, p. 9.

129. As quoted in Hamel, *Völkischer Verband*, p. 126, and *Handelswacht* 21 (1914): 167.

130. Ibid., 39 (1932): 254; "Im Kampf um das deutsche Schrifttum," 1931 flyer in Box 561, Forschungsstelle; *Handelswacht* 23 (1926): 16.

131. Advertisements on dust jacket of Münchhausen's *Deutsche Gedenk- und Weihestätten* (JFLV, 1926), and Dungen's *Adelsherrschaft im Mittelalter* (JFLV, 1927).

132. Bollmus, *Das Amt Rosenberg*, pp. 27–28.

133. See Graham, "Science and Values." Graham believes the different ideological directions of German and Russian eugenics indicates that science is not as "value free" as is commonly thought, but rather tends to take on the values of the social setting in which it is conducted. This may be so. However, the existence of a radical right-wing and a radical left-wing brand of eugenics may also indicate a basic similarity of intent between Russian communist and German neoconservative racists—namely, the (totalitarian?) longing to create not only a spiritually and socially but also a biologically "new man."

134. Advertisement on back cover of Dungen, *Adelsherrschaft im Mittelalter* (JFLV, 1927).

135. Advertisement for *Deutschlands Erneuerung* in Gottschald, *Deutsche Nameskunde* (JFLV, 1932).

136. *LKD*, p. 198.

137. See Hitler's comments in honor of Lehmann's seventieth birthday in 1934, as reprinted in *Fünfzig Jahre JFLV*, p. 171.

138. The Bauer-Fischer-Lenz book, for example, became a recognized standard text on genetics in respected medical circles. (See Bronder, *Bevor Hitler Kam*, p. 309, and Field, "Nordic Racism," p. 528.)

139. Pulzer, *Rise of Political Anti-Semitism*, p. 5.

140. *Tat* 14 (1922/23): 607ff.

141. On the anti-Semitic ideology and activities of the DHV, see Hamel, *Völkischer Verband*, pp. 14–68; Pulzer, *Rise of Political Anti-Semitism*, pp. 219–21; and Mosse, *Crisis of German Ideology*, pp. 258–61.

142. *Handelswacht* 35 (1928): 117.

143. Copy of Christian Winter's letter of 21 July 1931 to E. Maril, in DHV Mappe, Forschungsstelle; Zimmermann, "Rudolf Mosse gegen DHV," p. 187.

144. Habermann, "DHV in Kampfe," p. 30, DHV Archive; Pezold, "Zum Bericht der Deutschen Allgemeinen Treuhänder . . . 30 Juni 1934," Pezold Nachlass; and Pezold's comments

in *Der Spiegel*, 25. Dec. 1950, p. 37. Stapel echoed these sentiments in another book he published with the HVA, *Die literarische Vorherrschaft der Juden* (1937). Morris's "German Nationalist Fiction" should be consulted on the anti-Semitic philosophy and publications of Stapel, the HVA, and the LMV.

145. See for example his letter to M. Moritz [pseudonym of Gottfried Zarnow], 9 Feb. 1931, Zarnow Nachlass. Zarnow had engaged a Jewish defense attorney for a libel suit, and Lehmann feared it would not only bring unfavorable publicity to the JFLV, but might cause the loss of the Nazis and other devoted readers of the house's anti-Semitic materials.

146. *LKD*, pp. 149, 163, 182, 244; *Deutschlands Erneuerung* 7 (1920): 454; Lehmann to Schemann, 9 Oct. 1929, Schemann Nachlass.

147. *LKD*, pp. 244, 182.

148. Ibid., pp. 243–44.

CHAPTER 8

1. *LKD*, p. 181.

2. *Tat* 10 (1918/19): 855.

3. *LW*, pp. 329, 340; *Tat* 10 (1918/19): 684, 855–57 and 14 (1922/23): 85; Diederichs, "Symbolik" (1924), p. 3; *Die geistigen Aufgaben von heute*, p. 67.

4. Diederichs, *Die geistigen Aufgaben der Zukunft* (1920), p. 10.

5. *PdG*, p. 1; *Tat* 10 (1918/19): 686–87, 956, 15 (1928/29): 475 and 17 (1925/26): 205; Diederichs, *Die geistigen Aufgaben der Zukunft* (1920), p. 12; *Wille und Gestaltung*, pp. 54–55; *Das deutsche Gesicht*, pp. 14–15.

6. *Tat* 18 (1926/27): 790; *Volkswerdung durch Mythos*, p. 11; Diederichs, "Geistige Krisis und Buch" (1929), p. 211; Diederichs to Blunck, 9 Oct. 1926, Blunck Nachlass.

7. Struve, *Elites Against Democracy*, p. 368 n. 50.

8. *LW*, p. 35.

9. Diederichs, "Die Lauensteiner Jubilatenwoche" (1923), p. 705; "Aufruf," 1923 flyer in Diederichs Archive.

10. Diederichs to H. Mutzenbecher, 17 Mar. 1919, and Diederichs to K. Sprengel, 15 Feb. 1923, Stadtbibliothek Dortmund; Diederichs to Dr. Fischer, Nov. 1922, and Driesmans to Diederichs, 14 May 1923, Diederichs Archive.

11. Advertisement for *Deutschlands Erneuerung* in Gottschald, *Deutsche Nameskunde* (JFLV, 1932); *LW*, p. 348; *Tat* 17 (1925/26): 609; *Volkswerdung durch Mythos*, pp. 12–13.

12. See Tönnies, *Gemeinschaft und Gesellschaft*. On the social and psychological origins and antimodern character of Tönnies's sociological theories, see Mitzman, "Tönnies and German Society," and *Sociology and Estrangement*, pp. 3–131.

13. *LW*, pp. 324–25, 354; *Tat* 10 (1918/19): 683, 877 and 19 (1927/28): 649–53; Diederichs, *Die geistigen Aufgaben der Zukunft* (1920), p. 7; *Wille und Gestaltung*, pp. 5–6; *Die Tätigkeit des Verlages 1914–1924*, Introduction; Diederichs as quoted in Becker, "Ein deutscher Verleger."

14. See the advertisement for this book in F. Haiser, *Freimaurer und Gegenmaurer im Kampf um die Weltherrschaft* (JFLV, 1924).

15. See Hock, *Deutscher Antikapitalismus*.

16. *LW*, pp. 351–55, 434; *Tat* 10 (1918/19): 77, 875, 11 (1919/20): 267, 12 (1920/21): 476 and 15 (1923/24): 210; Diederichs, *Die geistigen Aufgaben der Zukunft* (1920), pp. 9, 13; Diederichs, "Prognosse literarischen Entwicklungen" (1929), p. 15 and "Geistige Krisis und Buch" (1929), p. 210.

17. *Tat* 11 (1919/20): 70–71, 233.

18. Ibid., 10 (1918/19): 724, 773–74, 857; Diederichs, *Die geistigen Aufgaben der Zukunft* (1920), pp. 10–13.

19. See *Tat* 10 (1918/19): 721, 725.

20. Advertisement for *Psychologie des Sozialismus* in *Nicht Lesebücher*, p. 60.

21. For a brief discussion of Winnig's ideology, see McRandle, *Track of the Wolf*, pp. 95–100.

22. Lehmann to Winnig, 20 Nov. and 21 Dec. 1926, Lehmann Archive.

23. *LW*, p. 434; *Tat* 10 (1918/19): 725, 875, 956, 11 (1919/20): 70, 233, 267, 269, 294, 615 and 14 (1922/23): 237.

24. *LW*, pp. 351–52, 355, 434; *Tat* 10 (1918/19): 84, 855–57, 12 (1920/21): 534; Diederichs to E. Lissauer, 24 Apr. 1919, Diederichs Archive.

25. See Hoepke, *Deutsche Rechte und der italienische Faschismus*, and Petersen, "Italienische Faschismus aus Sicht der Weimarer Republik."

26. In 1923 Diederichs believed he had met his "Mussolini," a radical right-wing Social Democrat. The publisher convinced him to go to the Ruhr to speak to workers there on the need for a strong sense of national solidarity. (Diederichs to E. Schmitt, 27 Feb. 1923, Diederichs Archive.)

27. *Tat* 18 (1926/27): 789; Diederichs to E. Schmitt, 27 Jan. 1925, Diederichs Archive. For further evidence that Diederichs rejected the notion of a führer as the solution to Germany's crisis, see *Tat* 19 (1927/28): 653, and *Wille und Gestaltung*, p. 4.

28. *LKD*, pp. 231, 245.

29. Hoepke, *Deutsche Rechte und der italienische Faschismus*, pp. 31ff.

30. Stapel, "The Coming Conservative Revolution," p. 172.

31. Just how close is not altogether clear. While Lehmann, as detailed above in pp. 157–58, was active in many of the Munich organizations which contained early Nazis and which were direct forerunners of the Nazi party, there is some question as to whether he ever actually joined the party at this time. Maser (*Frühgeschichte der NSDAP*, p. 177) claims Lehmann did enroll and received a membership number of 878. The publisher's somewhat reserved stance during the 1923 beer hall putsch casts some doubt on his association with the Nazi party at the time, however. Most importantly, the biographical sketch *LKD*, published by Lehmann's widow in 1935, makes no mention of Lehmann's membership in the party in the early 1920s; on the contrary, Lehmann's widow rather apologetically explains that Lehmann, although formally a member of the *Deutschnationale Volkspartei* in the 1920s, "sympathized" with and often "helped" the NSDAP (*LKD*, p. 70).

32. *LKD*, pp. 230–31.

33. Ibid., pp. 265–66.

34. Lehmann, "Warum wählt das nationale Deutschland im zweiten Wahlgang Adolf Hitler?" reprinted in ibid., pp. 267–73.

35. See Morris, "German Nationalist Fiction," chap. 5.

36. Kessler, *Stapel*, p. 126.

37. Sätze 3 & 4 of "Sechs Sätze zur Entwicklung des Verlagsunternehmungen des D.H.V. (18 June 1931)," Pezold Nachlass. Also discussed in Kessler, *Stapel*, pp. 126ff.

38. Gerhard, *Um Reiches Zukunft*, p. 209.

39. Hitler's copy of Stapel's autographed book can be found in Hitler Library collection, Rare Books Division, Library of Congress.

40. *Tat* 10 (1918/19): 642–46, 953.

41. See Braatz, "Two Neo-Conservative Myths," and Neurohr, *Der Mythos vom Dritten Reich*.

42. Copy of DHV *Juristische Abteilung* circular "Informationsrundschreiben über den politischen Sensationsprozess um den Buchtitel *Das dritte Reich*" (4 March 1931), in DHV Mappe, Forschungsstelle.

43. Ibid.
44. Ibid.
45. *LKD*, pp. 79–80.
46. Reprinted in *Fünfzig Jahre JFLV*, p. 171.
47. Ibid., pp. 155ff.
48. Morris, "German Nationalist Fiction," chap. 5.
49. Ibid., and Flemmer, *Verlage in Bayern*, p. 193.
50. See Wulf, *Literatur und Dichtung im Dritten Reich*, p. 58, and Kessler, *Stapel*, pp. 238ff.
51. Sieh, *Hamburger Nationalistenklub*, p. 37 n. 41. On the activities of Habermann and Günther, see Hoffmann, *Widerstand, Staatsstreich, Attentat*.
52. "HAVA Auseinandersetzung" file (1949), in Stapel Nachlass.
53. Atzenbeck, "Diederichs' Werk und Vermächtnis," pp. 128–29.

CHAPTER 9

1. See for example Fleischer, *Die Wichtigkeit des Buchhandels*, pp. 30–31, and Thomas Mann's "Festrede" for the 100th anniversary of the Reclam Verlag in 1928, as quoted in Widmann, *Der deutsche Buchhandel*, 1:251.
2. Fleischer, *Wichtigkeit des Buchhandels*.
3. Friedrich Gogarten, in *Im Zeichen des Löwen*, p. 161. For a similar comment by Gertrud le Fort, see *SBZ*, p. 232.
4. Lazarsfeld & Merton, "Mass Communication," p. 116.
5. Lazarsfeld & Menzel, "Mass Media and Personal Influence," p. 95; Katz, "Diffusion of New Ideas," pp. 77, 83; Katz & Lazarsfeld, *Personal Influence*, pp. 31–32.
6. See Maser's *Hitler's Mein Kampf*, p. 7; Richards, *The German Bestseller*, pp. 55ff.
7. The few titles which could boast sales of approximately 500,000 or more in twentieth-century Germany included (besides *Mein Kampf*): *Im Westen Nichts Neues, Der Wehrwolf, Volk ohne Raum*, the virulently anti-Semitic novel *Die Sünde wider das Blut* by A. Dinter (who also published works with the HVA), and W. Flex's war novel *Ein Wanderer zwischen Zwei Welten*. Dinter's and Flex's novels both sold more than 680,000 copies.
8. See Ward, *Book Production, Fiction, and German Reading Public*; Fullerton, "German Book Markets"; and Schenda, *Volk ohne Buch*. On right-wing fiction in the twentieth century, see Morris, "German Nationalist Fiction."
9. See Monaco, *Cinema and Society*, pp. 115–46.
10. Hitler may well have educated himself on racial and military matters by means of the publications of the JFLV and the HVA. Albert Krebs, who worked in the DHV and who was a member of the Nazi party, asserted that "from various conversations with Hitler, I discovered that the publishing activity of the DHV made a deep impression on him. The importance of that activity he saw, above all, as the creation of a cultural and political position of strength over against the huge influence which the Jews exercised over the German press during the Weimar era. Only in the fields of political and military literature, however, was Hitler actually acquainted with specific books produced by the DHV's publishing firms." (Krebs, *Tendenzen und Gestalten*, p. 147.) In Hitler's personal library, now located in the Library of Congress, can be found some seven books which had been published by the HVA prior to 1933; four of these deal specifically with military matters and World War I. Hitler's library also contains Beenken's *Was Wir verloren haben*, five books issued by the EDV (including Dwinger's two war novels), and fifty-seven pre-1933 titles from the J. F. Lehmanns Verlag, twenty of which deal with race and racial hygiene and seventeen of which treat the war and military affairs. It is true that the vast majority of Hitler's books were neither

acquired nor read by him; they were unsolicited gifts sent to the Nazi party leader (later Head of State) by authors and publishers. One of the GSV books, for example, had been sent to Hitler by Heinrich Stalling, Jr. who had inscribed a personal dedication to Hitler. Of the fifty-seven JFLV books in the Hitler library, forty-seven were sent by Lehmann personally and contain dedications to Hitler such as "Dedicated to Herr Hitler as thanks for his work in enlightening the German *Volk*," or "To the prophet of the Third Reich."

11. Berg, "Das Mäzenatentum," p. 145.

12. As quoted in Menz, *Der deutsche Buchhandel* (2nd ed.), p. 28.

13. Karl Scheffler, "Berufsidealismus," in *Navigarre Necesse Est: Eine Festgabe zum 50. Geburtstages von Anton Kippenberg* (Leipzig, 1924), as quoted in de Mendelssohn, *S. Fischer*, p. 47.

14. Fischer believed that "nurturing literary art . . . is one of the most personal duties of a publisher. In this area it is a matter of recognizing and promoting latent cultural forces. Fostering talent . . . requires the greatest personal activity on the part of the publisher and the marshaling of all his abilities. . . . The publisher, as a man who is prompted to place his money and his efforts behind nonmaterial values, longs to be a discoverer: he wants to help bring new values to light and, as an organizational entreprenuer, wants to create new values." (*S. Fischer Verlag Almanach*, p. 24.)

15. Karl Scheffler, *Die fetten und die mageren Jahre* (Munich, 1946), as quoted in Hiller, *Sozialgeschichte von Buch*, p. 7.

16. On the nature of patronage, see Hauser, *Sozialgeschichte der Kunst*; Haskell, "Patronage"; Laurenson & Swingewood, *Sociology of Literature*, pp. 91–141; and Collins, *Authorship in the Days of Johnson* and *The Profession of Letters*.

17. *Deutschlands Erneuerung* 7 (1920): 457.

18. *SBZ*, p. 41.

19. See Göpfert, "Bemerkungen über Buchhändler zur Zeit der Aufklärung"; Möller, *Aufklärung in Preussen*; and Ost, *Nicolais Allgemeine Deutsche Bibliothek*.

20. Schulze, *Buchhandel und geistigen Strömungen*; Hermann, "Die Buchstadt Leipzig"; Läuter, "Anfänge sozialistischen Verlagstätigkeit."

21. Johann, *Buchverlage des Naturalismus*; de Mendelssohn, *S. Fischer*; Grothe, "Neue Rundschau des Verlages S. Fischer"; Redlich, "German Literary Expressionism"; and Göpfert, "Der expressionistische Verlag."

22. Göbel, "Ernst Rowohlt Verlag," and "Kurt Wolff Verlag." Wolff's comment was made in his letter of 29 March 1921 to Rene Schickele, in *Briefwechsel eines Verleger*.

23. The first copyright law covering the entire Deutscher Bund was passed in November 1837. Revisions of the law were made after unification, in April 1871 and January 1876. Only with the 1886 Universal Copyright Convention of Berne, however, was literary piracy finally eliminated in Europe. See Goldfriedrich, *Geschichte des Deutschen Buchhandels*, 4:166–84, 453–83; Gieske, *Entwicklung des deutschen Urheberrechts*; and Bappert, *Wege zum Urheberrecht*.

24. Pascal, *From Naturalism to Expressionism*, p. 279; also Fullerton, "German Book Markets," pp. 322ff.

25. Eckertz in *Schriftsteller, Verleger, Publikum*, p. 26.

26. See Kron, *Schriftsteller und Schriftstellerverbände*.

27. Ludwig Havatny, "Der Kampf der Erfolg," in *Schriftsteller, Verleger, Publikum*, p. 72; Meyer-Dohm, *Buchhandel als kulturwirtschaftliche Aufgabe*, p. 27.

28. On the "culture industry" and the publisher's role within it, see Menz, *Kulturwirtschaft*; Meyer-Dohm, "Wissenschaftliche Literatur als Marktobjekt"; and Paul Ernst's comments in *Schriftsteller, Verleger, Publikum*, pp. 32–33.

Bibliography

I. PRIMARY SOURCES

A. Unpublished Archival Materials
  Bayreuth
    Richard Wagner Gedenkstätte der Stadt Bayreuth
    Houston Stuart Chamberlain Nachlass
  Burg Ludwigstein
    Archiv der Deutschen Jugendbewegung
    EDV Mappe
    Gustav Wyneken Nachlass
  Coblenz
    Bundesarchiv
    Albert Krebs Nachlass
    Rudolf Pechel Nachlass
    Gottfried Traub Nachlass
    Hermann Ullmann Nachlass
    Gottfried Zarnow [M. E. Moritz] Nachlass
  Cologne
    Eugen Diederichs Verlag Archive
  Dortmund
    Stadt- und Landesbibliothek
    Wilhelm Deimann Nachlass
    Handschriftenabteilung
  Freiburg im Breisgau
    Universitätsbibliothek
    Karl Ludwig Schemann Nachlass
  Hamburg
    Deutscher Handels- und Industrieangestellten-Verbandes (DHV) Archive
    Forschungsstelle für die Geschichte des Nationalsozialismus in Hamburg
    DHV Diller 11/22
    DHV Mappe
    Box 561: DHV
  Hamburg-Sülldorf
    Wilhelm Stapel Nachlass (in possession of Pastor Hennig Stapel)
  Karlsruhe
    Badische Landesbibliothek
    Leopold Ziegler Nachlass

Kiel
  Schleswig-Holsteinische Landesbibliothek
    Hans F. Blunck Nachlass
    Gustav Frenssen Nachlass
    Ferdinand Tönnies Nachlass
Marbach am Neckar
  Deutsches Literaturarchiv und Schiller Nationalmuseum
    Paul Ernst Nachlass
    Wilhelm Hertz Nachlass
    Hermann Hesse Nachlass
    Gustav Pezold/Langen-Müller Verlag Nachlass
Marburg
  Universitätsbibliothek
    Paul Natorp Nachlass
Merseburg
  Deutsches Zentralarchiv, Historische Abteilung II
    Max Weber Nachlass
Munich
  Bayerische Staatsbibliothek
    Otto Crusius Nachlass
    G. Christian Petzet Nachlass
  J. F. Lehmanns Verlag Archive
Washington, D.C.
  Library of Congress, Rare Book Division
    Hitler Library
B. Interviews
  Niels Diederichs (Cologne, November 1972)
  Ulf Diederichs (Cologne, 1972–73)
  Hermann Schumacher (Hamburg, May 1976)
  Otto Spatz (Munich, February 1973)
  Hennig Stapel (Hamburg, April 1973)
C. Catalogs and Yearbooks of the Neoconservative Houses
  Bericht und Abrechnung des D. H. V. für die Geschäftsjahre 1909 und 1910. Hamburg: 1911.
  D. H. V. Rechenschaftsbericht für 1929. Hamburg: Hanseatische Verlagsanstalt, 1930.
  D. H. V. Rechenschaftsbericht für 1930. Hamburg: Hanseatische Verlagsanstalt, 1931.
  D. H. V. Rechenschaftsbericht für 1931. Hamburg: Hanseatische Verlagsanstalt, 1932.
  Das deutsche Gesicht: Ein Weg zur Zukunft. Zum XXX. Jahr des Verlages. Jena: Eugen Diederichs Verlag, 1926.
  Der Verlag Eugen Diederichs in Jena. Jena: Eugen Diederichs Verlag, 1904.
  Die geistigen Aufgaben von heute, morgen und übermorgen: Ein Verlagsverzeichnis in sechs Gruppen. Jena: Eugen Diederichs Verlag, 1927.
  Die Kulturbewegung Deutschlands im Jahre 1913. Jena: Eugen Diederichs Verlag, 1913.
  Die Neuerscheinungen des Verlages im Jahre 1912. Jena: Eugen Diederichs Verlag, 1912.
  Die Tätigkeit des Verlages während des letzten Jahrzehnts, 1914–1924. Jena: Eugen Diederichs Verlag, 1924.
  Ein deutscher Verlag: Heinrich Beenken Verlag 1888–1938. Edited by Ernst H. Lehmann. Berlin: Heinrich Beenken Verlag, 1938.
  Einhundertfünfzig Jahre Verlag Gerhard Stalling 1789–1939. Edited by Eugen Roth. Oldenburg: Gerhard Stalling Verlag, 1939.
  175 Jahre Stalling: Eine Erinnerungsschrift. Oldenburg: Gerhard Stalling Verlag, 1965.

Eugen Diederichs, Verleger, Buchgestalter, Publizist: Katalog zur Ausstellung in der Stadtbücherei im Wilhelmpalais 26. April—12. Mai 1968. Stuttgart, 1968.
Fünfundsiebzig Jahre J. F. Lehmanns Verlag. Munich: J. F. Lehmanns Verlag, 1965.
Fünfzig Jahre J. F. Lehmanns Verlag 1890–1940. Munich: J. F. Lehmanns Verlag, 1940.
Heinrich Stalling, Ein deutscher Verleger: Zum 70. Geburtstag des Geheimen Kommerzierrats Dr. med. h. c. Heinrich Stalling. Oldenburg: Gerhard Stalling Verlag, 1935.
Im Memoriam: Eugen Diederichs. Jena: Privatdruck, 1930.
Im Zeichen des Löwen: Für Eugen Diederichs LX. Jahr am XXII. Juni MCMXXVII. Jena: Privatdruck, 1927.
Jahrbuch für deutschnationale Handlungsgehilfen. Hamburg: Hanseatische Verlagsanstalt, 1921.
Jena und Weimar: Ein Almanach des Verlages Eugen Diederichs in Jena. Jena: Eugen Diederichs Verlag, 1908.
Neuerscheinungen Politik/Antike/Renaissance: Bücher-Verzeichnis. Jena: Eugen Diederichs Verlag, 1911.
Nicht Lesebücher sondern Lebensbücher. Jena: Eugen Diederichs Verlag, 1925.
60 Jahre Eugen Diederichs Verlag: Ein Almanach. Düsseldorf: Eugen Diederichs Verlag, 1956.
Stirb und Werde: Ein Arbeitsbericht über 30 jährigen Verlagstätigkeit auf religiösen Gebiete 1899–1929. Jena: Eugen Diederichs Verlag, 1929.
Verlagsverzeichnis 1944. Hamburg: Hanseatische Verlagsanstalt, 1944.
Vierzig Jahre Dienst am Deutschtum 1890–1930. Munich: J. F. Lehmanns Verlag, 1930.
Volkswerdung durch Mythos und Geschichte: Ein Verlagsverzeichnis. Jena: Eugen Diederichs Verlag, 1928.
Von der Wissenschaft zur Lebensgestaltung: Bücher zur Lebensdeutung/Naturwissenschaften/ Geschichte/Sozialen Fragen/Volkserziehung/Humanität. Jena: Eugen Diederichs Verlag, 1910.
Wege zu deutscher Kultur: Eine Einführung in die Bücher des Verlages. Jena: Eugen Diederichs Verlag, 1908.
Wille und Gestaltung: Ein Almanach zur 25. jährigen Bestehen des Verlages. Jena: Eugen Diederichs Verlag, 1921.
Zum 25. jährigen Gründungstag von J. F. Lehmanns Verlag. Munich: J. F. Lehmanns Verlag, 1915.
Zu neuer Renaissance: Ein Sendschreiben. Leipzig: Eugen Diederichs Verlag, 1900.
Zur Erhöhung des Lebensgefühls: Bücher zu den modernen literarischen Bewegung. Jena: Eugen Diederichs Verlag, 1910.
Zur Kultur der Seele 1896–1906: Verlagsbericht. Jena: Eugen Diederichs Verlag, 1906.
Zur Neuorientierung der deutschen Kultur nach dem Kriege: Richtlinien in Gestalt eines Bücher-Verzeichnisses. Jena: Eugen Diederichs Verlag, 1916.
D. Journals and Newspapers of the Neoconservative Houses
Archiv für Rassen- und Gesellschaftsbiologie
Bühne und Welt
Das deutsche Gesicht. Vierteljahresberichte aus dem Verlage Eugen Diederichs in Jena
Deutsche Handelswacht
Deutsches Volkstum
Deutschlands Erneuerung
Diederichs Löwe
Der Hansische Bücherbote
Herdefeuer
Der Ochs von Lauenstein

Die Tat
Der Türmer
Volk und Rasse
Der Zopfabschneider
E. Writings of the Neoconservative Publishers
Beenken, Heinrich, ed. *Was wir verloren haben.* Berlin, 1920.
―――. *Land in Ketten: Geraubtes deutsches Land.* Berlin, 1932.
Diederichs, Eugen. "Erzieht der Buchhandel Charaktere?" *Unser Blatt* 21 (1894):
175–76.
―――. "Uber die Hebung des Standesbewusstseins." *Unser Blatt* 24 (1894): 199–201.
―――. "Einigkeit und Recht und Freiheit." *Unser Blatt* 17 (1895): 133–36.
―――. "Auf welchem Wege ist eine wirtschaftliche Besserung zu erreichen?" *Unser
Blatt* 22 (1895): 172–74.
―――. "Zum 1. April." *Unser Blatt* 6 (1896): 45–46.
―――. "In Canossa." *Naumburger Kreisblatt,* 48 no. 138 (14 June 1896).
―――. "Am Strand." *Naumburger Kreisblatt,* 48 no. 179 (1 Aug. 1896).
―――. "Bei den Meergöttern Böcklins." *Naumburger Kreisblatt,* 48 no. 209 (5 Sept.
1896).
―――. "In der Republik von San Marino." *Naumburger Kreisblatt,* 48 no. 281 (29 Nov.
1896).
―――. "Rom." *Naumburger Kreisblatt,* 49 no. 80 (4 Apr. 1897).
―――. "Sils-Maria und Friedrich Nietzsche." *Berliner Tageblatt,* 8 Aug. 1908.
―――. "Zur Psychologie des Sortiments." *Börsenblatt für den deutschen Buchhandel* 76
(1909): 10971–73.
―――. "Das Elend der Kritik." *Der Bücherwurm* 1 (1910): 4–6.
―――. "Weltausstellung im Lichte des Buchhandels." *Allgemeine Buchhändlerzeitung* 17
(17 Nov. 1910): 631–32.
―――. "Der Einzelne und der Staat." *Verlagsprospekt für "Politische Bibliothek."* Jena,
1911.
―――. "Zum Kampf um die Fraktur." *Börsenblatt für den deutschen Buchhandel* 78
(1911): 12260–62.
―――. "Sollen wir die Fraktur abschaffen?" *Jahrbuch des deutschen Werkbundes.* Jena,
1912.
―――. "Verlegerische Aufgaben." *Der Volkserzieher* 16 (1912): 193–94.
―――. "Brief des Verlegers." *Die Aktion* 3 (1913): 1160–62.
―――. "Jugendentwicklung oder Jugendkultur? Freundesworte zu 'Freideutsche
Jugend: Festschrift zur Jahrhundertfeier auf dem Hohen Meissner' [1913]." In
Grundschriften der deutschen Jugendbewegung, edited by Werner Kindt, pp. 94–96.
Düsseldorf, 1963.
―――. "Über die Notwendigkeit akademischer Vorbildung." *Studentische Monatshefte
vom Oberrhein,* no. 7 (1913): 10–12.
―――. "Buchhändler und Idealismus." In *Festbuch zur Pfingsttagung deutscher
Buchhandlungsgehilfen auf der BUGRA, 1914 in Leipzig,* pp. 108–10. Leipzig, 1914.
―――. "Der Buchhändler Beruf und die Fragen der modernen Kulturentwicklung."
In *Pfingsttagung deutscher Buchhandlungsgehilfen: Zwei Vorträge,* pp. 4–12. Berlin, 1914.
―――. "Gibt es Bibliophilen?" *Deutscher Bibliophilen-Kalendar, 1914,* pp. 66–69.
―――. "Die Abtrünnigen?" *Börsenblatt für den deutschen Buchhandel* 82 (1915): 42–44.
―――. "Krieg und Ewigkeitsglaube." *Christliche Welt* 29 (Aug. 1915).
―――. *Die geistigen Aufgaben der Zukunft: Eine Ansprache an die Leipziger Buchhand-
lungsgehilfen.* Leipzig, 1920.

————. "Über die Zukunft des deutschen Buches." *Deutsche Presse* 9 (9 Dec. 1921): 3.

————. "Es muss anders werden." *Börsenblatt für den deutschen Buchhandel* 89 (1922): 576–78.

————. "Die Lauensteiner Zusammenkunft." *Börsenblatt für den deutschen Buchhandel* 89 (1922): 1361–63, 1397–1409.

————. "Das Echo der Lauensteiner Tagung." *Börsenblatt für den deutschen Buchhandel* 89 (1922): 1550–52.

————. "Lauensteiner Winterlager." *Börsenblatt für den deutschen Buchhandel* 90 (1923): 118–20.

————. "Kalkulations- und Honorarfragen im Verlag." *Börsenblatt für den deutschen Buchhandel* 90 (1923): 180–82.

————. "Sommerakademien für den Jungbuchhandel." *Börsenblatt für den deutschen Buchhandel* 90 (1923): 332–33.

————. "Die Launesteiner Jubilatenwoche." *Börsenblatt für den deutschen Buchhandel* 90 (1923): 701–5.

————. "Die Sommerakademien des Jungbuchhandels." *Börsenblatt für den deutschen Buchhandel* 90 (1923): 1282–85.

————. "Berufslehre." *Börsenblatt für den deutschen Buchhandel* 90 (1923): 7227–28.

————. "Am Scheideweg." *Deutsche Allgemeine Zeitung*, 25 Dec. 1923.

————. "Die geistige Krisis des Buches." *Magdeburger Zeitung*, 1 July 1924.

————. "Symbolik." *Der Zopfabschneider* 3 (1924): 1–3.

————. "Die Idee 'Lauenstein.'" *Der Zopfabschneider* 5 (1924): 21–24.

————. "Zur inneren Krise aller Buchhändlerorganisationen." *Der Zopfabschneider* 5 (1924): 34–36.

————. "Vor dreissig Jahren." In *Festschrift E. R. Weiss*, pp. 15–21. Leipzig, 1925.

————. "Der schlafende Verlag." *Börsenblatt für den deutschen Buchhandel* 92 (1925): 4563–65.

————. "Sommerakademien für den Jungbuchhandel 1925." *Börsenblatt für den deutschen Buchhandel* 92 (1925): 4720–22.

————. "Vorschlag zur Gründung eines 'Kulturamtes' unter dem Protektorat des Börsenvereins." *Börsenblatt für den deutschen Buchhandel* 92 (1925): 9735–37.

————. "Eindrücke von Dreissigacker." *Börsenblatt für den deutschen Buchhandel* 92 (1925): 11451–52.

————. "Zur wirtschaftlichen Notlage." *Börsenblatt für den deutschen Buchhandel* 92 (1925): 19474–75.

————. "Über die Zukunft des deutschen Buches." *Der Ochs von Lauenstein* 1 (1925): 2–4.

————. "Über Sommerakademien für den Buchhandel." *Der Ochs von Lauenstein* 1 (1925): 11–14.

————. "Jungbuchhandel und Sommerakademie." *Der Ochs von Lauenstein* 3/4 (1925): 1–6.

————. "Schlusswort." *Der Ochs von Lauenstein* 3/4 (1925): 80–87.

————. "Zukunftsgedanken eines Kulturverlegers über deutsche Geistigkeit." *Neue Freie Presse* (Vienna), 3 Oct. 1926.

————. "Bericht über die 5. Lauensteiner Tagung." *Börsenblatt für den deutschen Buchhandel* 93 (1926): 639–40.

————. "Die Fortbildungsfrage im Jungbuchhandel." *Börsenblatt für den deutschen Buchhandel* 93 (1926): 746–47.

————. "Gegenwart und Zukunft: Ein Schlusswort zur wirtschaftlichen Lage." *Der Ochs von Lauenstein* 5 (1926): 29–32.

————. "Vom Verlegerberuf." *Das deutsche Gesicht* 1 (1926): 4–8.

———. "Ein deutscher Verleger: Werdegang und Bekenntnis." *Frankfurter Zeitung*, 24 Oct. 1927.

———. "Der Aufmarsch der Interessenverbände für die 50 jährige Schutzfrist." *Börsenblatt für den deutschen Buchhandel* 94 (1927): 242–43.

———. "Organische Gesetze geistiger Lebens und die Schutzfrist." *Börsenblatt für den deutschen Buchhandel* 94 (1927): 269–72.

———. "Gedanken zur Buchkrisis." *Der Ochs von Lauenstein* 7 (1927): 8–10.

———. "Die heutige geistige Krisis und das Buch." *Börsenblatt für den deutschen Buchhandel* 96 (1929): 209–12.

———. "Der Tag des Buches als Kampftag gegen Entseelung." *Börsenblatt für den deutschen Buchhandel* 96 (1929): 299.

———. "Prognose der literarischen Entwicklungen." *Diederichs Löwe* 1 (1929): 13–15.

———. "Eine sachliche Beschwerde an die geistige Schicht des deutschen Volkes." *Kölner Universitäts-Zeitung* 13 no. 4 (1930): 6–7.

———. *Leben und Werk: Ausgewählte Briefe und Aufzeichnungen.* Edited by Lulu von Strauss und Torney-Diederichs. Jena, 1936.

———. *Aus meinem Leben.* Jena, 1938.

———. *Selbstzeugnisse und Briefe von Zeitgenossen.* Edited by Ulf Diederichs. Düsseldorf, 1967.

Lehmann, Julius F., ed. *Deutschlands Zukunft bei einem guten und bei einem schlechten Frieden.* Munich, 1917.

———. "Berechnung in fremder Valuta." *Börsenblatt für den deutschen Buchhandel* 89 (1922): 1104.

———. *Verleger J. F. Lehmann: Ein Leben im Kampf für Deutschland.* Edited by Melanie Lehmann. Munich, 1935.

Pezold, Gustav. "Aus 10 jähriger Nachkriegssortimentererfahrungen und neueren Verlagsarbeit." In *Buch und Beruf im neuen Staat: Elf Reden gehalten auf einem Jungbuchhändlertreffen,* edited by Karl H. Bischoff, pp. 47–60. Bremen, 1933.

Stapel, Wilhelm. "Die grosse Aufregung. Was geht der Albert Langen Verlag die deutschnationalen Handlungsgehilfen an?" *Deutsche Allgemeine Zeitung* no. 301 (5 July 1931).

———. "Literarische Diktatur des DHV?" *Deutsche Handelswacht* 38 (1931): 217–19.

———. "The Coming Conservative Revolution." *The English Review* 53 (1931): 166–72.

F. Memoirs, Correspondence, and Documents

Blüher, Hans. *Werke und Tage: Geschichte eines Denkers.* Munich, 1953.

Blunck, Hans F. *Licht auf den Zügeln: Lebensbericht, Band 1.* Mannheim, 1953.

Chamberlain, Houston Stuart. *Briefe.* 2 vols. Munich, 1918.

Class, Heinrich. *Wider den Strom.* Leipzig, 1932.

Deuerlein, Ernst, ed. *Der Hitler-Putsch: Bayerische Dokumente zum 8./9. November 1923.* Stuttgart, 1962.

Heuss, Theodor. *Erinnerungen 1905–1933.* Tübingen, 1963.

Hitler, Adolf. *Mein Kampf.* Translated by Ralph Mannheim. Boston, 1943.

Holm, Korfiz. *ich-kleingeschrieben: Heitere Erlebnisse eines Verlegers.* Munich, 1932.

Kindt, Werner, ed. *Grundschriften der deutschen Jugendbewegung.* Düsseldorf, 1963.

———, ed. *Die Wandervogelzeit: Quellenschriften zur deutschen Jugendbewegung, 1896–1919.* Cologne & Düsseldorf, 1968.

Krebs, Albert. *Tendenzen und Gestalten der NSDAP: Erinnerungen an die Frühzeit der Partei.* Stuttgart, 1959.

Widmann, Hans, ed. *Der deutsche Buchhandel in Urkunden und Quellen.* 2 vols. Hamburg, 1965.

Wolff, Kurt. *Briefwechsel eines Verlegers 1911–1963*. Edited by Bernhard Zeller and E. Otten. Frankfurt, 1966.

G. Other Contemporary Literature

Bechly, Hans. *Die Deutschnationale Handlungsgehilfenbewegung und die politische Parteien.* Hamburg, 1911.

Bernstein, Eduard. *Die Voraussetzungen des Sozialismus und die Aufgaben der Sozial-demokratie.* Reinbeck, 1969.

Bischoff, Diedrich. *Deutsche Gesinnung.* Jena, 1914.

Borchardt, Rudolf. *Die deutsche Literatur im Kampf um Ihr Recht.* Munich, 1931.

Freyer, Hans. *Revolution von Rechts.* Jena, 1931.

Habermann, Max. *Die Erziehung zum deutschen Menschen.* Hamburg, 1924.

Haeckel, Ernst. *Monism as Connecting Religion and Science.* Translated by J. Gilchrist. London, 1894.

Lehmann, Friedrich. *Wir von der Infanterie.* Munich, 1929.

Muthesius, Hermann. *Der Werkbund: Arbeit und Zukunft.* Jena, 1914.

Natorp, Paul. *Deutscher Weltberuf.* Jena, 1918.

Nietzsche, Friedrich. *Beyond Good and Evil.* Translated by M. Cowan. Chicago, 1955.

————. *Unzeitgemässe Betrachtungen, Erstes Stück: David Strauss, der Bekenner und der Schrifsteller.* Munich, 1964.

————. *The Will to Power.* Translated and edited by Walter Kaufmann. New York, 1967.

Richter, Werner. "Die literarische Diktatur des Deutschnationalen Handlungsgehilfen-Verbandes." *Berliner Tageblatt*, 19 June 1931.

S. Fischer Verlag Almanach, Das 25. Jahr. Berlin, 1911.

Schaack, Wilhelm. *Wie und was wir geworden sind: Die deutschnationale Handlungsgehil-fenbewegung, Ihr Werdegang.* Hamburg, 1903.

Schriftsteller, Verleger, und Publikum, Eine Rundfrage: Zehnjahreskatalog Georg Müller Verlag. Munich, 1913.

Schuron, Hermann. *Die Deutschnationaler Handlungsgehilfen-Verband zu Hamburg: Sein Werdegang und seine Arbeit.* Jena, 1914.

Stellrecht, H. *Trotz Allem: Ein Buch der Front.* Munich, 1931.

Tönnies, Ferdinand. *Gemeinschaft und Gesellschaft.* 1887.

Weber, Max. *From Max Weber: Essays in Sociology.* Edited by Hans H. Gerth and C. Wright Mills. Oxford, 1958.

————. *The Protestant Ethic and the Spirit of Capitalism.* Translated by Talcott Parsons. New York, 1958.

Werbe- und Merkbüchlein des Alldeutschen Verbandes. 7th ed. Munich, 1903.

Zimmermann, Albert. *Der D. H. V.: Sein Werden, Wirken, und Wollen.* Hamburg, n.d. [1929–30].

————. "Rudolf Mosse gegen DHV." *Mitteilungen des allgemeinen deutschen Buchhand-lungsgehilfen Verbandes* 30 (July 1931): 185–88.

Zweig, Stefan. "Lob der deutschen Verleger." *Börsenblatt für den deutschen Buchhandel* 80 (1913): 573–74, 611.

II. SECONDARY LITERATURE

Albertin, Lothar. *Nationalismus und Protestantismus in der österreichischen Los-von-Rom Bewegung um 1900.* Inaugural dissertation, Cologne, 1953.

Anchor, Robert. *Germany Confronts Modernization: German Culture and Society 1790–1890.* Lexington, Mass., 1972.

Anderson, Eugene N. "German Romanticism as an Ideology of Cultural Crisis." *Journal of the History of Ideas* 2 (1941): 301–17.

Andler, Charles. *Le pangermanisme philosophique 1800 à 1914.* Paris, 1917.

Anstett, Jean-Jacques. "Paul de Lagarde." In *The Third Reich*, edited by the International Council for Philosophical and Humanistic Studies, pp. 148–202. London, 1955.

Atzenbeck, C. "Eugen Diederichs Werk und Vermächtnis." *Scholle* 13 (1936): 127–29.

Bappert, W. *Wege zum Urheberrecht. Die geschichtliche Entwicklung des Urheberrechtsgedankes.* Frankfurt, 1962.

Barclay, David E. "A Prussian Socialism? Wichard von Moellendorf and the Dilemmas of Economic Planning in Germany, 1918–1919." *Central European History* 11 (1978): 50–82.

Barker, R. J. "The Sociological Function of Intellectuals in Modern Society: A Study of Some Social Movements in Post-War Germany." Ph.D. dissertation, London School of Economics and Political Science, 1936.

Basler, Otto. "Amerikanismus: Geschichte eines Schlagwortes." *Deutsche Rundschau* 224 (1930).

Becker, O. H. "Ein deutscher Verleger." *Der Türmer* 38 (1936): 82.

Benz, Richard. "Sechzig Jahre Eugen Diederichs Verlag." *Welt und Wort* 10 (1956): 335.

Berg, Leo. "Das Mäzenatentum." *Das Magazin: Monatsschrift für Musik, Kunst, und Literatur* 77 (1908): 145–47.

Berghahn, Volker R. *Germany and the Approach of War in 1914.* London, 1973.

——————. *Rüstung und Machtpolitik: Zur Anatomie des Kalten Krieges vor 1914.* Düsseldorf, 1973.

——————. *Der Tirpitz-Plan: Genesis und Verfall einer innenpolitischen Krisenstrategie unter Wilhelm II.* Düsseldorf, 1971.

Bergmann, Klaus. *Agrarromantik und Grossstadtfeindschaft.* Meisenheim, 1970.

Betz, Anton. "Paul N. Cossmann und die Münchener Publizistik." *Publizistik* 10 (1965): 376–81.

Bieber, H. "Neuromantik." In *Reallexikon der deutschen Literaturgeschichte*, edited by Paul Merker and W. Stammler. 3 vols., 2:495–96. Berlin, 1926–28.

Biechele, Eckhard. *Der Kampf um die Gemeinwirtschaftskonzeption des Reichswirtschaftsministeriums im Jahre 1919: Eine Studie zur Wirtschaftspolitik unter Reichswirtschaftsminister Rudolf Wissell in der Frühphase der Weimarer Republik.* Inaugural dissertation, Berlin, 1973.

Bleuel, H., and Klinnert, E. *Deutsche Studenten auf dem Weg ins Dritten Reich.* Gütersloh, 1967.

Böhm, Ekkehard. *Überseehandel und Flottenbau. Hanseatische Kaufmannschaft und deutsche Seerüstung 1879–1902.* Düsseldorf, 1972.

Bolle, Fritz, "Darwinismus und Zeitgeist." In *Das wilhelminische Zeitalter*, edited by Hans Joachim Schoeps, pp. 235–87. Stuttgart, 1967.

Bollmus, Reinhard. *Das Amt Rosenberg und seine Gegner: Zum Machtkampf im nationalsozialistischen Herrschaftssystem.* Stuttgart, 1970.

Bollnow, Otto F. *Die Lebensphilosophie.* Berlin, 1958.

Bonhard, Otto. *Geschichte des Alldeutschen Verbandes.* Berlin, 1920.

Booms, Hans. *Die Deutschkonservative Parteien: Preussische Charakter, Reichsauffassung, Nationalbegriff.* Düsseldorf, 1954.

Borinski, Fritz, and Milch, Werner. *Jugendbewegung: The Story of German Youth 1896–1933.* London, 1945.

Bowen, Ralph. *German Theories of the Corporate State: With Special Reference to the Period 1870–1919.* New York, 1947.

Braatz, Werner E. "Two Neo-Conservative Myths in Germany 1919–32: The 'Third Reich' and the 'New State.' " *Journal of the History of Ideas* 32 (1971): 569–84.

Broermann, Herbert. *Der Kunstwart in seiner Eigenart, Entwicklung, und Bedeutung.* Inaugural dissertation, Berne, 1934.

Bronder, Dietrich. *Bevor Hitler Kam.* Hannover, 1964.

Brunschwig, Henri. *La crise de l'état prussien à la fin du XVIIIe siècle et la genèse de la mentalité romantique.* Paris, 1947.

Brunzel, Hans Paul. "Die 'Tat' 1918–1933. Ein publizistischer Angriff auf die Verfassung von Weimar innerhalb der 'Konservativen Revolution.' " Dissertation, mimeographed. Bonn, 1952.

Buchwald, Reinhardt. "Eugen Diederichs und die Volksbildungsarbeit." *Hefte für die Büchereiwesen* 15 (Feb./Mar. 1931): 61–66.

Byrnes, Robert F. "The French Publishing Industry and Its Crisis in the 1890s." *Journal of Modern History* 23 (1951): 232–42.

Campbell, Joan. *The German Werkbund: The Politics of Reform in the Applied Arts.* Princeton, 1978.

Carsten, F. L. " 'Volk ohne Raum': A Note on Hans Grimm." *Journal of Contemporary History* 2 (1967): 221–27.

Class, Heinrich. "J. F. Lehmann und der Alldeutsche Verband." *Deutschlands Erneuerung* 19 (1935): 258–61.

Coellen, Ludwig. *Neuromantik.* Jena, 1906.

Collins, A. S. *Authorship in the Days of Johnson.* London, 1927.

———. *The Profession of Letters: A Study of the Relation of Author to Patron, Publisher and Public 1780–1832.* London, 1928.

Conrad-Martius, H. *Utopien der Menschenzüchtung: Der Sozialdarwinismus und seine Folgen.* Munich, 1955.

Coyner, S. J. "Class Consciousness and Consumption: The New Middle Class in the Weimar Republic." *Journal of Social History* 10 (1977): 310–31.

Craig, Gordon A. *Germany 1866–1945.* New York, 1978.

Croner, Fritz. "Die Angestelltenbewegung nach der Währungsstabilisierung." *Archiv für Sozialwissenschaft und Sozialpolitik* 60 (1928): 103–46.

Cysarz, Herbert. *Zur Geistesgeschichte des Weltkriegs: Die dichterischen Wandlungen des deutschen Kriegsbilds, 1910–1930.* Saale, 1931.

Dahrendorf, Ralf. *Society and Democracy in Germany.* Garden City, N.Y., 1969.

Darnton, Robert. *The Business of the Enlightenment: A Publishing History of the Encyclopédie, 1775–1800.* Cambridge, Mass., 1979.

———. "The Encylopédie Wars in Prerevolutionary France." *American Historical Review*, 76 (1973): 1331–52.

———. "Reading, Writing, and Publishing in Eighteenth Century France: A Case Study in the Sociology of Literature." In *Historical Studies Today*, edited by Felix Gilbert and S. Graubard, pp. 238–80. New York, 1972.

Demant, Ebbo. *Von Schleicher zu Springer: Hans Zehrer als politischer Publizist.* Mainz, 1971.

Diederichs, Ulf. "Marketing um die Jahrhundertwende—Eugen Diederichs." *Buchmarkt* 2 (Mar./Apr. 1969): 93–103.

Diehl, James M. *Paramilitary Politics in Weimar Germany.* Bloomington, Ind., 1977.

Dietrich, A. "Der Verleger Eugen Diederichs." *Der Ring. Politische Wochenschrift* 1 (1928): 558–59.

Dietze, Klaus. "Eugen Diederichs." In *Handbuch der Zeitungswissenschaft*, edited by W. Heide, 1:825–28. Leipzig, 1940.

————. *Eugen Diederichs und seine Zeitschriften.* Würzburg, 1940.

Domandi, Mario. "The German Youth Movement." Ph.D. dissertation, Columbia University, 1960.

Dreyfuss, Carl. *Beruf und Ideologie der Angestellten.* Munich, 1933.

Ecksteins, Modris. *The Limits of Reason: The German Democratic Press and the Collapse of Weimar Democracy.* London, 1975.

Edmundson, Nelson. "The Fichte Society: A Chapter in Germany's Conservative Revolution." *Journal of Modern History* 28 (1966): 161–80.

Ehmcke, F. H. "Erinnerungen an Eugen Diederichs." *Gutenberg Jahrbuch* 6 (1931): 328–35.

Elster, Hanns M. "Fünfundzwanzig Jahre Eugen Diederichs Verlag." *Börsenblatt für den deutschen Buchhandel* 88 (1921): 1368–70.

Emmerich, Wolfgang. *Zur Kritik der Volkstumsideologie.* Frankfurt, 1971.

Engelhard, Erich. "Die Angestellten." *Kölner Vierteljahresheft für Soziologie* 10 (1932): 479–520.

Epstein, Klaus. *The Genesis of German Conservatism.* Princeton, 1966.

————. "Review of Kurt Sontheimer, *Antidemokratisches Denken in der Weimarer Republik.*" *Historische Zeitschrift* 197 (1963): 657–66.

"Eugen Diederichs." *Börsenblatt für den deutschen Buchhandel* 94 (1927): 761–63.

"Eugen Diederichs' 'Neue Tat' und die Kolportageromantik." *Der Ring. Politische Wochenschrift* 2 (1929): 880.

Fenske, Hans. *Konservatismus und Rechtsradikalismus in Bayern nach 1918.* Bad Homburg, 1969.

Fest, Joachim. *The Face of the Third Reich: Portraits of the Nazi Leadership.* Translated by Michael Bullock. New York, 1970.

Field, Geoffrey G. "H. S. Chamberlain: Prophet of Bayreuth." Ph.D. dissertation, Columbia University, 1972.

————. "Nordic Racism." *Journal of the History of Ideas* 38 (1977): 523–40.

Fischer, Fritz. *Griff Nach der Weltmacht: Der Kriegszielpolitik des kaiserlichen Deutschlands.* 3d rev. ed. Düsseldorf, 1964.

Fischer, F. W. *Die Angestellten, ihre Bewegung und ihre Ideologie.* Inaugural dissertation, Heidelberg, 1931.

Fischer, K. A. "J. F. Lehmann, München." *Deutsche Arbeit* 35 (1935): 322–24.

Fischli, B. "Monsieur la Capital und Madame la Terre: Zur ideologischen Funktion des völkisch-faschistischen Heimatsstücks (1897–1933)." *Diskurs* 3 (1973): 23–50.

Fleischer, R. A. *Die Wichtigkeit des Buchhandels.* Kassel & Basel, 1953.

Flemmer, Walter. *Verlage in Bayern.* Pullach, 1974.

Franz-Willing, Georg. *Die Hitlerbewegung: Der Ursprung, 1919–1922.* Berlin, 1962.

Frecot, Janos. "Die Lebensreformbewegung." In *Das wilhelminische Bildungsbürgertum: Zur Sozialgeschichte seiner Ideen,* edited by Klaus Vondung, pp. 138–52. Göttingen, 1976.

Freedman, Ralph. *Hermann Hesse: Pilgrim of Crisis, A Biography.* New York, 1978.

Friederich, Werner P. *History of German Literature.* 2d ed. New York, 1961.

Fritzsche, K. *Politische Romantik und Gegenrevolution, Fluchtwege in der Krise der bürgerlichen Gesellschaft: Das Beispiel des 'Tat-Kreises'.* Frankfurt, 1975.

Fuller, Leon W. "The War of 1914 as Interpreted by German Intellectuals." *Journal of Modern History* 14 (1942): 145–60.

Fullerton, Ronald A. "The German Book Markets, 1815–1888." Ph.D. dissertation, University of Wisconsin, 1975.

Gasman, Daniel. *The Scientific Origins of National Socialism: Social Darwinism in Ernst Haeckel and the German Monist League.* London, 1971.

Gatzke, Hans. *Germany's Drive to the West: A Study of Germany's Western War Aims During the First World War.* Baltimore, 1950.

Gay, Peter. *The Dilemma of Democratic Socialism: Eduard Bernstein's Challenge to Marx.* New York, 1952.

———. *Weimar Culture: The Outsider as Insider.* New York, 1968.

Gerhard, Walter [pseudonym]. *Um des Reiches Zukunft: Nationale Widergeburt oder politische Reaktion?* Freiburg, 1932.

Gerstenberger, Heide. "Konservatismus in der Weimarer Republik." In *Rekonstruktion des Konservatismus*, edited by Gerd-Klaus Kaltenbrunner, pp. 331–46. Freiburg, 1972.

———. *Der revolutionäre Konservatismus–Ein Beitrag zur Analyse des Liberalismus.* Berlin, 1969.

Gerstenhauer, M. R. *Der völkische Gedanke in Vergangenheit und Zukunft: Aus der Geschichte der völkischen Bewegung.* Leipzig, 1933.

Getzeny, Heinrich. "Das Jubiläum einer Kulturbewegung." *Hochland* 19 (1922): 700–713.

Gewerkschaftsbund der Angestellten. *Die wirtschaftliche und soziale Lage der Angestellten.* Berlin, 1911.

Gieske, Ludwig. *Die geschichtliche Entwicklung des deutschen Urheberrechts.* Göttingen, 1957.

Glum, Friedrich. *Konservatismus im 19. Jahrhundert.* Bonn, 1963.

———. *Philosophen im Spiegel und Zerrspiegel: Deutschlands Weg in den Nationalismus und Nationalsozialismus.* Munich, 1954.

Göbel, Wolfram. "Der Ernst Rowohlt Verlag 1910–1913: Seine Geschichte und seine Bedeutung für die Literatur seiner Zeit." *Archiv für Geschichte des Buchwesens* 14 (1974): 465–608.

———. "Der Kurt Wolff Verlag 1913–1930: Expressionismus als verlegerische Aufgabe." *Archiv für Geschichte des Buchwesens* 15 (1975): 521–962.

Goldfriedrich, J., and Kapp, Friedrich. *Geschichte des deutschen Buchhandels.* 4 vols. Vol. 4, *Von Beginn der Fremdherrschaft bis zur Reform des Börsenvereins im neuen Deutschen Reiche (1805–1889).* Leipzig, 1913.

Göpfert, Herbert G. "Bemerkungen über Buchhändler und Buchhandel zur Zeit der Aufklärung in Deutschland." *Wolfenbütteler Studien zur Aufklärung* 1 (1974): 69–83.

———. "Der expressionistische Verlag: Versuch einer Übersicht." *Brannenburger Vorträge*, 1962, pp. 43–69.

———. "Zur Geschichte des Buchhändlerischen Selbstverständnisses: Eugen Diederichs." *Bertelsmann-Briefe* 57 (1968): 2–6.

Gordon, Harold J. *Hitler and the Beer Hall Putsch.* Princeton, 1972.

Graham, Loren R. "Science and Values: The Eugenics Movement in Germany and Russia in the 1920s." *American Historical Review*, 82 (1977): 1133–64.

Grauthoff, Otto. *Die Entwicklung der modernen Buchkunst in Deutschland.* Leipzig, 1901.

Groh, Dieter. *Russland und das Selbstverständnis Europas: Ein Beitrag zur europäischen Geistesgeschichte.* Neuwied, 1961.

Grothe, Wolfgang. "Die Neue Rundschau des Verlages S. Fischer: Ein Beitrag zur Publizistik und Literaturgeschichte der Jahre von 1890 bis 1925." *Archiv für Geschichte des Buchwesens* 4 (1961/62): 809–996.

Gumbel, Emil. *Acht Jahre politische Justiz.* Berlin, 1927.

———. *Von Fememord zur Reichskanzlei.* Heidelberg, 1962.

———. *"Verräter verfallen der Feme": Opfer, Mörder, Richter 1919–1920.* Berlin, 1929.

Günther, H. F. K. "Erinnerungen an J. F. Lehmann." *Deutschlands Erneuerung* 19 (1935): 277–79.

Guratzsch, Dankwart. *Macht durch Organisation: Die Grundlegung des Hugenbergischen Presseimperiums.* Gütersloh, 1974.

Haas, Willy. "Meine Meinung." *Die literarische Welt* 2 (1926): 2.

Halsted, John B., ed. *Romanticism.* New York, 1969.

Hamel, Iris. *Völkischer Verband und nationale Gewerkschaft: Der Deutschnationale Hand-*

lungsgehilfen-Verband, 1893–1933. Frankfurt, 1967.

Hampe, Peter. "Sozioökonomische und psychische Hintergründe der bildungsbürgerliche Imperialbegeisterung." In *Das wilhelminische Bildungsbürgertum: Zur Sozialgeschichte seiner Ideen,* edited by Klaus Vondung, pp. 67–79. Göttingen, 1976.

Hannover, H., and Hannover, E. *Politische Justiz 1918–1933.* Frankfurt, 1966.

Hartenstein, Wolfgang. *Die Anfänge der Deutschnationalen Volkspartei 1918–1920.* Düsseldorf, 1962.

Haskell, Francis. "Patronage." In *Encyclopedia of World Art,* 15 vols., 11:118–35. New York, 1959–68.

Hauser, Arnold. *Sozialgeschichte der Kunst und Literatur.* Munich, 1969.

Heckart, Beverly. *From Bassermann to Bebel: The Grand Bloc's Quest for Reform in the Kaiserreich 1900–1914.* New Haven, 1975.

Hecker, H. *'Die Tat' und ihr Osteuropabild 1909–1939.* Cologne, 1974.

Hermann, Eva. "Die Buchstadt Leipzig und ihre Rolle bei der Vorbereitung der bürgerlichen Revolution von 1848 in Ungarn." *Beiträge zur Geschichte des Buchwesens* 1 (1965): 53–251.

Hertzman, Lewis. *DNVP: Right-Wing Opposition to the Weimar Republic, 1918–1924.* Lincoln. Neb., 1963.

Hesse, Hermann. "Der Verlag Eugen Diederichs." *März* 3 (1909): 318–20.

Heuss, Theo. "Wilhelm Stapel: Zum sechzigsten Geburtstag." *Frankfurter Zeitung,* 27 Oct. 1942.

Hiller, Helmut. "Buch- und Verlagswesen als Lehrgegenstand der Publizistik?" *Börsenblatt für den deutschen Buchhandel.* N.S. 20 (1964): 1720–22.

————. *Zur Sozialgeschichte von Buch und Buchhandel.* Bonn, 1966.

Hirsch, Helmut. *Der 'Fabier' Eduard Bernstein: Zur Entwicklungsgeschichte des evolutionären Sozialismus.* Bonn, 1977.

Hock, Wolfgang. *Deutscher Antikapitalismus: Der ideologische Kampf gegen die freie Wirtschaft im Zeichen der grossen Krise.* Frankfurt, 1960.

Hoepke, Klaus-Peter. *Die deutsche Rechte und der italienische Faschismus: Ein Beitrag zum Selbstverständnis und zur Politik von Gruppen und Verbände der deutschen Rechte.* Düsseldorf, 1968.

Höfele, Karl Heinrich. "Selbstverständnis und Zeitkritik des deutschen Bürgertums vor dem ersten Weltkrieg." *Zeitschrift für Religions- und Geistesgeschichte* 8 (1956): 40–56.

Hoffmann, H. H. *Der Hitler-Putsch: Krisenjahre deutscher Geschichte 1920–1924.* Munich, 1964.

Hoffmann, Peter. *Widerstand, Staatsstreich, Attentat: Der Kampf der Opposition gegen Hitler.* Frankfurt, 1974.

Holt, Niles Robert. "Ernst Haeckel's Monistic Religion." *Journal of the History of Ideas* 32 (1971): 265–80.

————. "The Social and Political Ideas of the German Monist Movement, 1871–1914." Ph.D. dissertation, Yale University, 1967.

Hoyer, Franz Alfons. *Die "Werkleute auf Haus Nyland:" Darstellung und Würdigung eines Dichterkreises.* Inaugural dissertation, Freiburg, 1941.

Hüttig, Helmut. *Die politische Zeitschriften der Nachkriegszeit in Deutschland.* Magdeburg, 1928.

Jantzen, Hinrich. "Eugen Diederichs." In *Namen und Werke: Biographien und Beiträge zur Soziologie der Jugendbewegung,* 10 vols., 2:81–90. Frankfurt, 1974.

Jarausch, Konrad. *The Enigmatic Chancellor: Bethmann Hollweg and the Hubris of Imperial Germany.* New Haven, 1973.

Jasper, G. *Der Schutz der Republik: Studien zur staatlichen Sicherung der Demokratie in der Weimarer Republik, 1922–1930.* Tübingen, 1963.

Jenny, E. *Die Heimatskunstbewegung.* Inaugural dissertation, Berne, 1934.

Jerussalemski, A. S. *Der deutsche Imperialismus: Geschichte und Gegenwart.* Berlin, 1968.

Johann, Ernst. *Die deutsche Buchverlage des Naturalismus und der Neuromantik.* Weimar, 1935.

Johannsen, Harro. *Der Revisionismus in der deutschen Sozialdemokratie 1890 bis 1914.* Inaugural dissertation, Hamburg, 1954.

Jonas, Erasmus. *Die Volkskonservativen 1928–1933: Entwicklung, Struktur, Standort, und politische Zielsetzung.* Düsseldorf, 1965.

Jones, Larry Eugene. "Between the Fronts: The German National Union of Commercial Employees from 1928 to 1933." *Journal of Modern History* 48 (1976): 462–82.

————. "The Crisis of White-Collar Interest Politics: *Deutschnationaler Handlungsgehilfen-Verband* and the *Deutsche Volkspartei* in the World Economic Crisis." In *Industrielles System und politische Entwicklung in der Weimarer Republik,* edited by Hans Mommsen, D. Petzina, and B. Weisbrod, pp. 811–23. Düsseldorf, 1973.

Jovy, E. M. *Deutsche Jugendbewegung und Nationalsozialismus.* Cologne, 1952.

Kaltenbrunner, Gerd-Klaus, ed. *Rekonstruktion des Konservatismus.* Freiburg, 1972.

Katz, Elihu. "The Diffusion of New Ideas and Practices." In *The Science of Human Communication,* edited by Wilbur Schramm, pp. 77–93. New York, 1963.

————, and Lazarsfeld, Paul. *Personal Influence: The Part Played by People in the Flow of Mass Communications.* New York, 1964.

Kaufman, Walter. *Monarchism in the Weimar Republic.* New York, 1953.

Kessler, Heinrich. *Wilhelm Stapel als politischer Publizist: Ein Beitrag zur Geschichte des konservativen Nationalismus zwischen den beiden Weltkriegen.* Nuremberg, 1967.

Ketelsen, Uwe-Karsten. *Völkisch-nationale und nationalsozialistische Literatur in Deutschland, 1890–1945.* Stuttgart, 1976.

von Klemperer, Klemens. "On Austrofascism." *Central European History* 11 (1978): 313–17.

————. *Germany's New Conservatism: Its History and Dilemma in the Twentieth Century.* 2d rev. ed. Princeton, 1968.

Kober, A. H. "Ein Kulturverlag." *Ostdeutsche Monatshefte* 4 (1923): 73–76.

Kocka, Jürgen. "The First World War and the 'Mittelstand': German Artisans and White Collar Workers." *Journal of Contemporary History* 8 (1973): 101–23.

————. *Klassengesellschaft im Krieg: Deutsche Sozialgeschichte 1914–1918.* Göttingen, 1973.

————. "Zur Problematik der Angestellten 1914–1933." In *Industrielles System und politische Entwicklung in der Weimarer Republik,* edited by Hans Mommsen, D. Petzina, and B. Weisbrod, pp. 792–811. Düsseldorf, 1973.

————. *Unternehmensverwaltung und Angestelltenschaft am Beispiel Siemens 1847–1914.* Stuttgart, 1969.

————. "Vorindustrielle Faktoren in der deutschen Industrialisierung: Industrialbürokratie und 'neuer Mittelstand.'" In *Das kaiserliche Deutschland,* edited by Michael Stürmer, pp. 265–86. Düsseldorf, 1970.

Köhler, W. "Verlag Eugen Diederichs." *Protestanten Blatt,* 9 April 1913.

Kohn, Hans. *The Mind of Germany: Education of a Nation.* New York, 1960.

————. "Romanticism and the Rise of German Nationalism." *Review of Politics* 12 (1950): 443–472.

Köllmann, Wolfgang. "The Process of Urbanization in Germany at the Height of the Industrialization Period." *Journal of Contemporary History* 4 (1969): 59–76.

Köster, Hans. "Jugendbewegung—Lauenstein Kreis—Anfänge des Jungbuchhandels." *Börsenblatt für den deutschen Buchhandel.* N.S. 22 (1966): 757–63.

Koszyk, Kurt. *Deutsche Presse 1914–1945.* Berlin, 1972.

————, and Pruys, K. H. *dtv Wörterbuch zur Publizistik.* Frankfurt, 1969.

Krabbe, Wolfgang. *Gesellschaftsveränderung durch Lebensreform: Strukturmerkmale einer sozialreformerischen Bewegung in Deutschland der Industrialisierungsperiode.* Göttingen, 1974.

Kratzsch, Gerhard. *Kunstwart und Dürerbund: Ein Beitrag zur Geschichte der Gebildeten im Zeitalter des Imperialismus.* Göttingen, 1969.

Krause, Manfred. "Zur Rolle der Mittelschichten in der Auseinandersetzung zwischen Arbeiterklasse und Bourgeoisie gegen Ende der Weimarer Republik." *Revue Allemagne* 4 (1974): 23–28.

Kreiler, K., ed. *Traditionen deutscher Justiz: Die grosse politische Prozesse der Weimarer Zeit.* Berlin, 1977.

Kron, Friedhelm. *Schriftsteller und Schriftstellerverbände: Schriftstellerberuf und Interessenpolitik 1842–1973.* Stuttgart, 1976.

Kruck, Alfred. *Geschichte des Alldeutschen Verbandes 1890–1939.* Wiesbaden, 1954.

Kühn, Lenore. "Ein königlicher Verleger." *Das deutsche Wort* 13 (1937): 26–33.

Kupisch, Karl. "The 'Luther Renaissance.'" *Journal of Contemporary History* 2 (1967): 39–49.

Kurucz, Jenö. *Struktur und Funktion der Intelligenz während der Weimarer Republik.* Berlin, 1967.

Labedz, Leopold, ed. *Revisionism.* New York, 1962.

Landauer, Carl. "The Bavarian Problem in the Weimar Republic, 1918–1923." *Journal of Modern History* 16 (1944): 93–115, 205–23.

Lane, Barbara. *Architecture and Politics in Germany, 1918–1945.* Cambridge, Mass., 1968.

Laqueur, Walter. "The Role of the Intelligentsia in the Weimar Republic." *Social Research* 39 (1972): 213–27.

———. *Young Germany: A History of the German Youth Movement.* London, 1962.

Latourette, Kenneth S. *Christianity in a Revolutionary Age: A History of Christianity in the 19th and 20th Centuries.* 2 vols. Vol. 2, *The 19th Century in Europe: The Protestant and Eastern Churches.* Grand Rapids, Mich., 1959.

Laubenthal, Wilhelm. *Der Gedanke einer geistigen Erneuerung Deutschlands im deutschen Schrifttum von 1871 bis zum Weltkrieg.* Frankfurt, 1938.

Laurenson, Diana, and Swingewood, Alan. *The Sociology of Literature.* London, 1972.

Läuter, Peter. "Die Anfänge des sozialistischen Verlagstätigkeit in Deutschland (1844–1900)." *Beiträge zur Geschichte des Buchwesens* 2 (1966): 169–243.

Lazarsfeld, Paul, and Merton, R. K. "Mass Communication, Popular Taste, and Organized Social Action." In *The Communication of Ideas,* edited by Lyman Bryson, pp. 95–118. New York, 1964.

———, and Menzel, Herbert. "Mass Media and Personal Influence." In *The Science of Human Communication,* edited by Wilbur Schramm, pp. 94–115. New York, 1963.

Lebovics, Herman. *Social Conservatism and the Middle Classes in Germany, 1914–1933.* Princeton, 1969.

Lederer, Emil. *Die Privatangestellten in der modernen Wirtschaftsentwicklung.* Tübingen, 1912.

Lees, Andrew. "Debates About the Big City in Germany, 1890–1914." *Societas* 5 (1975): 31–47.

Lehmann, Friedrich. "Mein Oheim J. F. Lehmann." *Deutschlands Erneuerung* 19 (1935): 267–72.

Leisen, Adolf. *Die Ausbreitung des völkischen Gedankes in der Studentenschaft der Weimarer Republik.* Inaugural dissertation, Heidelberg, 1964.

Leopold, John A. *Alfred Hugenberg: The Radical Nationalist Campaign Against the Weimar Republic.* New Haven, 1977.

Lepsius, M. Rainer. *Extremer Nationalismus: Strukturbedingungen vor der nationalsozialistischen Machtergreifung.* Stuttgart, 1966.

Lersch, Philip. *Lebensphilosophie der Gegenwart.* Berlin, 1932.

von der Leyen, Friedrich. "Eugen Diederichs." In *Neue deutsche Biographie,* 3:637–38. Berlin, 1957.

Liebe, Werner. *Die Deutschnationale Volkspartei 1918–1924.* Düsseldorf, 1956.
Lohalm, Uwe. *Völkischer Radikalismus: Die Geschichte des deutschvölkischen Schutz- und Trutzbundes 1919–1923.* Hamburg, 1970.
Lougee, Robert W. *Paul de Lagarde, 1827–1891: A Study of Radical Conservatism in Germany.* Cambridge, Mass., 1962.
Löwenthal, Leo. "Die Auffassung Dostojewskis im Vorkriegsdeutschland." *Zeitschrift für Sozialforschung* 3 (1934): 344–81.
Lübbe, Hermann. *Politische Philosophie in Deutschland: Studien zu ihrer Geschichte.* Munich, 1974.
Ludwig, Kurt. "Tatkreis 1929–1933." In *Die bürgerlichen Parteien in Deutschland 1830–1945,* edited by Dieter Fricke, et al., 2:672–75. Leipzig, 1970.
Lutzhöft, Hans-Jürgen. *Der nordische Gedanke in Deutschland, 1920–1940.* Stuttgart, 1971.
McRandle, James H. *The Track of the Wolf: Essays on National Socialism and Its Leader, Adolf Hitler.* Evanston, Ill., 1965.
Maier, Charles S. *Recasting Bourgeois Europe: Stabilization in France, Germany, and Italy in the Decade After World War I.* Princeton, 1975.
Mannheim, Karl. "Das konservative Denken: Beiträge zur Werde des politisch-historischen Denkens in Deutschland." *Archiv für Sozialwissenschaft* 57 (1927): 68–142, 470–95.
von Martin, Alfred. "Weltanschauliche Motive in altkonservativen Denken." In *Deutscher Staat und deutsche Parteien: Beiträge zur deutschen Parteien- und Geistesgeschichte, Friedrich Meinecke zum 60. Geburtstag dargebracht,* pp. 47–95. Munich, 1922.
Martini, Fritz. *Deutsche Literaturgeschichte.* 7th rev. ed. Stuttgart, 1965.
Maser, Werner. *Die Frühgeschichte der NSDAP: Hitlers Weg bis 1924.* Frankfurt, 1965.
———. *Hitler's 'Mein Kampf'.* Munich, 1966.
Mauersberger, Volker. *Rudolf Pechel und die "Deutsche Rundschau": Eine Studie zur konservativ-revolutionären Publizistik in der Weimarer Republik (1918–1933).* Bremen, 1971.
May, Arthur J. *The Hapsburg Monarchy 1867–1914.* New York, 1960.
de Mendelssohn, Peter. *S. Fischer und sein Verlag.* Frankfurt, 1970.
Mennekes, F. *Die Republik als Herausforderung: Konservatives Denken in Bayern zwischen Weimarer Republik und antidemokratischer Reaktion (1918–1925).* Berlin, 1973.
Menz, Gerhard. *Der deutsche Buchhandel: Vierundzwanzig Lebensbilder führender Männer des Buchhandels.* Leipzig, 1925 and Gotha, 1942.
———. "Eugen Diederichs. 22.6.1867–10.9.1930." *Börsenblatt für den deutschen Buchhandel* 97 (1930): 885–86.
———. *Kulturwirtschaft.* Leipzig, 1933.
———. *Die Zeitschrift, ihre Entwicklung und ihr Lebensbedingungen.* Stuttgart, 1928.
———. "Zeitschriftenverlegerpersönlichkeiten IX. Eugen Diederichs." *Der Zeitschriftenverleger* 44 (1942): 290–92.
Mertens, Carl. *Verschwörer und Fememörder.* Berlin, 1926.
Messer, August. *Die freideutsche Jugendbewegung.* 5th ed. Langensalza, 1924.
von Metnitz, Gustav. *Die deutsche Nationalbewegung 1871–1933.* Berlin, 1939.
Meyer, Henry C. *Mitteleuropa in German Thought and Action 1815–1945.* The Hague, 1955.
Meyer-Dohm, Peter. *Buchhandel als kulturwirtschaftliche Aufgabe.* Gütersloh, 1967.
———. "Wissenschaftliche Literatur als Marktobjekt." In *Das wissenschaftliche Buch,* edited by Peter Meyer-Dohm, pp. 13–36. Hamburg, 1969.
Mitzman, Arthur. *The Iron Cage: An Historical Interpretation of Max Weber.* New York, 1970.
———. *Sociology and Estrangement: Three Sociologists in Imperial Germany.* New York, 1973.
———. "Tönnies and German Society, 1887–1914: From Cultural Pessimism to the Celebration of the *Volksgemeinschaft.*" *Journal of the History of Ideas* 32 (1971): 507–24.
Mohler, Armin. *Die konservative Revolution in Deutschland 1918–1932: Grundriss ihrer*

Weltanschauungen. Stuttgart, 1950. 2d rev. ed. Düsseldorf, 1972.

Möller, H. *Aufklärung in Preussen: Der Verleger, Publizist und Geschichtsschreiber Friedrich Nicolai.* Berlin, 1975.

Monaco, Paul. *Cinema and Society: France and Germany in the Twenties.* New York, 1976.

Morris, Rodler. "German Nationalist Fiction and the 'Jewish Question' 1918–1933." Ph.D. dissertation in progress, University of North Carolina.

Mosse, George L. "The Corporate State and the Conservative Revolution in Weimar Germany." In *Germans and Jews: The Right, the Left, and the Search for a 'Third Force' in Pre-Nazi Germany,* pp. 116–43. New York, 1970.

———. *The Crisis of German Ideology: Intellectual Origins of the Third Reich.* New York, 1964.

———. *Toward the Final Solution: A History of European Racism.* New York, 1978.

Müller, J. *Die Jugendbewegung als deutsche Hauptrichtung neukonservativer Reformen.* Zürich, 1971.

Nasarski, Peter, ed. *Deutsche Jugendbewegung in Europa: Ein Bilanz.* Cologne, 1967.

Neumann, Sigmund. *Die Stufen des preussischen Konservatismus: Ein Beitrag zu Staats- und Gesellschaftsbild Deutschlands im 19. Jahrhundert.* Berlin, 1928.

Neurohr, Jean F. *Der Mythos vom Dritten Reich: Zur Geistesgeschichte des Nationalsozialismus.* Stuttgart, 1957.

Neven du Mont, Reinhold. *Die Kollektivierung des literarischen Konsums in der modernen Gesellschaft durch die Arbeit der Buchgemeinschaften.* Inaugural dissertation, Freiburg im Breisgau, 1961.

Nolte, Ernst. "Germany." In *The European Right, A Historical Profile,* edited by Hans Rogger and Eugene Weber, pp. 261–307. Berkeley, 1965.

Oschilewski, Walter G. "Charakterköpfe des Buchhandels: Eugen Diederichs—Der Vater des Jungbuchhandels." *Der Junge Buchhandel 1955,* no. 9 (Beilage zum *Börsenblatt für den deutschen Buchhandel,* no. 70 [2 Sept. 1955]): J60–61.

———. "Eugen Diederichs: Ein Beitrag zur Geschichte der neuen deutschen Buchkunst." *Imprimatur* 9 (1940): 17–32.

———. "Eugen Diederichs und die deutsche Buchkunst." *Archiv für Buchgewerbe* 73 (1936): 399–416.

———. "Eugen Diederichs und sein Werk." *Deutscher Kulturwart* 4 (1937): 515–18.

———. *Eugen Diederichs und sein Werk.* Jena, 1936.

———. *Zeitungen in Berlin im Spiegel der Jahrhunderte.* Berlin, 1975.

Ost, Günther. *Friedrich Nicolais Allgemeine Deutsche Bibliothek.* Berlin, 1928.

Osteraas, Leena K. "The New Nationalists: Front Generation Spokesmen in the Weimar Republic." Ph.D. dissertation, Columbia University, 1972.

Paetel, Karl O. *Jugend in der Entscheidung: 1913–1933–1945.* Bad Godesberg, 1963.

———. *Jugendbewegung und Politik.* Bad Godesberg, 1961.

Paquet, Alfons. "Eugen Diederichs: Zu seinem 60. Geburtstag." *Frankfurter Zeitung,* 28 June 1927.

Pascal, Roy. *From Naturalism to Expressionism: German Literature and Society 1880–1918.* London, 1973.

Petersen, Jens. "Der italienische Faschismus aus der Sicht der Weimarer Republik." *Quellen und Forschungen aus italienischen Archiven und Bibliotheke* 55–56 (1976): 315–60.

Petzold, Joachim. *Die Dolchstosslegende: Eine Geschichtsfälschung im Dienst des deutschen Imperialismus und Militarismus.* Berlin-Ost, 1963.

———. *Konservative Theoretiker des deutschen Faschismus: Jungkonservative Ideologen in der Weimarer Republik als geistige Wegbereiter der faschistischen Diktatur.* East Berlin, 1977. (Appeared in the West as *Wegbereiter des deutschen Faschismus: Die Jungkonservativen in der Weimarer Republik.* Cologne, 1978.)

Pfeiler, William K. *War and the German Mind.* New York, 1941.

Phelps, Reginald H. "'Before Hitler Came': Thule Society and *Germanen Orden.*" *Journal of Modern History* 35 (1963): 245–61.

von Pigenot, Ludwig. "Gleitwort." In *Hölderlin-Vermächtnis,* by Norbert von Hellingrath. Munich, 1936.

Poliakov, Leon. *The Aryan Myth: A History of Racist and Nationalist Ideas in Europe.* New York, 1974.

Poor, Harold. "City versus Country: Anti-Urbanism in the Weimar Republic." *Societas* 6 (1976): 177–92.

Prang, Helmuth. "Neuromantik." In *Merker Reallexikon der deutschen Literaturgeschichte,* edited by W. Kohlschmidt and W. Mohr, 2 vols., 2:678–80. Berlin, 1965.

Pross, Harry. *Jugend Eros Politik.* Berne, 1964.

———. *Literatur und Politik: Geschichte und Programme der politisch-literarischen Zeitschriften im deutschen Sprachgebiet seit 1870.* Olten & Freiburg, 1963.

Pruemm, Karl. "Das Erbe der Front." In *Die deutsche Literatur im Dritten Reich,* edited by Horst Denkler and Karl Pruemm, pp. 138–64. Stuttgart, 1976.

———. *Literatur des soldatischen Nationalismus der 20er Jahre (1918 bis 1933).* Kronberg, 1974.

Pulzer, Peter G. J. *The Rise of Political Anti-Semitism in Germany and Austria.* New York, 1964.

Raabe, Felix. *Der bündische Aufbruch 1918–1923.* Bad Godesberg, 1963.

———. *Die bündische Jugend: Ein Beitrag zur Geschichte der Weimarer Republik.* Stuttgart, 1961.

Rapp, Adolf. *Der deutsche Gedanke: Seine Entwicklung im politischen und geistigen Leben seit dem 18. Jahrhundert.* Bonn, 1920.

Rauschning, Hermann. *The Conservative Revolution.* New York, 1941.

Réal, Jean. "The Religious Conception of Race: Houston Stuart Chamberlain and Germanic Christianity." In *The Third Reich,* edited by the International Council for Philosophical and Humanistic Studies, pp. 243–86. London, 1955.

Redlich, Fritz. "German Literary Expressionism and Its Publishers." *Harvard Library Bulletin* 18 (1969): 143–68.

Regener, Edgar A. "Verlagskultur." *Erwina* 13 (1906): 111–24.

Richards, Donald Day. *The German Bestseller in the 20th Century: A Complete Bibliography and Analysis 1915–1940.* Berne, 1968.

Ringer, Fritz K. *The Decline of the German Mandarins: The German Academic Community, 1890–1933.* Cambridge, Mass., 1969.

Rogger, Hans. "Was There a Russian Fascism? The Union of Russian People." *Journal of Modern History* 36 (1964): 398–415.

Romein, J. "Über den Konservatismus als historischer Kategorie." In *Wesen und Wirklichkeit des Menschen: Festschrift für Helmuth Plessner,* pp. 215–44. Göttingen, 1957.

Rosenhaupt, Hans Wilhelm. *Der deutsche Dichter um die Jahrhundertwende und seine Abgelöstheit von der Gesellschaft.* Berne, 1939.

Rossbacher, K. "Programm und Romane der Heimatskunstbewegung: Möglichkeiten sozialgeschichtlicher und soziologischer Analyse." *Sprachkunst* 5 (1974): 301–26.

Rosteutscher, J. H. W. *Die Wiederkunft des Dionysos: Der naturmystische Irrationalismus in Deutschland.* Berne, 1947.

Rüschemeyer, Dietrich. "Modernisierung und die Gebildeten im kaiserlichen Deutschland." *Kölner Zeitschrift für Soziologie und Sozialpsychologie* 16 (1972): 515–29.

Ryan, Lawrence. *Friedrich Hölderlin.* Stuttgart, 1962.

Schauer, Georg Kurt. *Deutsche Buchkunst 1890 bis 1960.* Vol. 1. Hamburg, 1963.

Schenda, Rudolf. *Volk ohne Buch: Studien zur Sozialgeschichte des populären Lesestoffes 1770–1910.* Munich, 1977.

Schenk, H. G. *The Mind of the European Romantics.* Garden City, N.Y., 1969.

Schierer, Herbert. *Das Zeitschriftenwesen der Jugendbewegung: Ein Beitrag zur Geschichte der Jugendzeitschrift.* Berlin, 1938.

Schilling, Konrad. *Beiträge zu einer Geschichte des radikalen Nationalismus in der wilhelminischen Ära 1890–1909.* Inaugural dissertation, Cologne, 1967.

Schmidt, Georg. "Eugen Diederichs und die Jugendbewegung." *Der Jungdeutsche,* 28 Oct. 1930.

Schmidt, Klaus Werner. "Die Tat (1909–1939)." In *Deutsche Zeitschriften des 17. bis 20. Jahrhunderts,* edited by Heinz-Dietrich Fischer, pp. 349–63. Pullach, 1973.

Schoeps, Hans Joachim, ed. *Das wilhelminische Zeitalter.* Stuttgart, 1967.

Scholten, O. F. "Deutsche Verleger, so und anders." Sonderdruck aus *Deutsche Handelswacht,* n. d.

Schönfelder, G. "Zum Gedächtnis Eugen Diederichs." *Börsenblatt für den deutschen Buchhandel* 107 (1940): 322.

Schönhoven, Klaus. *Die Bayerische Volkspartei 1924–1932.* Düsseldorf, 1972.

Schottelius, H., and Deist, W. *Marine und Marinepolitik in kaiserlichen Deutschland 1871–1914.* Düsseldorf, 1972.

Schottenloher, Karl. *Bücher bewegten die Welt.* 2 vols. Stuttgart, 1951.

Schramm, Albert. "Eugen Diederichs und das schöne Buch." *Taschenbuch für Bücherfreunde* 1 (1925): 98–103.

Schücking, Levin. *Die Soziologie der literarischen Geschmacksbildung.* 2d ed. Leipzig, 1931.

Schüddekopf, Otto E. *Die deutsche Innenpolitik im letzten Jahrhundert und der konservative Gedanke.* Brunswick, 1951.

————. *Linke Leute von Rechts: Die nationalrevolutionären Minderheiten und der Kommunismus in der Weimarer Republik.* Stuttgart, 1960.

Schüler, Winfried. *Der Bayreuther Kreis von seiner Entstehung bis zum Ausgang der wilhelminischen Ära.* Munich, 1971.

Schulz, Gerd. "Eugen Diederichs und das Börsenblatt: Eine Betrachtung zum 22. Juni 1967." *Börsenblatt für den deutschen Buchhandel* 23 (1967): 1312–19.

Schulze, Friedrich. *Der deutsche Buchhandel und die geistigen Strömungen der letzten hundert Jahre.* Leipzig, 1925.

Schwabe, Klaus. "Anti-Americanism with the German Right, 1917–1933." *Amerikastudien* 21 (1976): 89–107.

————. *Wissenschaft und Kriegsmoral: Die deutschen Hochschullehrer und die politische Grundfragen des ersten Weltkrieges.* Göttingen, 1969.

Schwarz, Wilhelm J. *War and the Mind of Germany.* Berne, 1975.

Schwend, Karl. *Bayern zwischen Monarchie und Diktatur.* Munich, 1954.

Schwierskott, Hans-Joachim. *Arthur Moeller van den Bruck und der revolutionäre Nationalismus in der Weimarer Republik.* Göttingen, 1962.

von See, Klaus. *Die Ideen von 1789 und die Ideen von 1914. Deutsches Volkstumsdenken zwischen Französischer Revolution und Erstem Weltkrieg.* Wiesbaden, 1975.

von Seggern, Christina B. "The *Alldeutscher Verband* and the German *Nationalstaat.*" Ph.D. dissertation, University of Minnesota, 1974.

Seidelmann, Karl. *Bund und Gruppe als Lebensform deutscher Jugend: Versuch einer Erscheinungskunde des deutschen Jugendleben in der ersten Hälfte des 20. Jahrhunderts.* Munich, 1955.

————. *Die deutsche Jugendbewegung.* Bad Heilbronn, 1966.

Siebert, F. "J. F. Lehmann." *Akademische Blätter* 50 (1935): 51, 84.

Sieh, Hans G. K. *Der Hamburger Nationalistenklub: Ein Beitrag zur Geschichte der christlich-konservativen Strömungen in der Weimarer Republik.* Inaugural dissertation, Mainz, 1963.

Siefert, Hermann. *Der bündische Aufbruch 1918–1923.* Bad Godesberg, 1963.

————. *Untersuchungen zur Entstehung und Frühgeschichte der bündischen Jugend.* Munich, 1961.

Sinzheimer, H., and Fraenkel, Ernst. *Die Justiz in der Weimarer Republik.* Neuwied, 1968.

Sippell, Margarete Elisabeth. *Julius Friedrich Lehmann–München als Zeitschriftenverleger.* Inaugural dissertation, Leipzig & Borna, 1940.

Smith, Woodruff. *The German Colonial Empire.* Chapel Hill, 1978.

Soergel, A. *Dichtung und Dichter der Zeit.* Rev. ed. Düsseldorf, 1961.

Sontheimer, Kurt. *Antidemokratisches Denken in der Weimarer Republik: Die politische Ideen des deutschen Nationalismus 1918–1933.* Munich, 1962.

———. "Der Tatkreis." *Vierteljahreshefte für Zeitgeschichte* 7 (1959): 229–60.

Speier, Hans. *Die Angestellten vor dem Nationalsozialismus: Ein Beitrag zum Verständnis der deutschen Sozialstruktur 1918–1933.* Göttingen, 1977.

Stackelberg, J. Roderick. "The Politics of Self-Congratulation: A Critique of *Völkisch* Idealism in the Works of Stein, Lienhard, and Chamberlain." Ph.D. dissertation, University of Massachusetts, 1974.

Stappenbacher, Susi. *Die deutschen literarischen Zeitschriften in den Jahren 1918–1925 als Ausdruck geistiger Strömungen.* Inaugural dissertation, Erlangen, 1962.

Stark, Gary D. "Entrepreneurs of Ideology: Neo-Conservative Publishers in Germany, 1890–1933." Ph.D. dissertation, Johns Hopkins University, 1974.

Steinberg, Jonathan. *Yesterday's Deterrent.* London, 1965.

Steinberg, Michael S. *Sabers and Brown Shirts: The German Students' Path to National Socialism 1918–1933.* Chicago, 1977.

Steinhausen, Georg. *Deutsche Geistes- und Kulturgeschichte von 1870 bis zur Gegenwart.* Halle, 1931.

Stern, Fritz. *The Politics of Cultural Despair: A Study in the Rise of the Germanic Ideology.* Garden City, N.Y., 1965.

Stern, Guy. *War, Weimar, and Literature: The Story of the Neue Merkur 1914–1925.* University Park, Penn., 1971.

Stern, Howard. "The Organisation 'Consul.'" *Journal of Modern History* 35 (1963): 20–32.

Stöckel, Günther. *Osteuropa und die Deutschen: Geschichte und Gegenwart einer spannungsreichen Nachbarschaft.* Oldenburg, 1967.

zu Stolberg-Wernigerode, Otto Graf. *Die unentschiedene Generation: Deutschlands konservative Führungsschichte am Vorabend des ersten Weltkriegs.* Munich, 1968.

Struve, Walter. *Elites Against Democracy: Leadership Ideals in Bourgeois Political Thought in Germany, 1890–1933.* Princeton, 1973.

———. "Hans Zehrer as a Neoconservative Elite Theorist." *American Historical Review* 70 (1965): 1035–57.

Theisen, Helmut. *Die Entwicklung zum nihilistischen Nationalismus in Deutschland 1918 bis 1933.* Inaugural dissertation, Basel, 1955.

Thimm, Annelise. *Flucht in der Mythos: Die Deutschnationale Volkspartei und die Niederlage von 1918.* Göttingen, 1969.

Turner, Henry A. "Fascism and Modernization." In *Reappraisals of Fascism*, edited by Henry A. Turner, pp. 117–39. New York, 1975.

Unseld, Siegfried. *Der Autor und sein Verleger.* Frankfurt, 1978.

"Der Verlag Eugen Diederichs in Jena." *Bücherkunde der Reichsstelle zur Förderung des deutschen Schrifttums* 3 (1936): 8–10.

"Der Verlag J. F. Lehmann in München." *Bücherkunde der Reichsstelle zur Förderung des deutschen Schrifttums* 3 (1936): 89–92.

Vermeil, Edmond. *Doctrinaires de la révolution allemande 1918–1938.* Paris, 1938.

———. "The Origin, Nature and Development of German Nationalist Ideology in the 19th and 20th Centuries." In *The Third Reich*, edited by the International Council for Philosophical and Humanistic Studies, pp. 3–111. London, 1955.

Vesper, Reinhold. "Würdige Feierstunde des Eugen Diederichs Verlages." *Börsenblatt für den deutschen Buchhandel* 103 (1936): 833.

Viebig, Kurd. *Die Entstehung und Entwicklung der Freikonservativen und der Reichspartei.* Weimar, 1920.

Vondung, Klaus. "Deutsche Apokalypse 1914." In *Das wilhelminische Bildungsbürgertum: Zur Sozialgeschichte seiner Ideen,* edited by Klaus Vondung, pp. 153–71. Göttingen, 1976.

————, ed. *Das wilhelminische Bildungsbürgertum: Zur Sozialgeschichte seiner Ideen.* Göttingen, 1976.

————. "Zur Lage der Gebildeten in der wilhelminischen Zeit." In *Das wilhelminische Bildungsbürgertum: Zur Sozialgeschichte seiner Ideen,* edited by Klaus Vondung, pp. 20–33. Göttingen, 1976.

Waite, Robert G. L. *Vanguard of Nazism: The Free Corps Movement in Postwar Germany 1918–1923.* New York, 1969.

Ward, Alfred. *Book Production, Fiction, and the German Reading Public 1740–1800.* London, 1974.

Weber, Marianne. *Max Weber: Ein Lebensbild.* Tübingen, 1926.

Wehler, Hans-Ulrich. "Sozialdarwinismus im expandierenden Industrie-Staat." In *Deutschland in der Weltpolitik des 19. und 20. Jahrhunderts: Fritz Fischer zum 65. Geburtstag,* edited by Immanuel Geiss and B. J. Wendt, pp. 133–42. Düsseldorf, 1973.

Weichardt, Walter. "Eugen Diederichs." *Der Bücherwurm* 7 (1921): 98–100.

Wels, Benno. "Eugen Diederichs, Verlag in Jena." *Tribüne,* 1912.

Wernecke, K. *Der Wille zur Weltgeltung: Aussenpolitik und Öffentlichkeit im Kaiereich am Vorabend des Ersten Weltkrieges.* Düsseldorf, 1970.

Werner, Lothar. *Der Alldeutsche Verband 1890–1918.* Berlin, 1935.

Wertheimer, Mildred. *The Pan-German League 1890–1914.* New York, 1924.

von Westarp, Graf. *Konservative Politik im letzten Jahrzehnt des Kaiserreiches.* 2 vols. Berlin, 1935.

Westphal, Otto. *Feinde Bismarcks: Geistige Grundlagen der deutschen Opposition 1848–1918.* Munich, 1930.

Whiteside, Andrew G. *The Socialism of Fools: George Ritter von Schönerer and Austrian Pan-Germanism.* Berkeley, 1975.

Willey, Thomas E. *Back to Kant: The Revival of Kantianism in German Social and Historical Thought, 1860–1914.* Detroit, 1978.

Winzen, Peter. *Bülows Weltmachtpolitik: Untersuchungen zur Frühphase seiner Aussenpolitik 1897–1901.* Boppard, 1977.

Wulf, Joseph. *Literatur und Dichtung im Dritten Reich.* Gütersloh, 1963.

Ziemer, R., and Wolf, R. *Wandervogel und Freideutsche Jugend.* Bad Godesberg, 1961.

Zimmermann, P. *Der Bauernroman: Antifeudalismus—Konservatismus—Faschismus.* Stuttgart, 1975.

Zimmermann, Werner G. *Bayern und das Reich 1918–1923.* Munich, 1953.

Zmarzlick, Hans-Günther. "Social Darwinism in Germany, Seen as an Historical Problem." In *Republic to Reich: The Making of the Nazi Revolution,* edited by Hajo Holborn, pp. 435–74. New York, 1972.

Index of Authors, Periodicals, and Publishing Firms

(*See* and *See also* references in bold face refer to General Index)

Adolf Klein Verlag, 12

A. Duncker Verlag, 13

Albatros Verlag, 27

Albert Langen–Georg Müller Verlag, 32, 237, 254–55 (n. 37), 256 (n. 68), 284 (n. 126); creation of, 29; and Krause affair, 53–56; antirationalist publications, 176; Nordic publications, 191; "hearth and homeland" publications, 194; publications on imperial expansion, 204–5; anti-Semitic publications, 210, 285 (n. 144); after 1933, 230–32; commercial aspects, 258 (n. 99). *See also* Hanseatic Publishing Institute; **Pezold, Gustav**

Albert Langen Verlag, 16, 238, 260 (n. 117); acquired by Hanseatic Publishing Institute, 28, 29, 254 (n. 34); and Krause affair, 53–56; publications on imperial expansion, 204; anti-Semitic publications, 210; commercial aspects, 254 (n. 35)

Alter, Junius [pseud. of Franz Sontag], 129, 272 (n. 29)

Andersen, Hans Christian, 93

Andreas-Salomé, Lou, 18, 178

Angriff, Der, 230

Anthropologische Revue, 90

Archiv für Rassen- und Gesellschaftsbiologie, 200, 238

Arnim, Bettina von, 85

Aufbruch, 138

Auf Gut Deutsch, 11

Aufmarsch Verlag. *See* Verlag der Aufmarsch

August Scherl Verlag, 10, 28, 254 (n. 37)

Avenarius, Ferdinand, 10, 45, 259 (n. 115); and Eugen Diederichs, 17, 78–79, 97, 252 (n. 4)

Avenarius Verlag. *See* Eduard Avenarius Verlag

Baader, Johannes, 137, 274 (n. 56)

Baeck, Leo, 209

Bang, Paul, 168, 169, 259 (n. 110), 277 (n. 36)

Banse, Ewald, 221

Bartels, Adolf, 59, 79, 97, 98, 241, 255 (n. 42)

Barthel, Max, 126, 218

Bauer, Erwin, 207, 284 (n. 138)

Beck'sche Verlagsbuchhandlung. *See* C. H. Beck'sche Verlagsbuchhandlung

Beenken Verlag. *See* Heinrich Beenken Verlag

Behringer, F., 217

Benninghoff, Ludwig, 161, 183

Benno Filser Verlag, 27

Benz, Richard, 182

Bergson, Henri, 17, 68–69

Berliner Tageblatt, 53–55

Bernoulli, Carl Albrecht, 60

Bernstein, Eduard, 102

Beumelburg, Werner, 152, 161, 241

B. G. Teubner Verlag, 200

Bischoff, Diedrich, 92

Bley, F., 119

Blüher, Hans, 105, 138, 210

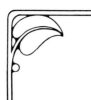

General Index

(*See* and *See also* references in bold face refer to Index of Authors, Periodicals, and Publishing Firms)

Aliens: influence of, 121, 205–7, 210. *See also* Anti-Semitism; Jews; Racial ideology
Alldeutscher Verband. *See* Pan-German League
Anthropological Society, 130, 237, 238
Anthroposophical Society, 74
Anthroposophy, 74. *See also* Religion
Anti-Americanism, 52, 134, 177
Anticapitalism, 216–17. *See also* Corporatism; Reform: social and economic; Socialism: need for a new
Anti-English sentiment, 119, 126–27
Antimaterialism, 63–64, 174–77. *See also* Idealism
Antirationalism, 66–69, 70, 137–38, 174–76. *See also* Life-philosophy; Mysticism; Vitalism
Anti-Semitism, 23–24, 51, 121, 130, 141, 149, 157–58, 161, 165, 166, 171, 208–10, 285 (nn. 144, 145). *See also* Jews; Racial ideology
Antiurbanism, 96–97, 193–94, 268 (n. 150). *See also* "Blood and Soil" ideology; "Hearth and Homeland" movement; Peasantry
Arndt, E. M., 19
Art, 76–81, 137, 181–82, 283 (n. 101)
Association for Germanic Volk Character and Racial Research, 201, 237, 238
Austria, 116, 117, 149, 270 (n. 16)
Austria-Hungary, 115, 127, 201
Author evenings: Langen-Müller Verlag, 37, 237
Authors, 3–4, 235–49 passim

Barth, Karl, 180
Barth, Theodor, 99, 100, 101
Bäumer, Gertrud, 273 (n. 47)
Bavarian Peoples party, 188
Bayreuth Circle, 11, 182, 237, 259 (n. 115) *See also* **Chamberlain, Houston Stuart**; Wagner, Richard
Bechly, Hans, 24, 27, 229
Beenken, Heinrich: and Friedrich Zillessen Verlag, 32; professional ethos, 35; opposition to Versailles peace settlement, 160–61, 287 (n. 10); and *Volk*-conservatism, 189; general contributions to the neoconservative movement, 235–46 passim. *See also* **Heinrich Beenken Verlag**
Beer hall putsch, 170, 254 (n. 31), 286 (n. 31). *See also* Hitler, Adolf; National Socialism
Below, Georg von, 259 (n. 110)
Beneficial Society 1914 in Jena, 135
Bestsellers, 241–42, 287 (n. 7)
Bethmann-Hollweg, Theobald von, 128–31, 271 (n. 13), 272 (n. 28)
"Blood and Soil" ideology, 15, 195. *See also* Antiurbanism; Peasantry; Racial ideology
Book clubs, 29–30. *See also* **German Home Library**
Book graphics, 79, 238, 240
Book trade. *See* Publishing industry
Bothmer, Graf, 272 (n. 26)
Bott, Karl, 27, 28
"Break With Rome" movement, 115–17, 239. *See also* Pan-German League; Religion

324 · General Index

264 (n. 74), 265 (n. 75). *See also* Antirationalism; Religion

Nationalism, radical, 5, 111–32, 186–211
National Military Archive, 150
National Socialism, 5, 9, 10, 11, 25, 151,
162, 163, 167, 170, 220, 239, 254 (nn. 31,
37), 259 (n. 110), 277 (n. 16), 279 (n. 67),
283 (n. 101), 285 (n. 145), 286 (n. 31), 287
(n. 10), 288 (n. 10); and Krause affair,
54–56; and the neoconservative publishers, 222–27; and the "Third Reich"
controversy, 225–27; policy toward neoconservative publishing firms after 1933,
228–34. *See also* Hitler, Adolf
National Socialist German Workers party.
See National Socialism
Naturalism, 86, 252 (n. 4)
Naumann, Friedrich, 99, 101, 127
Navalism, 117–19
Naval Office, 119
Nazism. *See* National Socialism
Neoconservatism: nature of, 4–9; contrasted
with traditional conservatism, 5–9, 125,
212–13; relation to publishers and pub-
lishing industry, 9–14; journals of, 41–50;
contributions of publishers to, 235–46;
dissemination of, as reflected in book
sales, 240–43. *See also* Pessimism, cul-
tural; Nationalism, radical; *Völkisch*
ideology
Neoromanticism, 85–88, 183. *See also*
Romanticism
"New Flock," 184–85
Nicolai, Friedrich, 246
Niekisch, Anna, 11
Niekisch, Ernst, 11
Nietzsche, Friedrich, 58, 59–60, 62, 63,
104, 138
Nietzsche-Forster, Elisabeth, 60
Nobel prize, 19, 69, 194, 240
Nordic ideology, 90, 93–94, 139, 140, 191–
93, 237, 274 (n. 72). See also *Völkisch*
ideology
Nordic Ring, 201

Organic state, 213–14. *See also* Reform:
political

Pan-German League, 24, 43, 44, 49, 112–19

passim, 121, 123, 124, 127, 128, 130, 132,
157, 202, 238, 239, 277 (nn. 15, 18)
Pankok, Bernhard, 265 (n. 86)
Pantheism, 74–75, 137. *See also* Religion
Papen, Franz von, 167
Patriotic Beneficial Society 1914 in
Thuringia, 135, 238
Patronage, 3, 243–49
Peasantry, 98, 194–95. *See also* Anti-
urbanism
Pechel, Rudolf, 11, 47
Periodicals. *See* Journals
Pessimism, cultural, 5, 52, 58–110, 120–24,
132–48, 172–85
Pezold, Gustav, 258 (n. 99), 284 (n. 126);
appointed director of Georg Müller
Verlag, 28, 254 (n. 34); director of
Langen-Müller Verlag, 29, 255 (n. 41),
260 (n. 117); professional ethos, 35–41
passim; and German publishing industry,
53, 256 (n. 68), 257 (n. 85); and Krause
affair, 53–56, 262 (n. 154); and Grimm's
Volk ohne Raum, 204–5; opposes alien
influence, 206, 210; after 1933, 230; gen-
eral contributions to the neoconservative
movement, 235–46 passim; early political
activity, 254 (n. 31). *See also* **Albert
Langen–Georg Müller Verlag; Georg
Müller Verlag; Hanseatic Publishing
Institute**
Plenge, Johann, 273 (n. 39)
Pöhner, Ernst, 279 (n. 67)
Progressive party, 21
Progressive Peoples party, 45, 100
Prussia, 165–67, 199
Prussian Academy of Writers, 194
Prussian Emergency Association for
German Scholarship, 199
Publishers, neoconservative, 9–14; com-
mercial aspects, 16–18, 20–21, 27, 252
(n. 5), 258 (n. 99); professional ethos,
34–41; and neoconservative journals,
41–50; and the German publishing in-
dustry, 50–57; after 1933, 228–34; gen-
eral contributions to the neoconservative
movement, 235–46; compared to patrons,
243–46. *See also* Beenken, Heinrich;
Diederichs, Eugen; **Eugen Diederichs
Verlag; Gerhard Stalling Verlag; Hanseatic Publishing Institute; Heinrich**